SÜDTIROL

ITALIA

FARM HOLIDAYS IN SOUTH TYROL

Here, timeless country hospitality is a tradition.

Away from the grind of daily life, immersed in a friendly country atmosphere, you can breathe the fresh country air and fragrance of age-old traditions, savour freshly-bottled wine in the company of the farmer, watch the harvester at work picking fruit off the trees and carrying it home like in the old days. Take your children to pet the newborn calf in our stables, or watch the farmer's wife preparing delicious country-fresh bread.

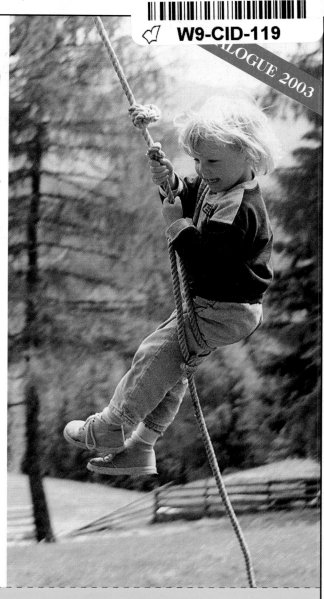

For more information on a real down-to-earth holiday, ring 0039 / 0471 / 999308 or send us this coupon by fax or post. Our fax number is 0039 / 0471 / 981171. Our address is Unione Agricoltori e Coltivatori diretti sudtirolesi, Via Macello 4/D, 39100 Bolzano. You will also find more information at: www.redrooster.it / E-mail: info@redrooster.it

Name _ _ _ _ _ _ _ _ _ _ _ _ _ _ _ _ _ _ _

Address _ _ _ _ _ _ _ _ _ _ _ _ _ _ _ _ _

_ _

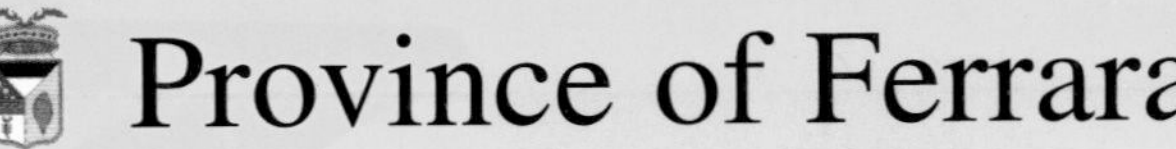

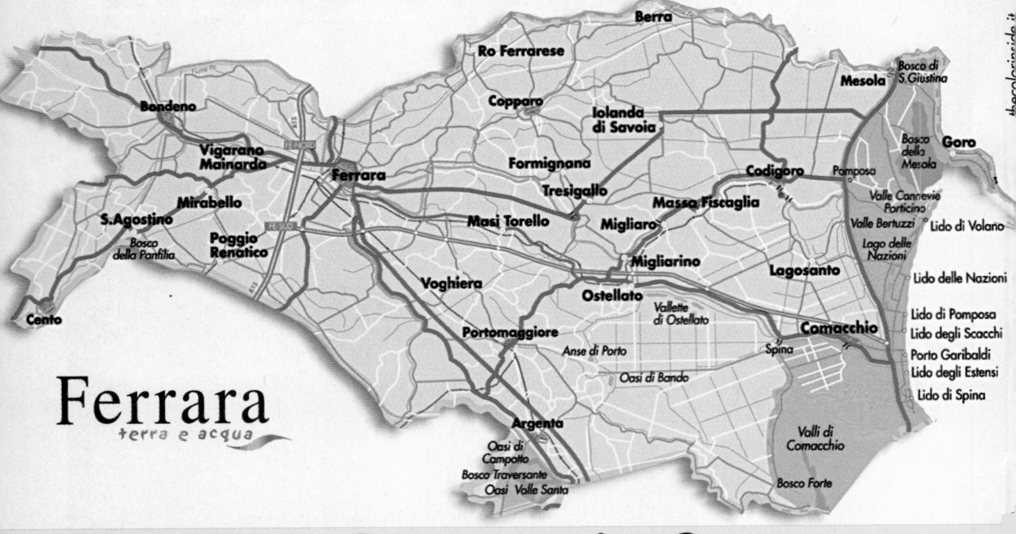

www.ferrarainfo.com

ALLA CEDRARA
Via Aranova, 104
Località Porotto - (Fe)
Tel. 0532 593033
Fax 0532 772293
www.allacedrara.it
agriturismo@allacedrara.it
posti letto 7

AL PALAZ
Via S. Giacomo, 86
località Masi Torello
Tel. 0532 816013
Fax 0532 816656
www.alpalaz.it
alpalaz@alpalaz.it
posti letto 14

BELVEDERE
Via Ostellato, 1
località Migliarino
Tel./Fax 0533 52138
posti letto 13

CA' LAURA
Via Cristina, 70
località Bosco Mesola - Mesola
Tel./Fax 0533 794372
www.calaura.it
info@calaura.it
posti letto 15

CAMPELLO
Via Zarabotta, 3
località Codigoro
Tel./Fax 0533 713665
www.agriturismocampello.it
supermarcy@inwind.it - posti letto 16

CA' SPINAZZINO
Via Taglione, 5
località Spinazzino - (Fe)
Tel. 0532 725035
remo.scaramagli@ntt.it
posti letto 12

CA' VECIA
Via Nuova Corriera, 166
Località Bosco Mesola
Mesola
Tel 0533 794600
posti letto 7

LA CASA DI CAMPAGNA
Via Nuova, 9
località Renazzo
Cento
Tel. 051 909005
posti letto 16

LA MIGLIARA
Via Provinciale Centese, 187
località S.Bianca
Bondeno
Tel./Fax 0532 893595
www.lamigliara.it
micsucci@tin.it
posti letto 8

LA ROCCHETTA
Via Rocca, 69
località S. Egidio - (Fe)
Tel. 0532 725824
Fax 0532 729084
www.larocchetta.com
larocchetta@larocchetta.com
posti letto 33

LE CASETTE
Via Virgiliana, 137
località Burana
Bondeno
Tel./Fax 0532 880736
fondocasette@libero.it
posti letto 16

LE PRADINE
Corso Italia, 537
località Mirabello
Tel. 0532 847630
Fax 0532 358098
www.lepradine.it
pradine@tin.it
posti letto 16

NOVARA
Via Ferrara, 61
località Dogato - Ostellato
Tel./Fax 0533 651097
www.agriturismonovara.it
info@agriturismonovara.it
posti letto 14

PRATO POZZO
Via Rotta Martinella, 34/a
località Anita
Argenta
Tel./Fax 0532 801058
pratopozzo@jumpy.it
posti letto 16

QUIETO VIVERE
Viale Raffaello, 96
località Lido di Spina
Tel. 0533 333559
Fax 0533 318189
posti letto 2

VAL CAMPOTTO
Via Maria Margotti, 2
località Campotto
Argenta
Tel. 0532 800516
Fax 0532 319413
www.valcampotto.it
agriturismo@valcampotto.it
posti letto 15

Turismo rurale
CORTE DOSSELLO
Via Briccola,7
Località Massafiscaglia (Fe)
Tel. 0533 539017
Fax 0532 606268
effegigf@tin.it
posti letto 9

Turismo rurale
VILLA BELFIORE
Via Pioppa, 27
località Ostellato
Tel. 0533 681164
Fax 0533 681172
www.villabelfiore.it
agriturismobelfiore@libero.it
posti letto 37

Ask for your complimentary Guidebook **"Holidays 2003"**
of the province of Ferrara **agriturismo@provincia.fe.it**

i **Ferrara Castello Estense Tel. (+39) 0532 299303 - Fax (+39) 0532 212266 - infotur@provincia.fe.it**
Comacchio P.zza Folegatti, 28 - Tel. (+39) 0533 310161 - iat@comune.comacchio.fe.it

Italian Farm Vacations

The Guide to Countryside Hospitality

TOURING CLUB OF ITALY

Touring Club Italiano
President and Chairman: Roberto Ruozi
General Manager: Guido Venturini

Touring Editore
Managing Director: Guido Venturini
General Manager: Alfieri Lorenzon
Editorial Manager: Michele D'Innella

International Department
Fabio Pittella
fabio.pittella@touringclub.it

Senior Editor: Viviana Arrigoni
Translation: Buysschaert & Malerba (David Stanton, Nicola Hawkins)
Map Design: Touring Club Italiano
Cover picture: "Toscana, nearby of Pienza", Bruno Morandi (Agency: Franca Speranza)

Advertising Manager: Claudio Bettinelli
Local Advertising: Progetto
www.progettosrl.it - info@progettosrl.it

Printing: Grafiche Mazzucchelli - Settimo Milanese (MI)
Binding: Torriani & C. - Cologno Monzese (MI)

Distribution
USA/CAN - Publishing Group West
UK/Ireland - Portfolio Books

Touring Club Italiano, corso Italia 10, 20122 Milano
www.touringclub.it

Code L2AAE
ISBN 88-365-2038-4

Printed in March 2003

Summary

Farmhouse Holidays in Italy
A Resource for the Future

Thanks to Italy's beautiful landscapes and rich cultural heritage, rural tourism has now started to play an important role in the nation's economy.

Trips to the country are an age-old custom because our grandparents, or even their grandparents, used to pay visits to farmers, who were also very often their friends. The highest level of sales promotion the farmers reached was perhaps the display on the public highway of a leafy bough to announce, at the beginning of spring, the sale of the surplus produce in the farm's storehouse. This precedent is worth mentioning because in the agricultural world changes always occur very gradually, in this case stimulated by the need to give better prospects to a system of farming that was in crisis with regard to both its results and its identity. This was therefore the primary motivating factor that led firstly to the birth of a new activity and then to its quantitative growth and, finally, to its evolution to increasingly professional forms of tourist accommodation.

Are there advantages for everyone in farmhouse holidays?

In 2000 the farmhouse holiday business in Italy registered over 10 million bed-nights, with an annual turnover of around 490 million euros. These figures confirm its validity both as a means of supplementing the farmers' incomes and as incentive for the renovation of the farm buildings. Farmhouses abandoned for years have been given a new lease of life as tourist accommodation, at the same time providing the financial resources for the necessary improvements. In addition to these advantages in terms of property and budget, there has also been progress in the production cycle with the introduction of new crops and new types of stockbreeding geared to both catering and recreational activities. An even more wide-ranging effect regards handicrafts, gastronomy and in general everything concerned with traditional rural culture, which has certainly been given a boost by tourism. Moreover, farmhouse holidays are environment-friendly because the farmers have learned to treat the landscape as an economic resource; their activity has ceased to be mere exploitation of the land, as has often been the case in the past, and becomes its management for tourist purposes by making it more accessible and enhancing its quality with the reintroduction of the indigenous flora and fauna. And farmhouse holidays are also advantageous for guests, who spend less than they would in conventional accommodation and often find them more enjoyable, especially at the height of the tourist season.

Rural holidays in five points

After these introductory remarks, it is worth considering the situation in Italy with regard to the five main points regulating farmhouse holidays:

1. only farmers can run farmhouse accommodation;

2. the farming activity must play a more important role than tourism;

3. the tourist facilities must be housed in converted rural buildings;

4. the guests' rooms must be on the farm itself;

5. the catering must mainly make use of the farm's produce.

It is evident that the legislator's main concern was that of providing the necessary incentives for farms and, at the same time, of discouraging forms of tourist accommodation not closely linked to the rural environment. Although the concept is clear on paper, it is not easy to apply it in a world that ranges from the inaccessible vineyards of the Cinque Terre to huge estates controlled by large companies. Returning to the figures, in 2000 there were over 9,000 establishments providing farmhouse accommodation (just over one per cent of all Italian firms (with a total of 105,000 beds. These are respectable figures, although the European totals, with 100,000 establishments and peaks of 30,000 in France and 15,000 in Austria, highlight the fact that this country is still lagging behind.

What does the future hold for farmhouse accommodation in Italy?

What the statistics do not reveal is that almost half of the establishments providing farmhouse accommodation are concentrated in just three regions: Trentino-Alto Adige, Tuscany and Umbria. In other words, some areas are on a par with the other European countries, while the rest of Italy is still far behind. In some cases, the accommodation is of a hotel standard, in others it is, to say the least, somewhat rustic. This is the case with, above all, Tuscany, which has developed forms of accommodation that are so refined as to raise suspicions that the agricultural activity has been kept going simply as a façade. What is one to make of certain farmhouses, now the homes of well-to-do outsiders, that can only be called farms because they are surrounded by olive groves? And how should we interpret the conversion into tourist accommodation of whole hamlets located on some of the larger estates?

From the guest's point of view, however, the question is, all things considered, of secondary importance: those who opt for farmhouse holidays are only in search of a beautiful place in the country offering high-quality facilities (even if this pushes up the price). The farming community, too, seems to have willingly adapted to the new trend. But analysts of this phenomenon still have their doubts: maybe the genuine farmhouse accommodation of yesteryear was better?

How to consult the guide

• The 1,293 establishments presented in the guide represent, in regional order, around 15% of the total farm holiday enterprises available in Italy. Based on primarily qualitative and geographical criteria, the selection has been made using research and constant monitoring methods (surveys, local collaboration and inspections), aimed at offering the public a tool which is both useful and independent.
• The information given is that supplied by the owners of the properties themselves, verified both on site by surveyors, and at the editing stage of the publication by TCI experts. Errors in transmitting the information, or printing, and last minute variations cannot be excluded. It is therefore indispensable to telephone well in advance, in order to check availability, possible dates when the establishment may be closed, prices and categories, and to make reservations.

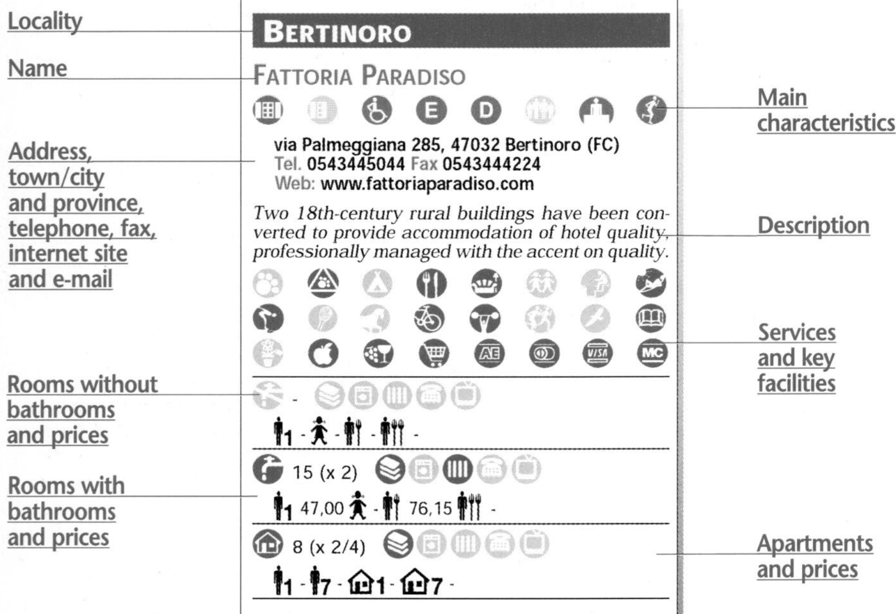

Prices

All prices are referred to the tariffs recorded in Summer 2002; they relate to the peak rates and are purely indicative. It is therefore strongly recommended to check prices at the time of booking.

Map indications

All the localities which contain at least one farm holiday mentioned in the guide are highlighted in the regional map to be found at the beginning of each chapter, in order that readers can easily identify the establishments' geographical position in each zone.

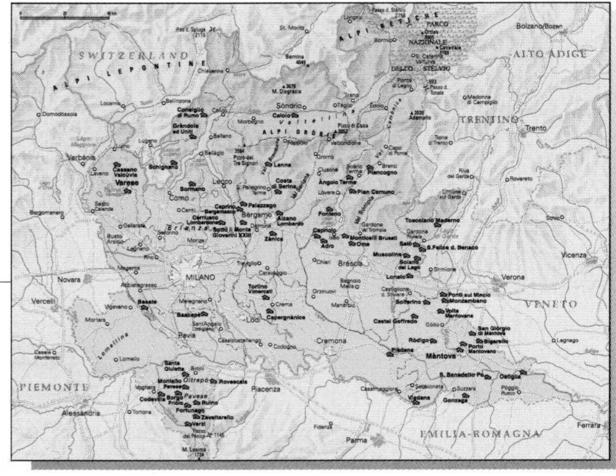

The symbols

The wide range of symbols used, specifically created for this guide, supply extensive information which is quick and easy to follow. The line of red symbols refers to information of more general interest (opening times, proximity to sea or lake, etc.), the three lines with blue symbols list the principal structure and facility details. When a symbol is "lit up" ( ), this signifies that the corresponding characteristic or facility is present: if the symbol is not "lit up" ( ), this means that it is not provided. The final six lines record the price tariffs, referred to respectively as: rooms without bathrooms (first two lines), rooms with bathrooms (third and fourth lines), apartments (fifth and sixth lines).

Main characteristics

In addition to general information (opening times, facilities for the disabled, languages spoken), this indicates whether the structure is more suited to families, or to sporty or cultural holidays.

- Open all year round
- Seasonal opening (closed for a period of at least three months)
- Wheelchair facilities for the disabled
- English spoken
- German spoken
- Suitable for families with children
- Suitable for smart holidays
- Suitable for sporty holidays

Services and key facilities offered

Illustrates the key facilities: restaurant, areas for children, sports' facilities, credit cards, etc..

- Dogs allowed
- Dogs allowed by pre-arranged agreement
- Areas equipped for tents and/or caravans
- Restaurant
- Communal areas
- Play areas and/or equipment for children
- Sauna
- Solarium
- Swimming pool
- Tennis court(s)
- Riding-school or facilities for horse-riding
- Bicycle hire
- Sports' facilities
- Organised sports activities
- Naturalistic activities/courses
- Cultural activities/courses
- Certified organic crops
- Farm cultivation (vegetable crops, fruit, cereals)
- Wine production
- Farm produce sold directly
- American Express accepted
- Diner's card accepted
- Visa card accepted
- Mastercard accepted

Accommodation and prices

For each category (rooms without bathrooms, with bathrooms, apartments), the total number of rooms is specified next to the symbol, with the number of places in brackets. Additional services are also highlighted (laundry, central heating), etc.

- Rooms without bathrooms (number of people)
- Rooms with bathrooms (number of people)
- Apartments (number of people)
- Laundry available
- Washing machine
- Central heating
- Telephone in the room
- Television in the room
- 1 Price per person per day
- Price per child per day
- Half board price per day
- Full board price per day
- 7 Price per person per week
- 1 Apartment hire per day
- 7 Apartment hire per week

PARCO NAZIONALE DELLA MAJELLA

Park Headquarters
Via Occidentale 4/6 - 66016 Guardiagrele (CH)
Tel. 0871 80371 - Fax 0871 800340

Planning office
Piazza Alberto Duval Casa Nanni - 67030 Campo di Giove (AQ)
Tel 0864 40851 - Fax 0864 4085350
e-mail: info@parcomajella.it - http://www.parcomajella.it

A Park which is all mountain, the Holy Mother Mountain of the green Abruzzi, in the heart of Central Italy in the most inaccessible and wildest part of the Apennines. A place that was very dear to pope Celestine V and many hermits, where naturalistic rarities live in perfect harmony with masterpieces of art, culture, history and man's work, generating a majestic and harmonious setting which instils a sense of peace and releases a profound spirituality.
The Park of the bear, the chamois, the otter, and the dotterel, the Park of the vast high-altitude plains and wild imposing canyons, but also the Park of the hermits, abbeys, tholi and historical centres of Pescocostanzo, Pacentro, Palena and Guardiagrele, the pottery of Rapino and Guardiagrele, the terracotta figures of Pacentro, the carved wood of Pretoro, the fabrics of Taranta Peligna, the copper and iron of Guardiagrele, the jewellery of Sulmona, Pescocostanzo and Guardiagrele, the lacework of Pescocostanzo.

A Park for life and for the biodiversity of life, respected in its sacredness with an immensely valuable natural, historical and cultural patrimony which the young National Park, founded only a few years ago but already sufficiently well-established, is striving to organise its use and education about the environment increasingly better, and to preserve intact or reinforce its fundamental values for future generations to enjoy.

ABRUZZO

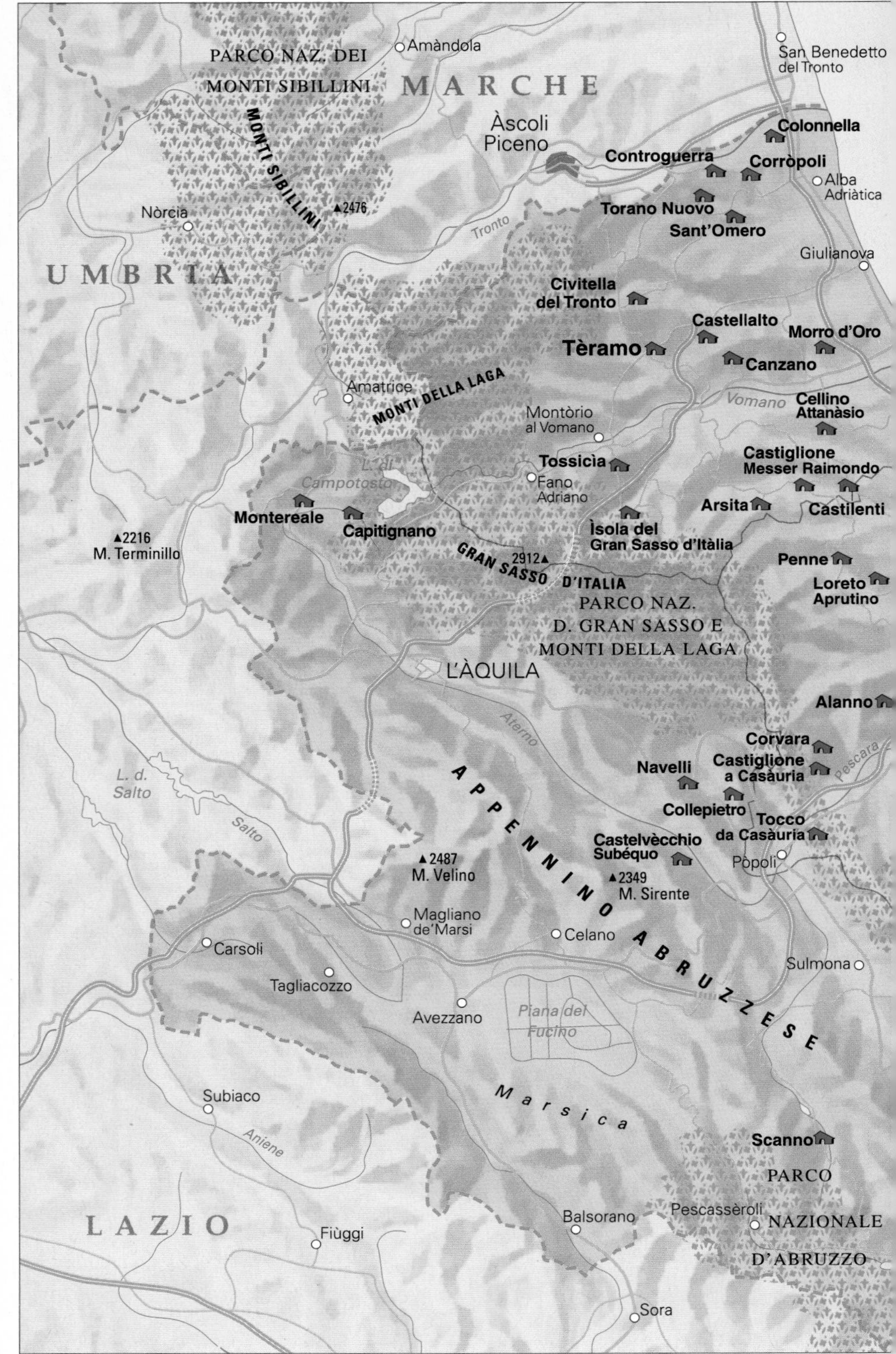

PARCO NAZ. DEI MONTI SIBILLINI
MONTI SIBILLINI
Amàndola
MARCHE
San Benedetto del Tronto
Àscoli Piceno
Colonnella
Controguerra
Corròpoli
Alba Adriàtica
Torano Nuovo
Sant'Omero
Nòrcia
2476
Tronto
Giulianova
UMBRIA
Civitella del Tronto
Castellalto
Morro d'Oro
Tèramo
Canzano
Amatrice
MONTI DELLA LAGA
Vomano
Cellino Attanàsio
Montòrio al Vomano
Tossicìa
Castiglione Messer Raimondo
L. di Campotosto
Fano Adriano
Arsita
Castilenti
Montereale
Capitignano
Ìsola del Gran Sasso d'Itàlia
2216
M. Terminillo
GRAN SASSO D'ITALIA
2912
Penne
Loreto Aprutino
PARCO NAZ. D. GRAN SASSO E MONTI DELLA LAGA
L'ÀQUILA
Aterno
Alanno
Corvara
Pescara
Castiglione a Casàuria
Navelli
L. d. Salto
APPENNINO ABRUZZESE
Collepietro
Tocco da Casàuria
Salto
Castelvècchio Subéquo
Pòpoli
2487
M. Velino
2349
M. Sirente
Magliano de'Marsi
Celano
Carsoli
Sulmona
Tagliacozzo
Avezzano
Piana del Fucino
Marsica
Subiaco
Aniene
Scanno
PARCO NAZIONALE D'ABRUZZO
LAZIO
Balsorano
Pescassèroli
Fiùggi
Sora

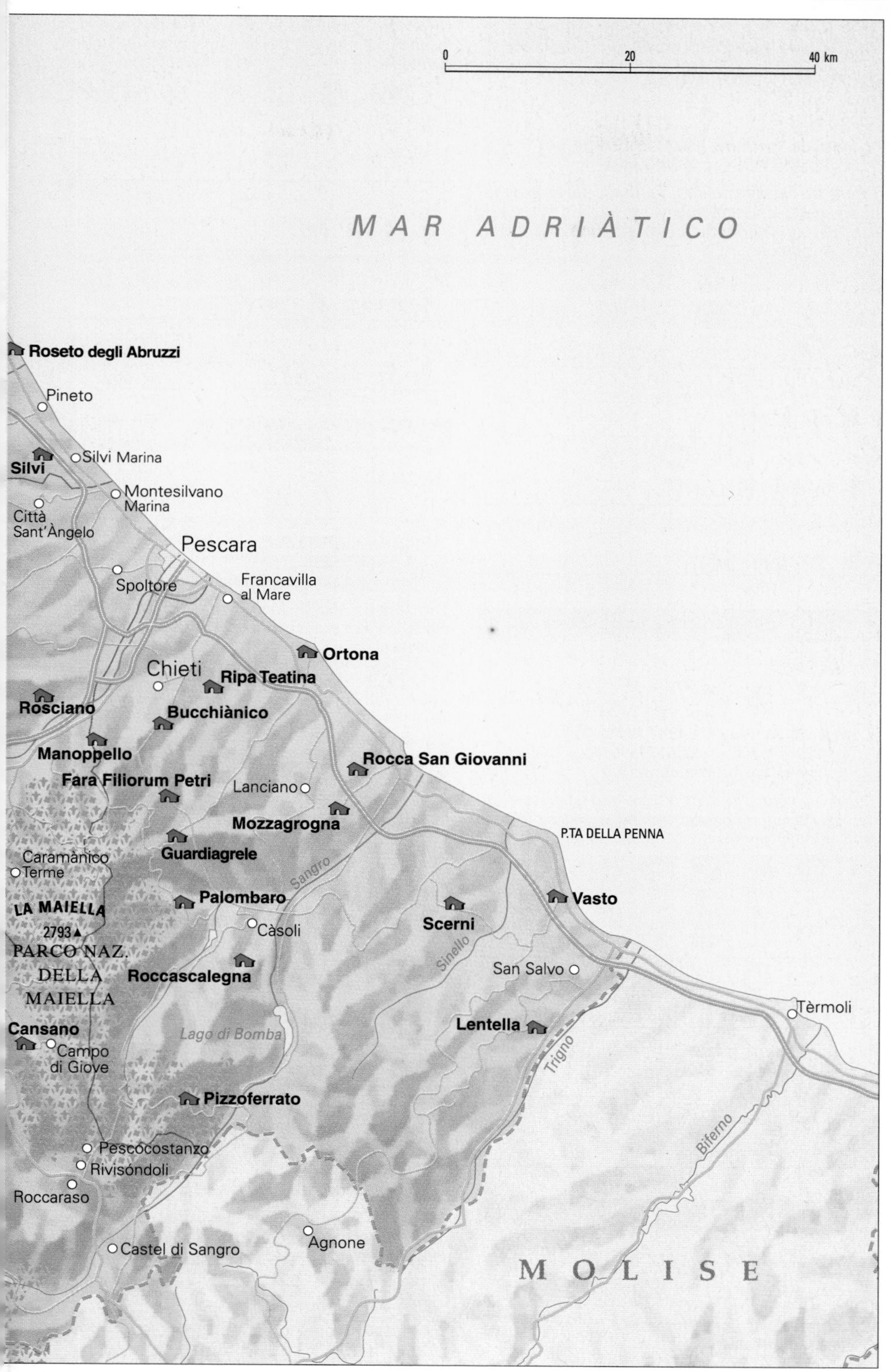
0
20
40 km
MAR ADRIÀTICO
Roseto degli Abruzzi
Pineto
Silvi
Silvi Marina
Montesilvano Marina
Città Sant'Àngelo
Pescara
Spoltore
Francavilla al Mare
Ortona
Chieti
Ripa Teatina
Rosciano
Bucchiànico
Manoppello
Rocca San Giovanni
Fara Filiorum Petri
Lanciano
Mozzagrogna
P.TA DELLA PENNA
Guardiagrele
Caramànico Terme
Sangro
Palombaro
Vasto
LA MAIELLA
2793
Càsoli
Scerni
PARCO NAZ. DELLA MAIELLA
Roccascalegna
Sinello
San Salvo
Tèrmoli
Lentella
Cansano
Lago di Bomba
Campo di Giove
Trigno
Pizzoferrato
Biferno
Pescocostanzo
Rivisóndoli
Roccaraso
Agnone
Castel di Sangro
MOLISE

ALANNO

VALLE ROSA DEL CIGNO

contrada Sperduto, 65020 Alanno (PE)
Tel. 0858573495 Fax 0858573801

This is an excellent choice for those seeking quality and good taste: the rooms are located in the low outbuilding, the kitchen and dining-room in the large farmhouse.

-
1 - - -

3 (x 2/4)
1 30,00 - 43,00 -

-
1 - 7 - 1 - 7 -

ARSITA

DI MARCO

contrada Pantane 1, 64031 Arsita (TE)
Tel. 0861995208 Fax 0861995957
Web: www.agriturismoabruzzo.it

This is an organic farm with crops and pasturage and two excellently renovated farmhouses close to each other. Riding courses are available on request.

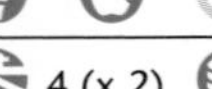    

4 (x 2)
1 20,66 14,46 33,57 -

-
1 - - -

-
1 - 7 - 1 - 7 -

BUCCHIANICO

CASA BIANCA

contrada Cese Colle Torino 34,
66011 Bucchianico (CH)
Tel. 0871381887 Fax 0871381887

On the hill facing the village, where the property is located, simple yet welcoming accommodation is available.

-
1 - - -

4 (x 2)
1 20,00 - 31,00 -

-
1 - 7 - 1 - 7 -

CANSANO

AGRIPARK

at Renaro, 67030 Cansano (AQ)
Tel. 3334791838
Web: www.abruzzo.agriturismo.it

The Maiella Massif looms up behind this accommodation that is ideal for both the keen hiker and the gourmet.

6 (x 2/4)
1 31,00 16,00 - -

-
1 - - -

-
1 - 7 - 1 - 7 -

CANZANO

L'ANTICO FRANTOIO

at Santa Lucia, via Colle di Corte 14,
64020 Canzano (TE)
Tel. 086157904
E-mail: lantico.frantoio@tiscali.it

Situated in the hills and surrounded by olives and acacias, this farmhouse dating from 1880 has outbuildings provided with modern comforts and wide terraces.

-

1 - - - -

-

1 - - - -

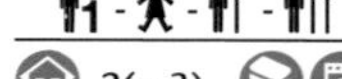

2(x 3)

1 20,66 7 - 1 - 7 -

Capitignano

La Canestra

at Aglioni, via S. Rocco 40,
67014 Capitignano (AQ)
Tel. 0862901243 Fax 086287312215
E-mail: lacanestra@libero.it

Three farmhouses provide accommodation in this village; in addition to enjoying the local specialities, guests may explore the area on the back of a donkey.

2 (x 2)

1 21,00 - 36,00 -

3 (x 2)

1 21,00 - 36,00 -

-

1 - 7 - 1 - 7 -

Castellalto

San Cipriano

at Castelnuovo Vomano, contrada San Cipriano,
64020 Castellalto (TE)
Tel. 086157160 Fax 086157160
E-mail: agritancredi@virgilio.it

This pleasant building located on the edge of a vineyard has well-kept, bright rooms and external spaces where guests may relax.

-

1 - - - -

-

1 - - - -

4(x 2)

1 - 7 - 1 50,00 7 -

Castelvecchio Subequo

Casa Sole

contrada Colanamini,
67024 Castelvecchio Subequo (AQ)
Tel. 0864797206 Fax 0864797206
E-mail: silveridonato@tin.it

This farm is noted for its welcoming and informal accommodation, as well as for the cultivation of saffron and other specialist crops.

-

1 - - - -

3 (x 2)

1 23,50 - 37,00 -

-

1 - 7 - 1 - 7 -

Castiglione a Casauria

Acquaviva

contrada Acquaviva 1,
65020 Castiglione a Casauria (PE)
Tel. 085880786 Fax 085880786

Located in the upper Pescara Valley, with a superb view of the surrounding area, this is a simple cottage, brick-built with wood-lined interiors.

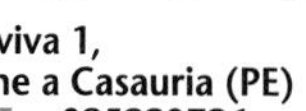

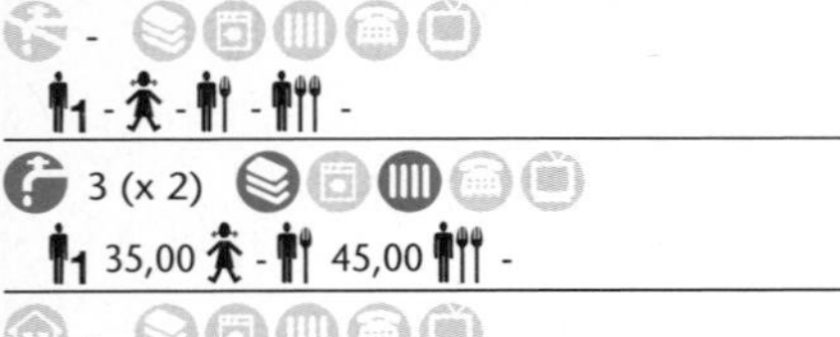

Castiglione Messer Raimondo

Colle San Giorgio

at San Giorgio,
64034 Castiglione Messer Raimondo (TE)
Tel. 0861990492 Fax 0861990492
E-mail: collegiorgio@tin.it

In the hills close to the Gran Sasso, this stone farmhouse has knotty beams and solid wood tables where wholesome local dishes are served.

4 (x 2)

1 20,00 - 35,00 -

La Ginestra

at San Giorgio, contrada Valloni 12,
64034 Castiglione Messer Raimondo (TE)
Tel. 0861990140 Fax 0861990140
E-mail: didomfran@tiscali.it

Guests are accommodated in this recently built farmhouse, furnished in early 20th-century style, standing in the middle of a farm with a pond.

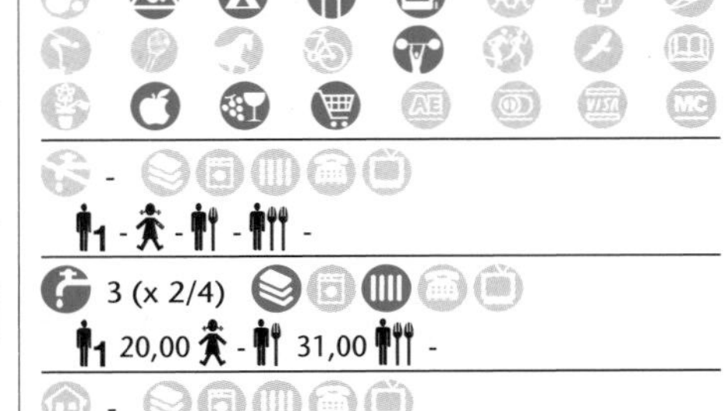

3 (x 2/4)

1 20,00 - 31,00 -

Castilenti

Le Lepri

at Villa San Romualdo, contrada Lepre,
64035 Castilenti (TE)
Tel. 0861996245
E-mail: le.lepri@ciaoweb.it

The Gran Sasso dominates the area, but all around there are historic towns and villages to visit, with plenty of opportunities to savour the excellent cuisine.

3 (x 2)

1 21,00 16,00 - -

Cellino Attanasio

Il Melograno

contrada Valviano 11, 64036 Cellino Attanasio (TE)
Tel. 0861659041 Fax 0861659041
E-mail: az.ilmelograno@libero.it

The name of this establishment reveals what is has to offer: organic farming and its products served at table, while natural materials were used for the renovation of the farmhouse.

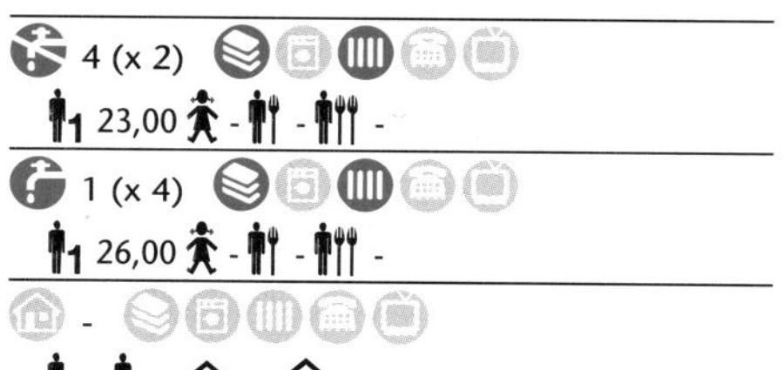

4 (x 2)

1 23,00 - -

1 (x 4)

1 26,00 - -

-

1 - 7 - 1 - 7 -

Civitella del Tronto

De Angelis Corvi

at Sant'Eurosia, 64010 Civitella del Tronto (TE)
Tel. 3476834628 Fax 0736252854
E-mail: deangelis.am@libero.it

Two fine farmhouses in stone and brick provide accommodation almost on the border between the Marches and Abruzzo; the accent is on simplicity and there's a wonderful view.

9 (x 1/2)

1 30,00 15,00 -

-

1 - - -

-

1 - 7 - 1 - 7 -

Masseria Priori

at Villa Passo, 64010 Civitella del Tronto (TE)
Tel. 0861917634 Fax 0861917634
Web: www.masseriapriori.it

At the centre of the farm is a charming 18th-century house with thick stone walls and huge vaults adding a flavour of history to the holiday.

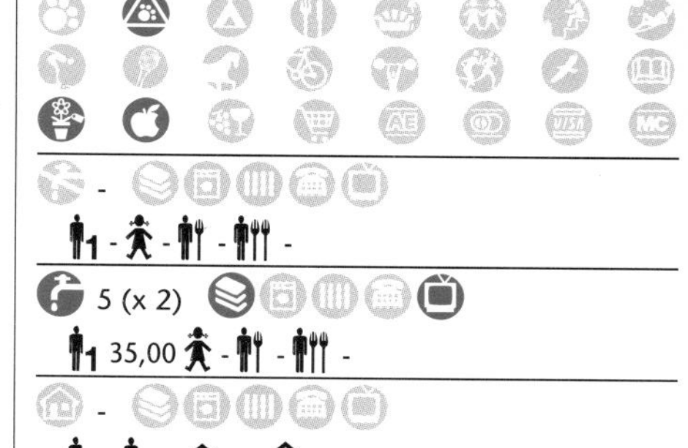

-

1 - - -

5 (x 2)

1 35,00 - -

-

1 - 7 - 1 - 7 -

Collepietro

La Fonte

via La Fonte, 67020 Collepietro (AQ)
Tel. 0862955131 Fax 0862955131
Web: http://digilander.libero.it/agriturismo-lafonte

Located in the heart of the Abruzzo Apennines, noted for their peaceful atmosphere and pure air, this recently opened farmhouse accommodation is simple but very clean and tidy.

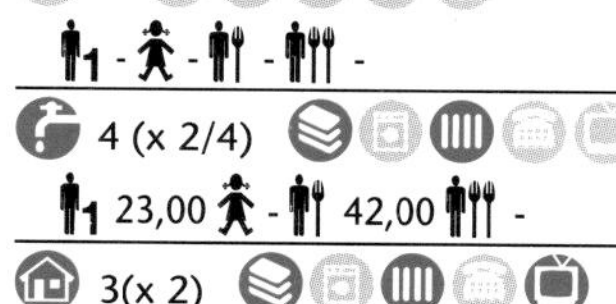

-

1 - - -

4 (x 2/4)

1 23,00 - 42,00 -

3(x 2)

1 - 7 - 1 - 7 590,00

Colonnella

Masseria Barnabei

contrada Vallecupa, S.P. (provincial road) Collonnella-Controguerra 30, 64012 Colonnella (TE)
Tel. 0861797330 Fax 0861761045
Web: www.masseriabarnabei.com

This accommodation is on the border with the Marches in an area renowned for the production of the Controguerra wine, and it's just a stone's throw from the sea.

\-

1 - - -

\-

1 - - -

8 (x 3/4)

1 - 7 - 1 150,00 7 -

Controguerra

Gioie di Fattoria

contrada San Biagio 13,
64010 Controguerra (TE)
Tel. 086189606 Fax 086189606
Web: www.gioiedifattoria.it

In the hills, this accommodation is in an early 20th-century farmhouse, rebuilt in rustic style; its large terrace commands views of the Gran Sasso and the sea.

\-

1 - - -

\-

1 - - -

4(x 4)

1 - 7 - 1 68,00 7 -

Lu Feschiuole

at San Giuseppe, 64010 Controguerra (TE)
Tel. 0861856630 Fax 0861856630
Web: www.agriturismo.com/lufeschiuole

In the pleasant Val Vibrata, amid olive groves and vineyards, there's a friendly welcome in well-equipped farmhouse accommodation where a range of recreational activities are available.

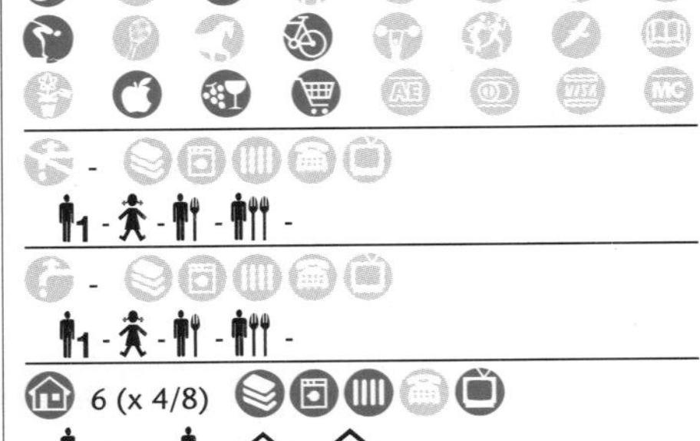

\-

1 - - -

\-

1 - - -

6 (x 4/8)

1 30,00 7 - 1 - 7 -

Corropoli

Gli Olmi

at Ravigliano 80, 64013 Corropoli (TE)
Tel. 0861856596 Fax 0861856596
Web: www.agriturismo.abruzzo.it

This complex of rural buildings located in the hills offers attractive modern rooms within easy reach of the beaches at Alba Adriatica and Villa Rosa.

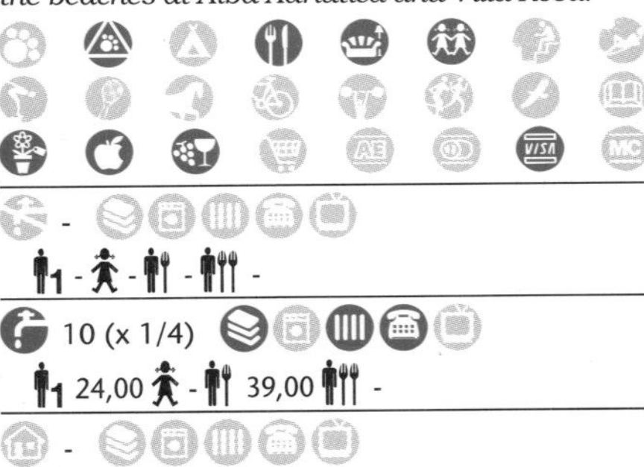

\-

1 - - -

10 (x 1/4)

1 24,00 - 39,00 -

\-

1 - 7 - 1 - 7 -

Corvara

L'Aperegina

contrada Pretara 1, 65020 Corvara (PE)
Tel. 0858889351 Fax 0858889351
Web: www.laperegina.com

At the foot of the Gran Sasso, simple but cosy accommodation is available in delightful rooms; beekeeping is the farm's main activity.

\-

1 - - -

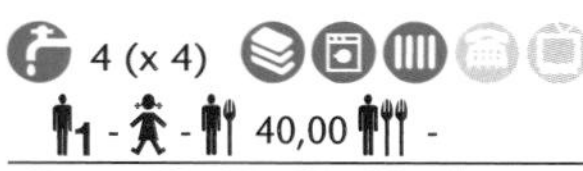
4 (x 4)

1 - - 40,00 -

1 - 7 - 1 - 7 -

Fara Filiorum Petri

L'Antico Tratturo

at Piana Masseria, 66010 Fara Filiorum Petri (CH)
Tel. 0871706066
Web: www.agriturismo.abruzzo.it

Set in the hills, a recently renovated stone cottage provides simple but comfortable (accommodation complete with fireplace).

1 - - -

5 (x 2)

1 31,00 - 52,00 -

1 - 7 - 1 - 7 -

Guardiagrele

Casino di Caprafico

at Caprafico, 66016 Guardiagrele (CH)
Tel. 0871897492 Fax 0871897492

Guests are accommodated in an 18th-century cottage; recently renovated, it has preserved all of its old-world charm.

1 - - -

1 - - -

3 (x 2/4)

1 - 7 - 1 - 7 560,00

Isola del Gran Sasso d'Italia

San Giovanni ad Insulam

at San Giovanni ad Insulam,
64045 Isola del Gran Sasso d'Italia (TE)
Tel. 0861210211
Web: www.sangiovanniadinsulam3000.it

This fine old stone farmhouse, where the frequent motif of the arch is a reminder that it was once a stopping-place for pilgrims, is ideal for all those who are fascinated by the past.

1 - - -

2 (x 2/4)

1 23,50 - - -

1(x 5)

1 - 7 - 1 68,00 7 -

Lentella

Il Bosco degli Ulivi

contrada Fonte Puteo, 66050 Lentella (CH)
Tel. 0873321116
Web: www.agriturismo.abruzzo.it

Amid olive groves, there's a warm welcome with accommodation in simple farm buildings. The sea is just ten minutes away (a bathing hut and beach umbrella are included in the price).

1 - - -

2 (x 2/8)

1 23,50 7 - 1 - 7 -

Loreto Aprutino

Ai Calanchi

contrada Fiorano, 65014 Loreto Aprutino (PE)
Tel. **0854214473** Fax **0854214473**

On top of a hill, with a row of cypresses in the background, this pleasant farmhouse has an atmosphere of monastic peace.

1 - - -

4 (x 2)

1 31,00 - 42,00 -

2(x 4)

1 - 7 - 1 114,00 7 -

Le Magnolie

contrada Fiorano 83, 65014 Loreto Aprutino (PE)
Tel. **0858289534** Fax **0858289534**
Web: **www.lemagnolie.com**

Located in a panoramic position on a hill, these two cottages dating from the 17th century have period furniture and are also equipped for banquets.

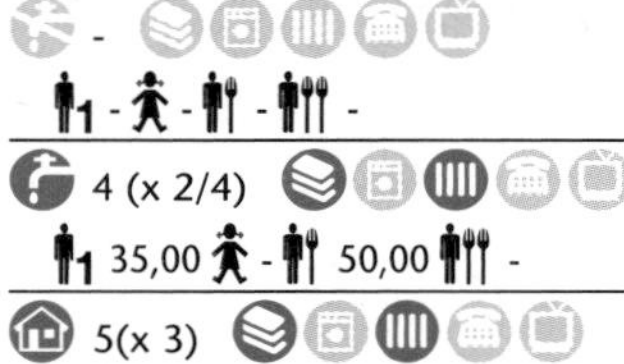

4 (x 2/4)

1 35,00 - 50,00 -

5(x 3)

1 - 7 - 1 120,00 7 -

Manoppello

Villa Pardi

at Cappuccini, 65024 Manoppello (PE)
Tel. **0854712289** Fax **0854712289**
Web: **www.villapardi.it**

This is a complex comprising an 18th-century shooting-lodge and two renovated cottages, well furnished and equipped with air-conditioning.

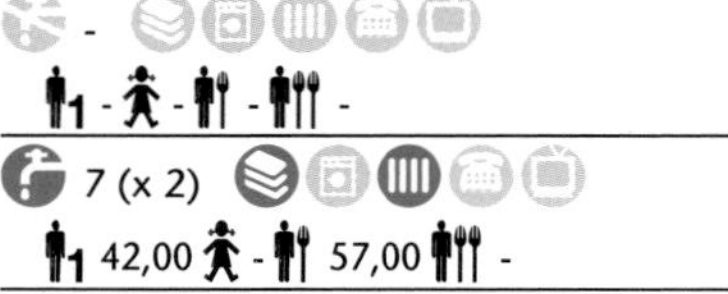

7 (x 2)

1 42,00 - 57,00 -

1 - 7 - 1 - 7 -

Montereale

Montorselli

at Cesaproba, contrada Ranaglie,
67015 Montereale (AQ)
Tel. **0862901848**

Woods of chestnut, conifer and beech clothe the slopes of the Gran Sasso, where this recently built farmhouse stands.

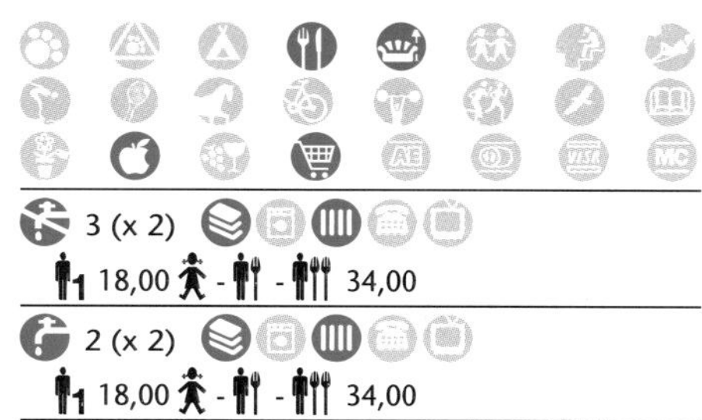

3 (x 2)

1 18,00 - - 34,00

2 (x 2)

1 18,00 - - 34,00

-

1 - 7 - 1 - 7 -

Morro d'Oro

Ponte Murato

contrada Ponte Murato 26, 64020 Morro d'Oro (TE)
Tel. 0858041171 Fax 0858041577
Web: www.agriturismopontemurato.it

These are rooms with a view over the well-cultivated rolling farmland of the lower Vomano Valley; but for lovers of wilder landscapes, the slopes of the Gran Sasso are close at hand.

-

1 - - -

-

1 - - -

3 (x 2/5)

1 - 7 - 1 93,00 7 491,00

Mozzagrogna

La Vigna

contrada Rosciavizza 27, 66030 Mozzagrogna (CH)
Tel. 0872712250 Fax 0872712250

This rural residence is surrounded by vineyards and olive groves in the hills extending inland from the sea. The view ranges from the Adriatic coast to the Sangro Valley and the Maiella Massif.

-

1 - - -

-

1 - - -

1(x 8)

1 26,00 7 - 1 - 7 -

Navelli

Casa Verde

at Civitaretenga, corso Umberto I 7,
67020 Navelli (AQ)
Tel. 0862959163 Fax 0862959163

Guests get a very warm welcome in this rural residence on the Piano di Navelli, an area noted for the cultivation of saffron.

-

1 29,00 - 40,00 -

6 (x 1/4)

1 29,00 - 40,00 -

-

1 - 7 - 1 - 7 -

Ortona

Agriverde

at Villa Caldari, via Monte Maiella 118,
66020 Ortona (CH)
Tel. 0859032101 Fax 0859031089
Web: www.agriverde.it

An attractive group of buildings surround a 19th-century villa where the restaurant, ample communal spaces and fitness centre are located.

\-
1 - - -

12 (x 1/4)
1 38,00 - 50,00 -

\-
1 - 7 - 1 - 7 -

PALOMBARO

L'ULIVETO

via Limiti di Sotto 38, 66010 Palombaro (CH)
Tel. 0871895348 Fax 0871895201
Web: www.agriturismo.com/uliveto

Guests are accommodated in a hospitable rural residence opposite the village of Palombaro, which stands on a hill sheltered by the Maiella Massif.

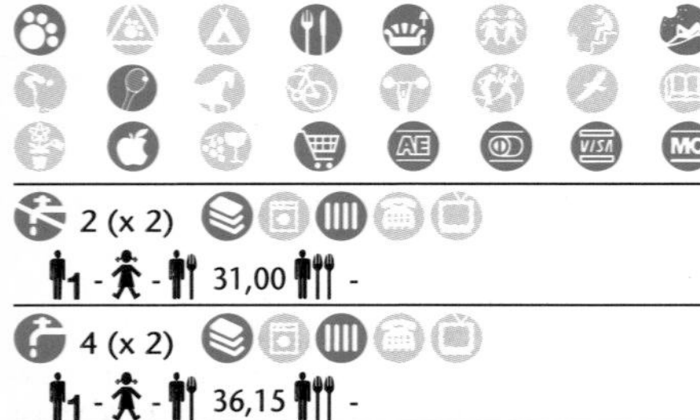

2 (x 2)
1 - - 31,00 -

4 (x 2)
1 - - 36,15 -

\-
1 - 7 - 1 - 7 -

PENNE

IL PORTICO

contrada Colle Serangelo 26, 65017 Penne (PE)
Tel. 0858210775 Fax 0858210775
Web: web.tiscali.it/ilportico

The name refers to the shady garden where guests may indulge in convivial pleasures and laze in the summer months.

4 (x 2/4)
1 17,00 - 34,00 -

3 (x 2)
1 18,00 - 36,00 -

\-
1 - 7 - 1 - 7 -

LA VENTILARA

contrada Trofigno, 65017 Penne (PE)
Tel. 085823374 Fax 085823374

A special feature of this farm is the enthusiasm of the owner of the house, who successfully organises kite competitions and trips on donkeys.

2 (x 4)
1 20,00 - - -

\-
1 - - -

\-
1 - 7 - 1 - 7 -

TENUTA SIGILLO

contrada Mallo 23, 65017 Penne (PE)
Tel. 08528102

Accommodation is available both in a recently refurbished farmhouse and in the main house, where the communal spaces are also situated.

4 (x 2)

1 21,00 - - -

3 (x 2)

1 21,00 - - -

-

1 - 7 - 1 - 7 -

Pizzoferrato

Antica Taverna

via Fannini 3, 66040 Pizzoferrato (CH)
Tel. **0872946255** Fax **0872946255**
E-mail: **dimatteo56@genie.it**

One of the special features of this farmhouse accommodation is the chance to explore on horseback the ancient cattle-tracks leading to the heart of the Maiella Massif.

-

1 - - - -

4 (x 2)

1 - - 30,00 -

-

1 - 7 - 1 - 7 -

Ripa Teatina

La Capezzagna

contrada Santo Stefano,
66010 Ripa Teatina (CH)
Tel. **0871398040** Fax **0871398040**
Web: **www.lacapezzagna.it**

Guests on this farm dedicated to quality wine-growing are accommodated in small suites with charming names and dine together with the family.

-

1 - - - -

3 (x 4)

1 30,99 - 46,48 -

-

1 - 7 - 1 - 7 -

Rocca San Giovanni

La Chiave

contrada Pocafeccia 10,
66020 Rocca San Giovanni (CH)
Tel. **0871563971**

This tastefully renovated farmstead lies in the verdant setting of a fruit and vegetable farm. The excellent cuisine is particularly recommended.

3 (x 2/4)

1 20,00 - 35,00 -

-

1 - - - -

-

1 - 7 - 1 - 7 -

ROCCASCALEGNA

IL GELSO

at Capriglia, via della Bonifica 6,
66040 Roccascalegna (CH)
Tel. **0872987526** Fax **0872987207**
Web: **www.ilgelso.3000.it**

A great location for a holiday in the Sangro Valley, which winds up from Fossacesia to the slopes of the Maiella Massif; don't miss Signora Giovanna's tasty traditional dishes.

\-
 1 - - -

3 (x 2/4)
 1 15,80 - 34,10 -

1(x 2)
 1 - 7 - 1 78,00 7 -

IL NESPOLO

contrada Capriglia 54, 66040 Roccascalegna (CH)
Tel. **0872987439** Fax **0872987439**
E-mail: **ilnespolo@inwind.it**

Accommodation is provided in two recently refurbished farmhouses; thanks to the skilful cook, the cuisine is particularly outstanding.

\-
 1 - - -

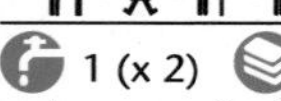  1 (x 2)
1 31,00 - 46,00 -

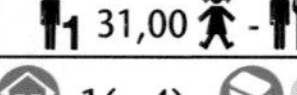 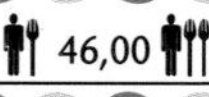 1(x 4)
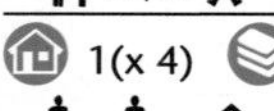  1 - 7 - 1 124,00 7 -

MAJA

contrada Aia di Rocco 73, 66040 Roccascalegna (CH)
Tel. **0872987315** Fax **0872987315**

With its splendid position, this pleasant farmhouse, remodernised in harmony with its rural setting, offers a warm welcome.

\-
 1 - - -

\-
1 - - -

1(x 8)
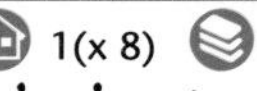  1 - 7 - 1 65,00 7 -

ROSCIANO

FIOR DI PESCO

at Villa San Giovanni, contrada Feudo 5,
65020 Rosciano (PE)
Tel. **0858505760** Fax **0858505760**
E-mail: **az.agr.fiordipesco@katamail.com**

This farmhouse accommodation is quite unusual: it's more a seaside villa than a rural residence, with its balconies, arcades and large paved areas for sunshades and tables.

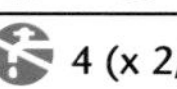   

4 (x 2/4)
1 26,00 - - 52,00

\-
1 - - -

\-
1 - 7 - 1 - 7 -

ROSETO DEGLI ABRUZZI

DI NICOLA DUNATILL

via Nazionale 7,
64026 Roseto degli Abruzzi (TE)
Tel. **0858992180**
E-mail: **dunatill@inwind.it**

This farm is well known for its production of Trebbiano and Montepulciano d'Abruzzo wines, while its olive oil is first rate.

\-

1 - - -

\-

1 - - -

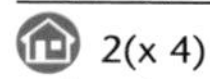 2(x 4)

1 - 7 - 1 - 7 750,00

Sant'Omero

La Meridiana

contrada Santa Maria a Vico,
64027 Sant'Omero (TE)
Tel. 0861786336 Fax 0861786336
Web: www.agriturismolameridiana.it

Within easy access of the sea, the mountains and various towns, this pleasant accommodation allows its guests to savour the joys of country life.

\-

1 - - -

\-

1 - - -

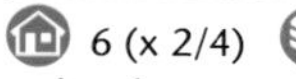 6 (x 2/4)

1 - 7 - 1 51,00 7 -

Scanno

Le Prata

at Le Prata, 67038 Scanno (AQ)
Tel. 0864747263

For holidays in a natural setting in the Tasso Valley, this recently renovated farmhouse offers comfortable accommodation.

\-

1 - - -

3 (x 2/4)

1 - - 35,00 -

\-

1 - 7 - 1 - 7 -

Scerni

Fattoria dell'Uliveto

contrada Ragna 59, 66020 Scerni (CH)
Tel. 0873914173 Fax 0873914173
Web: www.ventricina.com

In the pleasant setting of the hills just near the coast are these two splendidly renovated farmhouses, with a large arcade giving onto the countryside.

\-

1 - - -

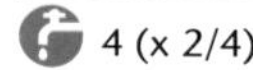 4 (x 2/4) 

1 28,00 15,00 45,00 -

\-

1 - 7 - 1 - 7 -

Silvi

Le Macine

contrada Cerrano 36, 64028 Silvi (TE)
Tel. 0859354033 Fax 0854225071
Web: www.agriturismolemacine.it

Located in the hills behind the coast, where wheat, fruit and olives are grown, these four farm buildings form a small country 'village' within sight of the sea.

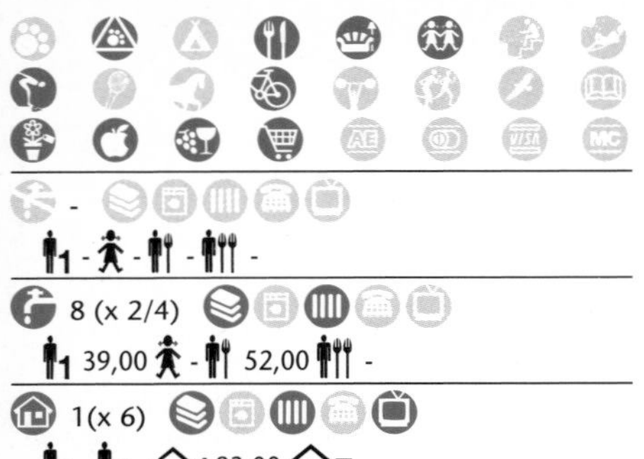

\-

1 - - -

8 (x 2/4)

1 39,00 - 52,00 -

1(x 6)

1 - 7 - 1 83,00 7 -

Teramo

Ginestrella

at Miano, contrada Colli, 64100 Teramo
Tel. **3283427479** Fax **0861246152**
Web: **www.ginestrella.it**

In a splendid setting, this farmhouse is now dedicated to rural tourism in accordance with the tenets of ecological architecture.

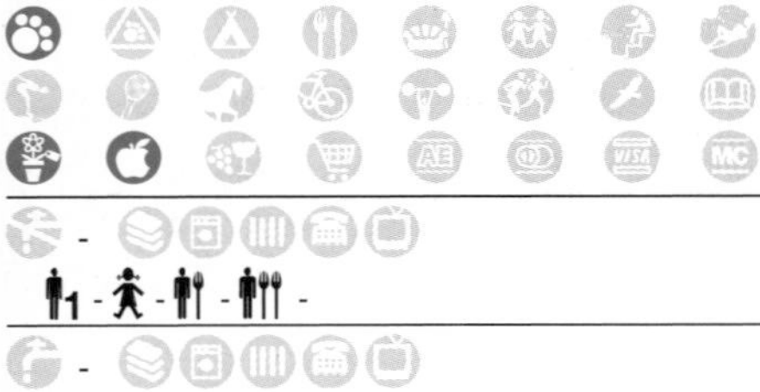

\-

1 - - -

\-

1 - - -

4(x 2)

1 - 7 - 1 120,00 7 -

Le Macine

at Poggio Cono, 64020 Teramo
Tel. **0861555227**

Accommodation is available in this renovated but authentically rural building, in contact with people accustomed to working on the land and proud of it too.

\-

1 - - -

3 (x 4)

1 21,00 - 31,00 -

\-

1 - 7 - 1 - 7 -

Tocco da Casauria

L'Oliveto

contrada S. Anna, 65028 Tocco da Casauria (PE)
Tel. **0858809178** Fax **085880538**
Web: **www.agricolturaoggi.com/agriturismololiveto**

Recent rebuilding has provided this accommodation with a portico and loggias, bright, well-equipped rooms and areas with a gazebo and tables.

\-

1 - - -

\-

1 - - -

2(x 8)

1 - 7 - 1 105,00 7 -

Madonna degli Angeli

contrada Madonna degli Angeli 7,
65028 Tocco da Casauria (PE)
Tel. **0854223813** Fax **0854223813**
E-mail: **lorenzo.depompeis@tin.it**

Careful conservation work has preserved the fascinating atmosphere of this post-house, where guests are now accommodated.

\-

1 - - -

-

1 - - -

4 (x 2/4)

1 - 7 - 1 75,00 7 -

Torano Nuovo

Villa Fiore

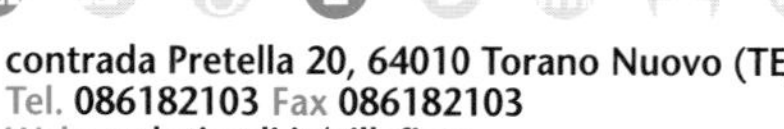

contrada Pretella 20, 64010 Torano Nuovo (TE)
Tel. 086182103 Fax 086182103
Web: web.tiscali.it/villafiore

This rural residence is the result of the restoration of an old farmhouse; it has a small restaurant serving local dishes and rooms looking out onto the valley.

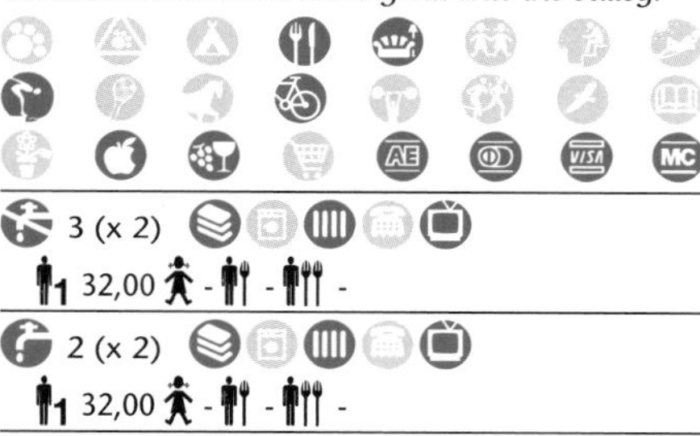

3 (x 2)

1 32,00 - -

2 (x 2)

1 32,00 - -

2(x 5)

1 - 7 - 1 128,00 7 -

Tossicia

Il Borghetto

contrada Viola 3, 64049 Tossicia (TE)
Tel. 0861698498 Fax 1782240585
Web: www.il-borghetto.com

This farmhouse offering accommodation in the higher hills has been renovated, but its solid late 19th-century appearance and the original materials have been preserved.

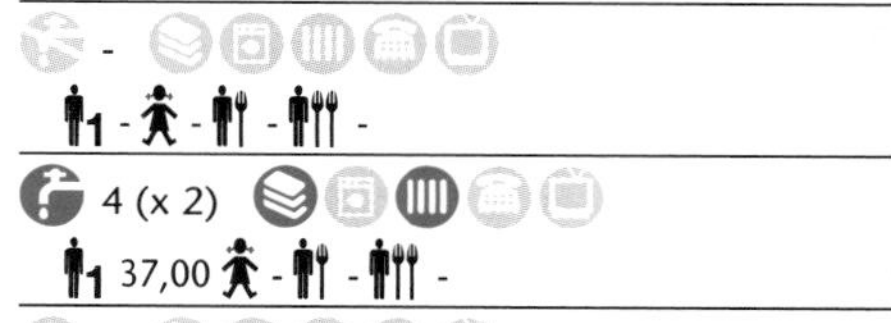

-

1 - - -

4 (x 2)

1 37,00 - -

-

1 - 7 - 1 - 7 -

Il Cerquone

contrada Cerquone 10, 64049 Tossicia (TE)
Tel. 0861698097 Fax 0861699719
Web: www.turismoverde.it

Located in the hills at the foot of the mountains, this farmhouse in 18th-century style, with its stone portal and severe lines, offers high quality accommodation.

-

1 - - -

5 (x 2)

1 25,00 - -

-

1 - 7 - 1 - 7 -

Vasto

Pozzitello

contrada Buonanotte, 66054 Vasto (CH)
Tel. 0873549888 Fax 0873549888

Amid fields of sunflowers and irises, two well-equipped stone farmhouses offer comfortable accommodation with a patio and an attractive garden.

-

1 - - -

-

1 - - -

7 (x 2/8)

1 - 7 - 1 135,00 7 -

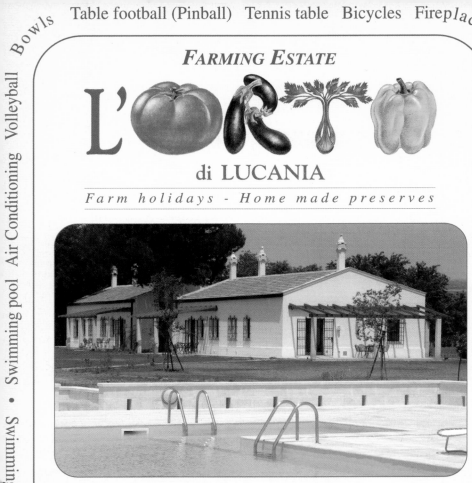

BASILICATA

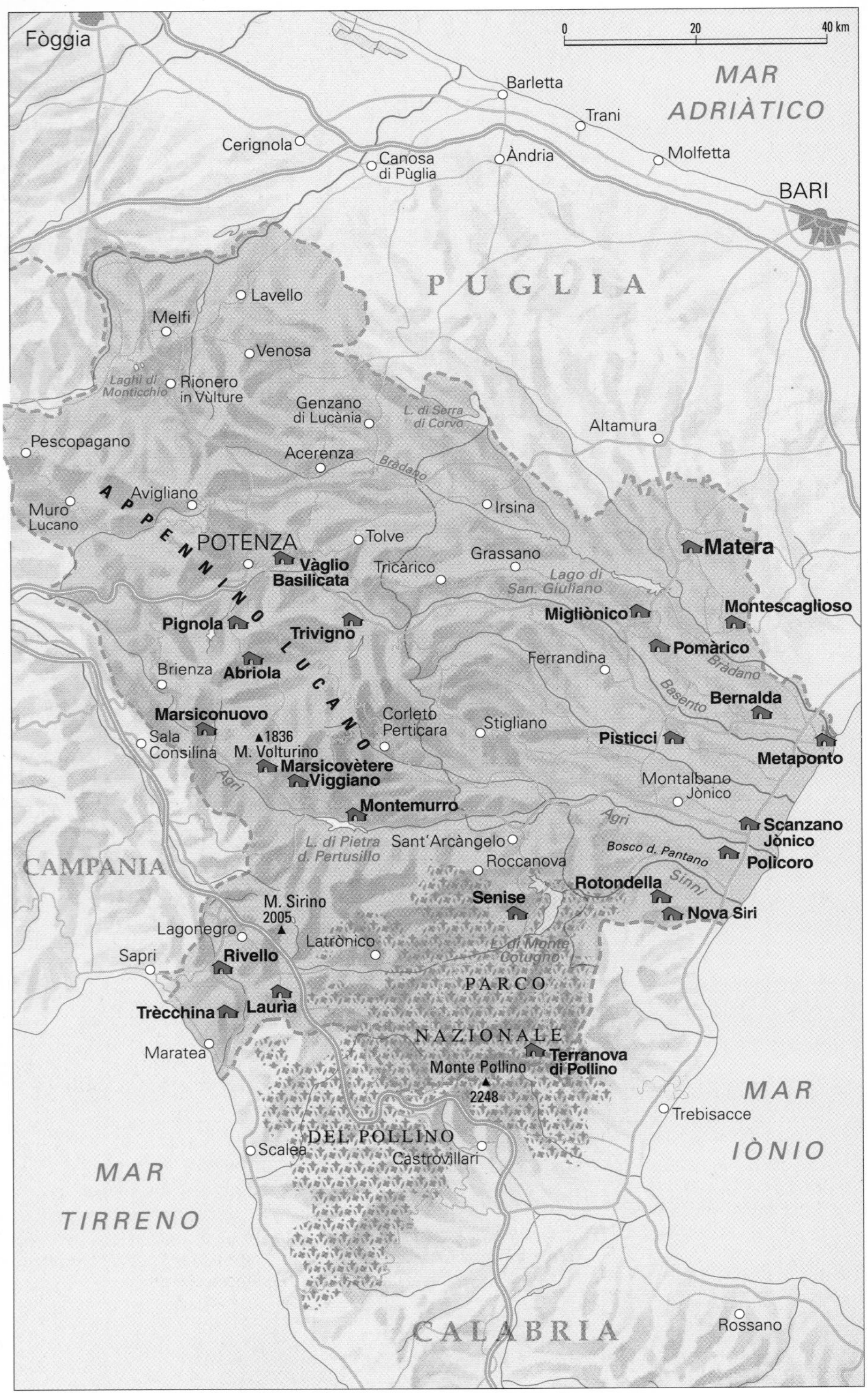

0
20
40 km
Fòggia
Barletta
Trani
MAR
ADRIÀTICO
Cerignola
Canosa
di Pùglia
Àndria
Molfetta
BARI
PUGLIA
Lavello
Melfi
Venosa
Laghi di
Monticchio
Rionero
in Vùlture
Genzano
di Lucània
L. di Serra
di Corvo
Altamura
Pescopagano
Acerenza
Bràdano
APPENNINO LUCANO
Muro
Lucano
Avigliano
Irsina
POTENZA
Tolve
Matera
Vàglio
Basilicata
Tricàrico
Grassano
Lago di
San. Giuliano
Pignola
Trivigno
Migliònico
Montescaglioso
Pomàrico
Brienza
Abriola
Ferrandina
Bràdano
Basento
Bernalda
Marsiconuovo
Corleto
Perticara
Stigliano
Sala
Consilina
1836
M. Volturino
Pisticci
Metaponto
Agri
Marsicovètere
Viggiano
Montalbano
Jònico
Montemurro
Agri
Scanzano
Jònico
L. di Pietra
d. Pertusillo
Sant'Arcàngelo
Bosco d. Pantano
Policoro
CAMPANIA
Roccanova
Sinni
Rotondella
Senise
M. Sirino
2005
Nova Siri
Lagonegro
Latrònico
L. di Monte
Cotugno
Sapri
Rivello
PARCO
Trècchina
Lauria
NAZIONALE
Terranova
di Pollino
Maratea
Monte Pollino
2248
MAR
Trebisacce
DEL POLLINO
Scalea
Castrovillari
IÒNIO
MAR
TIRRENO
CALABRIA
Rossano

ABRIOLA

LA DOLCE VITA

 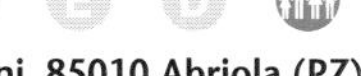

contrada Valloni, 85010 Abriola (PZ)
Tel. 0971923524
Web: www.aziendelucane.org/ladolcevita

In a mountain setting, this accommodation is ideal for those wanting to explore the surrounding countryside and see a working farm at close quarters.

 -
 1 - - -

 9 (x 1/2)
1 21,00 - 42,00 -

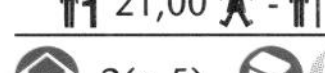 2(x 5) 
 1 25,00 7 - 1 - 7 -

BERNALDA

RELAIS MASSERIA CARDILLO

strada Basentana at km 97.5,
75012 Bernalda (MT)
Tel. 0835748992 Fax 0835748994
Web: www.masseriacardillo.it

Located in the Piana di Metaponto, this accommodation offers a warm atmosphere and modern comforts, as do the flats located in the outbuildings.

-
 1 - - -

 10 (x 2)
1 55,00 - 68,00 -

-
1 - 7 - 1 - 7 -

SALIERNO DI BIASE ALESSANDRINA

at Torremare, 75012 Bernalda (MT)
Tel. 0835543055

In both the modern farmhouse in the countryside and an old renovated building in the village, the rooms are rustic but functional.

-
1 - - -

-
1 - - -

 3(x 4)
1 - 7 - 1 83,00 7 -

LAURIA

SOLE VERDE

 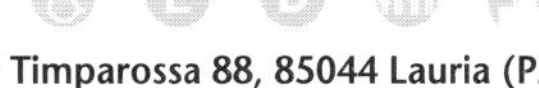

contrada Timparossa 88, 85044 Lauria (PZ)
Tel. 0973825208

Located in the open countryside with a wood behind it, this accommodation in a refurbished farmhouse comprises two one-roomed flats.

\-

1 - - -

\-

1 - - -

2(x 3)

1 - 7 - 1 51,50 7 -

Marsiconuovo

Vignola

contrada Capo d'Acqua 11,
85052 Marsiconuovo (PZ)
Tel. 0975342511 Fax 0975344003

This renovated farmhouse dating from 1860 has a large restaurant; it's the ideal starting-point for walking tours of the surrounding area.

\-

1 - - -

4 (x 4)

1 15,00 - 26,00 -

1(x 4)

1 - 7 - 1 18,00 7 -

Marsicovetere

Il Querceto-La terra di Nancy

contrada Barricelle 70,
85050 Marsicovetere (PZ)
Tel. 097569339 Fax 097569907
Web: www.ilquerceto.it

This farm, which is called 'La Terra di Nancy', uses organic methods to produce wholesome food and organizes workshops on this theme.

\-

1 - - -

6 (x 2/4)

1 42,00 - 57,00 -

1(x 4)

1 - 7 - 1 260,00 7 -

Matera

Matinelle

contrada Le Matinelle, 75100 Matera
Tel. 0835307343 Fax 0835307343
Web: www.lematinelle.com

This typical rural house, which has been refurbished, offers rooms of various types located in the former stables; these are provided with air-conditioning and are furnished in traditional style.

\-

1 - - -

8 (x 1/4)

1 30,00 - 45,00 -

-

1 - 7 - 1 - 7 -

Metaponto

Casa Ricotta

S.S. (state road) 106 at km 448, podere 81,
75010 Metaponto (MT)
Tel. 0835741214

Ideal for a holiday close to the sea, the countryside and archaeological remains, this functional modern building has a restaurant serving the farm's own produce.

-

1 - - - -

-

1 - - - -

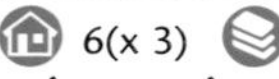 

6(x 3)

1 57,00 7 - 1 - 7 -

MacchiAgricola

S.S. (state road) 106 at km 444,
75010 Metaponto (MT)
Tel. 0835582193 Fax 0835470194
Web: www.macchiagricola.com

Surrounded by citrus groves, this farmhouse on the Ionian Coast has welcoming and comfortable rooms with their own little garden or veranda.

-

1 - - - -

-

1 - - - -

18 (x 2/4)

1 47,00 7 - 1 - 7 -

San Marco

at San Marco, S.S. (state road) 175 at km 34,
75010 Metaponto (MT)
Tel. 0835747050 Fax 0835747070
Web: www.sifor.it/aziende/sanmarco

This accommodation, located in a commanding position, offers a view as far as the sea; it is divided into two separate blocks, with the restaurant and services in a new building.

-

1 - - - -

5 (x 2/4)

1 34,00 - 42,00 -

8 (x 4/5)

1 - 7 - 1 - 7 774,69

Miglionico

San Giuliano

contrada Foggia di Lupo, 75010 Miglionico (MT)
Tel. 0835559183 Fax 0835559183
Web: www.san-giuliano.com

This farmhouse accommodation, situated near Lake San Giuliano, has recently renovated buildings with modern conveniences.

-

1 - - -

8 (x 2)

1 25,00 - 40,00 -

1(x 4)

1 - 7 - 1 - 7 500,00

Montemurro

Robilotta Giovanni

contrada Castelluccio, 85053 Montemurro (PZ)
Tel. **0975354070** Fax **0971753411**
E-mail: **diesell@libero.it**

This accommodation is ideal for an active holiday: during walks along the ancient cattle-tracks you can pick wild raspberries and strawberries and, later in the year, mushrooms and truffles.

-

1 - - -

6 (x 1/2)

1 25,00 - 35,00 -

2 (x 4/5)

1 - 7 - 1 100,00 7 -

Montescaglioso

L'Orto di Lucania

contrada Dogana, 75024 Montescaglioso (MT)
Tel. **0835202195** Fax **0835207008**
Web: **www.ortodilucania.it**

This accommodation, with its modern, well-equipped farmhouses, has an environment-friendly approach to agriculture.

-

1 - - -

-

1 - - -

6(x 4)

1 - 7 - 1 110,00 7 698,00

Pierro Emilia

at Menzane Fiumicello,
75024 Montescaglioso (MT)
Tel. **0835200406** Fax **0835208141**

Located in the Bradano Valley, this farm has three modern apartments in a pleasant building surrounding a grassy area.

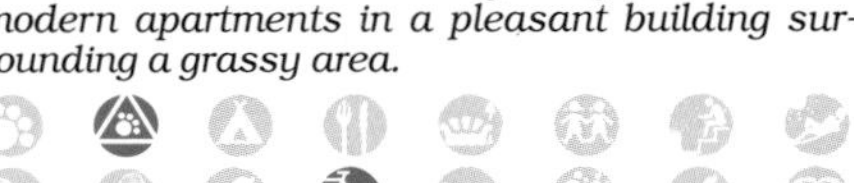

-

1 - - -

-

1 - - -

3(x 4)

1 20,00 7 - 1 - 7 -

Nova Siri

La Collinetta

contrada Pietra del Conte, 75020 Nova Siri (MT)
Tel. **0835505175** Fax **0835505175**
Web: **www.starttel.it**

Just five kilometres from the sea, this pleasant rural accommodation is housed in an old building where two restaurants provide a warm welcome.

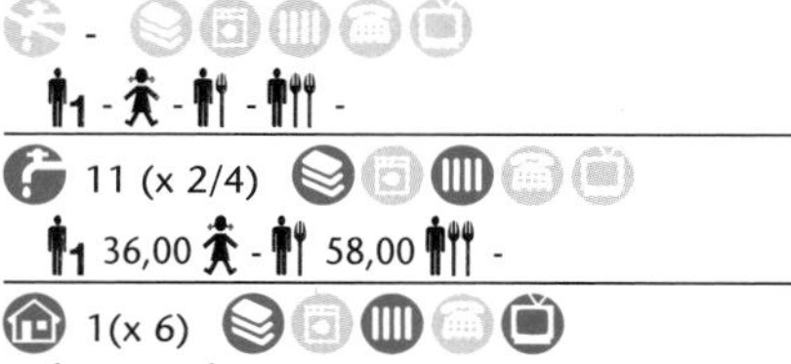

11 (x 2/4)

36,00 - 58,00 -

1(x 6)

36,00 - 1 - 7 -

Pignola

La Fattoria sotto il Cielo

contrada Petrucco, 85010 Pignola (PZ)
Tel. 0971420166 Fax 0971486000
Web: www.lafattoriasottoilcielo.it

This superb accommodation is situated in an elegant rural setting, and the restaurant plays a major role. Nearby is the Lago Pantano di Pignola Nature Reserve.

6 (x 2)

30,00 - 43,00 -

1 - 7 - 1 - 7 -

Pisticci

I Caselli

contrada Giumenteria, 75020 Pisticci (MT)
Tel. 0835470206 Fax 0998277055

Pleasant accommodation is available in this peaceful house located close to the orchards, olive groves and market gardens in the countryside surrounding a village.

3 (x 4/5)

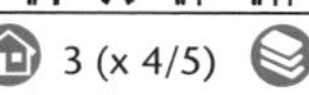

1 - 7 - 1 70,00 7 -

San Teodoro Nuovo

at Marconia, contrada San Teodoro Nuovo, 75020 Pisticci (MT)
Tel. 0835470042 Fax 0835470042
Web: www.santeodoronuovo.com

Top quality accommodation is available in this elegant 18th-century house and its outbuildings in the middle of a farm of 150 hectares where citrus fruit, olives, cereals and other crops are grown.

9 (x 2/6)

1 31,00 7 - 1 - 7 -

Policoro

Ricciardulli

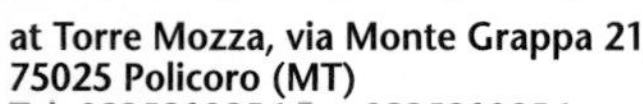

at Torre Mozza, via Monte Grappa 21,
75025 Policoro (MT)
Tel. **0835910256** Fax **0835910256**

Located in an area specialising in market gardening, this accommodation is in utilitarian self-contained flats close to the modern farmhouse.

\-

1 - - -

\-

1 - - -

3 (x 4/8)

1 - 7 - 1 - 7 700,00

Pomarico

Lama di Palio

contrada Lama di Palio, 75016 Pomarico (MT)
Tel. **0835552359**

In an isolated position, amid the fragrance of the Mediterranean scrub, these recently constructed buildings offer modern conveniences and a restaurant.

\-

1 - - -

\-

1 - - -

2(x 4)

1 - 7 - 1 77,00 7 -

Rivello

Leo Nicolina

contrada Fiumicello 42, 85040 Rivello (PZ)
Tel. **097346339**

Accommodation is available in modern rooms (a kitchen is available for those staying at least a month); there's also a camping area, a restaurant and a large terrace.

5 (x 2)

1 13,00 - 26,00 -

\-

1 - - -

\-

1 - 7 - 1 - 7 -

Tre Forni

contrada Campo di Monaco 1,
85040 Rivello (PZ)
Tel. **097346549**

Signor Pietro gives his guests a very warm welcome; the outstanding feature of holidays here is the traditional rural atmosphere of the surroundings.

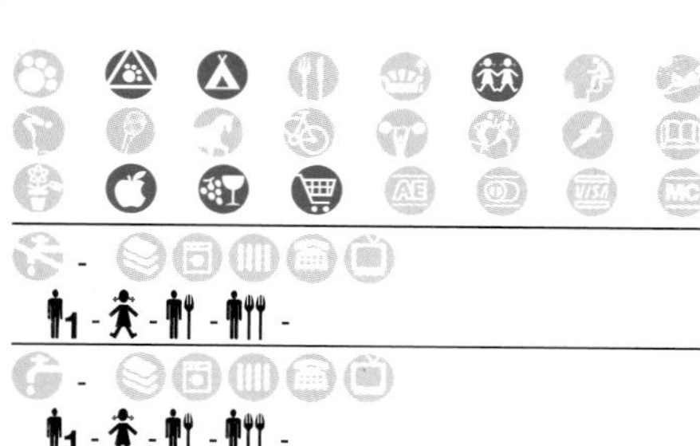

\-

1 - - -

\-

1 - - -

5(x 2)

1 18,00 7 - 1 - 7 -

Rotondella

Il Pago

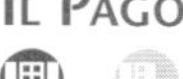

contrada Trisaia Pantanello 7,
75026 Rotondella (MT)
Tel. **0835848090** Fax **0835848097**
Web: **www.heraclea.it/ilpago**

Located in the Piana di Trisia, just a few kilometres from the sea, each of these recent, functional buildings has its own independent access to the garden.

\-

1 - - -

4 (x 4)

1 25,00 - 39,00 -

\-

1 - 7 - 1 - 7 -

Scanzano Jonico

Agata Giuseppe

at Terzo Cavone, via Roma 10,
75020 Scanzano Jonico (MT)
Tel. **0835954649**

Welcoming accommodation is provided in clean, airy rooms with modern conveniences; in the evenings dances and dinners are regularly organised in the open air.

\-

1 - - -

\-

1 - - -

4(x 5)

1 - 7 - 1 60,00 7 -

Bufaleria

via Monviso 61, 75020 Scanzano Jonico (MT)
Tel. **0835954287**
Web: **www.simar.net/web/cal/bufa-ita.htm**

These small flats have large arcades where guests can relax and enjoy their meals together, with fruit provided free by the farm.

\-

1 - - -

\-

1 - - -

5(x 4)

1 - 7 - 1 52,00 7 -

Senise

Casale Donnaperna

contrada Timpone, 85038 Senise (PZ)
Tel. **0973686729** Fax **0973686729**
Web: **www.donnaperna.it**

This accommodation in an 18th-century house is noteworthy for the elegant setting, the refined cuisine and the range of services available.

- 2 (x 1/2)

85,00 - 95,00 -

4 (x 4/8)

340,00 - -

Terranova di Pollino

La Garavina

at Casa del Conte,
85030 Terranova di Pollino (PZ)
Tel. 097393395 Fax 097393395
E-mail: lagaravina@tin.it

This farmhouse accommodation is in the mountains, in the heart of the Monte Pollino National Park, a true paradise for nature lovers.

- -

5 (x 2/4)

21,00 - - 46,48

1(x 5)

10,00 - - -

Trecchina

La Colla

contrada Colla, 85049 Trecchina (PZ)
Tel. 0973826067

In the hills just inland from Maratea, a trim fenced lawn welcomes guests, reflecting this carefully well-kept accommodation.

- -

- -

3(x 6)

- - - 581,00

Trivigno

La Foresteria di San Leo

contrada San Leo 11, 85018 Trivigno (PZ)
Tel. 0971981157 Fax 0971442695

In this establishment housed in an ancient Benedictine hermitage, the accommodation reflects the atmosphere of its setting and the food is vegetarian.

- -

5 (x 2/4)

39,00 - - 68,00

- - - -

Vaglio Basilicata

La Dimora dei Cavalieri

contrada Tataseppe 1, 85010 Vaglio Basilicata (PZ)
Tel. 0971487466 Fax 0971487907
Web: www.dimoracavalieri.it

The outstanding feature of this old farmhouse offering comfortable accommodation is the excellent cuisine combining tradition with innovation.

-

1 - - - -

5 (x 2/4)

1 30,00 21,00 45,00 -

1(x 3)

1 30,00 7 - 1 - 7 -

VIGGIANO

AGRICOLA PISANI

contrada San Lorenzo, 85059 Viggiano (PZ)
Tel. 097561076 Fax 0975352000
E-mail: biopisani@tiscali.it

Surrounded by orchards, this two-storey building is divided into two large flats where guests are accommodated in comfort.

-

1 - - - -

-

1 - - - -

2(x 2)

1 18,00 7 - 1 - 7 -

CALABRIA

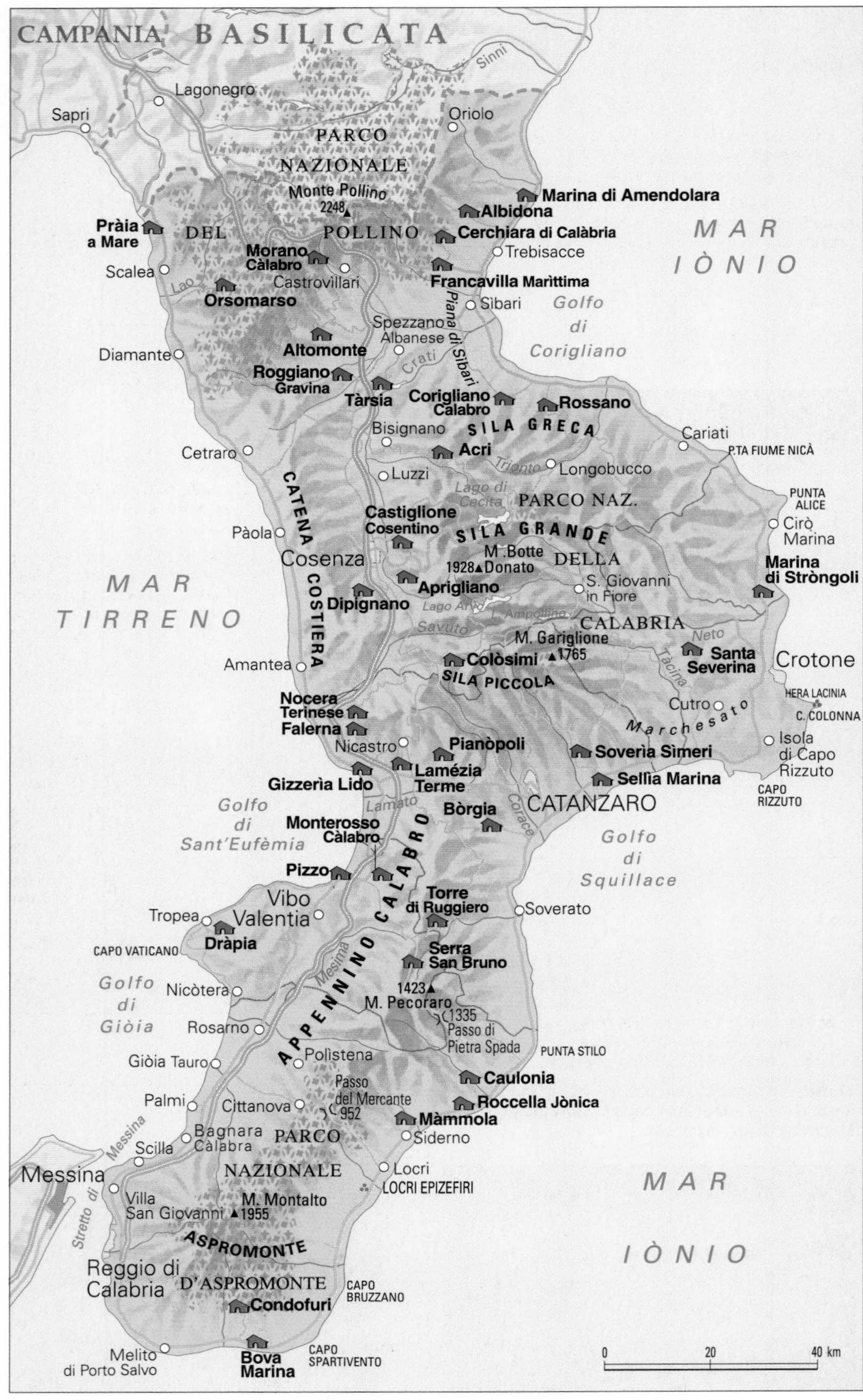
CAMPANIA
BASILICATA
Sinni
Lagonegro
Sapri
Oriolo
PARCO
NAZIONALE
Monte Pollino
2248
DEL
POLLINO
Marina di Amendolara
Albidona
Pràia a Mare
Cerchiara di Calàbria
Trebisacce
Morano Càlabro
Castrovillari
Scalea
Lao
Orsomarso
Francavilla Marìttima
MAR
IÒNIO
Sìbari
Piana di Sibari
Golfo
di
Corigliano
Spezzano Albanese
Altomonte
Diamante
Crati
Roggiano Gravina
Tàrsia
Corigliano Calabro
Rossano
Bisignano
SILA GRECA
Cariati
P.TA FIUME NICÀ
Cetraro
Acri
Trionto
Longobucco
Luzzi
Lago di Cecita
PARCO NAZ.
PUNTA ALICE
CATENA COSTIERA
Castiglione Cosentino
SILA GRANDE
Cirò Marina
Pàola
M. Botte Donato
1928
DELLA
Cosenza
Marina di Stròngoli
MAR
TIRRENO
Aprigliano
S. Giovanni in Fiore
Dipignano
Lago Arvo
Ampollino
CALABRIA
Savuto
Neto
M. Gariglione
1765
Santa Severina
Crotone
Amantea
Colòsimi
Tàcina
SILA PICCOLA
HERA LACINIA
Nocera Terinese
Cutro
C. COLONNA
Falerna
Marchesato
Nicastro
Pianòpoli
Isola di Capo Rizzuto
Soverìa Sìmeri
Lamézia Terme
Gizzerìa Lido
Sellìa Marina
CAPO RIZZUTO
Golfo
di
Sant'Eufèmia
Lamato
Bòrgia
CATANZARO
Corace
Monterosso Càlabro
Golfo
di
Squillace
Pizzo
APPENNINO CALABRO
Vibo Valentia
Torre di Ruggiero
Tropea
Soverato
Dràpia
CAPO VATICANO
Serra San Bruno
Mesima
Golfo
di
Giòia
Nicòtera
1423
M. Pecoraro
Rosarno
1335
Passo di Pietra Spada
Polìstena
PUNTA STILO
Giòia Tauro
Caulonia
Passo del Mercante
952
Palmi
Cittanova
Roccella Jònica
Màmmola
Bagnara Càlabra
PARCO
Siderno
Messina
Scilla
NAZIONALE
Locri
Messina
LOCRI EPIZEFIRI
Villa San Giovanni
M. Montalto
1955
MAR
Stretto di Messina
ASPROMONTE
IÒNIO
Reggio di Calabria
D'ASPROMONTE
CAPO BRUZZANO
Condofuri
Melito di Porto Salvo
Bova Marina
CAPO SPARTIVENTO
0
20
40 km

Acri

Santa Maria di Macchia

contrada Macchia di Baffi 73, 87041 Acri (CS)
Tel. 0984946165 Fax 0984955124
E-mail: gennaro.baffi@tiscali.it

This is an excellent address for a relaxing holiday in the typical cottages of the higher hills. They have simple, bright rooms and there's always a friendly welcome.

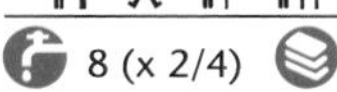 -

1 - - -

8 (x 2/4)

1 20,50 - 36,00 -

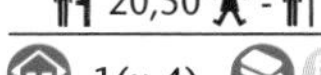

1(x 4)

1 21,00 7 - 1 - 7 -

Albidona

Masseria Torre di Albidona

at Piana della Torre, 87070 Albidona (CS)
Tel. 0981507944 Fax 0981507944
E-mail: torredialbidona@supereva.it

These comfortable flats, with a view of the sea, are located in old stone farmhouses surrounded by the Mediterranean scrub.

 -

1 - - -

-

1 - - -

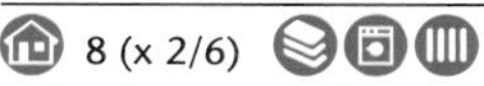

8 (x 2/6)

1 - 7 - 1 - 7 775,00

Altomonte

La Quercia

contrada Boscari, 87042 Altomonte (CS)
Tel. 0981946232 Fax 0981946232
Web: www.agrilaquercia.it

This accommodation is provided by a number of old buildings that have been restored.The centre is 5 km away, and the sea, the mountains and the remains of the ancient Sybaris are within a radius of 20 km.

-

1 - - -

4 (x 2/4)

1 20,00 - 35,00 -

-

1 - 7 - 1 - 7 -

Le Farnie

contrada S. Anna, 87042 Altomonte (CS)
Tel. 0981948786 Fax 0981948786
Web: www.paginegialle.it/agriturismolefarnie

This farmhouse has been skilfully renovated with a wide veranda commanding splendid views, traditional furnishings and tasteful fittings.

\-
1 - - -

5 (x 2)
1 25,00 - 40,00 -

\-
1 - 7 - 1 - 7 -

Aprigliano

Piccole Vigne

contrada San Nicola, 87051 Aprigliano (CS)
Tel. 0984423891 Fax 0984422309

In a fine position on the upper reaches of the River Crati, this refurbished 19th-century country house is largely devoted to wine-growing.

2 (x 2)
1 26,00 - 33,50 -

\-
1 - - -

\-
1 - 7 - 1 - 7 -

Borgia

Borgo Piazza

at Vallo di Borgia, 88021 Borgia (CZ)
Tel. 0961391326 Fax 0961391326
Web: www.ponterio.3000.it

This large farm in a splendid position on Squillace Bay offers accommodation in its well-kept guest-house with period furniture.

\-
1 - - -

8 (x 1/4)
1 38,00 - 56,00 -

1(x 4)
1 - 7 - 1 - 7 619,75

Bova Marina

La Spina Santa

via Spina Santa, 89035 Bova Marina (RC)
Tel. 0965761012 Fax 0965761012
Web: www.laspinasanta.com

Just a stone's throw from the sea, with a magnificent view of Etna, this holiday accommodation is in an old manor house surrounded by shady palm trees.

\-
1 - - -

10 (x 2)
1 35,00 - 45,00 -

1(x 4)
1 - 7 - 1 - 7 420,00

Castiglione Cosentino

Caldeo

contrada Fontana 28,
87040 Castiglione Cosentino (CS)
Tel. 0984442575 Fax 0984442575
Web: www.italyinholiday.it

Situated in a large modern building attached to the original nucleus dating from the 18th-century, the rooms have views of the Crati Valley and Cosenza.

 -

1 - - -

 8 (x 2/4)

1 21,00 - 42,00 -

-

1 - 7 - 1 - 7 -

Caulonia

Domolà

via Cappelleri 52, 89041 Caulonia (RC)
Tel. 0964863604 Fax 0964863604
Web: web.tiscali.it/agriturismo-domola

Guests are accommodated in the farmhouses near the main building: on no account should you miss the unspoilt scenery of the Aspromonte National Park.

-

1 - - -

5 (x 2)

1 22,00 - 40,00 -

7 (x 2/3)

1 22,00 7 - 1 - 7 -

Cerchiara di Calabria

Acampora

at Piana, contrada Milizia,
87070 Cerchiara di Calabria (CS)
Tel. 0981991320
Web: web.tiscali.it/agriturismoacampora

Located on the slopes of Monte Sellaro, this establishment is run by advocates of organic farming, noted for their warmth and hospitality.

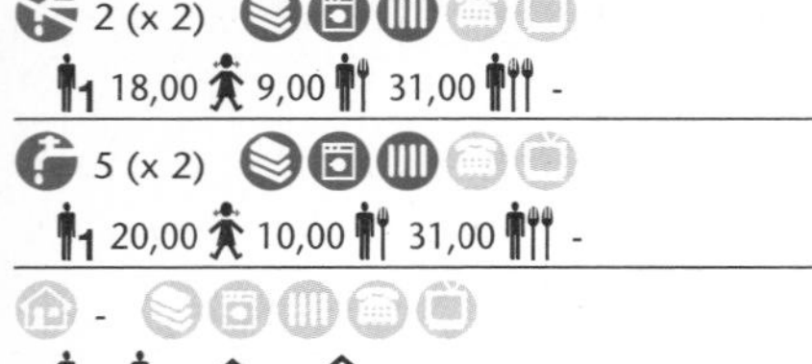

2 (x 2)

1 18,00 9,00 31,00 -

5 (x 2)

1 20,00 10,00 31,00 -

-

1 - 7 - 1 - 7 -

Colosimi

La Baita

contrada Silicella, 87050 Colosimi (CS)
Tel. 0984392802

In the splendid setting of the Sila Piccola plateau, surrounded by market gardens and orchards, this accommodation is in a renovated cottage or four delightful wooden chalets.

-

1 - - - -

-

1 - - - -

5 (x 2/6)

1 23,00 7 - 1 - 7 -

Condofuri

Il Bergamotto

at Amendolea, 89030 Condofuri (RC)
Tel. 0965727213 Fax 0965727213

In the Aspromonte National Park, an agricultural village has been carefully restored to provide tourist accommodation: the restaurant serves delicious dishes using local produce.

11 (x 2/4)

1 16,00 - 26,00 -

-

1 - - - -

-

1 - 7 - 1 - 7 -

Corigliano Calabro

Al Vecchio Biroccio da Giorgio

contrada Frassa, 87065 Corigliano Calabro (CS)
Tel. 0983854233 Fax 0983854233
Web: www.calabriaweb/agriturismoalvecchio biroccio.it

Citrus and olive groves surround this accommodation, while higher up the timeless manna ash grows in profusion.

-

1 - - - -

3 (x 2)

1 39,00 - 49,00 -

-

1 - 7 - 1 - 7 -

Dipignano

Foresta Sottana

contrada Foresta, 87045 Dipignano (CS)
Tel. 0984621574 Fax 0984621574
Web: www.forestasottana.it

The accommodation is in two stone cottages that have been renovated with care and good taste; the rooms are comfortable and atmospheric, and the Tyrrhenian is only half an hour away.

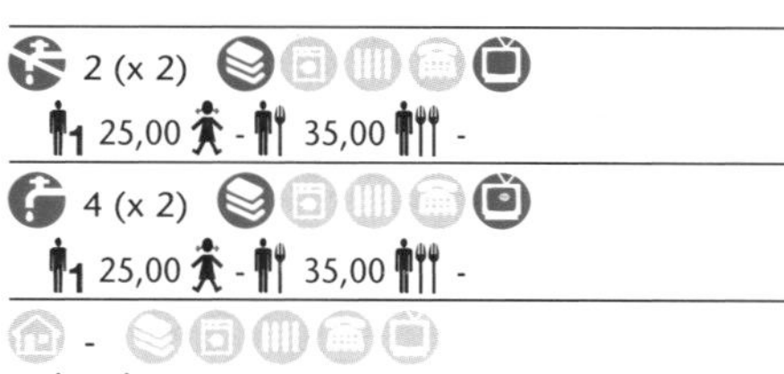

Drapia

Torre Galli

contrada San Rocco Moccina 1, fondo Moccina 1, 89862 Drapia (VV)
Tel. 096367254 Fax 096367254
E-mail: torregalli@hotmail.com

Located in a lemon-grove, these 18th-century cottages have been carefully renovated and furnished with both antiques and elements of hi-tech design.

-
1 - - -
3 (x 2/4)
1 41,00 - 54,00 -

-
1 - 7 - 1 - 7 -

Falerna

Villella

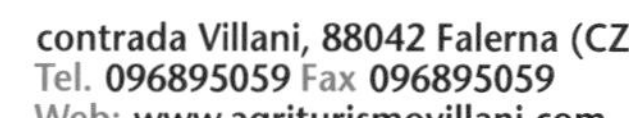

contrada Villani, 88042 Falerna (CZ)
Tel. 096895059 Fax 096895059
Web: www.agriturismovillani.com

In this refurbished old farmhouse among the olive groves in the hills is a restaurant with walls in bare stone, a large fireplace and traditional kitchen utensils.

-
1 - - -
4(x 4)
1 20,00 7 - 1 - 7 -

Francavilla Marittima

La Mandria

contrada Sferracavallo 89,
87072 Francavilla Marittima (CS)
Tel. 0981992576 Fax 0981992576
E-mail: agrilamandria@tiscali.it

Located in the Monte Pollino National Park, this establishment comprises a sheepfold restored with a taste for rustic detail and a modern building with comfortable rooms.

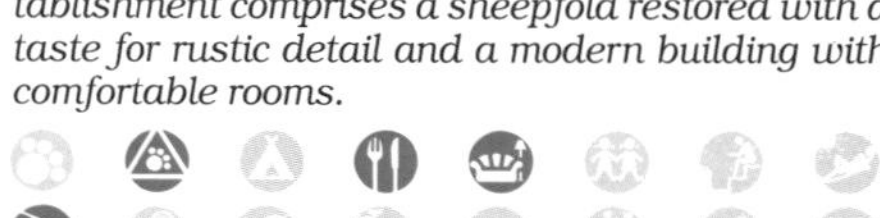

-
1 - - -
8 (x 2)
1 30,00 - 60,00 -
4(x 4)
1 - 7 - 1 - 7 600,00

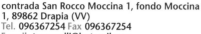

Gizzeria Lido

Torre dei Cavalieri di Malta

contrada Santa Caterina,
88040 Gizzeria Lido (CZ)
Tel. 0968466208 Fax 0968466208
Web: www.torredeicavalieri.it

The rooms in this establishment have an atmosphere of bygone days; the owner is able to communicate his passion for the land and the animals to his guests.

 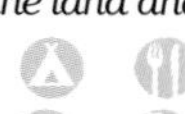   

-

1 - - -

 7 (x 1/4) 
1 23,24 - -

 4(x 4) 

1 - 7 - 1 72,30 7 -

Lamezia Terme

Tenuta Feudo de' Medici

at Sambiase, contrada Felicetta,
88046 Lamezia Terme (CZ)
Tel. 096821012 Fax 098621012
Web: www.de-medici.it

The accommodation is in an imposing 18th-century farmhouse with a lived-in air about it. Adjacent are the ancient olive-press and centuries-old olive grove producing excellent oil.

-
1 - - -

-
1 - - -

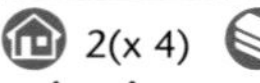 2(x 4)  
1 - 7 - 1 21,00 7 -

Trigna

at Sant'Eufemia Lamezia, contrada Trigna,
88040 Lamezia Terme (CZ)
Tel. 0968209034 Fax 0968209034
Web: www.agriturismotrigna.it

Located on the Tyrrhenian Sea, with the Ionian close by, this accommodation offers comfortable self-contained rooms in the former stables.

 -
1 - - -

 10 (x 2/4) 
1 33,00 - 52,00 -

2(x 3)

1 - 7 - 1 66,00 7 450,00

Mammola

Cannazzi

contrada Cannazzi, 89045 Mammola (RC)
Tel. **0964418023**

Commanding splendid views, these rustic rooms are located in an old cottage strategically positioned between the Ionian and Tyrrhenian seas; the excellent cuisine is not to be missed.

\-

1 - - -

3 (x 2)

1 20,00 - 30,00 -

4 (x 2/6)

1 18,00 7 - 1 - 7 -

Marina di Amendolara

La Lista

contrada Lista, 87070 Marina di Amendolara (CS)
Tel. **0981915445** Fax **0981915445**
Web: **www.lalista.it**

'Turismo mare e campagna' (seaside and country holidays) is the slogan of this establishment on the Ionian Coast, with accommodation in a number of former farmhouses.

\-

1 - - -

\-

1 - - -

13 (x 2/9)

1 - 7 - 1 - 7 420,00

Marina di Strongoli

Dattilo

contrada Dattilo, 88815 Marina di Strongoli (KR)
Tel. **0962865613** Fax **0962865613**
Web: **www.dattilo.it**

Only a kilometre from the sea, amid olive and citrus groves and vineyards, this is a splendid 17th-century farmhouse surrounded by self-contained chalets with fireplaces and flower-bedecked terraces.

\-

1 - - -

\-

1 - - -

8(x 2)

1 26,00 7 - 1 - 7 -

Monterosso Calabro

Villa Velia

contrada Liddio, 89819 Monterosso Calabro (VV)
Tel. **0963325039** Fax **0963325039**
E-mail: **anparisi@libero.it**

Guests may choose between the main house and the attractive annexe for a holiday offering opportunities for interesting excursions or bathing in the sea.

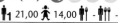

2 (x 2)

1 21,00 14,00 - -

\-

1 - - -

1(x 4)

1 - 7 - 1 83,00 7 -

Morano Calabro

La Locanda del Parco

contrada Mazzicanino, 87016 Morano Calabro (CS)
Tel. 098131304 Fax 098131304
Web: www.lalocandadelparco.com

In the heart of the Monte Pollino National Park, this modern and well-organised establishment has a particularly attractive restaurant, with a fireplace and a display of old artefacts.

-

1 - - -

6 (x 2/4)

1 31,00 - 47,00 -

2(x 4)

1 31,00 7 - 1 - 7 -

Nocera Terinese

Vota

at Campodorato, contrada Vota 3,
88047 Nocera Terinese (CZ)
Tel. 096891517
Web: www.agrivota.it

Those staying in this simple accommodation will get a warm welcome from the family running it, who have a passion for the land (the animals reared here include the black Calabrian pig).

-

1 - - -

8 (x 2)

1 28,50 - 50,00 -

2(x 4)

1 28,50 7 - 1 - 7 -

Orsomarso

I Cedri

at Bonicose, 87022 Orsomarso (CS)
Tel. 096226548
E-mail: ellegipi@libero.it

Courtesy and a passion for their work are the characteristics of the owners of this establishment; the rooms are in an 18th-century cottage that has been refurbished and provided with modern comforts.

-

1 - - -

6 (x 2/4)

1 35,00 - - -

1(x 4)

1 - 7 - 1 - 7 840,00

Pianopoli

Le Carolee

contrada Gabella 1, 88040 Pianopoli (CZ)
Tel. 096835076 Fax 096835076
Web: www.lecarolee.it

This hillside farm producing olives, citrus fruit and cork has orderly rooms in the French style; the swimming pool is surrounded by extensive grassy areas.

\-

1 - - -

8 (x 2)

1 48,00 - 58,00 -

\-

1 - 7 - 1 - 7 -

\-

1 - - -

\-

1 - - -

6 (x 2/6)

1 70,00 7 - 1 - 7 -

Pizzo

Agrimare

at Colamaio, 89812 Pizzo (VV)
Tel. 0963534880 Fax 0817146480

These small white villas with patios and lawns, located in a vast citrus grove adjacent to the sea, have direct access to the beach, where the bathing-hut and deck-chairs are free of charge.

Praia a Mare

Nappi

at Piano delle Vigne, via Marco Polo 10,
87028 Praia a Mare (CS)
Tel. 098574305
Web: www.agrinappi.it

On a hill farm commanding a splendid view, a number of old rural buildings have been restored into flats and a restaurant.

\-

1 - - -

\-

1 - - -

5 (x 4/6)

1 - 7 - 1 - 7 1.113,00

Roccella Jonica

Agriclub Placido Le Giare

at Marano, S.S. (state road) 106 at km 111,
89047 Roccella Jonica (RC)
Tel. 096485170 Fax 0964863115
Web: www.agriclublegiare.it

In a verdant setting close to the beach, this is a small paradise on earth with self-contained chalets. Diving sessions are also organised.

\-

1 - - -

1 (x 2)

1 50,00 - 70,00 -

11(x 2)

1 50,00 7 315,00 1 - 7 -

ROGGIANO GRAVINA

SANTA LUCIA

contrada Santa Lucia, 87017 Roggiano Gravina (CS)
Tel. **0984507019** Fax **0984507019**
E-mail: **slucia@mixer.antares.it**

This imposing farmhouse, which has preserved its 18th-century appearance, offers refurbished rooms and flats furnished in rustic style.

\-

1 - - -

4 (x 2)

1 21,00 - 39,00 -

2(x 8)

1 - 7 - 1 166,00 7 -

ROSSANO

COZZO DI SIMARI

at Crocicchia, via Cozzo di Simari 8, 87068 Rossano (CS)
Tel. **0983520896** Fax **0983520896**

Offering rooms with a view in the hills just inland from the Ionian Coast, this establishment is close to the beaches of Sibari Bay and the mountains of the Sila Greca and Monte Pollino.

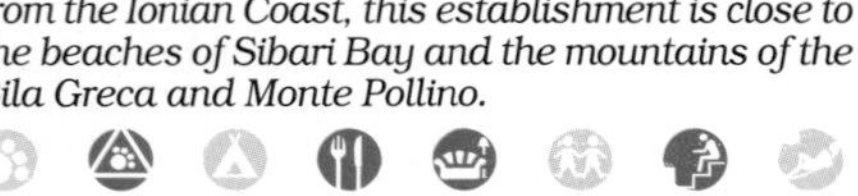

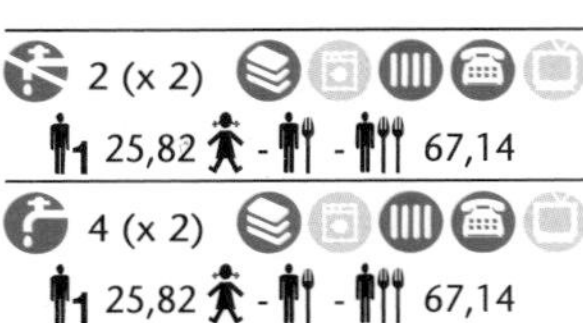

2 (x 2)

1 25,82 - - 67,14

4 (x 2)

1 25,82 - - 67,14

\-

1 - 7 - 1 - 7 -

FELLINO

contrada Fellino, 87068 Rossano (CS)
Tel. **0983514859** Fax **0983514859**

The pleasure of a holiday on this old farm, restored in a truly exemplary manner, is made complete by the discovery of the flavours of its kitchen garden.

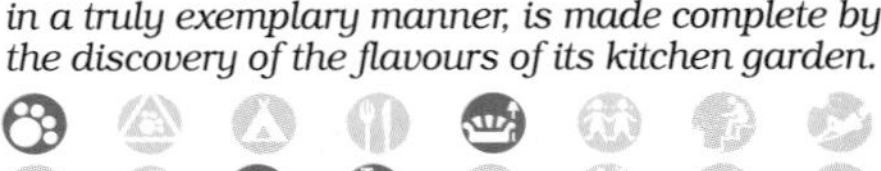

\-

1 - - -

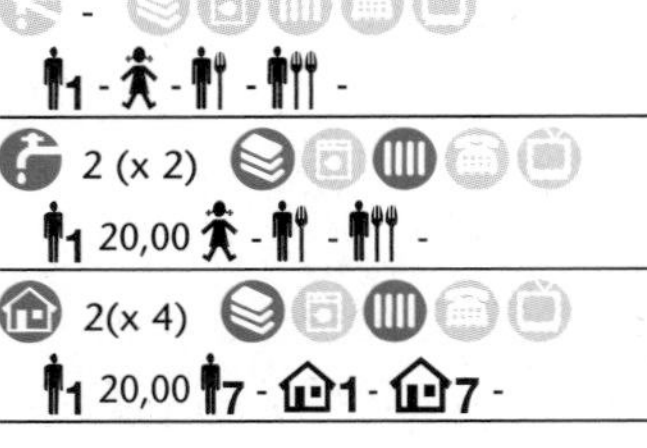

2 (x 2)

1 20,00 - - -

2(x 4)

1 20,00 7 - 1 - 7 -

Il Giardino di Iti

at Amica, 87068 Rossano (CS)
Tel. 098364508 Fax 098364508
Web: www.giardinoiti.it

Floors in terracotta and old beams, fireplaces and ancient stones, the scent of the lemon trees... all these features contribute in recreating an atmosphere of bygone times.

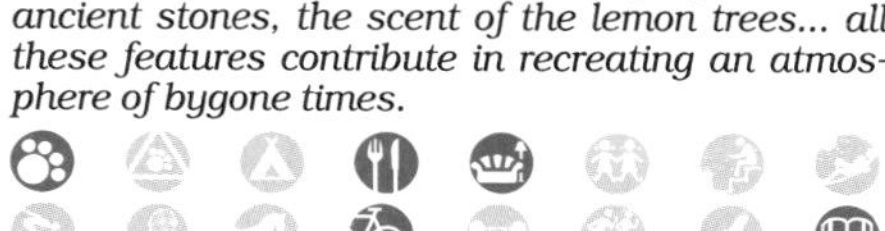

2 (x 2)

1 37,00 - 47,00 -

10 (x 2)

1 39,00 - 49,00 -

-

1 - 7 - 1 - 7 -

Le Colline del Gelso

contrada Gelso - Mazzei 18, 87067 Rossano (CS)
Tel. 0983569136 Fax 0983569136
Web: www.lecollinedelgelso.com

Accommodation is available in comfortable flats in a rural residence that has been carefully renovated using local stone and hand-made bricks.

-

1 - - - -

4 (x 2)

1 48,00 35,00 60,00 -

6 (x 2/4)

1 48,00 7 - 1 - 7 -

Santa Severina

Il Querceto

at Cerzeto, 88832 Santa Severina (KR)
Tel. 096251101 Fax 096251467
E-mail: cicciomac@altavista.net

This accommodation has a vaguely colonial atmosphere, due both to the luxuriant vegetation and to the yellow walls and curved gratings of the buildings.

-

1 - - - -

6 (x 1/2)

1 25,82 - 36,15 -

3(x 3)

1 - 7 - 1 67,14 7 -

Sellia Marina

Contrada Guido

contrada Guido, 88050 Sellia Marina (CZ)
Tel. 0961961495 Fax 0961961495
Web: www.contradaguido.it

This refined residence is located in an 18th-century village. A beautiful pinewood separates the estate from its private beach.

3 (x 1/2)

1 65,00 - 80,00 -

10 (x 2)

1 70,00 - 85,00 -

1 - 7 - 1 - 7 -

Serra San Bruno

Fondo dei Baroni

at La Chiusa, 89822 Serra San Bruno (VV)
Tel. 096371706 Fax 0963772180
Web: www.fondodeibaroni.it

This accommodation is characterised by the profusion of natural materials in the furnishings and the use of woodland produce in the dishes served in the restaurant.

\-

1 - - -

4 (x 2)

1 30,99 - 38,73 -

4(x 4)

1 - 7 - 1 98,13 7 -

Soveria Simeri

Santacinnara

contrada Santa Cenere,
88050 Soveria Simeri (CZ)
Tel. 0961798456 Fax 0961798526
Web: www.santacinnara.it

The owners' house is situated in the centre of the farm; around it, forming a sort of village, the flats have been carefully converted from the former stables and storehouses.

\-

1 - - -

\-

1 - - -

7 (x 3/6)

1 26,00 7 - 1 - 7 -

Tarsia

Agri Club

contrada Camigliano, 87040 Tarsia (CS)
Tel. 0981952716 Fax 0981952655
E-mail: iarmenta@libero.it

Guests on this farm will discover one of Calabria's treasures: olive oil made from varieties of ancient trees that give it a unique flavour.

\-

1 - - -

7 (x 1/4)

1 23,00 - 30,00 -

1(x 4)

1 - 7 - 1 70,00 7 260,00

Torre di Ruggiero

I Basiliani

contrada San Basile, 88060 Torre di Ruggiero (CZ)
Tel. 0967938000 Fax 0967938000
Web: www.ibasiliani.com

This quality farmhouse accommodation, located on the watershed between the Ionian and Tyrrhenian seas, offers a babysitting service on request, and educational activities are provided for groups.

\-

1 - - -

10 (x 2/4)

1 37,00 20,00 52,00 -

2(x 3)

1 - 7 - 1 - 7 668,81

CAMPANIA

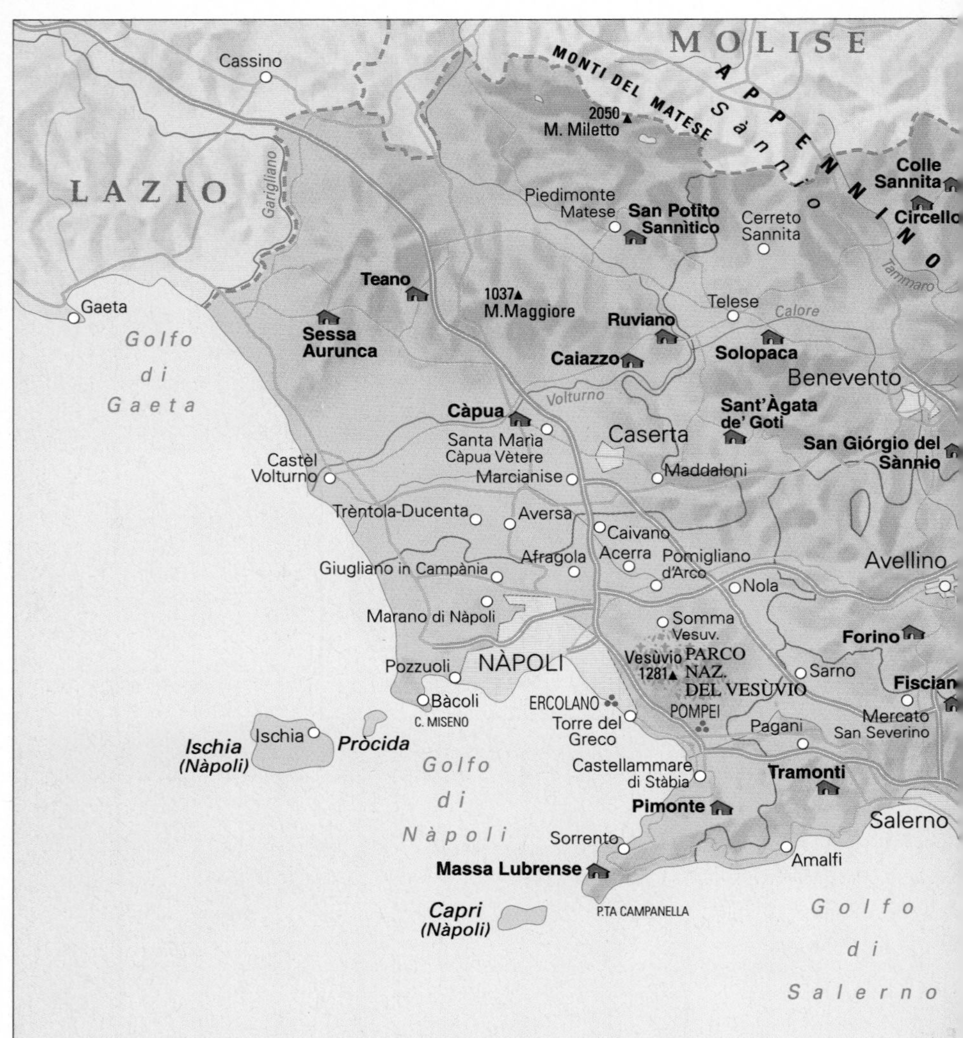
MOLISE
MONTI DEL MATESE
APPENNINO
Sànnio
2050
M. Miletto
Cassino
LAZIO
Garigliano
Piedimonte Matese
San Potito Sannìtico
Cerreto Sannita
Colle Sannita
Circello
Tammaro
Teano
1037
M.Maggiore
Telese
Calore
Gaeta
Sessa Aurunca
Ruviano
Solopaca
Caiazzo
Benevento
Golfo di Gaeta
Volturno
Càpua
Sant'Àgata de' Goti
Santa Marìa Càpua Vètere
Caserta
San Giórgio del Sànnio
Castèl Volturno
Marcianise
Maddaloni
Trèntola-Ducenta
Aversa
Caivano
Afragola
Acerra
Pomigliano d'Arco
Avellino
Giugliano in Campània
Nola
Marano di Nàpoli
Somma Vesuv.
Forino
Pozzuoli
NÀPOLI
Vesùvio 1281
PARCO NAZ. DEL VESÙVIO
Sarno
Fiscian
Bàcoli
C. MISENO
ERCOLANO
POMPEI
Mercato San Severino
Ischia
Ischia (Nàpoli)
Pròcida
Torre del Greco
Pagani
Golfo di Nàpoli
Castellammare di Stàbia
Tramonti
Pimonte
Salerno
Sorrento
Amalfi
Massa Lubrense
P.TA CAMPANELLA
Capri (Nàpoli)
Golfo di Salerno
MAR TIRRENO
0
20
40 km

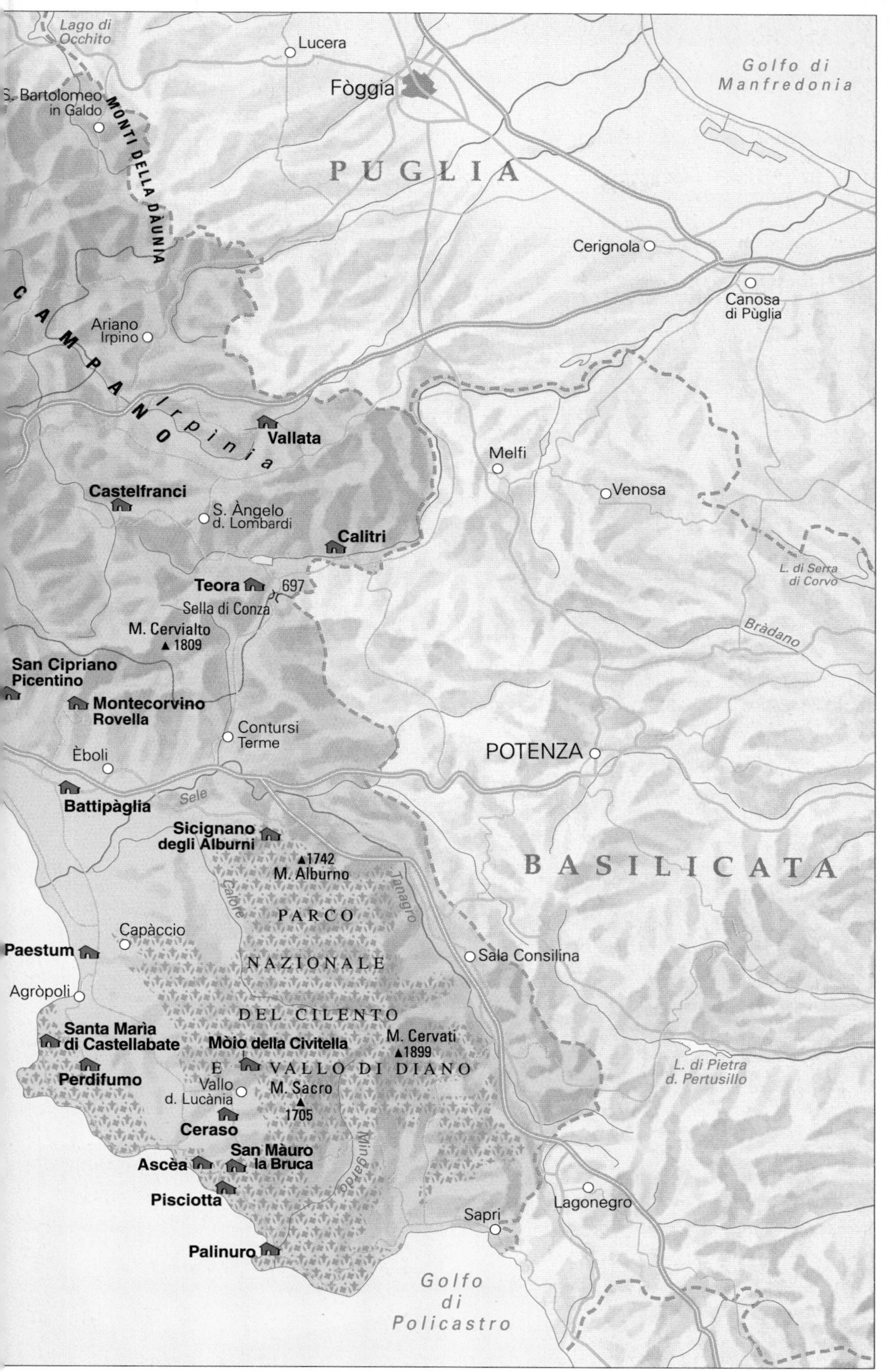
Lago di Occhito
Lucera
Fòggia
Golfo di Manfredonia
S. Bartolomeo in Galdo
MONTI DELLA DÀUNIA
PUGLIA
Cerignola
Canosa di Pùglia
CAMPANO
Ariano Irpino
Irpinia
Vallata
Melfi
Venosa
Castelfranci
S. Àngelo d. Lombardi
Calitri
L. di Serra di Corvo
Teora
697
Sella di Conza
M. Cervialto
1809
Bràdano
San Cipriano Picentino
Montecorvino Rovella
Contursi Terme
Èboli
POTENZA
Battipàglia
Sele
Sicignano degli Alburni
1742
M. Alburno
BASILICATA
Calore
Tanagro
PARCO NAZIONALE DEL CILENTO E VALLO DI DIANO
Capàccio
Paestum
Sala Consilina
Agròpoli
Santa Marìa di Castellabate
Mòio della Civitella
M. Cervati
1899
L. di Pietra d. Pertusillo
Perdifumo
Vallo d. Lucània
M. Sacro
1705
Ceraso
San Màuro la Bruca
Ascèa
Mingardo
Pisciotta
Lagonegro
Sapri
Palinuro
Golfo di Policastro

Ascea

Aurella

at Magnocavallo, via delle Erbe 1,
84046 Ascea (SA)
Tel. 0974977588 Fax 0974977588
E-mail: agriturismoaurella@libero.it

This farm, located on a hilltop in the Cilento National Park, dominates the remains of the ancient Greek city of Velia and the sea.

 -

1 - - -

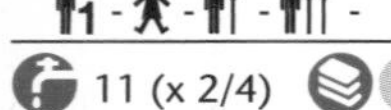 11 (x 2/4)

1 31,00 - 44,00 -

 1(x 4)

 1 - 7 - 1 70,00 7 -

Casa Leone

at Terradura, via Vittorio Emanuele 8,
84070 Ascea (SA)
Tel. 0974977003 Fax 0974978008
Web: www.cilento.de

The farmhouse is in the village, but its wide terraces face the estate where olives, figs and citrus fruit are grown.

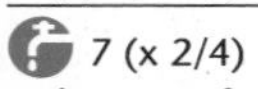 -

1 - - -

 7 (x 2/4) 

 1 32,00 20,00 48,00 -

2(x 2)

1 - 7 - 1 - 7 399,00

Iscairia

at Marina di Ascea, 84058 Ascea (SA)
Tel. 0974972241 Fax 0974972372
Web: www.iscairia.it

The owners of this accommodation share their lifestyle, which is dictated by a generous nature, with their guests (Iscaria does in fact mean 'happy island').

-

1 - - -

 10 (x 1/2)

1 42,00 - 62,00 -

-

1 - 7 - 1 - 7 -

Battipaglia

Antica Masseria La Morella

at Santa Lucia, via Fosso Stazione 3,
84090 Battipaglia (SA)
Tel. 082851008 Fax 081406630
Web: www.la-morella.it

In addition to its imposing main building (where the rooms for the guests are located), this two-hundred-year-old farm in the Piana del Sele has a church, stables, barns and an oven for baking bread.

 -

1 - - -

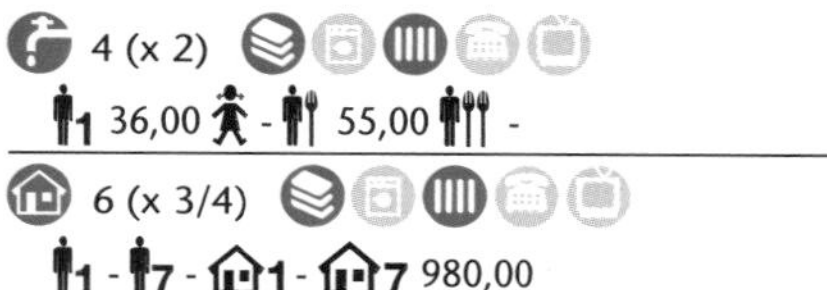

4 (x 2)

36,00 - 55,00 -

6 (x 3/4)

- - 1 - 7 980,00

Caiazzo

La Soppuntata

via Santa Lucia 6, 81013 Caiazzo (CE)
Tel. 0823862160 Fax 0823862160
E-mail: aziendaagrituristicalaso@tin.it

In this farmhouse, which has been refurbished with particular attention being paid to the details, a young family of nature lovers offers a warm welcome.

-

1 - - -

4 (x 1/2)

20,00 15,00 40,00 -

-

1 - 7 - 1 - 7 -

Le Campanelle

via Cameralunga 64, 81013 Caiazzo (CE)
Tel. 0823862487 Fax 0823862487

Amid green hills there's an informal and homely atmosphere in small self-contained apartments in a number of farmhouses situated close to the main residence.

-

1 - - -

-

1 - - -

4(x 2)

26,00 7 - 1 - 7 -

Calitri

Il Tufiello

contrada Tufiello, S.S. (state road) 399 at km 6, 83045 Calitri (AV)
Tel. 082738851 Fax 0815757604
Web: www.iltufiello.it

The accommodation is located in a white building in the centre of a farm growing cereals and sunflowers: there's a very friendly atmosphere and respect for nature.

-

1 - - -

4 (x 2)

25,00 - - -

3 (x 2/4)

1 - 7 - 1 104,00 7 -

Capua

Masseria Giòsole

via Giardini 31, 81043 Capua (CE)
Tel. 0823961108 Fax 0823627828
Web: www.masseriagiosole.com

The accommodation is provided in an old farmhouse where the large internal spaces and the green countryside sloping down towards the River Volturno induce the guests to indulge in domestic pleasures.

-

1 - - -

5 (x 2)

1 46,00 - 65,00 -

4 (x 4/8)

1 - 7 - 1 260,00 7 -

Castelfranci

Stella

at Braiole, 83040 Castelfranci (AV)
Tel. 082772012

This small farm in the peaceful countryside offers a warm welcome in spacious accommodation that has been carefully renovated and furnished in modern style.

-

1 - - -

4 (x 1/2)

1 25,00 - 55,00 -

2 (x 2/6)

1 - 7 - 1 50,00 7 -

Ceraso

La Petrosa

at Petrosa, via Fabbrica 25, 84052 Ceraso (SA)
Tel. 097461370 Fax 097479906
Web: www.lapetrosa.it

Country holidays for all tastes are available in the varied setting of the Palistro Valley: the accommodation ranges from the manor house to farmhouses and a campsite.

2 (x 2)

1 41,32 - 51,65 -

8 (x 2)

1 41,32 - 51,65 -

4 (x 5/6)

1 - 7 - 1 - 7 464,81

Circello

Taverna dei Liguri

contrada Macchia, 82020 Circello (BN)
Tel. 0824938222

The setting is the rolling hills where cereals and olives are grown. Located in open country, the farm offers its guests peaceful and homely surroundings.

-

1 - - -

10 (x 1/2)

1 18,00 - 41,00 -

-

1 - 7 - 1 - 7 -

Colle Sannita

Lisone

contrada Lisone 3, 82024 Colle Sannita (BN)
Tel. 0824931519 Fax 0824931519
E-mail: piacquadiocarmelo@tin.it

This hill farm provides large rooms with period furniture for holidays where guests come into direct contact with rural life.

-
$_1$ - - - -

4 (x 2)
$_1$ 20,00 10,00 30,00 -

-
$_1$ - $_7$ - $_1$ - $_7$ -

Fisciano

Barone Antonio Negri

at Gaiano, via Teggiano 8,
84084 Fisciano (SA)
Tel. 089958561 Fax 089958561

On a hillside close to the Monti Picentini Regional Park, an old rural residence has been renovated with a wonderful sense of tradition.

-
$_1$ 44,00 - 54,00 -

5 (x 2)
$_1$ 44,00 - 54,00 -

-
$_1$ - $_7$ - $_1$ - $_7$ -

Forino

Tenuta Monte Laura

via Due Principati, 83020 Forino (AV)
Tel. 0825762500 Fax 0825762500
Web: www.tenutamontelaura.it

This accommodation in an old farmhouse allows guests to relax in a natural setting; on offer here are courses on, for example, horse-riding, wine-making, herbalism and organic farming.

-
$_1$ - - - -

2 (x 2)
$_1$ 36,50 - 52,50 -

-
$_1$ - $_7$ - $_1$ - $_7$ -

Massa Lubrense

Agrimar

via Vincenzo Maggio 40, 80061 Massa Lubrense (NA)
Tel. 0818089682 Fax 0818089682
E-mail: agri_mar@libero.it

These bungalows are just twenty metres from the sea; guests will be delighted by the Neapolitan cuisine based on the farm's own produce.

-
$_1$ - - - -

6 (x 4)
$_1$ 36,00 18,00 - -

-
$_1$ - $_7$ - $_1$ - $_7$ -

Moio della Civitella

Civitella

at Pregliano, 84060 Moio della Civitella (SA)
Tel. 0828673051 Fax 0828679154
E-mail: lacivitella02@libero.it

This recently opened establishment offers comfortable accommodation, with wholesome food and opportunities for hiking and horse-riding.

5 (x 2)
1 35,00 25,00 45,00 -

\-
1 - - - -

\-
1 - 7 - 1 - 7 -

Montecorvino Rovella

Masseria Sparano

at Macchia, contrada Serroni,
84090 Montecorvino Rovella (SA)
Tel. 089981260 Fax 0898021740
Web: www.masseriasparano.it

Located in the Monti Picentini, this old-style farm is run by people who treat their guests like members of the family. The cuisine is based on produce grown using biodynamic methods.

\-
1 - - - -

3 (x 4)
1 37,00 - 57,00 -

\-
1 - 7 - 1 - 7 -

Monterovo

at Macchia, via Pazzulli 4,
84096 Montecorvino Rovella (SA)
Tel. 089981305 Fax 089982942
Web: www.turismoverde.it

This accommodation and restaurant is adjacent to stables with a riding-school, where there's a field equipped for horse jumping.

\-
1 - - - -

6 (x 2)
1 29,00 - 47,00 -

\-
1 - 7 - 1 - 7 -

Paestum

Seliano

via Seliano, 84063 Paestum (SA)
Tel. 0828724544 Fax 0828723634
Web: www.agriturismoseliano.it

This refined country house with facilities for high quality horse-riding is located in the centre of a vast rural complex that has been converted for rural tourism.

\-
1 - - - -

17 (x 2/4)
1 57,50 - 70,00 -

\-
1 - 7 - 1 - 7 -

Palinuro

Sant'Agata

at Sant'Agata Nord, 84064 Palinuro (SA)
Tel. 0974931716 Fax 0974931716

On a green hill the farmhouse, surrounded by arcades, has large rooms for the guests with balconies commanding splendid views.

\-
1 - - - -

7 (x 2)
1 - - 57,00 -

 2(x 4)

620,00

Perdifumo

Eucalipto

contrada Cafaro-Giungatelle,
84060 Perdifumo (SA)
Tel. 0974851995 Fax 0974851947
Web: www.agriturismoeucalipto.it

From the farm, renowned for its cuisine, a narrow road leads to the sea at Punta Licosa, a beautiful solitary spot.

 -

\-

19 (x 2/4)

33,00 - 51,00 -

2(x 5)

600,00

Pimonte

La Casa del Ghiro

at Franche, via San Nicola 15,
80050 Pimonte (NA)
Tel. 0818749241 Fax 0818749241

At the foot of the Monti Lattari and close to the Amalfi Coast, this establishment puts the accent on ecology and horse-riding in rustic but modern surroundings.

 -

\-

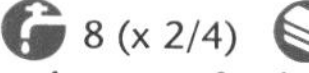 8 (x 2/4)

 35,00 - 55,00 -

 -

\-

Pisciotta

Principe di Vallescura

contrada Vallescura, 84066 Pisciotta (SA)
Tel. 0974973087 Fax 0974973031

This accommodation is on a huge farm growing olives and vines with splendid views of Palinuro Bay; on no account should the Greek temples at Paestum be missed.

\-

1 - - -

10 (x 2)

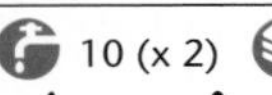

1 47,00 31,00 57,00 -

\-

1 - 7 - 1 - 7 -

Ruviano

Le Olive di Nedda

at Alvignanello, via Superiore Crocelle 14,
81010 Ruviano (CE)
Tel. 3488841276 Fax 0812451036
Web: www.olinedda.it

Near to an olive grove adjoining an oak wood, this farm is recommended for the warmth of its welcome and its excellent food.

\-

1 - - -

8 (x 2/4)

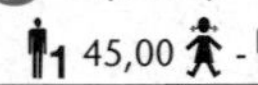

1 45,00 - 65,00 -

\-

1 - 7 - 1 - 7 -

San Cipriano Picentino

La Vecchia Quercia

at Nido, via Montevetrano 4,
84099 San Cipriano Picentino (SA)
Tel. 089882528 Fax 089882010
E-mail: lavecchia_quercia@tin.it

Two rural residences dating from the early 20th-century provide accommodation in the middle of the farm, where there are olive and citrus groves, vineyards, market gardens and woods.

\-

1 - - -

8 (x 1/4)

1 55,00 44,00 78,00 -

\-

1 - 7 - 1 - 7 -

San Giorgio del Sannio

Tufini

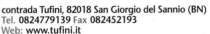

contrada Tufini, 82018 San Giorgio del Sannio (BN)
Tel. 0824779139 Fax 082452193
Web: www.tufini.it

This is a vast farm in a secluded area, ideal for those wanting to get away from the stress of city life. The rooms are furnished in simple, rustic style.

\-

1 - - -

4 (x 4)

1 - - 34,00 -

-

1 - 7 - 1 - 7 -

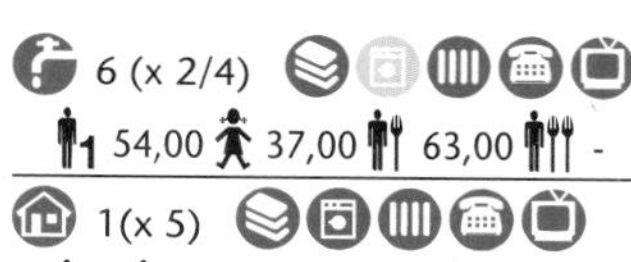

6 (x 2/4)

1 54,00 37,00 63,00 -

1(x 5)

1 - 7 - 1 220,00 7 1.400,00

San Mauro la Bruca

Prisco

contrada Valle degli Elci 2,
84070 San Mauro la Bruca (SA)
Tel. 0974974153 Fax 0974974928
Web: www.mieledelcilento.com

Just a few kilometres from the beaches of Palinuro and Marina di Camerota, this farmhouse accommodation is recommended by the Cilento National Park Board.

-

1 - - -

San Potito Sannitico

Quercete

   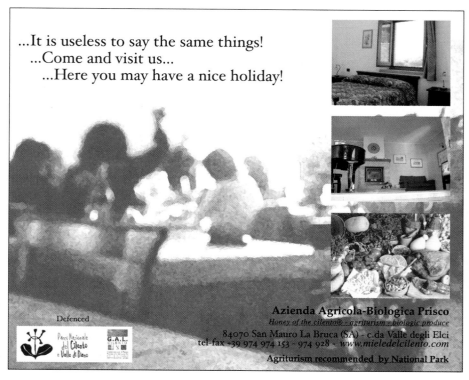

contrada Quercete, via Provinciale direction
Gioia Sannitica, 81010 San Potito Sannitico (CE)
Tel. 0823913881 Fax 0823785924
E-mail: quercete@tin.it

Part of this huge farm at the foot of the Monti del Matese is devoted to hazels and chestnuts; it provides its guests with rooms commanding wonderful views.

 -

1 - - -

 -

1 - - -

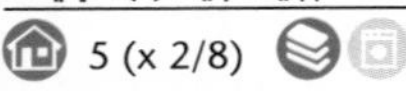 5 (x 2/8)

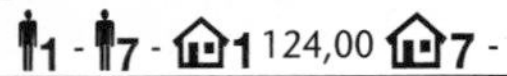

1 - 7 - 1 124,00 7 -

Sant'Agata de' Goti

Mustilli

via dei Fiori 20, 82019 Sant'Agata de' Goti (BN)
Tel. 0823717433 Fax 0823717619
Web: www.mustilli.com

This accommodation is provided in the centre of the village by a large wine-growing estate that has its headquarters in a splendid house dating from the 16th century.

2 (x 2)

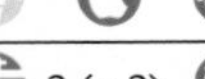 

1 33,75 - - 69,75

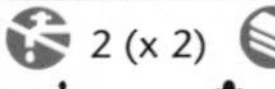   

4 (x 2)

1 33,75 - - 69,75

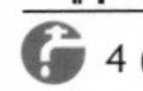  

-

1 - 7 - 1 - 7 -

Santa Maria di Castellabate

Annunziata

at Annunziata,
84072 Santa Maria di Castellabate (SA)
Tel. 0974961137

This old manor farm, with a church and dovecot, has been splendidly converted. The accommodation is in rooms furnished in a modern rustic style.

-

1 - - -

-

1 - - -

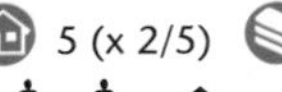 5 (x 2/5)

1 - 7 - 1 - 7 930,00

Podere Licosa

at Licosa,
84072 Santa Maria di Castellabate (SA)
Tel. 0974961137

This villa containing three apartments is just a stone's throw from the cliffs of Punta Licosa and is surrounded by pinewoods forming part of the Cilento National Park.

-

1 - - -

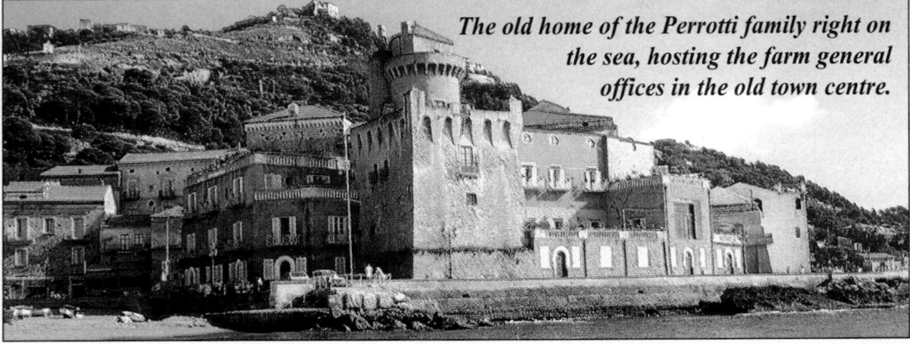

The old home of the Perrotti family right on the sea, hosting the farm general offices in the old town centre.

-
1 - - -

4 (x 4/8)

1 - 7 - 1 - 7 1.033,00

Sessa Aurunca

Aria Nova

at San Castrese, via Campo Felce S.S. 430,
81037 Sessa Aurunca (CE)
Tel. 0823706249 Fax 0823706249

This accommodation in a farmhouse, situated on a hill covered with orchards, assures peace and quiet in the rural atmosphere of bygone days.

-
1 - - -

2 (x 2)
1 25,00 - 43,00 -

2(x 4)
1 - 7 - 1 85,00 7 -

Sicignano degli Alburni

Sicinius

at Scorzo, contrada Piedi la Serra 7,
84029 Sicignano degli Alburni (SA)
Tel. 0828973763 Fax 0828973763
Web: www.sicinius.com

Although this accommodation is located in the hills, the mountains and sea are not far away and guests have a wide range of activities to choose from.

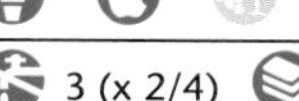

3 (x 2/4)
1 19,00 - 40,00 -

5 (x 4)
1 21,00 - 42,00 -

-
1 - 7 - 1 - 7 -

Solopaca

Masseria del Procaccia

at Varricello, via Procaccia 1,
82036 Solopaca (BN)
Tel. 0824971366 Fax 0824902956
Web: www.procaccia.it

The vineyards surrounding this building dating from the 18th century produce the famous Solopaca DOC wine; the Taburno-Camposauro Park is just a stone's throw away.

-
1 - - -

6 (x 1/2)
1 22,00 - 40,00 -

-
1 - 7 - 1 - 7 -

Teano

La Nuova Peschiera

at Peschiera, via XXVI Ottobre,
81057 Teano (CE)
Tel. 0823875521 Fax 0823875521
E-mail: lanuovapeschiera@yahoo.it

This accommodation is in a recently renovated cottage. There are opportunities for walking or riding tours in the Roccamonfina and Foce del Garigliano Regional Park.

-

1 - - -

4 (x 2/4)

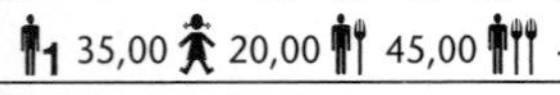

1 35,00 20,00 45,00 -

1(x 4)

1 35,00 7 - 1 - 7 -

Teora

Le Masserie di Corona

contrada Civita Superiore 29,
83056 Teora (AV)
Tel. 082751550 Fax 082751907
E-mail: terranostra@coldiretti.it

This vast farmhouse has been converted to provide comfortable rooms and a restaurant serving lamb and cheeses produced on the farm.

-

1 - - -

7 (x 2)

1 30,00 12,00 55,00 -

-

1 - 7 - 1 - 7 -

Tramonti

Mare e Monti

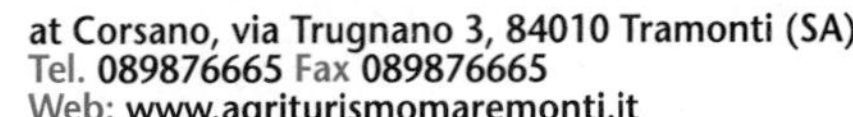

at Corsano, via Trugnano 3, 84010 Tramonti (SA)
Tel. 089876665 Fax 089876665
Web: www.agriturismomaremonti.it

This early 19th-century farmhouse with a homely atmosphere offers large rooms and rustic simplicity. Close at hand is the famous Amalfi Coast.

-

1 - - -

3 (x 2)

1 25,83 7,75 41,84 -

3(x 4)

1 - 7 - 1 72,30 7 -

Vallata

Masseria ai Pioppi della Corte

contrada Iazzano, 83059 Vallata (AV)
Tel. 082791043 Fax 082522443
E-mail: monaco@inopera.it

In this farmhouse, a true treasure trove of tradition, there is loving devotion to the home and an age-old sense of hospitality.

-

1 - - -

6 (x 2)

1 36,00 24,00 46,00 -

-

1 - 7 - 1 - 7 -

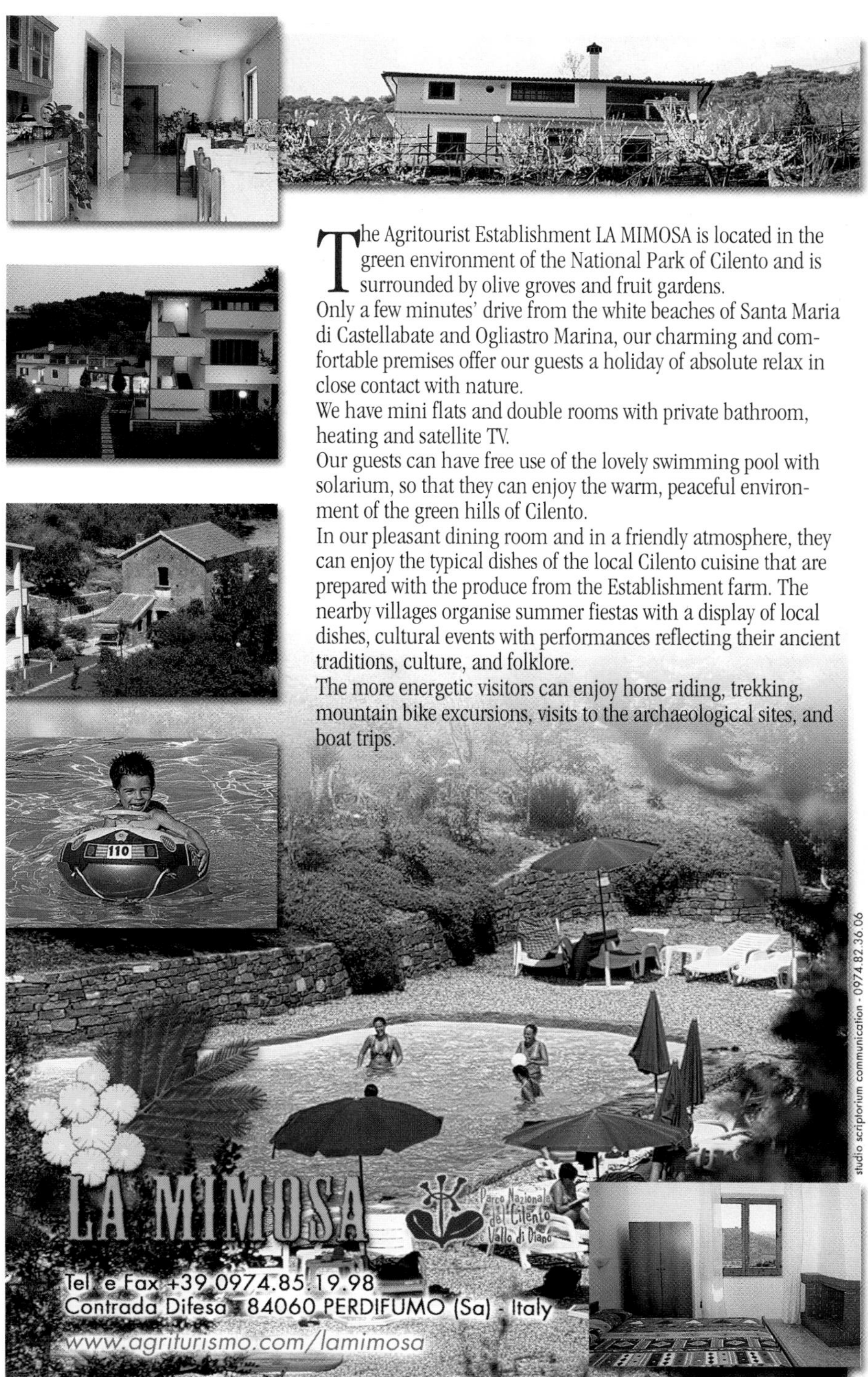
The Agritourist Establishment LA MIMOSA is located in the green environment of the National Park of Cilento and is surrounded by olive groves and fruit gardens.
Only a few minutes' drive from the white beaches of Santa Maria di Castellabate and Ogliastro Marina, our charming and comfortable premises offer our guests a holiday of absolute relax in close contact with nature.
We have mini flats and double rooms with private bathroom, heating and satellite TV.
Our guests can have free use of the lovely swimming pool with solarium, so that they can enjoy the warm, peaceful environment of the green hills of Cilento.
In our pleasant dining room and in a friendly atmosphere, they can enjoy the typical dishes of the local Cilento cuisine that are prepared with the produce from the Establishment farm. The nearby villages organise summer fiestas with a display of local dishes, cultural events with performances reflecting their ancient traditions, culture, and folklore.
The more energetic visitors can enjoy horse riding, trekking, mountain bike excursions, visits to the archaeological sites, and boat trips.
LA MIMOSA
Parco Nazionale del Cilento e Vallo di Diano
Tel. e Fax +39 0974.85.19.98
Contrada Difesa - 84060 PERDIFUMO (Sa) - Italy
www.agriturismo.com/lamimosa
studio scriptorium communication - 0974.82.36.06

EMILIA-ROMAGNA

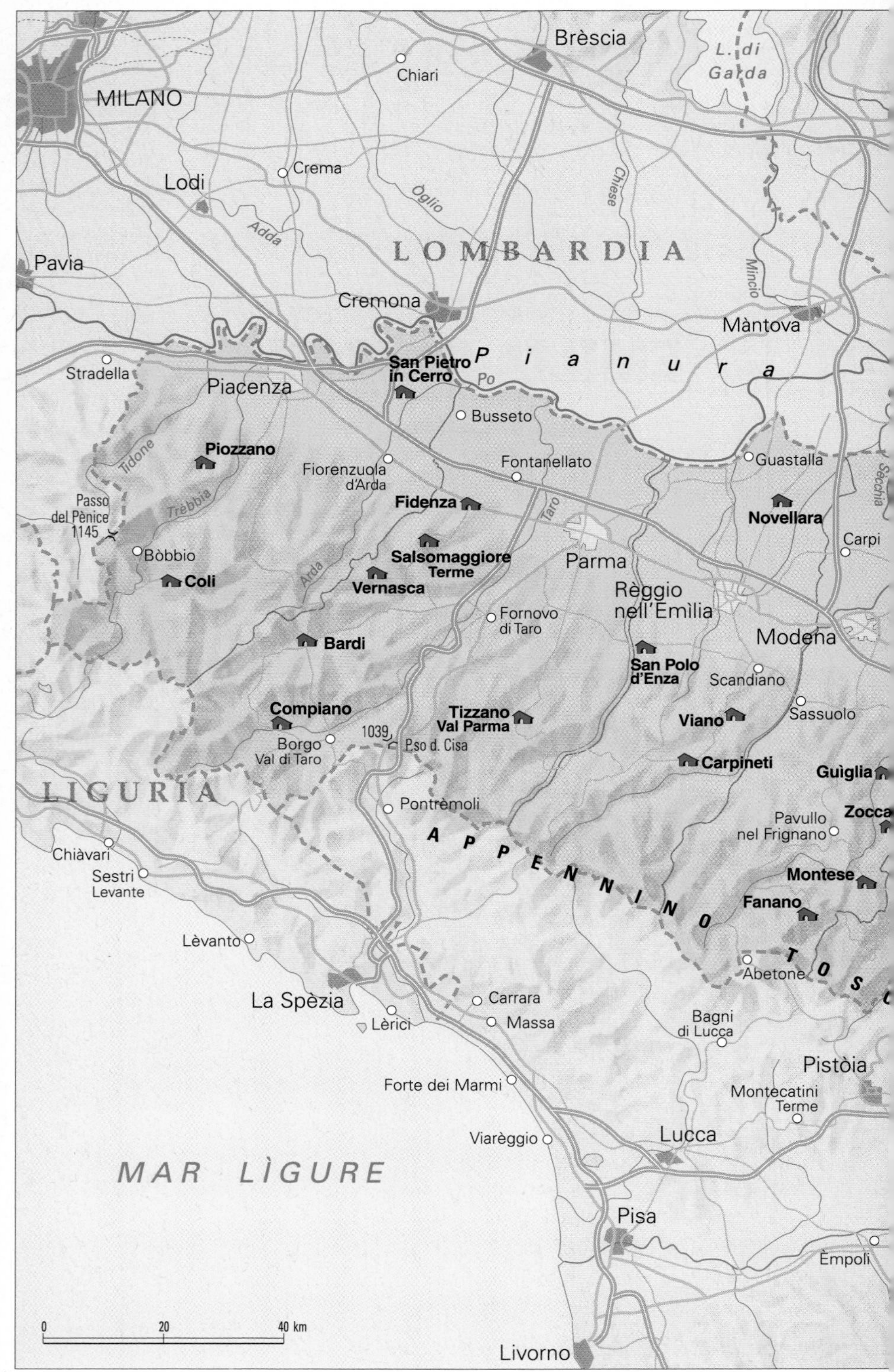

Brèscia
L. di Garda
Chiari
MILANO
Crema
Lodi
Òglio
Chiese
Adda
LOMBARDIA
Pavia
Mincio
Cremona
Màntova
Stradella
San Pietro in Cerro
Pianura
Po
Piacenza
Busseto
Piozzano
Tidone
Fiorenzuola d'Arda
Fontanellato
Guastalla
Sècchia
Passo del Pènice 1145
Trèbbia
Fidenza
Taro
Novellara
Carpi
Bòbbio
Salsomaggiore Terme
Parma
Coli
Arda
Vernasca
Règgio nell'Emìlia
Fornovo di Taro
Modena
Bardi
San Polo d'Enza
Scandiano
Sassuolo
Compiano
Tizzano Val Parma
Viano
Borgo Val di Taro
1039
P.so d. Cisa
Carpineti
Guìglia
LIGURIA
Pontrèmoli
Zocca
Pavullo nel Frignano
APPENNINO TOS
Chiàvari
Sestri Levante
Montese
Fanano
Lèvanto
Abetone
La Spèzia
Carrara
Lèrici
Massa
Bagni di Lucca
Pistòia
Forte dei Marmi
Montecatini Terme
Viarèggio
Lucca
MAR LÌGURE
Pisa
Èmpoli
0
20
40 km
Livorno

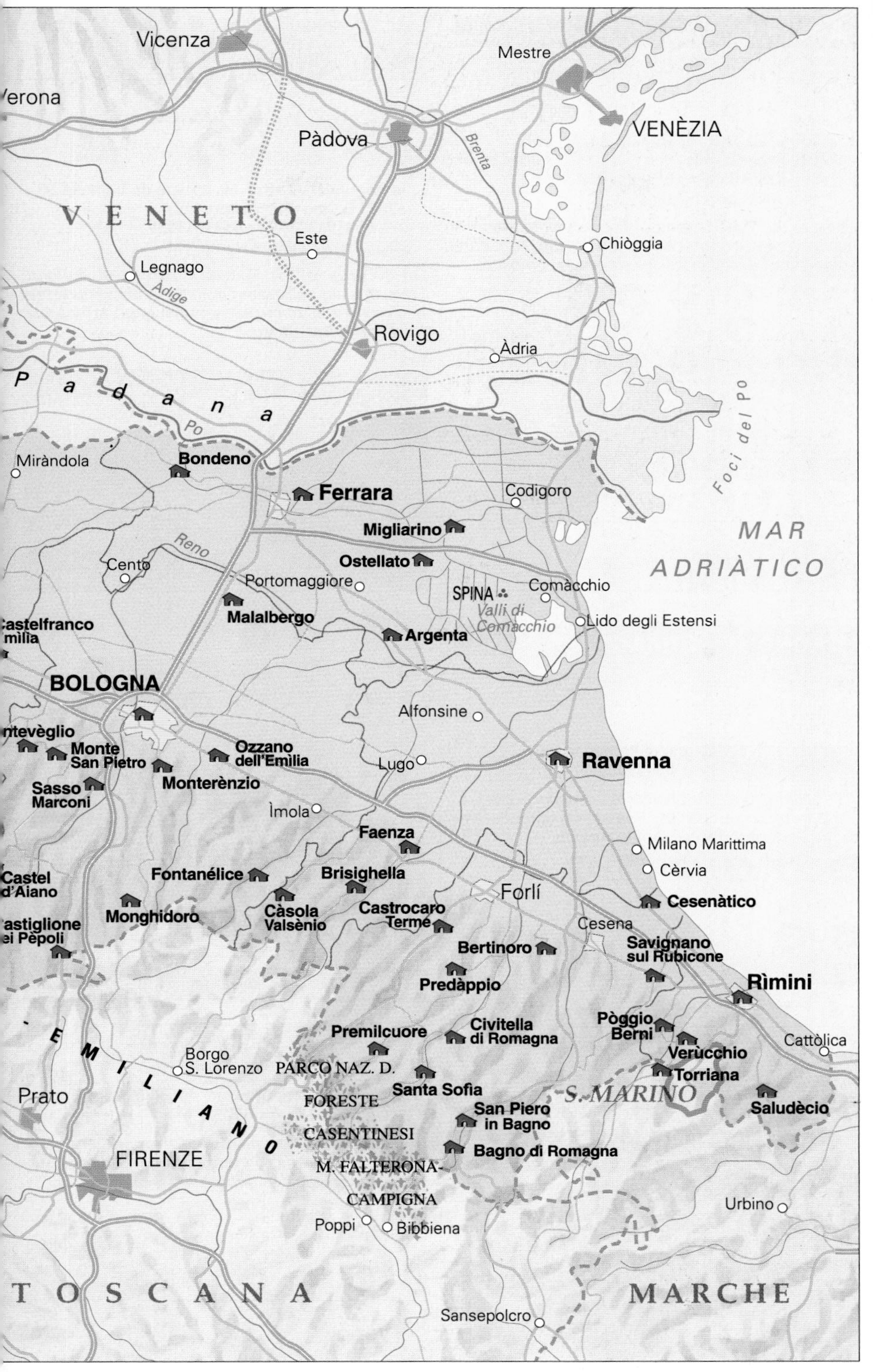
Vicenza
Verona
Mestre
VENÈZIA
Pàdova
Brenta
VENETO
Este
Chiòggia
Legnago
Àdige
Rovigo
Àdria
Padana
Po
Foci del Po
Miràndola
Bondeno
Ferrara
Codigoro
Migliarino
MAR ADRIÀTICO
Reno
Ostellato
Cento
Portomaggiore
SPINA
Comàcchio
Valli di Comacchio
Malalbergo
Lido degli Estensi
Castelfranco Emìlia
Argenta
BOLOGNA
Alfonsine
Monteveglio
Monte San Pietro
Ozzano dell'Emìlia
Lugo
Ravenna
Sasso Marconi
Monterènzio
Ìmola
Faenza
Milano Marittima
Cèrvia
Castel d'Aiano
Fontanélice
Brisighella
Forlí
Cesenàtico
Monghidoro
Càsola Valsènio
Castrocaro Terme
Castiglione dei Pèpoli
Cesena
Bertinoro
Savignano sul Rubicone
Predàppio
Rìmini
Premilcuore
Civitella di Romagna
Pòggio Berni
Verùcchio
Cattòlica
Borgo S. Lorenzo
PARCO NAZ. D. FORESTE CASENTINESI M. FALTERONA-CAMPIGNA
Santa Sofia
Torriana
EMILIANO
S. MARINO
Prato
San Piero in Bagno
Saludècio
FIRENZE
Bagno di Romagna
Urbino
Poppi
Bibbiena
TOSCANA
MARCHE
Sansepolcro

Argenta

Prato Pozzo Rifugio di Valle

at Anita, via Rotta Martinella 34/A,
44010 Argenta (FE)
Tel. 0532801058 Fax 0532801058
E-mail: pratopozzo@jumpy.it

Close to the Valli di Comacchio, accommodation is available in rooms in a converted hayloft (or in bungalows and dormitories), or else on a campsite.

-
1 - - -

8 (x 2/4)
1 - - - 46,00

-
1 - 7 - 1 - 7 -

Bagno di Romagna

Bacino

at Vessa, 47026 Bagno di Romagna (FC)
Tel. 0543912023 Fax 0543900638

This solitary stone farmhouse in the upper Savio Valley is located between the Foreste Casentinesi National Park and the coast of Romagna.

2 (x 4)
1 30,00 - 41,50 -

3 (x 2)
1 30,00 - 41,50 -

-
1 - 7 - 1 - 7 -

Mulino di Culmolle

at Poggio alla Lastra, via Mulino di Culmolle 50,
47021 Bagno di Romagna (FC)
Tel. 0543913039 Fax 0543913039
Web: www.mulinodiculmolle.it

On the edge of the Foreste Casentinesi National Park, this old mill dating from the 16th century has been converted to provide accommodation for those fond of the Apennines.

-
1 - - -

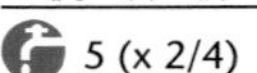

5 (x 2/4)
1 26,00 20,80 44,00 -

1(x 4)
1 - 7 - 1 156,00 7 -

Bardi

Il Castagneto

at Castagneto di Gravago, 43030 Bardi (PR)
Tel. 052577141 Fax 052577141

Comfortable rooms furnished in rustic style are available in a small group of stone cottages surrounded by old chestnut trees.

-
1 - - -

\-

1 - - -

4 (x 2/6)

1 25,00 7 140,00 1 - 7 -

Bertinoro

Fattoria Paradiso

via Palmeggiana 285, 47032 Bertinoro (FC)
Tel. **0543445044** Fax **0543444224**
Web: **www.fattoriaparadiso.com**

Two 18th-century rural buildings have been converted to provide accommodation of hotel quality, professionally managed with the accent on quality.

\-

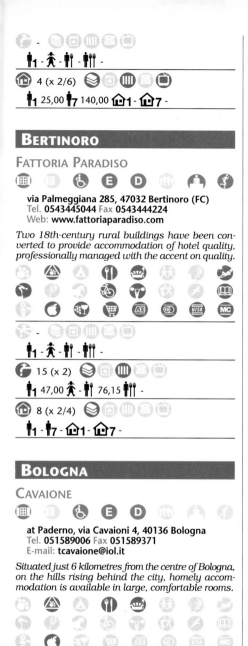

1 - - -

15 (x 2)

1 47,00 - 76,15 -

8 (x 2/4)

1 - 7 - 1 - 7 -

Bologna

Cavaione

at Paderno, via Cavaioni 4, 40136 Bologna
Tel. **051589006** Fax **051589371**
E-mail: **tcavaione@iol.it**

Situated just 6 kilometres from the centre of Bologna, on the hills rising behind the city, homely accommodation is available in large, comfortable rooms.

2 (x 2)

1 35,00 - - -

3 (x 2)

1 55,00 - - -

1(x 6)

1 40,00 7 - 1 - 7 -

Bondeno

La Migliara

at S. Bianca, via Provinciale Centese 187, 44012 Bondeno (FE)
Tel. **0532893595** Fax **0532893595**
Web: **www.lamigliara.it**

For those fond of the special atmosphere of the Po Valley, this rural residence has plenty of bicycles available for its guests. They can use them on the unsurfaced roads along the banks of the Po as far as Stellata.

\-

1 - - -

2 (x 2)

1 50,00 25,00 - -

3

1 - 7 - 1 70,00 7 -

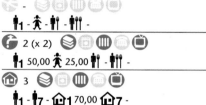

Brisighella

Corte dei Mori

at San Cassiano, via Valpiana 4, 48013 Brisighella (RA)
Tel. **054686489**
Web: **www.cortedeimori.com**

The accommodation is either in an old cottage or in a renovated hayloft, in the green hills between Emilia and Tuscany, facing the Lamone Valley.

2 (x 2)

1 27,00 20,00 37,00 -

4 (x 2)

35,00 25,00 45,00 -

-

1 - 7 - 1 - 7 -

Il Palazzo

via Baccagnano 11, 48013 Brisighella (RA)
Tel. **054680338** Fax **054680338**
Web: **www.ilpalazzo.net**

Near Brisighella and the thermal baths, the accommodation is in three houses provided with period furniture. The menu is vegetarian, with bread and focaccia baked in a wood-fired oven.

-

1 - - -

3 (x 4)

34,00 - 49,00 -

2(x 4)

1 - 7 - 1 130,00 7 600,00

Pedrósola

at San Cassiano, via S. Cassiano 95, 48020 Brisighella (RA)
Tel. **054686195** Fax **054686195**
Web: **www.pedrosola.it**

This farm devoted to the organic production of honey and soft fruit offers accommodation and activities for nature lovers.

-

1 - - - -

4 (x 1/4)

26,00 13,00 41,00 -

-

1 - 7 - 1 - 7 -

Relais Torre Pratesi

at Cavina, via Cavina 11, 48013 Brisighella (RA)
Tel. **054684545** Fax **054684558**
Web: **www.torrepratesi.it**

Ideal for a refined holiday in the atmosphere of a castle, the accommodation is available in the luxurious rooms of a 16th-century tower and the adjacent farmhouse.

-

1 - - - -

9 (x 2/4)

90,00 - 130,00 -

-

1 - 7 - 1 - 7 -

Relais Varnello

via Rontana 34, 48013 Brisighella (RA)
Tel. **054685493** Fax **054683124**
Web: **www.varnello.it**

In an area noted for its excellent climate and superb landscape, this modern rural accommodation has a beautiful garden.

\-

1 - - -

6 (x 2/4)

1 85,00 20,00 - -

\-

1 - 7 - 1 - 7 -

CARPINETI

CA' BRAGLIA

at Braglia di Poiago, via Braglia 101,
42033 Carpineti (RE)
Tel. 0522816418

This rural residence has been renovated preserving the traditional features: wooden beams, tiled floors and a kitchen with unplastered walls. The atmosphere is simple and friendly.

\-

1 - - -

\-

1 - - -

2(x 3)  

1 - 7 - 1 85,00 7 -

CASOLA VALSENIO

IL POGGIOLO

at Valdifusa, via Sintria 9,
48010 Casola Valsenio (RA)
Tel. 054673049 Fax 054673049

This accommodation is in a group of 14th-century buildings that have been restored preserving their original features and the unspoilt beauty of the surroundings.

\-

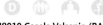

1 - - -

8 (x 2/4)

1 47,00 - 57,00 -

\-

1 - 7 - 1 - 7 -

LA CA' NOVA

at Baffadi, via Breta 29, 48010 Casola Valsenio (RA)
Tel. 054675177 Fax 054675177
Web: www.agriturcanova.it

In the hills near Faenza, in an area renowned for its herbs, guests are accommodated in carefully restored stone cottages near the River Senio.

\-

1 - - -

5 (x 2/4)

1 36,00 - 42,00 -

\-

1 - 7 - 1 - 7 -

CASTEL D'AIANO

LA FENICE

at Rocca di Roffeno, via Santa Lucia 29,
40040 Castel d'Aiano (BO)
Tel. 051919272 Fax 051919272
Web: www.lafeniceagritur.it

Guests staying in this 16th-century farmhouse will be in close contact with nature and the world of agriculture. They can also choose to spend memorable evenings in the old village tavern.

-

1 - - -

8 (x 2)

1 36,00 - 54,00 -

-

1 - 7 - 1 - 7 -

Castelfranco Emilia

Villa Gaidello Club

via Gaidello 18, 41013 Castelfranco Emilia (MO)
Tel. **059926806** Fax **059926620**
Web: **http://members.aol.com/gaidello**

This large farm, where organic methods have long been adopted, offers apartments with all modern conveniences in old farmhouses that have been renovated.

-

1 - - -

4 (x 1/2)

1 65,00 - - -

6(x 1)

1 - 7 - 1 227,00 7 -

Castiglione dei Pepoli

Ca' di Fatino

at Creda 169, 40030 Castiglione dei Pepoli (BO)
Tel. **053491801** Fax **053491801**
E-mail: **fatino@libero.it**

In the Apennines halfway between Bologna and Florence, this is an old rural residence that has been renovated in traditional style with special attention being paid to the details.

-

1 - - -

5 (x 2/4)

1 31,00 - 46,50 -

-

1 - 7 - 1 - 7 -

Castrocaro Terme

Sadurano

via Sadurano 45, 47011 Castrocaro Terme (FC)
Tel. **0543766643** Fax **0543766164**
Web: **www.sadurano.it**

In this vast estate, a completely renovated building offers its guests well-equipped rooms adjacent to a fitness centre.

-

1 - - -

8 (x 1/4)

1 28,00 - - -

-

1 - 7 - 1 - 7 -

Cesenatico

Ai Tamerici

via Mesolino 60, 47042 Cesenatico (FC)
Tel. **0547672730** Fax **0547672730**
E-mail: **tamerix@tiscali.it**

Just two kilometres from the sea, the rooms look out over beautiful green countryside, and guests can enjoy delicious dishes made from local produce.

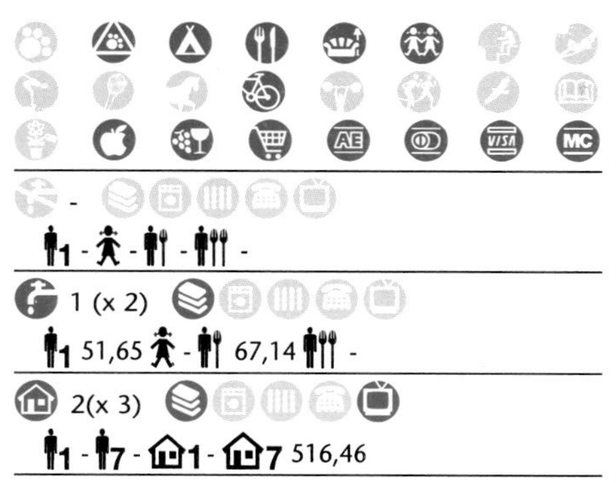

\-

1 - - - -

1 (x 2)

1 51,65 - 67,14 -

2(x 3)

1 - 7 - 1 - 7 516,46

Civitella di Romagna

Acero Rosso

at Seggio 5, 47012 Civitella di Romagna (FC)
Tel. 0543984035 Fax 0543983876
Web: www.acerorosso.com

Located in one of the valleys leading up to the Foreste Casentinesi National Park, this is a large farm devoted to organic crops and cattle-raising.

\-

1 - - - -

5 (x 2)

1 29,00 12,00 48,00 -

\-

1 - 7 - 1 - 7 -

Fattorie Faggioli - Ca' Bionda

at Cusercoli, via San Giovanni 42,
47010 Civitella di Romagna (FC)
Tel. 0543989101 Fax 0543989101
Web: www.fattoriefaggioli.it

In the Val Bidente, a model farm producing a variety of crops offers activities enabling guests to explore the countryside and learn about traditional rural lifestyles.

\-

1 - - - -

8 (x 2/4)

1 31,00 - 57,00 -

3 (x 4/6)

1 - 7 - 1 - 7 570,00

Coli

Tre Noci

at Fontana, 29020 Coli (PC)
Tel. 0523931020
Web: www.agritour.net

In the central Trebbia Valley, just a few kilometres from Bobbio, guests are accommodated in comfortable rooms in the former hayloft between the outbuildings surrounding the farmyard.

\-

1 - - - -

4 (x 4)

1 30,00 - 44,00 -

\-

1 - 7 - 1 - 7 -

Compiano

Carovane

at Bertoli, 43053 Compiano (PR)
Tel. 0525825324 Fax 0525825482
Web: www.carovane.com

This up-to-date farm, with five hundred hectares of woods, pasture and land under cultivation, offers large comfortable rooms furnished in rustic style.

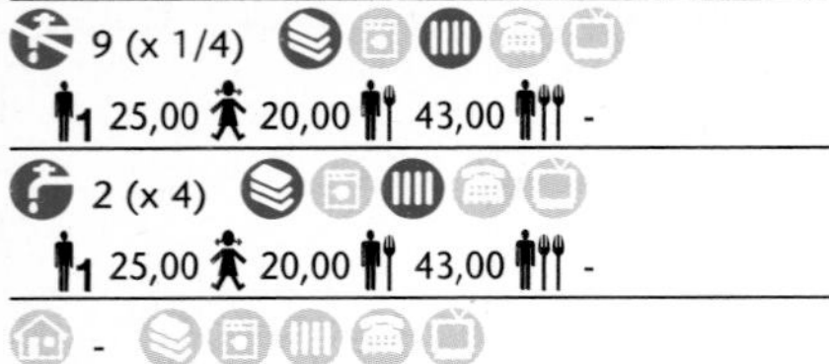

9 (x 1/4)
1 25,00 20,00 43,00 -

2 (x 4)
1 25,00 20,00 43,00 -

-
1 - 7 - 1 - 7 -

FAENZA

CA' DE' GATTI

at San Mamante, via Roncona 1, 48018 Faenza (RA)
Tel. 0546642202 Fax 0546642202
Web: www.mediagraph.it

Guests stay in a thousand-year-old building (there are traces of a Roman floor) surrounded by woods, vineyards and olive groves in the hills between Faenza and Brisighella.

-
1 - - -

3 (x 2/4)
1 38,00 - 51,00 -

2 (x 4/5)
1 - 7 - 1 80,00 7 -

LA SABBIONA

at Oriolo Fichi, via Oriolo 10, 48018 Faenza (RA)
Tel. 0546642142 Fax 0546642355
Web: www.lasabbiona.it

The accommodation is in an old farmhouse furnished in rustic style and in a modern annexe; it is possible to visit the winery and observe the processes of wine-making.

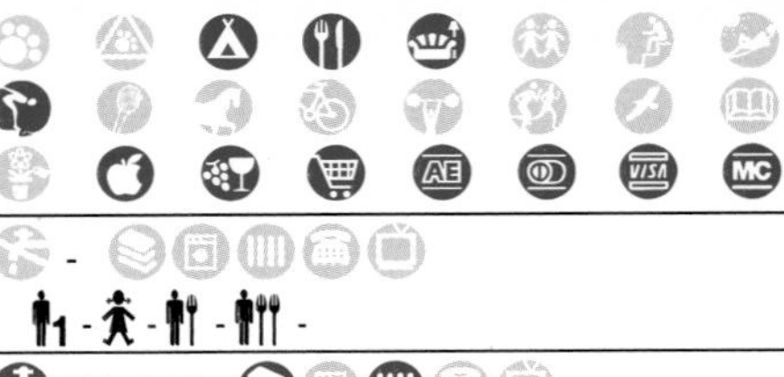

-
1 - - -

7 (x 1/4)
1 31,00 23,00 47,00 -

2 (x 3/6)
1 25,00 7 139,00 1 - 7 -

FANANO

DEL CIMONE LA PALAZZA

at Canevare, via Calvanella 710, 41020 Fanano (MO)
Tel. 053669311 Fax 053666631
Web: www.agriturismodelcimone.it

Set on a pleasant grassy slope, this stone cottage has been rebuilt to provide holiday accommodation, without in any way spoiling its original appearance.

-
1 - - -

13 (x 2/4)
1 36,00 - 50,00 -

3(x 4)
1 - 7 - 1 95,00 7 -

FERRARA

CA' SPINAZZINO

at Spinazzino, via Taglione 5, 44040 Ferrara
Tel. 0532725035 Fax 0532725035
E-mail: remo.scaramagli@tiscali.it

Set in the typical landscape of the plain of the Po, this large, rustic farmhouse dating from the early 20th century also offers camping facilities.

2 (x 2)
1 25,00 13,00 - -

-

1 - - -

4(x 3)

1 - 7 - 1 120,00 7 720,00

Fidenza

Il Tondino

at Tabiano Castello, via Tabiano 58,
43036 Fidenza (PR)
Tel. 052462106 Fax 052462106
Web: www.agriturismoiltondino.it

In a pleasant position and carefully renovated, the old farmhouse belonging to Tabiano Castle offers its guests peace and quiet and a friendly welcome.

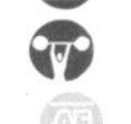

-

1 - - -

8 (x 2/4)

1 35,00 - -

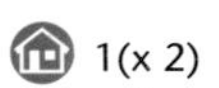

1(x 2)

1 - 7 - 1 90,00 7 -

Fontanelice

Ca' Monti

at Sassoleone, via Montemorosino 4,
40020 Fontanelice (BO)
Tel. 054297666 Fax 054297021
Web: www.camonti.it

The rooms are situated in the residence that, for generations, has belonged to the Monti family, who continue even today to welcome their guests with their proverbial cordiality.

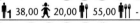

-

1 - - -

4 (x 2/4)

1 38,00 20,00 55,00 -

-

1 - 7 - 1 - 7 -

Guiglia

Ca' di Marchino

at Monteorsello, via Buzzeda 4,
41052 Guiglia (MO)
Tel. 059795582
Web: www.cadimarchino.it

This attractive stone cottage stands on the banks of a stream amid meadows that are ideal for easy walks or they can be explored on mountain bikes.

8 (x 2)

1 20,00 - 38,00 -

-

1 - - -

1(x 2)

1 - 7 - 1 55,00 7 350,00

MALALBERGO

IL CUCCO

at Altedo, via Nazionale 83,
40051 Malalbergo (BO)
Tel. 0516601124 Fax 0516601124
Web: www.ilcucco.it

In the plain close to Bologna, accommodation is available in an attractive late 19th-century farmhouse in a well-preserved agricultural setting.

-

1 - - -

5 (x 2)

1 72,00 - 88,00 -

-

1 - 7 - 1 - 7 -

MIGLIARINO

BELVEDERE

via Ostellato 1, 44027 Migliarino (FE)
Tel. 053352138 Fax 053352138

A new establishment in a handsome brick building dating from the early 19th century, which has even got a tower. It's in an excellent position for visiting Ferrara, Comacchio and the Po Delta.

5 (x 1/2)

1 31,00 - - -

1 (x 1)

1 31,00 - - -

1(x 4)

1 - 7 - 1 - 7 600,00

MONGHIDORO

LA CARTIERA DEI BENANDANTI

via Idice 13, 40063 Monghidoro (BO)
Tel. 0516551498 Fax 0516551498
Web: www.lacartiera.it

The name recalls the Middle Ages, the setting is that of the Bolognese Apennines; verdant and peaceful, these are the ideal surroundings for organic farming.

-

1 - - -

5 (x 1/2)

1 39,00 - 54,00 -

1(x 4)

1 - 7 - 1 - 7 315,00

MONTERENZIO

VILLAGGIO DELLA SALUTE PIÙ

via Sillaro 6, 40050 Monterenzio (BO)
Tel. 051929791 Fax 051929791
Web: www.villaggiodellasalute.it

It's difficult to say whether this is farmhouse accommodation or a beauty farm. This establishment is indeed unusual for its size and the variety and standard of the services it provides.

-

1 - - -

22 (x 1/2)
47,00 - 67,00 -

9 (x 2/6)
35,00 - -

Monte San Pietro

Tenuta Bonzara

at San Chierlo, via S. Chierlo 37/A,
40050 Monte San Pietro (BO)
Tel. 0516768324 Fax 051225772
Web: www.bonzara.it

This accommodation is in a completely restored village, with a shop selling local produce, a winery producing DOC wines and a museum devoted to agricultural traditions.

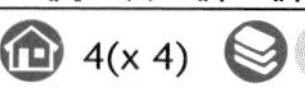

4(x 4)

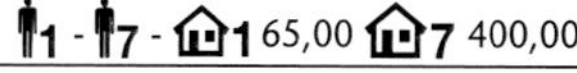

- - 65,00 400,00

Montese

Il Palazzino

at Maserno, via Lama 2500, 41055 Montese (MO)
Tel. 059980394 Fax 059980394
E-mail: ilpalazzino@libero.it

Growing various organic crops, this farm, with its woodland, is located near the village of Maserno; the accommodation is simple but comfortable and there's a restaurant with a veranda.

- - - -

4 (x 2)
25,00 - 38,00 -

1(x 4)
- - - 300,00

Monteveglio

Corte d'Aibo

via Marzatore 15, 40050 Monteveglio (BO)
Tel. 051832583 Fax 051832583
Web: www.cortedaibo.it

The 'Bolognese red' of the house stands out against its green surroundings; the building's main nucleus, where the rooms are located, dates from the 16th-century.

- - - -

4 (x 2)
45,00 - - -

- - - -

La Cavaliera

via Matilde di Canossa 13, 40050 Monteveglio (BO)
Tel. 051832595 Fax 051833126
E-mail: cavaliera@inwind.it

This very comfortable accommodation is in a refurbished farmhouse. The surroundings are homely and the restaurant also occupies an expanse of the garden.

4 (x 2)

65,00

La Stadira

via Acqua Fredda 17, 40050 Monteveglio (BO)
Tel. 051831429 Fax 051831429
Web: www.agriturismolastadira.it

The site is fascinating, with the abbey of Monteveglio and the village surrounding it. After taking a pleasant walk, guests will enjoy the excellent food in the restaurant and the comforts of hotel standard.

9 (x 1/2)

38,00 - 70,00 -

Novellara

Tenuta Riviera

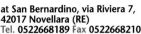

at San Bernardino, via Riviera 7,
42017 Novellara (RE)
Tel. 0522668189 Fax 0522668210
E-mail: riviera@riviera.it

Located in the plain near Reggio Emilia, this farm was founded by the Gonzaga on reclaimed land in 1650. It comprises the main villa and 18 cottages dating from various periods.

8 (x 4)

28,00

Ostellato

Belfiore

via Pioppa 27, 44020 Ostellato (FE)
Tel. 0533681164 Fax 0533681172
Web: www.agriturismobelfiore.com

In the heart of an area of special interest for its natural environment, the accommodation is in a large rural residence with comfortable, elegant rooms and a big garden adjoining a wood.

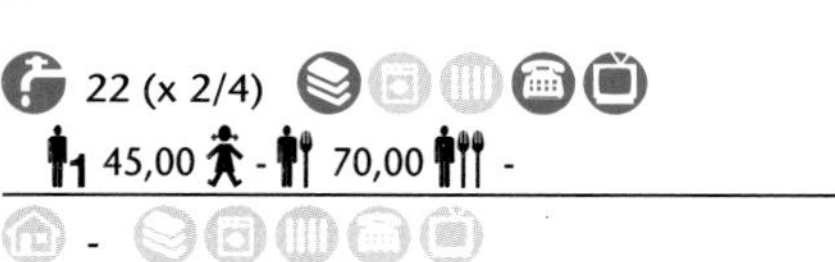
22 (x 2/4)
45,00 - 70,00 -

-
-7 - 1 - 7 -

Novara

at Dogato, via Ferrara 61, 44020 Ostellato (FE)
Tel. 0533651097 Fax 0533651097
Web: www.agriturismonovara.it

Close to the Po Delta Park, this is a 19th-century house with large comfortable rooms that are well heated in winter and cool in the summer.

      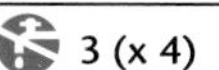  

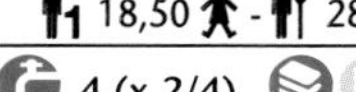
3 (x 4)
18,50 - 28,00 -

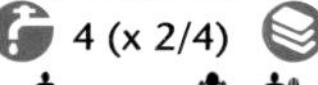
4 (x 2/4)
29,00 - 43,00 -

-
-7 - 1 - 7 -

Ozzano dell'Emilia

Dulcamara

at Settefonti, via Tolara di Sopra 78,
40064 Ozzano dell'Emilia (BO)
Tel. 051796643 Fax 0516511630
Web: www.coopdulcamara.it

Although close to the city, this farm in the Gessi Bolognesi Park has favoured organic agricultural methods and biodiversity.

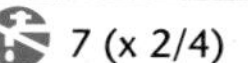   
7 (x 2/4)
30,00 15,00 42,00 -

-
- - - -

-
-7 - 1 - 7 -

Piozzano

I Pianoni

via Vallescura 11, 29010 Piozzano (PC)
Tel. 0523979422 Fax 0523979422
Web: www.pianoni.it

In this large hill farm producing meat and cheese, woods alternate with pasture and land under cultivation. The guests' rooms are in a secluded farmhouse.

-
- - - -

-
- - - -

1(x 8)
-7 - 1 - 7 250,00

Poggio Berni

Palazzo Astolfi

via Cella San Rocco 69, 47824 Poggio Berni (RN)
Tel. 0541688080 Fax 0541742050
E-mail: palazzo_astolfi@katamail.com

This farm centres on an old bishop's residence, now open to visitors and used for conferences. Rooms with a pleasant atmosphere are available in one of the renovated cottages.

-
- - - -

5 (x 1/2)
80,00 - - -

-

1 - 7 - 1 - 7 -

Palazzo Marcosanti

at Sant'Andrea, via Ripa Bianca 441,
47824 Poggio Berni (RN)
Tel. 0541629522 Fax 0541629522

In this imposing Malatesta fortress on a hill between Rimini and Cesena guests are accommodated in large rooms under the mansard roof; the cuisine is particularly refined.

-

1 - - - -

2 (x 2)

1 90,00 - - -

-

1 - 7 - 1 - 7 -

Predappio

Pian dei Goti

at Predappio Alta, via Montemirabello 2,
47010 Predappio (FC)
Tel. 0543921118
Web: www.piandeigoti.com

Situated on a hill farm in a basin with vineyards, meadows and woods, this recently refurbished farmhouse has large verandas.

-

1 - - - -

8 (x 2)

1 30,99 - - 61,97

-

1 - 7 - 1 - 7 -

Premilcuore

Agroippoturistica Ridolla

via Valbura, 47010 Premilcuore (FC)
Tel. 0543956829 Fax 0543956829
Web: www.ridolla.com

In an old building, this establishment also offers tours on horseback: the accommodation is in the farmhouse, where there's also a restaurant, or in the village and on the campsite.

4 (x 2)

1 16,00 - 42,00 -

3 (x 2)

1 18,00 - - -

7 (x 4/10)

1 20,00 7 - 1 - 7 -

Ravenna

L'Azdôra

at Madonna dell'Albero, via Vangaticcio 14,
48100 Ravenna
Tel. 0544497669 Fax 0544497669

One of the first centres for farmhouse holidays in the province of Ravenna, it has three buildings: two contain the rooms, in the third, more recent one is the award-winning restaurant.

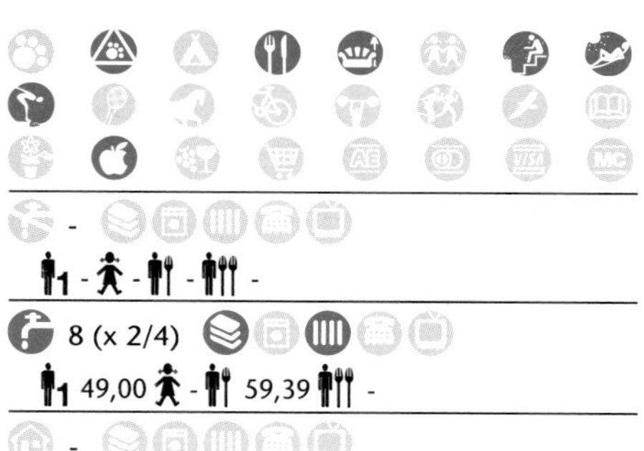

\-

1 - - -

8 (x 2/4)

1 49,00 - 59,39 -

\-

1 - 7 - 1 - 7 -

RIMINI

CASE MORI

at San Martino Monte L'Abbate, via Monte L'Abbate 9, 47851 Rimini
Tel. **0541731262** Fax **0541731262**
Web: **www.casemori.it**

These four farmhouses are on a farm growing cereals, vegetables and fruit close to the coast near Rimini, with areas of spontaneous vegetation and woodland.

\-

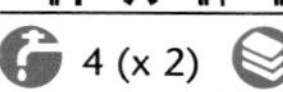

1 - - -

4 (x 2)

1 40,00 15,00 - -

\-

1 - 7 - 1 - 7 -

SALSOMAGGIORE TERME

ANTICA TORRE

at Cangelasio, case Bussandri 197, 43039 Salsomaggiore Terme (PR)
Tel. **0524575425** Fax **0524575425**
Web: **www.anticatorre.it**

A 15th-century tower overlooks this rural complex; in these peaceful, elegant surroundings, the atmosphere of a working farm has been preserved.

\-

1 - - -

9 (x 1/2)

1 35,00 - 52,00 -

\-

1 - 7 - 1 - 7 -

SALUDECIO

TORRE DEL POGGIO

at Poggio San Martino, via dei Poggi 2064, 47835 Saludecio (RN)
Tel. **0541857190** Fax **0541857190**

Just a few minutes' drive from Riccione, this former monastery is now a farm growing vines and olives that offers its guests rooms with modern conveniences.

\-

1 - - -

4 (x 1/2)

1 25,00 - - -

\-

1 - 7 - 1 - 7 -

SAN PIERO IN BAGNO

LE CORBAIE

at Monte Granelli Corbaie 13, via E. Ruscelli 27, 47026 San Piero in Bagno (FC)
Tel. **0543917111**
Web: **www.agriturismolecorbaie.it**

In a beautiful setting of wooded hills, this stone farmhouse with a tiled roof offers its guests one-roomed apartments, simply furnished with extra space provided by a raised platform.

\-
1 - - - -

\-
1 - - - -

5(x 4)
1 46,48 7 - 1 - 7 -

San Pietro in Cerro

La Valle

via Roma 17/1, 29010 San Pietro in Cerro (PC)
Tel. **0523839162** Fax **0523839162**

Dating from the 18th-century, this farm raising pigs, cattle and poultry provides excellent food and comfortable accommodation.

\-
1 - - - -

4 (x 1/4)
1 28,00 - - -

1(x 2)
1 - 7 - 1 60,00 7 360,00

San Polo d'Enza

Montefalcone

at Pontenovo, via Montefalcone 8,
42020 San Polo d'Enza (RE)
Tel. **0522874174** Fax **0522874174**
Web: **digilander.iol.it/aziendamontefalcone**

These stables in the hills overlooking the lower Enza Valley organise tours on horseback, including long distance trekking.

3 (x 1/2)
1 24,00 - 42,00 -

\-
1 - - - -

\-
1 - 7 - 1 - 7 -

Santa Sofia

Rio Sasso

via Forese 81/B, 47018 Santa Sofia (FC)
Tel. **0543970497** Fax **0543970497**

The accommodation is in a carefully renovated cottage, where guests can enjoy a holiday in a homely atmosphere, as well as the wholesome food.

\-
1 - - - -

12 (x 2)
1 26,00 - - 68,00

\-
1 - 7 - 1 - 7 -

Sasso Marconi

Le Conchiglie

at Lagune, via Lagune 76/1,
40037 Sasso Marconi (BO)
Tel. **0516750755** Fax **051840131**

A modern stock-raising farm that offers, in addition to its organic produce, a range of facilities and activities, a restaurant and accommodation in large renovated outbuildings.

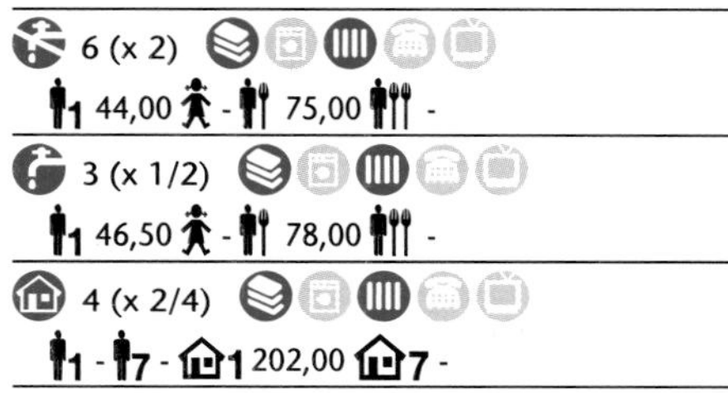

6 (x 2)
44,00 - 75,00 -

3 (x 1/2)
46,50 - 78,00 -

4 (x 2/4)
- - 202,00 -

Savignano sul Rubicone

I Portici

at Capanni, via Rubicone destra, II tratto 5500,
47039 Savignano sul Rubicone (FC)
Tel. 0541938143 Fax 0541938143
Web: www.agriturismoiportici.it

Close to the beaches of Romagna, this homely accommodation is in former outbuildings with a restaurant serving simple country fare, a campsite, a large garden, a swimming pool and a solarium.

-
- - -

5 (x 2)
32,00 - 45,50 -

2(x 4)
- - - 376,00

Tizzano Val Parma

Ca' D'Ranier

at Groppizioso 21,
43028 Tizzano Val Parma (PR)
Tel. 0521860304 Fax 0521860304

In a traditional farming environment, guests are accommodated in an old cottage. Holidays are organised for groups of at least ten children.

-
- - -

6 (x 2/4)
30,00 20,00 50,00 -

-
- - -

Casa Nuova

at Casanuova 1, 43028 Tizzano Val Parma (PR)
Tel. 0521868278 Fax 0521868278
Web: www.casa-nuova.com

From Parma, the road leads into the Apennines to this old tower-house, which stands out amid the greenery of the upper valley. Skiing is possible just ten kilometres away in winter.

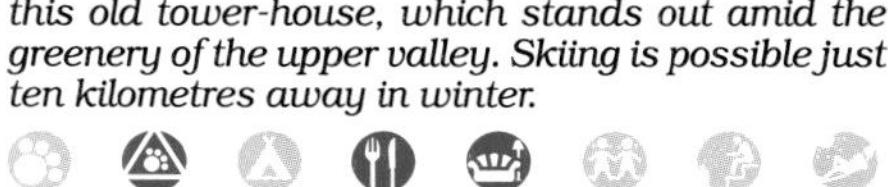

-
- - -

5 (x 2/4)
42,00 - 52,00 -

-
- - -

Torriana

Il Pomo Reale

via delle Fontane 17, 47825 Torriana (RN)
Tel. 0541675127 Fax 0541675127
E-mail: pomoreale@libero.it

This very comfortable accommodation is in the cool surroundings of the Marecchia Valley, halfway between the worldly pleasures of the Adriatic Coast and the medieval charm of Montefeltro.

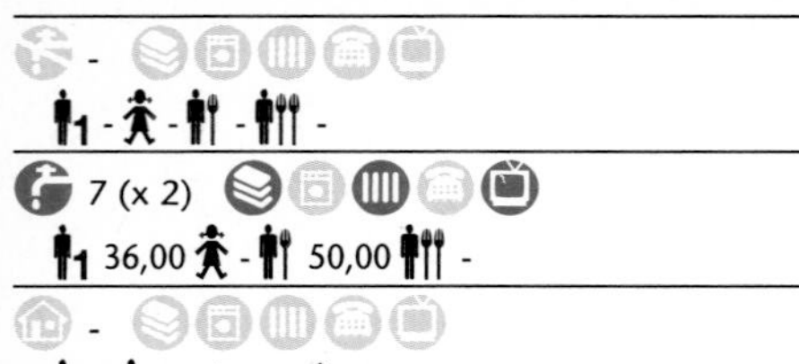

7 (x 2)

36,00 - 50,00 -

Vernasca

Cergallina

at Cergallina 1, 29010 Vernasca (PC)
Tel. 0523898289 Fax 0523898289
Web: www.cergallina.com

Thanks to Judith's verve and her husband Giorgio's cooking, there's a very warm welcome here; don't miss the tortelli and the ganassini in wine.

    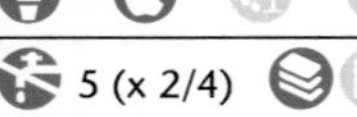 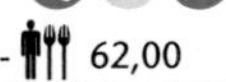 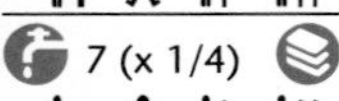 

5 (x 2/4)

- - - 62,00

7 (x 1/4)

- - - 77,00

- - - -

Verucchio

Le Case Rosse

at Villa Verucchio, via Tenuta Amalia 141,
47826 Verucchio (RN)
Tel. 0541678123 Fax 0541678876
Web: www.tenutaamalia.com

Offering a pleasant atmosphere and comfortable rooms, this late 18th-century farmhouse in the Marecchia Valley has been carefully renovated and has period furniture.

- - - -

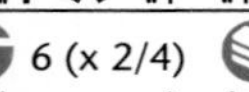 6 (x 2/4)  

36,00 - - -

1(x 7)

- 140,00 650,00

Viano

Cavazzone

at Regnano, via Cavazzone 4,
42020 Viano (RE)
Tel. 0522858100 Fax 0522858621
Web: www.cavazzone.it

This large farm dating from the late 19th century is built round a courtyard: although the architecture is austere, the combination of bare brick and stone is attractive.

- - - -

3 (x 4)

50,00 - - -

- - - -

Zocca

Tizzano

at Monteombraro, via Lamizze 1197,
41059 Zocca (MO)
Tel. 059989581
Web: www.agritizzano.it

Family-run accommodation is available in old buildings, including a tower-house, in a elevated position in the Panaro Valley; the rooms are rustic but comfortable.

- - - -

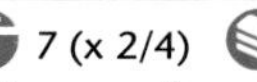 7 (x 2/4)  

18,00 13,00 31,00 -

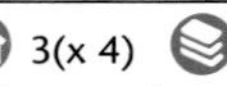 3(x 4)  

18,00 - - -

FRIULI-VENEZIA GIULIA

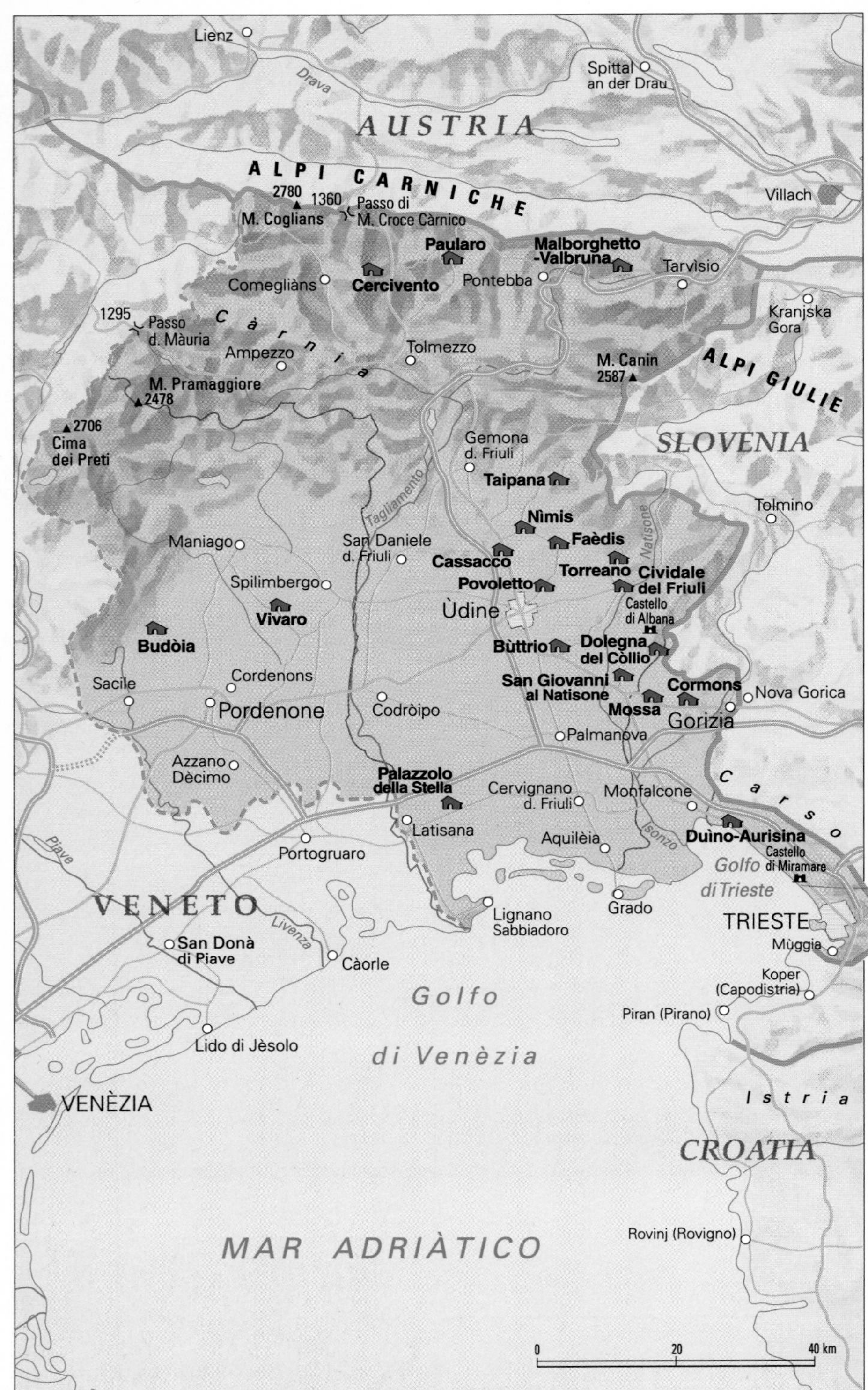
Lienz
Drava
Spittal an der Drau
AUSTRIA
ALPI CARNICHE
2780
1360
Passo di M. Croce Càrnico
M. Coglians
Villach
Paularo
Malborghetto -Valbruna
Tarvìsio
Comegliàns
Cercivento
Pontebba
Kranjska Gora
1295
Passo d. Màuria
Càrnia
Ampezzo
Tolmezzo
M. Canin 2587
ALPI GIULIE
M. Pramaggiore 2478
2706 Cima dei Preti
SLOVENIA
Gemona d. Friuli
Taipana
Tagliamento
Tolmino
Nìmis
Natisone
Maniago
San Daniele d. Friuli
Faèdis
Cassacco
Torreano
Cividale del Friuli
Spilimbergo
Povoletto
Ùdine
Castello di Albana
Vivaro
Budòia
Bùttrio
Dolegna del Còllio
San Giovanni al Natisone
Cormons
Sacile
Cordenons
Nova Gorica
Pordenone
Codròipo
Mossa
Gorizia
Palmanova
Azzano Dècimo
Palazzolo della Stella
Cervignano d. Friuli
Monfalcone
Carso
Latisana
Isonzo
Duino-Aurisina
Aquilèia
Portogruaro
Piave
Castello di Miramare
Golfo di Trieste
VENETO
Lignano Sabbiadoro
Grado
TRIESTE
Livenza
San Donà di Piave
Mùggia
Càorle
Koper (Capodistria)
Golfo di Venèzia
Piran (Pirano)
Lido di Jèsolo
VENÈZIA
Istria
CROATIA
Rovinj (Rovigno)
MAR ADRIÀTICO
0
20
40 km

Budoia

Piancavallo

at Dardago, via Pedemontana 40,
33070 Budoia (PN)
Tel. 0434653047
E-mail: agriturismopiancavallo@virgilio.it

Strongly oriented towards horse-riding, this farm offers riding courses and excursions on horseback, also for children outside the summer season.

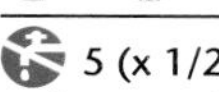 5 (x 1/2)  

 29,00 - - -

\-

\- - -

\-

\- - - -

Buttrio

Scacciapensieri

via Morpurgo 29, 33042 Buttrio (UD)
Tel. 0432674907 Fax 0432683924
Web: www.aziendagricolamarinadanieli.it

This handsome stone farmhouse on a hilltop not only provides accommodation but also has an elegant restaurant and a terrace shaded by large umbrellas.

\-

 - - -

 7 (x 1/4)  

59,00 - 78,00 -

\-

\- - - -

Cassacco

La Poce des Stries

at Montegnacco, 33010 Cassacco (UD)
Tel. 0432881343 Fax 0432851759

This late 19th-century cottage has been tastefully renovated. Udine is but a stone's throw away, while Venice, the lagoon and the Adriatic beaches can all be reached within an hour.

\-

 - - -

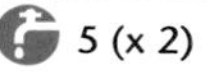 5 (x 2) 

38,75 - - -

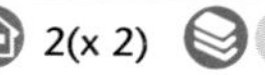 2(x 2)

 - - 77,50 -

Cercivento

Bosco di Museis

at Museis, 33020 Cercivento (UD)
Tel. 0433778822 Fax 043392330
Web: www.apicarnia.it

This farm produces fruit (including soft fruit) and everything the beehive has to offer; the accommodation is in comfortable wooden chalets in the middle of a wood.

- 1 - - -

- 1 - - -

6(x 2)

1 - 7 - 1 57,00 7 -

Cividale del Friuli

Rosa Rubini

at Spessa, via Case Rubini 3,
33040 Cividale del Friuli (UD)
Tel. 0432716141 Fax 0432716161
Web: www.villarubini.net

Surrounded by vineyards, the accommodation is available in modern apartments and recently renovated rooms furnished with antiques.

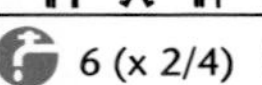
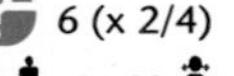

- 1 - - -

6 (x 2/4)

1 38,00 - - -

2(x 4)

1 - 7 - 1 77,50 7 -

Cormons

Casa Riz

at Giassico 18, 34170 Cormons (GO)
Tel. 048161362 Fax 048161362
Web: www.viniriz.it

Pleasant accommodation is available in simple surroundings, as one would expect in an organic farm serving wholesome food.

- 1 - - -

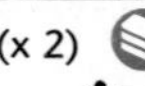

4 (x 2)

1 22,50 - - -

- 1 - 7 - 1 - 7 -

Kitzmüller Thomas

at Brazzano, via XXIV Maggio 56,
34071 Cormons (GO)
Tel. 048160853 Fax 048160853
E-mail: hans.kitzmueller@tin.it

Although the main building of this small wine-growing farm is just a stone's throw from the centre of the village, it is surrounded by a vineyard. To the rear are meadows and a small wood.

- 1 - - -

3 (x 2)

1 21,00 13,00 - -

1(x 3)

1 - 7 - 1 63,00 7 -

Dolegna del Collio

Venica & Venica

via Mernico 42, 34070 Dolegna del Collio (GO)
Tel. 048161264 Fax 0481639906
Web: www.venica.it

This farm, extending over four hills covered with vineyards, centres on an elegantly refurbished house, managed in an exemplary manner.

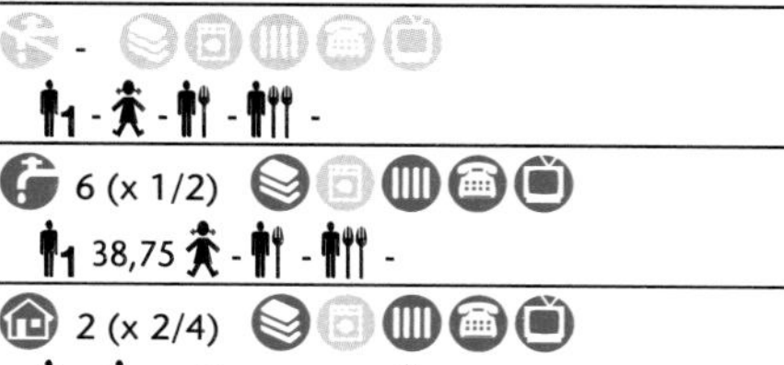

Duino-Aurisina

Mezzaluna

at Malchina 54/A, 34019 Duino-Aurisina (TS)
Tel. 040291529
Web: www.mezzalunanet.it

This accommodation in the fascinating setting of the Carso, close to Sistiana Bay and Trieste, is ideally located for trips across the border into Slovenia and Croatia.

\-

1 - - -

7 (x 2)

1 36,00 - -

\-

1 - 7 - 1 - 7 -

Radovic Nevo

at Aurisina 138/A, 34011 Duino-Aurisina (TS)
Tel. 040200173 Fax 040200173

The wines are produced organically - 'Natura magistra vitae' (nature is the master of life) is the owners' salutary motto - as are the meat and vegetables that are served at table.

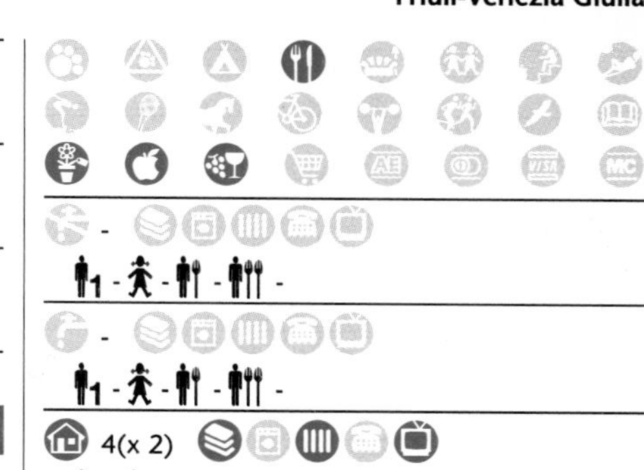

Terra del Carso

at San Pelagio 28/B, 34011 Duino-Aurisina (TS)
Tel. 040201056 Fax 040201056

"The sky, sea and land of the Carso" is the slogan of this farm; situated in the hills, its apartments have separate entrances.

\-

1 - - -

\-

1 - - -

4(x 2)

1 - 7 - 1 62,00 7 -

Faedis

Casa del Grivò

at Borgo Canal del Ferro 19, 33040 Faedis (UD)
Tel. 0432728638 Fax 0432728638
Web: www.grivo.has.it

In this establishment dedicated to non-smokers and dreamers, everything expresses the philosophy of the owners, from organic farming to the way it has been renovated.

1 (x 4)

1 26,00 - 40,00 -

-

1 - 7 - 1 - 7 -

MALBORGHETTO-VALBRUNA

MALGA PRIU

at Ugovizza, 33010 Malborghetto-Valbruna (UD)
Tel. **042860265**

Accommodation at high altitude is available in a chalet in Valcanale. Built of stone and wood, it is surrounded by meadows, land under cultivation and the splendid Tarvisio Forest.

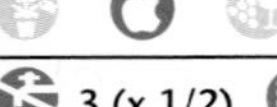 3 (x 1/2)  

1 20,50 - - 36,00

-

1 - - -

-

1 - 7 - 1 - 7 -

MOSSA

CODELLI

via dei Codelli 15, 34070 Mossa (GO)
Tel. **0481809285** Fax **0481880155**
E-mail: **codelli@libero.it**

The fulcrum of the estate is the 18th-century villa, while a nearby farmhouse, surrounded by vineyards, is reserved for the guests.

-

1 - - -

-

1 - - -

1(x 6) 

1 - 7 - 1 119,00 7 471,00

NIMIS

I COMELLI

   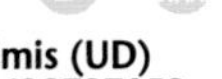

largo Diaz 8, 33045 Nimis (UD)
Tel. **0432790685** Fax **0432797158**

In a village amidst the vineyards and chestnut woods in the Prealpi Giulie (the foothills of the Julian Alps), the accommodation is provided by a beautiful late 19th-century cottage built of stone.

-

1 - - -

5 (x 2/4) 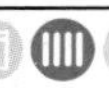

1 30,00 - - -

1 - 7 - 1 - 7 -

Palazzolo dello Stella

Tenuta Regina

at Piancada, Casali Tenuta Regina 8,
S.P. (provincial road) 122 at km 7.2,
33056 Palazzolo dello Stella (UD)
Tel. **0431587941** Fax **0431587941**
Web: **www.adriabella.com**

Everything a family needs for a relaxing holiday is available in the park surrounding the farmhouse. In addition, there's the sea, golf, thermal baths and historic cities.

-
1 - - -

-
1 - - -

8 (x 2/4)
1 - 7 - 1 220,00 7 -

Paularo

Sandri Salvatore

at Malga Val Bertat "Al Cippo", 33027 Paularo (UD)
Tel. **043370553** Fax **043370553**
E-mail: **agritursandri@libero.it**

In the area of the Comunità Montana della Carnia, simple accommodation is provided in two Alpine huts belonging to the farm: one is at high altitude, the other is in the village.

7 (x 1/2)
1 25,00 - - 42,00

4 (x 2)
1 25,00 - - 46,00

-
1 - 7 - 1 - 7 -

Povoletto

La Faula

at Ravosa, via Casali Faula 5,
33040 Povoletto (UD)
Tel. **0432666394** Fax **0432666032**
Web: **www.faula.com**

A wine-growing estate surrounds the farmhouse, which preserves its traditional appearance, while the accent is on environment-friendly agriculture and quality.

9 (x 2/4)

24,75 - 46,75 -

4 (x 2/4)

- - 72,50 -

Villa Corèn

at Siacco, via Cividale 1, 33040 Povoletto (UD)
Tel. 0432679078 Fax 0432679078
Web: www.villacoren.com

The apartments, with fireplaces and their own open space, are in the converted outbuildings. Accommodation is also available in the villa, amid frescoes and antique furniture.

2 (x 2)

32,50 - -

6 (x 2/4)

- - 90,00 -

San Giovanni al Natisone

Carlo Beria de Carvalho de Puppi

at Villanova del Judrio, via Giassico 2,
33048 San Giovanni al Natisone (UD)
Tel. 0432758000 Fax 0432758000

In the setting of the Colli Orientali and Collio, a refined rural holiday is to be had in an old country house dating from the 15th century.

3(x 3)

36,00 - - -

Casa Shangri-La

via Bolzano 60,
33048 San Giovanni al Natisone (UD)
Tel. 0432757844 Fax 0432746005
Web: www.madeinfriuli.com

In the heart of Friuli, this complex comprises accommodation and sports facilities on a huge wine-growing estate with the inevitable enoteca (wine shop).

6 (x 1/2)

62,00 - - -

Taipana

Campo di Bonis

at Campo di Bonis, 33040 Taipana (UD)
Tel. 0432788136 Fax 0432788246

"A touch of green silence" is the slogan of this farm set between large meadows, where there's a strong accent on touring on horseback.

\-

1 - - -

4 (x 2/4)

1 26,00 - - 47,00

1(x 8)

1 - 7 - 1 40,00 7 -

Torreano

Volpe Pasini

at Togliano, via Cividale 16,
33040 Torreano (UD)
Tel. 0432715151 Fax 0432715438
Web: www.volpepasini.net

In the heart of the Colli Orientali, amid the vineyards, seven rooms, tastefully furnished with original pieces from the villa, offer a holiday in hotel style.

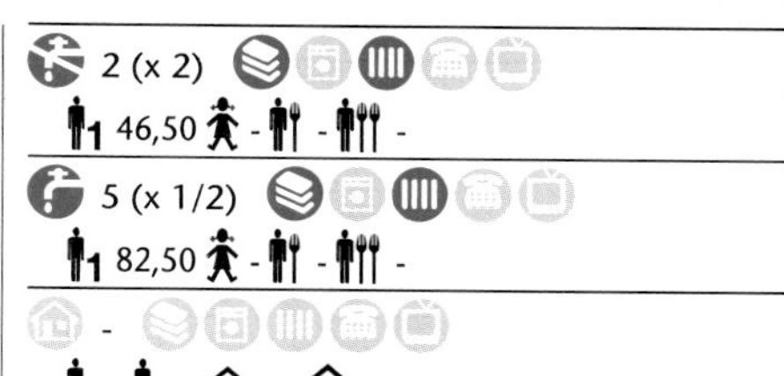

2 (x 2)

1 46,50 - - -

5 (x 1/2)

1 82,50 - - -

\-

1 - 7 - 1 - 7 -

Vivaro

Gelindo dei Magredi

via Roma 16, 33099 Vivaro (PN)
Tel. 042797037 Fax 042797515
E-mail: gelindodeimagredi@tin.it

The magredi are the typical alluvial lands of Friuli. The farm's name is a reminder of the warm welcome it offers and the pleasure of horse-riding and excursions in carriages.

\-

1 - - -

16 (x 1/2)

1 30,00 - - -

\-

1 - 7 - 1 - 7 -

LAZIO

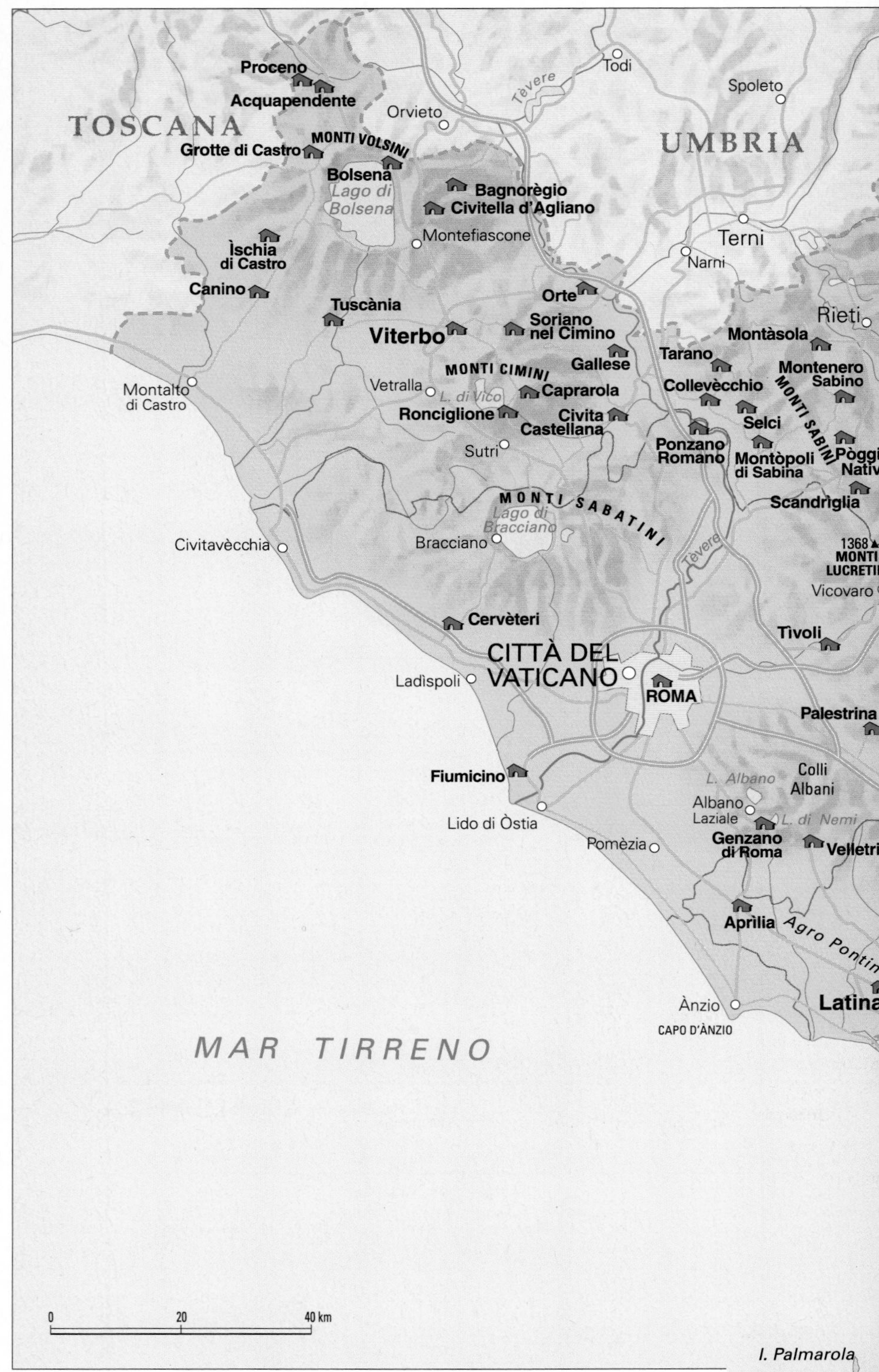
Proceno
Acquapendente
TOSCANA
Orvieto
Todi
Tèvere
Spoleto
UMBRIA
MONTI VOLSINI
Grotte di Castro
Bolsena
Lago di Bolsena
Bagnorègio
Civitella d'Agliano
Montefiascone
Terni
Narni
Ìschia di Castro
Canino
Orte
Tuscània
Soriano nel Cimino
Rieti
Viterbo
Montàsola
Gallese
Tarano
MONTI CIMINI
Montenero Sabino
Montalto di Castro
Vetralla
L. di Vico
Caprarola
Collevècchio
MONTI SABINI
Ronciglione
Civita Castellana
Selci
Ponzano Romano
Montòpoli di Sabina
Sutri
MONTI SABATINI
Lago di Bracciano
Scandrìglia
Civitavècchia
Bracciano
1368
MONTI LUCRETILI
Vicovaro
Cervèteri
Tìvoli
CITTÀ DEL VATICANO
ROMA
Ladìspoli
Palestrina
Fiumicino
L. Albano
Colli Albani
Albano Laziale
L. di Nemi
Lido di Òstia
Pomèzia
Genzano di Roma
Velletri
Aprìlia
Agro Pontino
Ànzio
Latina
CAPO D'ÀNZIO
MAR TIRRENO
0
20
40 km
I. Palmarola

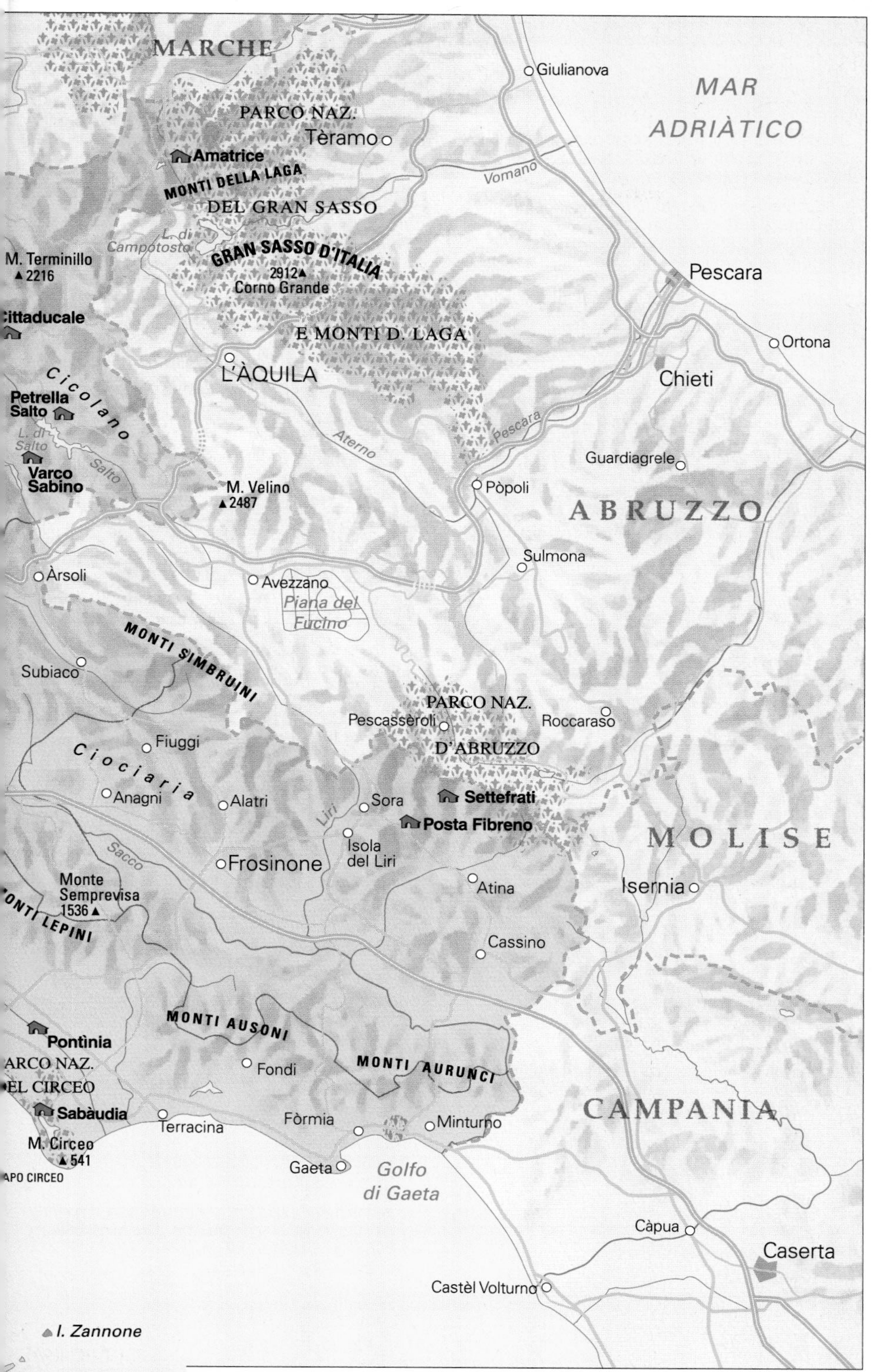

MARCHE
PARCO NAZ.
DEL GRAN SASSO
E MONTI D. LAGA
Tèramo
Amatrice
MONTI DELLA LAGA
Giulianova
MAR
ADRIÀTICO
Vomano
L. di
Campotosto
GRAN SASSO D'ITALIA
2912
Corno Grande
M. Terminillo
2216
Pescara
Ortona
Chieti
L'ÀQUILA
Cicolano
Petrella
Salto
L. di
Salto
Salto
Varco
Sabino
Aterno
Pescara
Guardiagrele
M. Velino
2487
Pòpoli
ABRUZZO
Sulmona
Àrsoli
Avezzano
Piana del
Fucino
MONTI SIMBRUINI
Subiaco
PARCO NAZ.
D'ABRUZZO
Pescassèroli
Roccaraso
Fiuggi
Ciociaria
Anagni
Alatri
Sora
Settefrati
Posta Fibreno
Liri
MOLISE
Isola
del Liri
Sacco
Frosinone
Atina
Isernia
Monte
Semprevisa
1536
MONTI LEPINI
Cassino
MONTI AUSONI
Pontìnia
Fondi
MONTI AURUNCI
CAMPANIA
Sabàudia
Terracina
Fòrmia
Minturno
M. Circeo
541
Gaeta
Golfo
di Gaeta
Càpua
Caserta
Castèl Volturno
I. Zannone
Is. di Ponza

6(x 5)

1 - 7 - 1 - 7 500,00

Acquapendente

Cerqueto

strada Falconiera, 01021 Acquapendente (VT)
Tel. 0763732106 Fax 0763732106
Web: www.cerqueto.it

This farmhouse dating from the second half of the 19th century has been renovated, but its original forms have been preserved; organic methods of farming have been in use here for some time.

 -

 1 - - -

 -

1 - - -

 6 (x 2/4)

1 - 7 - 1 - 7 774,69

Le Crete

via Cassia at km 129.4,
01021 Acquapendente (VT)
Tel. 0763734854 Fax 0763731525

A renovated farmhouse has been divided into self-contained apartments; next to it is a charming annexe, with its own open space.

 -

1 - - -

 -

1 - - -

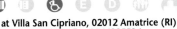

Amatrice

Amatrice

at Villa San Cipriano, 02012 Amatrice (RI)
Tel. 0746825536 Fax 0746825536
Web: www.agriturismoamatrice.com

The mountain scenery and the organisation make you think you're in Switzerland. The elegant buildings, with airy arcades, look out over impeccable lawns and hedges, and little lakes with swans.

 -

1 - - -

 11 (x 1/2) 

1 30,00 15,00 50,00 -

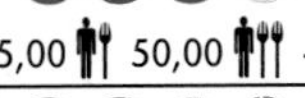 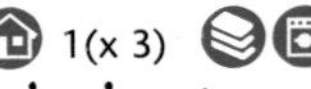 1(x 3) 

1 - 7 - 1 100,00 7 -

Aprilia

Tre Confini

at Campoverde, via Pantanelle 257,
04010 Aprilia (LT)
Tel. 0692746539 Fax 0692660044
Web: www.agrinet.it/treconfini

This is a wine-growing farm in the reclaimed Pontine Marshes (Agro Pontino in Italian). The airy modern building is in a verdant setting.

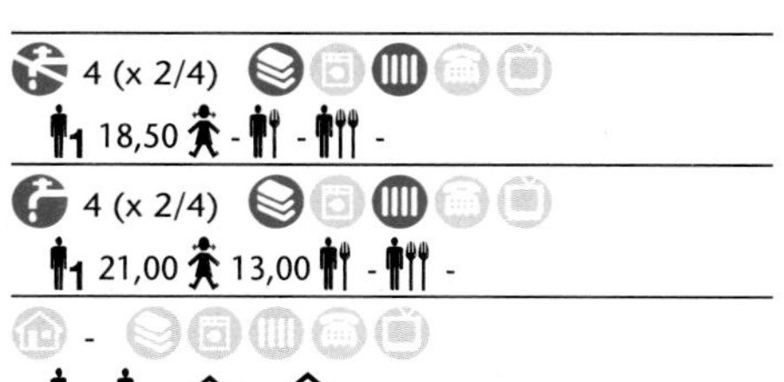

4 (x 2/4)

1 18,50 - - -

4 (x 2/4)

1 21,00 13,00 - -

-

1 - 7 - 1 - 7 -

BAGNOREGIO

SALLEGROTTE

at Vetriolo, 01022 Bagnoregio (VT)
Tel. **0761288298** Fax **0761288298**

Guests are accommodated in a number of renovated farmhouses in which the vernacular architecture has been preserved (one of them has a swimming pool).

-

1 - - - -

-

1 - - - -

6(x 2)

1 35,00 7 - 1 - 7 -

BOLSENA

BELVEDERE

at Belvedere 104, 01023 Bolsena (VT)
Tel. **0761798290** Fax **0761798290**
Web: **www.agritouristbelvedere**

Holiday accommodation is available in this family-run farm in a very peaceful setting amid vineyards and woods, with a splendid view of Lake Bolsena.

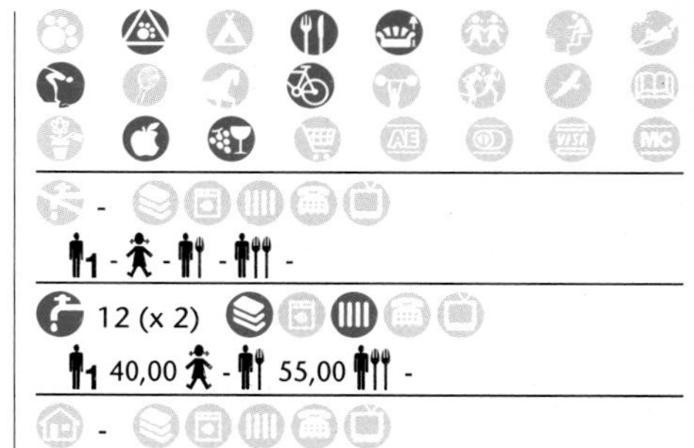

-

1 - - - -

12 (x 2)

1 40,00 - 55,00 -

-

1 - 7 - 1 - 7 -

LA RISERVA-MONTEBELLO

at Montebello, 01023 Bolsena (VT)
Tel. **0761798965** Fax **0761798965**
Web: **www.lariservamontebello.com**

Three stone farmhouses are located within a radius of one kilometre amid the rolling hills surrounding the lake, with its sparkling waters; sailing is possible here.

-

1 - - - -

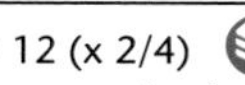  

12 (x 2/4)

1 54,00 - 81,00 -

-

1 - 7 - 1 - 7 -

MURACCIO

S.S. (state road) Cassia at km 110.3,
01023 Bolsena (VT)
Tel. **0761799005** Fax **0761780854**
E-mail: **agriturismo.muraccio@virgilio.it**

The farm is six kilometres away in the hills, while the accommodation is by the lake and is completely independent.

-

1 - - - -

-

1 - - - -

3 (x 2/5)

1 - 7 - 1 - 7 900,00

Podere Arlena

via Cassia at km 108.15, 01023 Bolsena (VT)
Tel. 0761799538 Fax 0761799538
Web: www.arlena.it

Accommodation is available in simply furnished apartments, all with verandas commanding superb views, in this 19th-century residence or its outbuildings.

\-

1 - - -

\-

1 - - -

8 (x 2/6)

1 - 7 - 1 150,00 7 1.200,00

Canino

Cerro Sughero

S.S. (state road) 312 at km 22.6,
01011 Canino (VT)
Tel. 0761437242 Fax 0761437242

In an area renowned for its olive oil, this estate is, in effect, a huge park where guests are free to ramble and ride mountain bikes.

\-

1 - - -

12 (x 4)

1 35,00 - - -

\-

1 - 7 - 1 - 7 -

Le Cascine

S.S. (state road) 312 at km 11.2,
01011 Canino (VT)
Tel. 0761438941 Fax 0761438941
Web: www.allecascine.it

Not far from the beaches of the Maremma, where it extends into Lazio, this modern establishment is of hotel standard. It has a swimming pool with a Jacuzzi.

\-

1 - - -

16 (x 2/4)

1 28,42 - - 56,85

\-

1 - 7 - 1 - 7 -

Caprarola

La Valle di Vico

at Valle di Vico, 01032 Caprarola (VT)
Tel. 3388018176
Web: www.lavalledivico.it

The farm is in the Lake Vico Nature Reserve. The self-contained apartments, which are all in the farmhouse, have solid wood furniture.

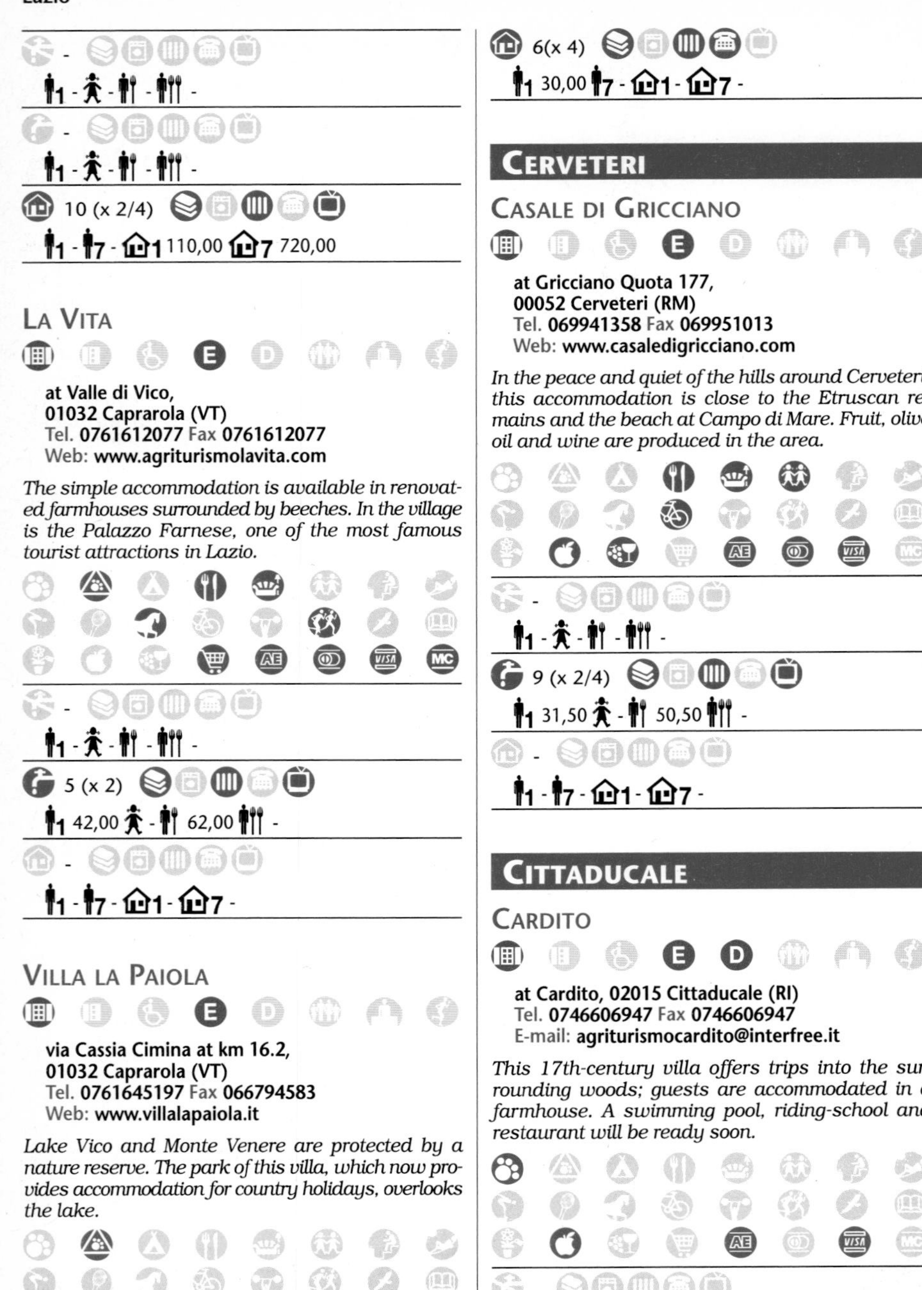

\-

1 - - -

\-

1 - - -

10 (x 2/4)

1 - 7 - 1 110,00 7 720,00

La Vita

E

at Valle di Vico,
01032 Caprarola (VT)
Tel. 0761612077 Fax 0761612077
Web: www.agriturismolavita.com

The simple accommodation is available in renovated farmhouses surrounded by beeches. In the village is the Palazzo Farnese, one of the most famous tourist attractions in Lazio.

\-

1 - - -

5 (x 2)

1 42,00 - 62,00 -

\-

1 - 7 - 1 - 7 -

Villa la Paiola

E

via Cassia Cimina at km 16.2,
01032 Caprarola (VT)
Tel. 0761645197 Fax 066794583
Web: www.villalapaiola.it

Lake Vico and Monte Venere are protected by a nature reserve. The park of this villa, which now provides accommodation for country holidays, overlooks the lake.

\-

1 - - -

\-

1 - - -

6(x 4)

1 30,00 7 - 1 - 7 -

Cerveteri

Casale di Gricciano

E

at Gricciano Quota 177,
00052 Cerveteri (RM)
Tel. 069941358 Fax 069951013
Web: www.casaledigricciano.com

In the peace and quiet of the hills around Cerveteri, this accommodation is close to the Etruscan remains and the beach at Campo di Mare. Fruit, olive oil and wine are produced in the area.

\-

1 - - -

9 (x 2/4)

1 31,50 - 50,50 -

\-

1 - 7 - 1 - 7 -

Cittaducale

Cardito

E D

at Cardito, 02015 Cittaducale (RI)
Tel. 0746606947 Fax 0746606947
E-mail: agriturismocardito@interfree.it

This 17th-century villa offers trips into the surrounding woods; guests are accommodated in a farmhouse. A swimming pool, riding-school and restaurant will be ready soon.

\-

1 - - -

\-

1 - - -

4 (x 2/4)

1 25,00 7 - 1 - 7 -

Civita Castellana

Casa Ciotti

via Terni 14, 01033 Civita Castellana (VT)
Tel. **0761513090** Fax **0761599120**
Web: **www.casaciotti.com**

This establishment is located in a 17th-century post-house, restored to its original splendour and provided with period furniture.

-

1 - - -

-

1 - - -

 10 (x 2/4) 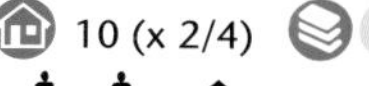

1 - 7 - 1 170,00 7 1.020,00
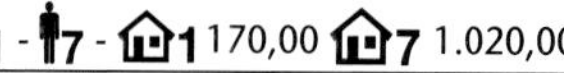

Civitella d'Agliano

Il Molinaccio

at Molinaccio 1, 01020 Civitella d'Agliano (VT)
Tel. **0761914438**

Careful renovation has turned this former mill into delightful holiday accommodation with the Rio Chiaro gurgling just a short distance away.

-
1 - - -

-
1 - - -

2 (x 4/6)
1 31,00 7 - 1 - 7 645,57

Collevecchio

Gianraffaele Pittalis

via Colli 3, 02042 Collevecchio (RI)
Tel. **0765578695** Fax **0765578695**

Amid the hills, this two-storied farmhouse has period furniture and a lounge with a fireplace and an arcade.

-
1 - - -

-
1 - - -

1(x 5) 
1 - 7 - 1 - 7 1.084,56

Fiumicino

Borgo di Tragliata

at Testa di Lepre, via del Casale di Tragliata, 00050 Fiumicino (RM)
Tel. **066687267** Fax **066687267**
Web: **www.tragliata.it**

In the Roman countryside, 17th-century farmhouses have been converted to provide accommodation. The rooms are airy and romantic, and various recreational activities are available.

-
1 - - -

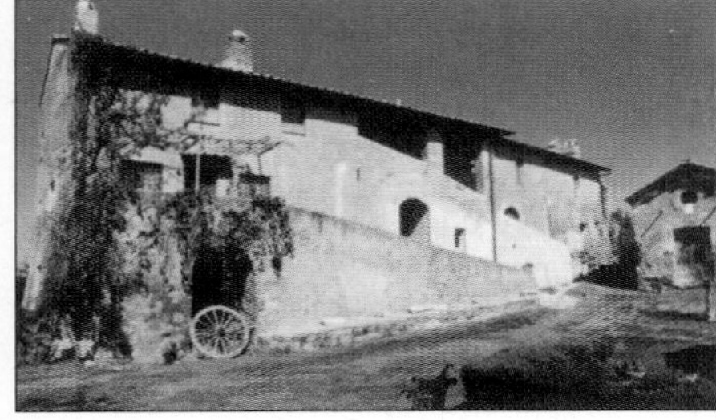

20 (x 2)
1 35,00 26,25 - -

7 (x 2/6)
1 - 7 - 1 271,11 7 -

Casale Doria Pamphilj

at Testa di Lepre, via O. Occioni,
00050 Fiumicino (RM)
Tel. 066689590 Fax 066689590
Web: www.doriapamphilj.it

This very recent establishment, which takes advantage of the height and light of an old barn to provide comfortable accommodation, has a name with historic overtones.

-
1 - - -

-
1 - - -

8 (x 2/4)
1 - 7 - 1 200,00 7 -

Gallese

Giulia di Gallese

at Il Piano, strada Cerreto, 01035 Gallese (VT)
Tel. 0761495510 Fax 0761495510
Web: www.giuliadigallese.com

This accommodation is in a recent building where there are a number of rooms for guests and a small apartment with cooking facilities.

-
1 - - -

7 (x 1/4)
1 51,60 - 61,90 -

1(x 3)
1 - 7 - 1 103,92 7 578,42

Genzano di Roma

Agropolis

at Landi, via S. Gennaro 2,
00045 Genzano di Roma (RM)
Tel. 069370335 Fax 069370335
Web: www.agropolisagriturismo.it

This elegant farmhouse with a friendly welcome commands a view extending from Monte Circeo and the Isole Pontine to the Monti Lepini.

-
1 - - -

12 (x 2/4)
1 30,00 - 51,00 -

-
1 - 7 - 1 - 7 -

Tre Palme

at Landi, strada Muti 73,
00045 Genzano di Roma (RM)
Tel. 069370286 Fax 069370286
Web: www.angelfire.com/nt/trepalme

Amid vineyards, olive groves and fields under other crops, the modern farmhouse with its attractive wooden furnishings is the ideal place for a relaxing country holiday.

-

1 - - -

2 (x 2)

1 20,00 - -

2(x 2)

1 - 7 - 1 - 7 498,00

Grotte di Castro

Castello di Santa Cristina

at Santa Cristina, 01025 Grotte di Castro (VT)
Tel. 076378011 Fax 076378011
Web: www.santacristina.it

"A delightful village in the heart of Tuscia" is how this establishment describes itself Lake Bolsena offers opportunities for bathing and watersports.

-

1 - - -

18 (x 1/2)

1 65,00 - -

8(x 4)

1 - 7 - 1 - 7 2.400,00

Ischia di Castro

Castro

at Ponte San Pietro, 01010 Ischia di Castro (VT)
Tel. 0761458769 Fax 0761458769
Web: www.primitaly.it/castro

This centre for tourism on horseback overlooks the splendid valley of the Fiora. There's period furniture and communal rooms with a pleasant atmosphere.

-

1 - - -

9 (x 2/4)

1 41,00 - 52,00 -

-

1 - 7 - 1 - 7 -

Le Chiuse

at Le Chiuse, 01010 Ischia di Castro (VT)
Tel. 0761424875 Fax 0761424875

In the land of the Etruscans, 25 km from the sea at Montalto di Castro and 20 km from the thermal baths at Saturnia, this accommodation is in a handsome tufa building.

-

1 - - -

12 (x 2/4)

1 35,00 - 70,00 -

-

1 - 7 - 1 - 7 -

Latina

Fattoria Prato di Coppola

at Borgo Sabotino, via del Mare at km 4.2,
04010 Latina
Tel. 0773273411 Fax 0773273412
E-mail: info@pratodicoppola.it

The apartments are in an old farmhouse that has been renovated and a more recent building. Nearby, the Ninfa Nature Reserve and the castle at Sermoneta are well worth a visit.

2 (x 2)

1 - - 38,00 -

-

1 - - -

6 (x 2/6)

1 - 7 - 1 110,00 7 -

MONTASOLA

MONTEPIANO

via Casalini 8, 02040 Montasola (RI)
Tel. 076563252 Fax 076563252
E-mail: montepiano@tin.it

The beauty of Sabina is unspoilt, with its wooded valleys and holy places ranging from Farfa Abbey to the Franciscan hermitages of the Rieti Basin.

-

1 - - -

-

1 - - -

4 (x 2/4)

1 - 7 - 1 172,00 7 805,00

MONTENERO SABINO

LE STREGHE

at Scrocco, 02040 Montenero Sabino (RI)
Tel. 0765324146 Fax 0765324146
Web: web.tiscali.it/lestregheagriturismo

Just an hour from Rome, this accommodation is in charming wooden chalets. There's a lively welcome from the two 'witches' who offer wholesome food and good cheer.

8 (x 2)

1 - - 42,00 -

-

1 - - -

-

1 - 7 - 1 - 7 -

Montopoli di Sabina

Rodeo

at Granari, via Caprareccia 6,
02034 Montopoli di Sabina (RI)
Tel. 0765279060 Fax 0765276783
Web: www.agriturismorodeo.com

In the Monti Sabini, the furnishings and country club atmosphere of this establishment are the ideal setting for a holiday with the accent on horse-riding.

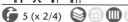

-

1 - - -

5 (x 2/4) 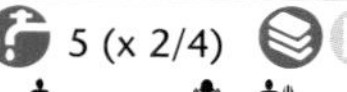 

1 26,00 - 42,00 -

-

1 - 7 - 1 - 7 -

Orte

La Chiocciola

at Seripola, 01028 Orte (VT)
Tel. 0761402734 Fax 0761490254
Web: www.lachiocciola.net

Luckily there are still people capable of converting a 15th-century farmhouse into tourist accommodation without spoiling its atmosphere.

-

1 - - -

8 (x 2/4)

1 55,00 - 76,00 -

-

1 - 7 - 1 - 7 -

Palestrina

Tao Center

via Colle Pastino, 00036 Palestrina (RM)
Tel. 069575670 Fax 069575670
Web: www.agriturismotaocenter.com

The activities available here range from the pleasures of life in the countryside to the practice of oriental disciplines and iridology, and the cuisine is satisfactory.

-

1 - - -

5 (x 2) 

1 - - 60,00 -

2 (x 5/4)    

1 - 7 - 1 - 7 619,00

Petrella Salto

Cooperativa Valle del Salto

at Cupaiolo, 02025 Petrella Salto (RI)
Tel. 0746526180 Fax 0746526208
Web: www.lazioagriturismo.com

In Cicolano, the isolated area of the Aniene Valley between Tivoli and the Piana del Fucino, this traditional farmhouse provides accommodation, while truffles are to be found in the woods.

-
1 - - -

-
1 - - -

10(x 4)
1 15,00 7 - 1 - 7 -

Poggio Nativo

Sant'Ilario sul Farfa

at Monte Santa Maria, via Colle,
02030 Poggio Nativo (RI)
Tel. 0765872410 Fax 0765872410
Web: www.santilariosulfarfa.it

An hour's drive from Rome, this holiday accommodation is in Sabina, close to the fascinating Farfa Abbey and Monti Lucretili Park.

-
1 - - -

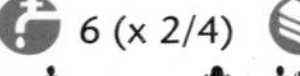
6 (x 2/4)
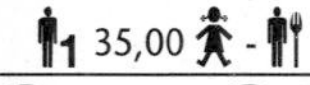
1 35,00 - 54,00 -

1(x 2)

1 - 7 - 1 - 7 723,00

Pontinia

Pegaso 2000

via Casanello, 04014 Pontinia (LT)
Tel. 0773853507 Fax 0773840415

The name reveals the owners' passion for horses. This is a modern building, surrounded by trees, in the reclaimed Pontine Marshes. There's an airfield for ultralights.

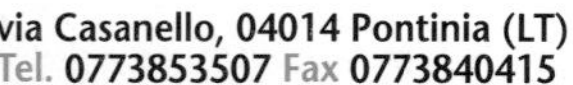

7 (x 2/4)
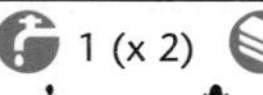   
1 24,00 - 42,00 -

1 (x 2)

1 27,00 - 45,00 -

-
1 - 7 - 1 - 7 -

Ponzano Romano

Monterone

contrada Monterone,
00060 Ponzano Romano (RM)
Tel. 0765338019 Fax 0765338019
Web: www.dipillo.it

Guests are accommodated in a converted outbuilding and a medieval watch-tower, and can take part in the farm's activities.

-
1 - - -

5 (x 2/4)

1 46,00 - 62,00 -

1(x 8)
1 - 7 - 1 206,00 7 1.154,00

Posta Fibreno

Tenuta Ducale La Pesca

via La Pesca 11, 03030 Posta Fibreno (FR)
Tel. 3355282107 Fax 0776891397
E-mail: agriturismolapesca@libero.it

Hiking, canoeing, a fishing school, bread-making weekends and courses of natural beauty treatments are but some of the recreational activities provided.

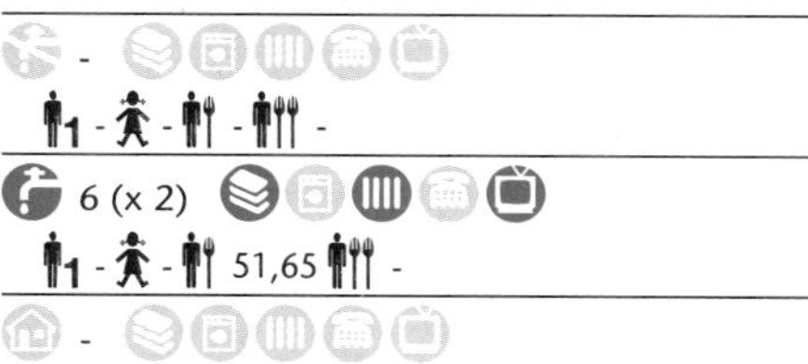

-
1 - - -

6 (x 2)
1 - - 51,65 -

-
1 - 7 - 1 - 7 -

Proceno

Il Molino

E D

corso Regina Margherita 70, 01020 Proceno (VT)
Tel. 0763711013 Fax 0763710036
Web: www.ilmolino.it

The accommodation is in two separate buildings: the Molino in a verdant valley by a stream, and the Caprino, in an open position commanding a fine view.

-
1 - - -

-
1 - - -

4 (x 2/10)
1 - 7 - 1 280,00 7 -

Roma

Borgo Bamboccio

E D

via della Giustiniana 990, 00189 Roma
Tel. 0630310113 Fax 0630350098

With its refined architecture, this complex overlooks the beautiful countryside around the remains of the city of Veii. The self-contained rooms are elegantly furnished and very comfortable.

-
1 - - -

-
1 - - -

3(x 4)
1 - 7 - 1 341,00 7 1.193,00

Cavendo Tutus

E D

via della Pisana 948/950, 00163 Roma
Tel. 0666156512 Fax 0666162970
E-mail: cavendotutus@mclink.it

For an unusual holiday in Rome, this is an oasis of greenery and peace, catering especially for those touring by bicycle (equipment is available for carrying out bicycle repairs).

-
1 - - -

-
1 - - -

10(x 2)
1 57,00 7 - 1 - 7 -

Lecanfore

E D

at Divino Amore, via P. Cavalloni 42, 00134 Roma
Tel. 0671350578 Fax 0671350562
Web: www.lecanfore.it

The centre of Rome is just a few kilometres away and the Appia Antica Archaeological Park is even closer. This early 20th-century farmhouse has been elegantly restored.

-
1 - - -

Lecanfore

Le Canfore Farm-House is placed in one of the most beautiful historical areas: in the middle of the Archaeological Park of Appia Antica, the Park of Roman Castles and the Divino Amore Sanctuary and, in the same time, very close to the centre of Rome.
Farm Holiday in Rome... archaeology and ecoturism through horse

and bike-riding along the wonderful Appia Antica and, for more trained people, up to the centre of Rome directly from Lecanfore farm-house.
The Farm-house, recently renewed in harmony with the countryside, is sorrounded by cerealyards, vineyards and olive goves.
Flats with different dimensions and rooms can be available for accomodation. All rooms are characterized by wooden beams and brick floors but also by modern comforts as air-conditioning and heating systems and satellite TV.
Horse-riding courses for adults and children are organized by the Fioranello Horse Centre thet is very close to the Farm house. By riding in the wonderful scenery rich in history and Roman culture, you can admire archaeological ruins and natural beauties and reach the Roman coast.
Close to: - Ciampino Airport Km. 3,8 - Fiumicino Airport Km. 25 - Line A Tube Station - Anagnina stop - Line B Tube Station - Eur Laurentina or Eur stops - Divino Amore Sanctuary Km. 5 - Archeological Park of Appia Antica Km. 2 - Tennis courts, football field, swimming pool and gym centre Km. 1 - Possibility of shuttle service - Bus n. 702 (direction Fioranello Road) 300 mts.

00134 Roma, via Pedica Cavalloni, 42 (via di Fioranello) - Tel. +39 06 71350578
Fax +39 06 71350562 - E-mail: agriturismo@lecanfore.it - www.lecanfore.it

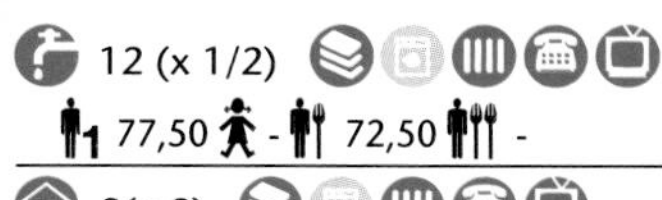

12 (x 1/2)

1 77,50 - 72,50 -

8(x 2)

1 - 7 - 1 154,94 7 919,29

Rodrigo De Vivar

at Ostia Antica, piazza della Rocca 18/19,
00119 Roma
Tel. 065652535 Fax 065652535
Web: www.rodrigodevivar.com

This farm, adjacent to the excavations, is oriented towards stock-raising and tourism on horseback. The accommodation is in rooms full of atmosphere.

-

1 - - -

14 (x 2/4)

1 200,00 - - -

3 (x 2/9)

1 - 7 - 1 270,00 7 -

Vivai Montecaminetto

via Sacrofanese 25, 00188 Roma
Tel. 0633615290 Fax 0633615290
Web: www.agriturismoroma.it

A pink house stands out against the greenery. From close quarters it turns out to be a villa with daring geometry. And there's a very friendly welcome.

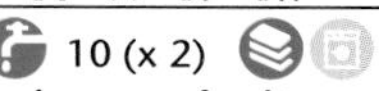

-

1 - - -

10 (x 2)

1 25,00 - 40,00 -

2(x 2)

1 25,00 7 - 1 - 7 -

Ronciglione

Trignano

via Cassia Cimina at km 25,
01037 Ronciglione (VT)
Tel. 0761628033 Fax 0761628033

On the slopes of the Monti Cimini, the farm, with its modern comforts, is an excellent base for tours on horseback and other kinds of excursion.

-

1 - - -

7 (x 2)

1 29,00 15,00 - -

2(x 4)

1 - 7 - 1 110,00 7 -

Sabaudia

Podere 1470

via Migliara 51, 04016 Sabaudia (LT)
Tel. 0773531052
Web: www.agriturismosabaudia.it

Located in the Circeo National Park, this farm is ideal for holidays focusing on nature, with trips to see the peregrines or round the lakes.

-
1 - - -

8 (x 1/2)
1 37,50 - -

-
1 - 7 - 1 - 7 -

SCANDRIGLIA

SANTO PAOLO ALTO

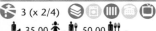

at Santo Paolo Alto 1,
02038 Scandriglia (RI)
Tel. **0765878767** Fax **0765878767**
E-mail: **egeo.minotti@libero.it**

This farmhouse has been restored according to the precepts of ecological architecture. The rooms with rustic furnishings look out over the Scandriglia Valley and the Monti Lucretili.

      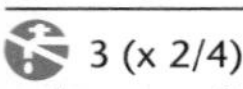   

3 (x 2/4)
1 35,00 - 50,00 -

-
1 - - -

-
1 - 7 - 1 - 7 -

SELCI

VALLEROSA

via Vallerosa 27, 02040 Selci (RI)
Tel. **0765519179** Fax **0765519179**
Web: **www.bytewise.it/vallerosa**

Guests are accommodated in the 19th-century villa and one of the renovated farmhouses; both the furnishings and swimming pool help to make their stay a pleasant one.

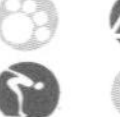        

-
1 - - -

-
1 - - -

7 (x 2/3)
1 - 7 - 1 165,00 7 -

SETTEFRATI

IL CASINO ROSSO

at Saranisco, S.P. (provincial road) for Settefrati,
03040 Settefrati (FR)
Tel. **0776695115**

'Unspoilt nature, forgotten aromas and tastes, sleep accompanied by birdsong and the chirping crickets': this is how this farm describes itself.

-
1 - - -

-
1 - - -

2(x 6)
1 - 7 - 1 100,00 7 500,00

Soriano nel Cimino

Parco dei Cimini

at Piangoli, strada Romana,
01038 Soriano nel Cimino (VT)
Tel. **0761752825** Fax **0761752266**
Web: **www.parcodeicimini.it**

In the heart of the Monti Cimini Park, amid woods of pine and chestnut, this elegant establishment is strongly oriented towards tourism on horseback.

-

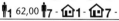

1 - - -

3 (x 2)

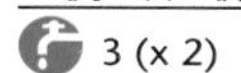 

1 31,00 - 52,00 -

3(x 2)

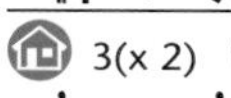 

1 62,00 7 - 1 - 7 -

Tarano

Le Fattorie Caracciolo

at Colle Campana, 02040 Tarano (RI)
Tel. **0765607731** Fax **0765609135**
Web: **www.fattoriecaracciolo.it**

Set in the wooded countryside, these three old farmhouses, with furnishings creating a romantic atmosphere, are close to the medieval village of Tarano.

-

1 - - -

-

1 - - -

7(x 2)

1 - 7 - 1 180,00 7 2.000,00

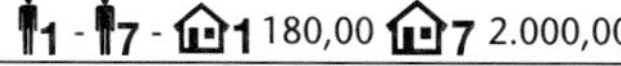

Tivoli

La Cerra

at Sant'Angelo in Valle Arcese, strada S. Gregorio at km 6.8, 00019 Tivoli (RM)
Tel. **0774411671** Fax **0774411229**

Surrounded by pinewoods in the hills, guests stay in renovated one-room apartments, which are self-contained and have period furniture, and in a number of bungalows in wood and masonry.

-

1 - - -

14 (x 4)

1 52,00 - -

-

1 - 7 - 1 - 7 -

Tuscania

Casa Caponetti

strada Quarticciolo 1, 01017 Tuscania (VT)
Tel. **0761435792** Fax **0761444247**
Web: **www.caponetti.com**

This place is a dream for both horses and their riders. The lady of the house is an expert cook and organises cookery courses with the accent on natural ingredients. The accommodation is in wooden chalets.

-

1 - - -

6 (x 2)

1 - - 70,00 -

-

1 - 7 - 1 - 7 -

Varco Sabino

La Ferrera

via Giovanni XXIII 5, 02020 Varco Sabino (RI)
Tel. **0765790110** Fax **0765790110**
Web: **www.laferrera.it**

In three rural buildings there are self-contained rooms of various sizes and levels of comfort; the excellent local dishes are based on meat produced on the farm.

\-

1 - - - -

6 (x 2/4)

1 32,00 - - 65,00

4 (x 5/4)

1 38,00 7 - 1 - 7 -

VELLETRI

IACCHELLI

via dei Laghi at km 15, 00049 Velletri (RM)
Tel. 069633256 Fax 0696143004

In the Castelli Romani Nature Park, this is a large complex consisting of low buildings around a square; there's an enormous restaurant.

\-

1 - - - -

5 (x 2)

1 42,00 - 65,00 -

5(x 4)

1 - 7 - 1 - 7 520,00

Viterbo

Il Rinaldone

at Rinaldone, strada Rinaldone 9, 01100 Viterbo
Tel. **0761352137** Fax **0761353116**
Web: **www.rinaldone.com**

Accommodation and meals are available in the elegant surroundings of an old house that has been carefully renovated and provided with modern facilities, including a swimming pool and tennis courts.

-

1 - - -

15 (x 2/4)

1 47,00 - 70,00 -

-

1 - 7 - 1 - 7 -

Tenuta Serpepe

strada Dogana 8, 01100 Viterbo
Tel. **3484114738** Fax **0761799203**
Web: **www.tenutaserpepe.it**

On this large organic farm with olive groves and cork-oaks, sheep yielding milk, Chianina cattle and Cinta Senese pigs are reared.

-

1 - - -

-

1 - - -

3 (x 4/6)

1 - 7 - 1 - 7 700,00

ASS.
ERBE AMICHE

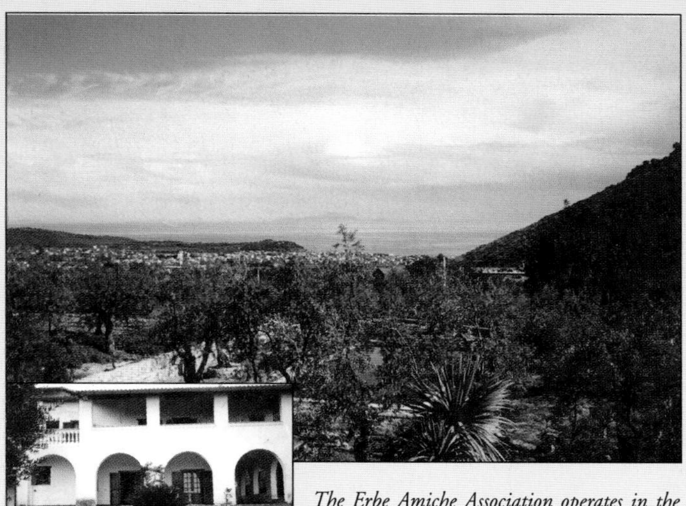

The Erbe Amiche Association operates in the country around Formia, in the heart of the Gaeta Gulf, 2 km away from the sea and 3 km from Mount Petrella; its premises can be used as a base for trips to Naples (70 km), Rome (100 km), the islands of Capri, Ponza, Ventotene and the archaeological excavations of Ercolano, Pompei and Cuma.
The Association offers the possibility of spending a holiday in contact with nature and a chance to see what the natural world has in store for us, for our own well being, with the following initiatives:
1) Visits to the Association's Botanical Garden, which systematically collects medicinal, aromatic and cosmetic plants of the Mediterranean flora, and explanations on their use.
2) Elements of organic farming, which aims at replacing chemicals with biological control means.
3) Demonstrations on how to prepare wholemeal bread, cheese made with natural rennet, cold pressed olive oil, and also wine and spumante, always using natural methods.
4) Elements of bee keeping, to obtain beehive products such as honey, pollen, propolis, etc., to cure and prevent various illnesses.
5) Rearing of farmyard animals in accordance with natural methods.
6) Farming courses for schools and association members.
The Association has 4 flats equipped with all comforts, plus swimming pool, tennis court, football field and riding course; you can also attend sailing, surfing and sea-going courses nearby.
Pets welcome.
Price per person: 23 euros. Discounts for groups and families, to be agreed.

ASS. ERBE AMICHE
Via T. Costa, 8 – Formia (LT) - Tel. +39 0771 22734 - 735262

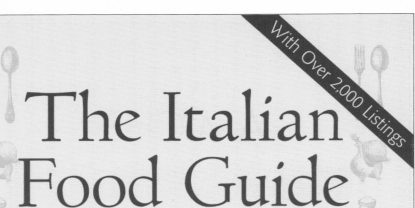

The Italian Food Guide

The Ultimate Guide to the Regional Foods of Italy

From the Touring Club of Italy, the country's foremost publisher of guidebooks for over **100** years.

TOURING CLUB OF ITALY

ISBN 8836525385 - 648pp - $ 24.95

LIGURIA

ALBENGA

IL COLLETTO

at Campochiesa, via Cavour 34,
17031 Albenga (SV)
Tel. 018221858 Fax 018221859
Web: www.ilcolletto.com

This estate is divided into three parts: firstly, there are the rooms and a garden with a swimming pool and gazebo; then the stables and a picnic area; finally, the farm and owners' house.

\-

1 - - - -

\-

1 - - - -

4(x 2)

1 40,00 7 210,00 1 - 7 -

ARENZANO

ARGENTEA

at Campo, via Vallerone 50, 16011 Arenzano (GE)
Tel. 0109135367 Fax 0109135367
E-mail: agriturismo.argentea@tiscali.it

The accommodation is in a 17th-century building that's recently been renovated; guests may relax on the beach, visit the Monte Beigua Nature Park or have a go at canyoning.

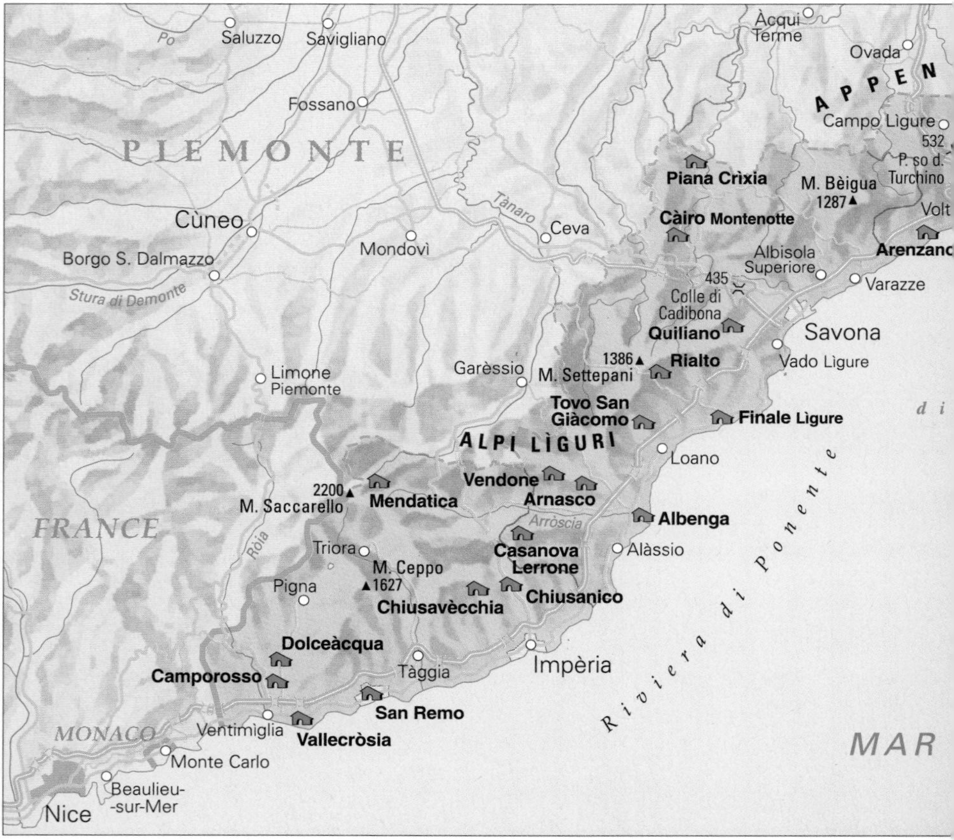

ARNASCO

IL CARRUGGIO

at Menosio, via Gallizi 6,
17032 Arnasco (SV)
Tel. 0182761182 Fax 0182570147
E-mail: ornella.bottero@tin.it

In a quiet village just inland from the coast, this cottage has been refurbished with modern comforts. Nearby is Albenga, with its charming medieval centre.

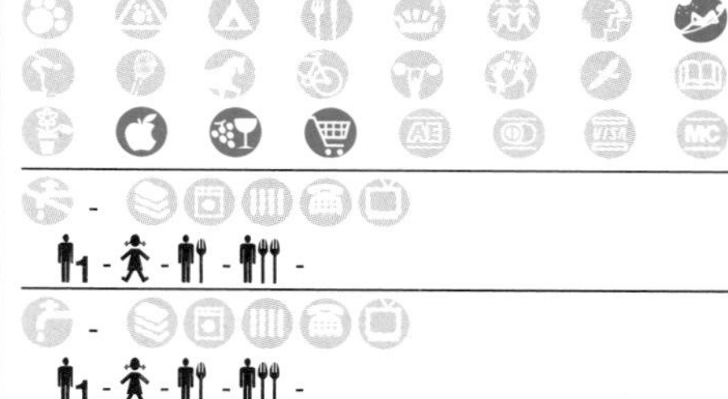

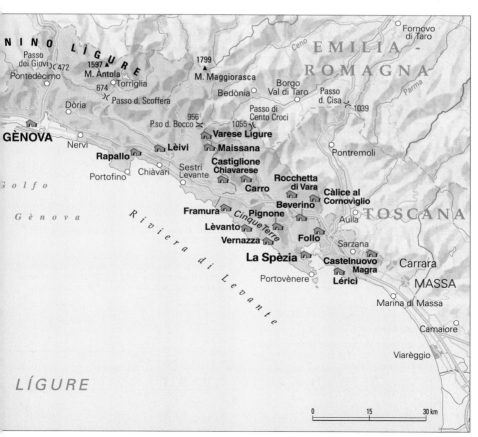

4 (x 4/5)

25,00 - 7 - 1 - 7 -

Beverino

Casa Villara

via Castagna Rossa 8, 19020 Beverino (SP)
Tel. 3498181269 Fax 0187884900
E-mail: casavillara@hotmail.com

Guests are accommodated in a sensitively renovated cottage; not surprisingly, its owners have opted for organic farming methods.

1 - - -

7 (x 2/4)

1 33,50 16,00 51,65 -

1 - 7 - 1 - 7 -

Pastani

via Pastani 19, 19020 Beverino (SP)
Tel. 0187883509 Fax 0187883509
Web: www.valdivara.com

In the peace and quiet of the woods there's just the right atmosphere - thanks also to Signora Angela's cooking - for a country holiday.

1 - - - -

4 (x 2)

1 32,50 - 45,00 -

1 - 7 - 1 - 7 -

Cairo Montenotte

Cascina del Vai

at Ville, strada Ville 140,
17014 Cairo Montenotte (SV)
Tel. 01950894 Fax 01950894

The old farm buildings have been renovated to provide accommodation, without, however, spoiling the pleasant atmosphere of the farmyard.

1 - - - -

7 (x 2/4)

1 38,00 - 50,00 -

1 - 7 - 1 - 7 -

Calice al Cornoviglio

Alpicella

at Bruscarolo, 19020 Calice al Cornoviglio (SP)
Tel. 0187935589

In the area of the Comunità Montana della Media Val di Vara, accommodation is available in a mountain hut with a view of the sea; it's in an isolated position, but is just a few kilometres from Calice.

1 (x 4)

1 32,00 - 42,00 -

1 (x 4)

1 32,00 - 42,00 -

\-

1 - 7 - 1 - 7 -

Camporosso

Il Bausco

at Brunetti, 18033 Camporosso (IM)
Tel. 0184206013 Fax 0184206851

In the area inland from Bordighera, palms, cypresses and olives are the pleasant setting of the renovated and well-equipped cottages providing accommodation.

\-

1 - - -

\-

1 - - -

3(x 2)

1 24,00 7 - 1 - 7 -

Carro

Ca' du Chittu

at Pavareto, isolato Camporione 25,
19012 Carro (SP)
Tel. 0187861205 Fax 0187861205
E-mail: caduchittu@virgilio.it

This is quality accommodation, as may be seen from the way this 19th-century cottage has been restored, the excellence of the cuisine and the farm's commitment to catering for educational visits.

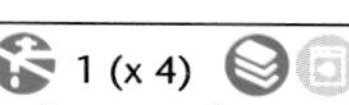

1 (x 4)

1 25,00 17,00 40,00 -

6 (x 2)

1 29,00 20,00 44,00 -

\-

1 - 7 - 1 - 7 -

Casanova Lerrone

Cascina il Poggio

at Marmoreo, via Poggio 97,
17033 Casanova Lerrone (SV)
Tel. 018274040

The farmhouse where the guests stay is in stone: the delightful rooms surround a small courtyard, with spacious new bathrooms and a garden.

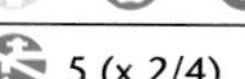 

5 (x 2/4)

1 25,00 - 30,00 -

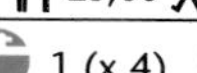 

1 (x 4)

1 30,00 - 37,00 -

\-

1 - 7 - 1 - 7 -

Castelnuovo Magra

Monteverde

via Molin del Piano 65, 19030
Castelnuovo Magra (SP)
Tel. 3392766699 Fax 0187770670
Web: www.agriturismomonteverde.it

A mother and her daughter, Anna and Virginia, have opted to live in the country and give their loving attention to this beautiful farm surrounded by olive trees.

\-

1 - - -

3 (x 2)

1 40,00 - -

4 (x 2/4)

1 - 7 - 1 180,00 7 1.000,00

Castiglione Chiavarese

La Terra di Mezzo

at Carmelo, 16030 Castiglione Chiavarese (GE)
Tel. 0185408461 Fax 0185408461
Web: www.laterradimezzo.net

This is an outpost of nature: the crops are certified as biodynamic and the house has been rebuilt using the materials and techniques of ecological architecture.

\-

1 - - -

3 (x 4)

1 26,00 13,00 -

\-

1 - 7 - 1 - 7 -

Monte Pù

at Monte Pù, 16030 Castiglione Chiavarese (GE)
Tel. 0185408027 Fax 0185408027

In the setting of the Val Petronio, amid vineyards, olive groves and the Mediterranean scrub, accommodation is available in three buildings with large communal spaces and attractive furnishings.

\-

1 - - -

9 (x 2/4)

1 35,00 - 51,00 -

2(x 4)

1 - 7 - 1 114,00 7 -

Chiusanico

Gli Orti

via Dian Castello 5/12,
18023 Chiusanico (IM)
Tel. 0183529030 Fax 0183296935
Web: www.gliorti.it

On this farm using organic methods, accommodation is available in two tastefully renovated and furnished cottages, pleasantly located by a stream where bathing is possible.

\-

1 - - -

\-

1 - - -

4 (x 4/6) 

1 - 7 - 1 95,00 7 630,00

Chiusavecchia

Le Casette

at Sarola, via XX Settembre,
18027 Chiusavecchia (IM)
Tel. 0183529025 Fax 0183766692
E-mail: laura.caleffi@uno.it

Located in the village of Sarola, just off the road climbing up from Imperia to Colle di Nava, this accommodation is ideal for a peaceful holiday close to the sea and the woods.

-
1 - - -

-
1 - - -

5 (x 4/6)
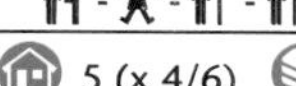 
1 - 7 - 1 90,00 7 570,00

Dolceacqua

Rifugio Alta Via

at Pozzuolo, strada militare La Colla-Gouta,
18035 Dolceacqua (IM)
Tel. 0184206754 Fax 0184206754
E-mail: silvdall@libero.it

Standing on a hillside, this stone house, simple in style but with a splendid view of the sea and mountains, has two horses available for experienced riders.

-
1 - - -

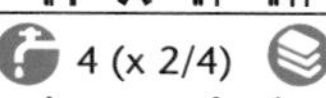

4 (x 2/4)
1 31,00 - 47,00 -

-
1 - 7 - 1 - 7 -

Terre Bianche-Locanda del Bricco

at Arcagna, 18035 Dolceacqua (IM)
Tel. 018431426 Fax 018431230
Web: www.terrebianche.com

This ancient tower overlooking the upper Nervia Valley above the medieval village of Dolceacqua commands a view extending from the highest peaks of the Maritime Alps to the sea.

-
1 - - -

7 (x 2)
1 57,00 - 73,00 -

-
1 - 7 - 1 - 7 -

Finale Ligure

Villa Piuma

at Perti, via Cappelletta Nuova 8,
17024 Finale Ligure (SV)
Tel. 019687030 Fax 019687030
Web: www.agriclub.it

Located 3 km from the beach at Finale, this 18th-century villa has been splendidly renovated and is partly used for holiday accommodation.

-
1 - - -

3 (x 2)
1 25,00 - - -

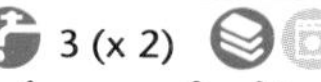

-
1 - 7 - 1 - 7 -

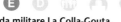

Follo

Carnea

at Carnea, via San Rocco 10, 19020 Follo (SP)
Tel. 0187947070 Fax 0187947070
E-mail: agriturismocarnea@hotmail.com

A holiday that is "out of this world" in the peace and quiet of the verdant surroundings, while the Cinque Terre, Portovenere and Lerici are close at hand.

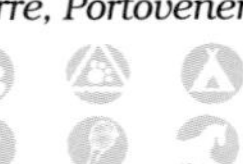   

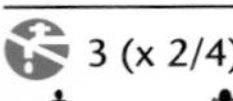 3 (x 2/4) 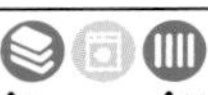

1 31,00 - 47,00 -

4 (x 2) 

1 31,00 - 47,00 -

-

1 - 7 - 1 - 7 -

Framura

La Caprarbia

at Le Fosse, 19014 Framura (SP)
Tel. 0187824282

The bright pink of a villa, with its arches and terraces, stands against the woods; there's also a small campsite equipped with solar panels.

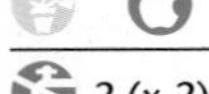   

2 (x 2)

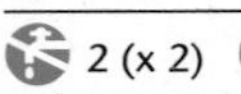 

1 20,00 - 33,00 -

 3 (x 2)

1 25,00 - - -

  1(x 2)

1 - 7 - 1 60,00 7 -

Genova

Pietre Turchine

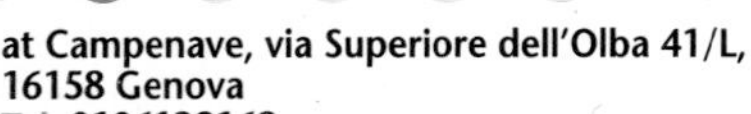

at Campenave, via Superiore dell'Olba 41/L, 16158 Genova
Tel. 0106139168

This is Liguria: just inland from Voltri, a stone's throw from Genoa, we are already amid the woods of the Monte Beigua Nature Park.

-

1 - - - -

3 (x 2)

1 42,00 - 50,00 -

-

1 - 7 - 1 - 7 -

La Spezia

Golfo dei Poeti - Fattorie Bedogni Von Berger

via Proffiano 34, 19123 La Spezia
Tel. 0187711053 Fax 0187711053
Web: www.agriturismogolfodeipoeti.com

Located on the Golfo dei Poeti, these two stone cottages have terraces supported by dry-stone walls, interiors with a pleasant atmosphere and two swimming pools with Jacuzzis.

-

1 - - - -

1 (x 2)

1 37,00 - - -

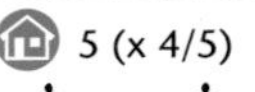  

5 (x 4/5)

1 55,00 7 - 1 - 7 -

Leivi

La Madre

at Garbuggi, via degli Ulivi 39, 16040 Leivi (GE)
Tel. 0185319529 Fax 0185319529
Web: www.lamadre.com

On this farm there's peace and quiet and fun for the children, including a swimming pool; close by is the Fontanabuona Valley and the Alta Via mountains.

-
1 - - -

-
1 - - -

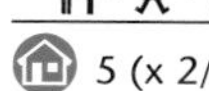 5 (x 2/6)  
1 30,00 7 - 1 - 7 -

Lerici

Gallerani

at Zanego 5, 19032 Lerici (SP)
Tel. 0187964057 Fax 0187964216
Web: www.cittadellaspezia.com

From the farm, amid the woods just inland from the sea, there's a panoramic view of the Golfo di La Spezia and Lerici; behind it is the Monte Marcello Nature Park.

2 (x 2)
1 40,00 - 55,00 -

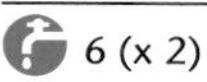 6 (x 2)  
1 40,00 - 55,00 -

-
1 - 7 - 1 - 7 -

Levanto

Il Frantoio

at Lavaggiorosso, via S. Sebastiano 10,
19015 Levanto (SP)
Tel. 0187803628 Fax 0187802568
Web: www.agriturismoilfrantoio.com

This accommodation is in a hamlet near Levanto that stands out among the olive trees; a narrow lane leads up to the farm in a sunny, panoramic position.

-
1 - - -

-
1 - - -

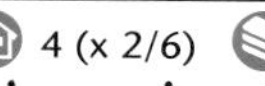 4 (x 2/6)   
1 41,00 7 - 1 - 7 -

Maissana

Giandriale

at Giandriale 5, 19010 Maissana (SP)
Tel. 0187840279 Fax 0187840156
Web: www.giandriale.it

In a nature reserve, the Giani family offer accommodation in orderly rooms with period furniture; they are in two buildings, both in stone, with a splendid view.

-
1 - - - -

6 (x 2)
1 26,00 - 41,32 -

2 (x 4/6)
1 31,00 7 - 1 - 7 -

Mendatica

Il Castagno

via San Bernardo 39, 18025 Mendatica (IM)
Tel. 0183328718

The accommodation is in the outbuildings of a farm attached to the traditions of the valley; the guests' rooms are comfortable and well-equipped.

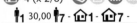

-
1 - - - -

2 (x 2)
1 30,00 - 42,00 -

4 (x 2/6)
1 30,00 7 - 1 - 7 -

Piana Crixia

La Celestina

at Gallareto, 17058 Piana Crixia (SV)
Tel. 019570292 Fax 0195704935
E-mail: lacelestina@libero.it

In the area of the Langhe Regional Park at Piana Crixia, accommodation is available in this three-storey farmhouse set in an excellent position.

4 (x 2)

1 20,00 - 40,00 -

1 (x 2)
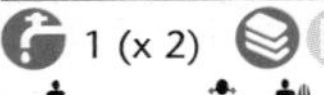

1 25,00 - 45,00 -

-
1 - 7 - 1 - 7 -

Pignone

5 Terre

at Gaggiola, 19020 Pignone (SP)
Tel. 0187888087

The hills behind the Cinque Terre offer peace and a cool climate. The accommodation is in new or renovated buildings, all of them well-equipped.

1 (x 2)
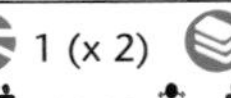

1 30,00 - 45,00 -

8 (x 2/4)
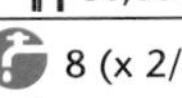

1 30,00 - 45,00 -

-
1 - 7 - 1 - 7 -

Quiliano

Casalina

at Montagna, via Chicchezza 7, 17047 Quiliano (SV)
Tel. 019887604

Not far from the city, this is a classic farm in the woods; the coolness and attractive rooms, furnished in Provençal style, encourage guests to take things easy.

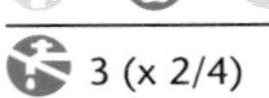

3 (x 2/4)
1 30,00 - - -

-
1 - - - -

-
1 - 7 - 1 - 7 -

Rapallo

La Bicocca

at Madonna Nera, salita S. Agostino 57,
16035 Rapallo (GE)
Tel. 0185272380 Fax 0185272380
Web: www.la-bicocca.it

The view is at its best at sunset, with the lights of Rapallo and the outline of the Monte di Portofino framing the Golfo del Tigullio.

 -

1 - - -

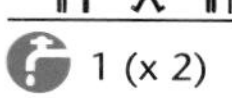 1 (x 2) 

 1 26,00 - -

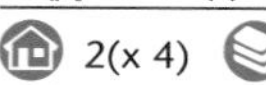 2(x 4) 

1 - 7 - 1 109,00 7 -

Rialto

La Ca' dell'Alpe

via Alpe 10, 17020 Rialto (SV)
Tel. 019688030 Fax 019688019
Web: www.agriturismofinaleligure.it

In the area near Finale, the farm is located amid the chestnut trees. Activities include walks of various degrees of difficulty and rock-climbing, without, obviously, forgetting the sea.

 -

1 - - -

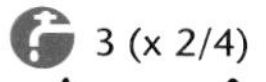 3 (x 2/4) 

 1 20,00 - 30,00 -

 2(x 4)

1 24,00 7 - 1 - 7 -

Rocchetta di Vara

Mare e Monti - Riomaggiore

at Saldino, 19020 Rocchetta di Vara (SP)
Tel. 3404174905 Fax 0187936448

The name almost says it all. The accommodation is in a renovated cottage in the woods, or else in the main building in Riomaggiore, in the centre of the village.

3 (x 2/4)

1 52,00 - 60,00 -

1 (x 2)

1 52,00 - 60,00 -

-

1 - 7 - 1 - 7 -

San Remo

Colle Mare

at Bussana, strada Collette Beulle 100,
18038 San Remo (IM)
Tel. 0184514252 Fax 0184514252

This modern villa with comfortable rooms and a large terrace facing the sea is the ideal solution for those visiting the Riviera di Ponente.

 5 (x 1/2) 

1 30,00 - 47,00 -

-

1 - - -

 1(x 3)

1 28,00 7 - 1 - 7 -

Tovo San Giacomo

Il Poggio

via Poggio 129, 17020 Tovo San Giacomo (SV)
Tel. 019637134
E-mail: agriturismoilpoggio@tiscali.it

The hamlet overlooks the valley; the complex comprises the restaurant, located in a 15th-century building, and the rooms, in a recent one.

4 (x 2)

26,00

Vallecrosia

Terre di Mare

via I Maggio 90, 18019 Vallecrosia (IM)
Tel. 0184255846
Web: www.terredimare.net

This recently built house belongs to a nursery specialising in ornamental plants with a large tropical garden close to the sea.

8 (x 2/4)

50,00 60,00

Varese Ligure

Il Gumo

at Gumo 69, 19028 Varese Ligure (SP)
Tel. 0187842282 Fax 0187842282
E-mail: ilgumo@tin.it

Surrounded by greenery and a colourful display of flowers, this farm offers comfortable accommodation furnished in traditional style.

1 (x 2)

34,00

1(x 4)

93,00 600,00

Il Pruno Selvatico

at Groppo Marzo 70/C, 19028 Varese Ligure (SP)
Tel. 0187842382 Fax 0187840956
Web: www.ilprunoselvatico.it

A holiday here is interesting from two points of view: the Alta Via of the Monti Liguria, which offers fresh air and mushrooms, and the sea between Sestri Levante and the Cinque Terre.

4 (x 2/4)

43,00 59,00

3(x 2)

1.150,00

Vendone

La Crosa

at Crosa 10, 17032 Vendone (SV)
Tel. 018276331 Fax 018276331
Web: www.lacrosa.it

Situated in an old hill village, a number of buildings surrounded by open spaces have been completely renovated to provide accommodation.

- 1 - - -

- 1 - - -

4 (x 2/4)

1 - 7 - 1 75,00 7 -

Vernazza

La Rocca

at Corniglia, via Fieschi 222, 19010 Vernazza (SP)
Tel. **0187812178**

The farmhouse is in the village, which is the first thing you'll want to explore; then you can take your pick between art and nature.

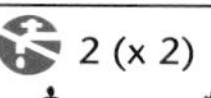

2 (x 2)

1 27,00 - - -

-

1 - - - -

1(x 3)

1 - 7 - 1 70,00 7 550,00

www.regione.liguria.it/conosc/4_natur/index.htm
www.parks.it

HANBURY Botanical Gardens Regional Protected Area (IM)
Tel. 0184 229507 - E-mail: info@cooperativa-omnia.com

ISOLA GALLINARA Regional Nature Reserve (SV)
Tel. 0182 541351 – fax 0182 554617

RIO TORSERO Regional Nature Reserve (SV)
Tel. 0182 990024 – fax 0182 991461

BERGEGGI Regional Nature Reserve (SV)
Tel. 019 257901 – fax 019 25790220
E-mail: b.ut@mail.comune.bergeggi.sv.it

BRIC TANA Regional Nature Park (SV)
Tel. 019 564007 – fax 019 564368
E-mail: ut.com.millesimo@libero.it

PIANA CRIXIA Regional Nature Park (SV)
Tel. 019 570021 – fax 019 570022
E-mail: pianacrixia@libero.it

BEIGUA Regional Nature Park (SV-GE)
Tel. 019 84187300 – fax 019 84187305
E-mail: beigua@tin.it

PRATORONDANINO Botanical Garden Provincial Protected Area (GE)
Tel. 010 54991 – fax 010 5499680

ANTOLA Regional Nature Park (GE)
Tel. 010 9761304 – fax 010 9760147
E-mail: antola@libero.it

PORTOFINO Regional Nature Park (GE)
Tel. 0185 289479 – fax 0185 285706
E-mail: enteparco.Portofino@libero.it

PORTOFINO State Marine Protected Area (GE)
Tel. 0185 289649 – fax 0185 293002
E-mail: amp.portofino@libero.it

AVETO Regional Nature Park (GE)
Tel. 0185 340311 – fax 0185 343370
E-mail: parco.aveto@comunic.it parcoaveto@libero.it

CINQUE TERRE National Park (SP)
CINQUE TERRE State Marine Protected Area (SP)
Tel. 0187 760000 – fax 0187 920866
E-mail: cmriomaggiore@castagna.it parconazionale5terre@libero.it

PORTOVENERE Regional Nature Park (SP)
Tel. 0187 794830 – fax 0187 794831
E-mail: atecnica@tin.it

MONTEMARCELLO-MAGRA (SP) Regional Nature Park
Tel. 0187 691071 – fax 0187 606738
E-mail: info@parcomagra.it

ALTA VIA DEI MONTI LIGURI Trekking Itinerary (GE)
Tel. 010 2471678 – fax 010 2471522
E-mail: unione.liguria@lig.camcom.it

Regional Tourist Board
Tel. 010 530821 – fax 010 5958507
E-mail: info.inliguria@liguriainrete.it

Accident Emergency Calls
Tel. **118**; 336 689316

Fire Emergency Calls
Tel. **1515**; 167807047

LOMBARDIA

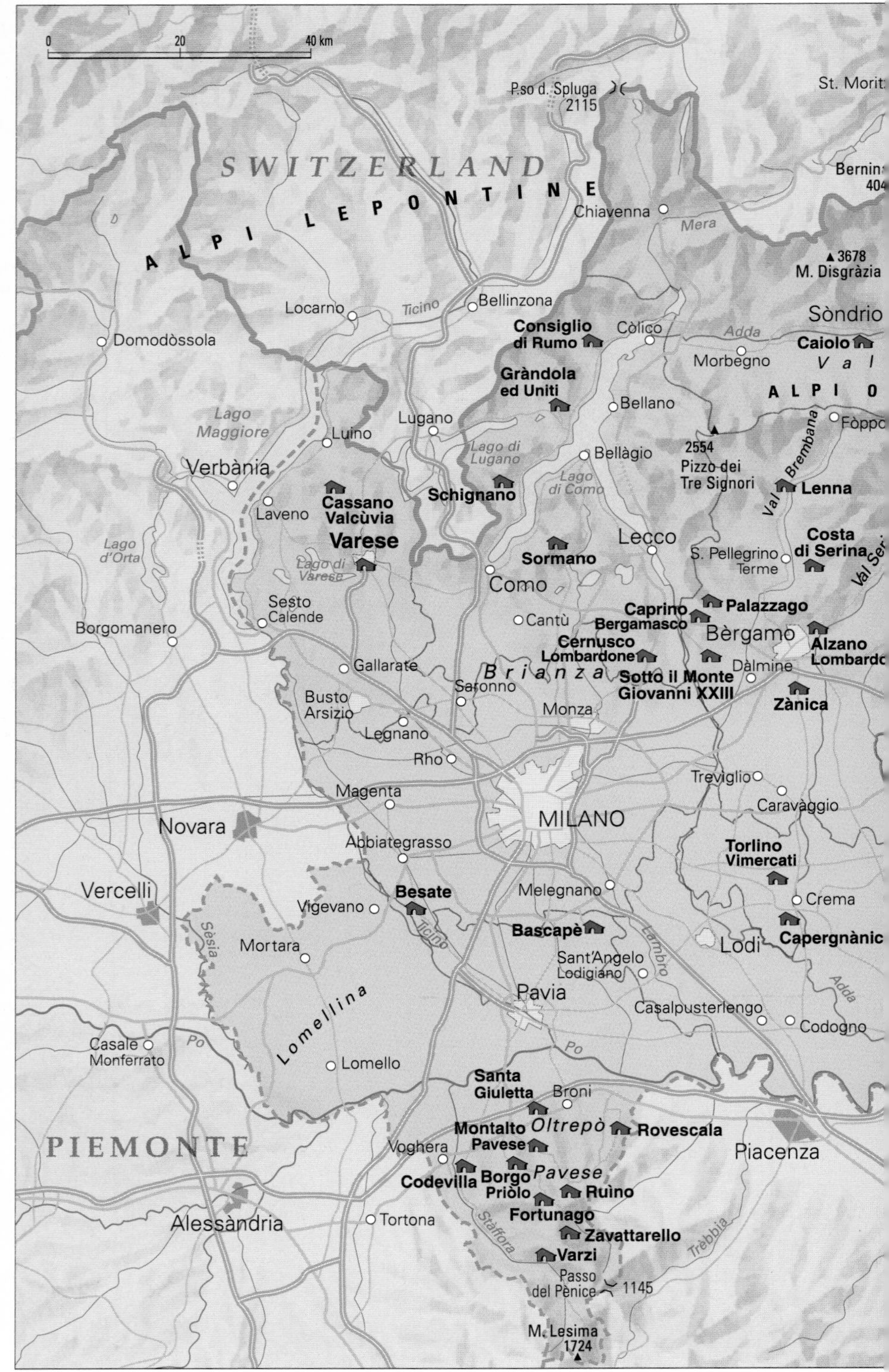

0
20
40 km
P.so d. Spluga
2115
St. Morit
SWITZERLAND
ALPI LEPONTINE
Bernin
Chiavenna
Mera
3678
M. Disgràzia
Locarno
Ticino
Bellinzona
Sòndrio
Domodòssola
Consiglio di Rumo
Còlico
Adda
Caiolo
Morbegno
Val
Gràndola ed Uniti
ALPI O
Bellano
Lago Maggiore
Lugano
Luino
Fòppo
Val Brembana
Lago di Lugano
Bellàgio
2554
Pizzo dei Tre Signori
Verbània
Lago di Como
Lenna
Laveno
Cassano Valcùvia
Schignano
Varese
Lago d'Orta
Lago di Varese
Lecco
Costa di Serina
Sormano
S. Pellegrino Terme
Como
Sesto Calende
Caprino Bergamasco
Palazzago
Borgomanero
Cantù
Bèrgamo
Alzano Lombardo
Cernusco Lombardone
Gallarate
Brianza
Sotto il Monte Giovanni XXIII
Dalmine
Saronno
Busto Arsizio
Zànica
Monza
Legnano
Rho
Treviglio
Magenta
Caravàggio
Novara
MILANO
Abbiategrasso
Torlino Vimercati
Vercelli
Melegnano
Besate
Crema
Vigevano
Bascapè
Sèsia
Ticino
Lambro
Mortara
Lodi
Capergnànic
Sant'Angelo Lodigiano
Adda
Pavia
Lomellina
Casalpusterlengo
Codogno
Casale Monferrato
Po
Po
Lomello
Santa Giuletta
Broni
Oltrepò Pavese
Montalto Pavese
Rovescala
PIEMONTE
Voghera
Piacenza
Codevilla
Borgo Priòlo
Ruìno
Fortunago
Tortona
Alessàndria
Staffora
Zavattarello
Trebbia
Varzi
Passo del Pènice
1145
M. Lesima
1724

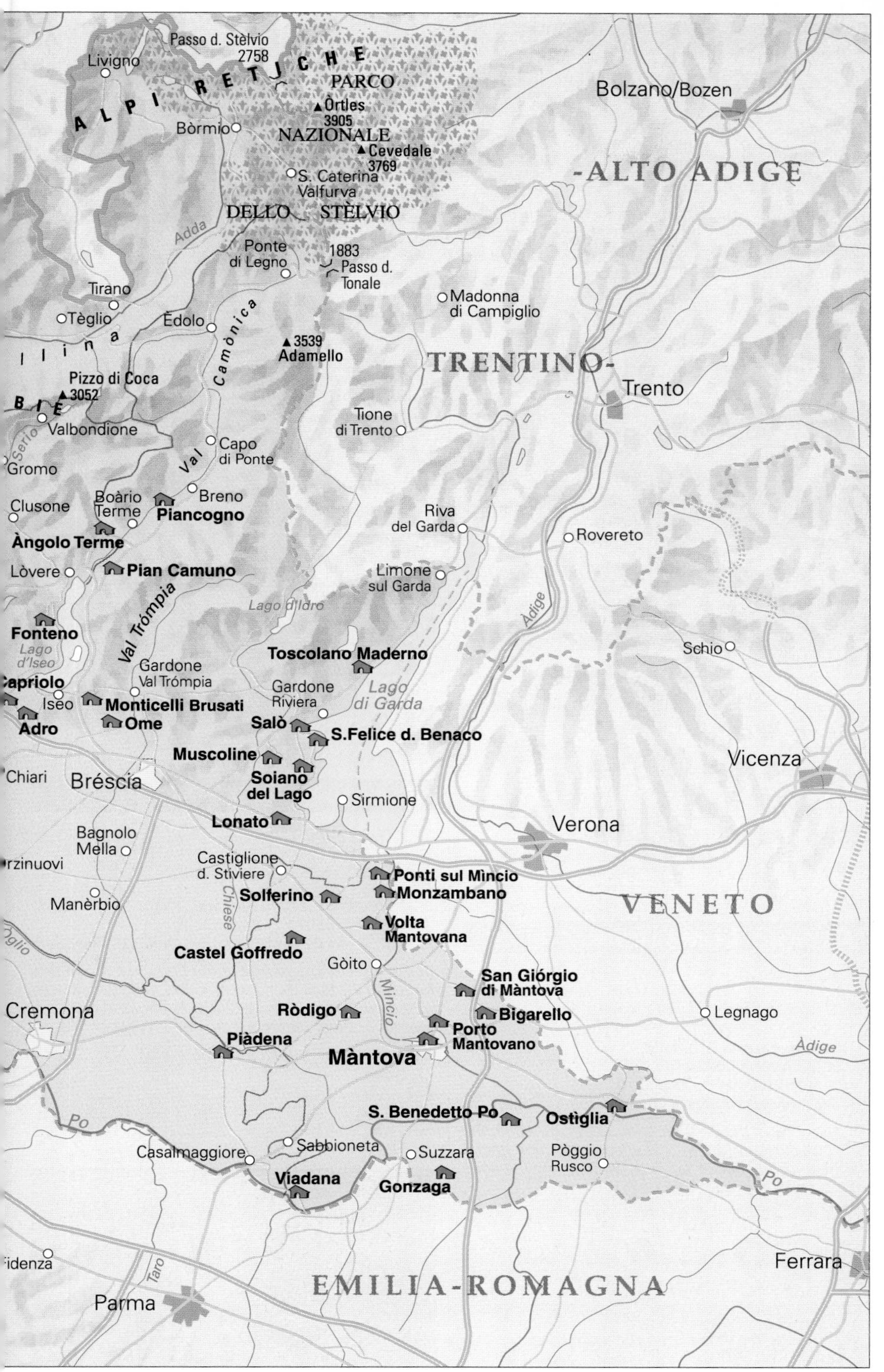

Passo d. Stèlvio
2758
Livigno
ALPI RETICHE
PARCO NAZIONALE DELLO STÈLVIO
Òrtles 3905
Bòrmio
Cevedale 3769
S. Caterina Valfurva
Bolzano/Bozen
TRENTINO-ALTO ADIGE
Adda
Ponte di Legno
1883
Passo d. Tonale
Tirano
Tèglio
Èdolo
Val Camònica
Madonna di Campiglio
3539 Adamello
Pizzo di Coca 3052
Valbondione
Trento
Tione di Trento
Capo di Ponte
Gromo
Breno
Boàrio Terme
Piancogno
Clusone
Àngolo Terme
Riva del Garda
Rovereto
Lòvere
Pian Camuno
Limone sul Garda
Val Trómpia
Lago d'Idro
Adige
Fonteno
Lago d'Iseo
Toscolano Maderno
Schio
Gardone Val Trómpia
Gardone Riviera
Lago di Garda
Iseo
Monticelli Brusati
Adro
Ome
Salò
S.Felice d. Benaco
Muscoline
Vicenza
Chiari
Bréscia
Soiano del Lago
Sirmione
Lonato
Verona
Bagnolo Mella
Castiglione d. Stiviere
Ponti sul Mìncio
Monzambano
Manèrbio
Solferino
VENETO
Chiese
Volta Mantovana
Castel Goffredo
Gòito
Mincio
San Giórgio di Màntova
Cremona
Ròdigo
Bigarello
Legnago
Porto Mantovano
Piàdena
Adige
Màntova
S. Benedetto Po
Ostiglia
Po
Sabbioneta
Casalmaggiore
Suzzara
Pòggio Rusco
Viadana
Gonzaga
Po
Ferrara
EMILIA-ROMAGNA
Taro
Parma

Adro

Cornaleto

via Cornaletto 2, 25030 Adro (BS)
Tel. 0307450554 Fax 0307450552
Web: www.cornaleto.it

On a hillside, amid the renowned vineyards of Franciacorta, this is modern farmhouse accommodation where the restaurant plays a particularly important role.

-
1 - - -

11 (x 2)
1 50,00 - -

3(x 2)
1 - 7 - 1 75,00 7 480,00

Alzano Lombardo

Ardizzone

at Nese, cascina Grumello,
24022 Alzano Lombardo (BG)
Tel. 035510060 Fax 035738703
Web: www.hobbyfarms.it

On the edge of the Colli Bergamaschi Park - with the city still close at hand - this accommodation is in a fortified farmhouse of the 16th century, amid woods of pine and coppiced trees.

-
1 - - -

-
1 - - -

5 (x 2/5)
1 23,25 7 - 1 - 7 -

Angolo Terme

Roccolo

at Colle Vareno, 25040 Angolo Terme (BS)
Tel. 034665290

This accommodation is at a high altitude, at the foot of the Pizzo della Presolana, with a splendid panoramic view. The rooms are simple but well-kept and comfortable.

-
1 - - -

8 (x 2)
1 24,00 - 37,00 -

-
1 - 7 - 1 - 7 -

Bascapè

Tenuta Camillo

   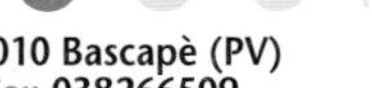

at Trognano, 27010 Bascapè (PV)
Tel. 038266509 Fax 038266509
Web: www.agriturismo.com/tenutacamillo

In the typical landscape of the Lombard plain, this large farm is built round a courtyard, with the owners' villa dating from the early 20th century and outbuildings; in addition, there's a swimming pool and lawn.

-
1 - - -

7 (x 2/4)
1 60,00 - - -

2 (x 2/6)
1 - 7 - 1 95,00 7 -

Besate

Cascina Caremma

E

via Cascina Caremma 1, 20080 Besate (MI)
Tel. 029050020 Fax 029050020
Web: www.caremma.com

Just 30 km from Milan, in the Ticino Valley Regional Park, this typical Lombard farmhouse is at the centre of a vast area of land under organic crops.

-
1 - - -

14 (x 1/4)
1 31,00 15,00 46,50 -

-
1 - 7 - 1 - 7 -

Bigarello

Il Galeotto

E

at Gazzo, via Galeotto 2, 46030 Bigarello (MN)
Tel. 0376229165 Fax 0376229165
Web: www.galeotto.supereva.it

The Mincio, Adige and Po have formed the landscape between Mantua, ruled by the Gonzaga, and Verona, where the Scaligeri held sway. At table, however, the protagonist is rice.

-
1 - - -

3 (x 2)
1 30,00 - 50,00 -

-
1 - 7 - 1 - 7 -

Borgo Priolo

Castello di Stefanago

at Stefanago, 27040 Borgo Priolo (PV)
Tel. 0383875227 Fax 0383875644
Web: www.castellodistefanago.it

A holiday with a special atmosphere is possible in this vast farm in the Oltrepò Pavese; in the centre of it is a medieval manor, admirably preserved.

-
1 - - -

6 (x 2)
1 38,00 - 49,00 -

4 (x 2/4)
1 - 7 - 1 208,00 7 -

Torrazzetta

at Torrazzetta 1, 27040 Borgo Priolo (PV)
Tel. 0383871041 Fax 0383871041
Web: www.torrazzetta.it

On the first hills of the Oltrepò Pavese, this large establishment combines the comfort of a hotel and the atmosphere of an old inn.

-
1 - - -

27 (x 2)
1 46,00 - 66,00 -

-
1 - 7 - 1 - 7 -

Caiolo

Ribuntà

at San Bernardo, 23010 Caiolo (SO)
Tel. 0342561297 Fax 0342561297

In the lower Valtellina, near the confluence of the Livrio and the Adda, the accommodation is in a rural building dating from the 15th century and a modern building.

\-

1 - - -

4 (x 4)

1 31,00 - 42,00 -

\-

1 - 7 - 1 - 7 -

Capergnanica

Cascina Arcobaleno

via SS. Trinità 14, 26010 Capergnanica (CR)
Tel. 0373238112 Fax 0373256919
Web: www.cascinarcobaleno.it

The main features of the countryside between the rivers Serio and Adda are poplars, farmhouses, little churches and their towers, watercourses and the croaking of frogs. It's ideal for families or groups of schoolchildren.

\-

1 - - -

4 (x 1/4)

1 40,00 - - -

2(x 2)

1 37,50 7 125,00 1 - 7 -

Caprino Bergamasco

Cascina Ombria

at Ombria, 24030 Caprino Bergamasco (BG)
Tel. 035781668 Fax 035781668

This farmhouse dating from 1613 was originally a Milanese outpost in Venetian territory. The rooms are tastefully furnished; on the ground floor there's a veranda giving onto a garden.

\-

1 - - -

3 (x 2)

1 35,00 - 55,00 -

\-

1 - 7 - 1 - 7 -

Capriolo

Ricci Curbastro & Figli

via Adro 37, 25031 Capriolo (BS)
Tel. 030736094 Fax 0307460558
Web: www.riccicurbastro.it

This late 19th-century rural building between the Oglio and Monte Alto is surrounded by the hills of Franciacorta, with 300 kilometres of paths and tracks suitable for mountain bikes.

-

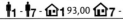

1 - - - -

-

1 - - - -

7 (x 2/4)

1 - 7 - 1 93,00 7 -

Cassano Valcuvia

Al Cavallino

road for Ferrera 50, 21030 Cassano Valcuvia (VA)
Tel. 0332995508 Fax 0332995885
Web: www.alcavallino.it

The peaceful, verdant Valcuvia is the ideal environment for tourism on horseback. This modern riding centre offers accommodation and riding weeks for children.

-

1 - - - -

6 (x 4)

1 37,00 31,00 52,00 -

-

1 - 7 - 1 - 7 -

Castel Goffredo

Colombare

via Casalmoro 20, 46042 Castel Goffredo (MN)
Tel. 0376779638 Fax 0376779169
Web: www.agriturismocolombare.it

This attractive farm is ideal for a peaceful holiday amid poplars and canals. In addition to providing a swimming pool and golf course (opening shortly) for its guests, it makes its own beer.

4 (x 1/2)

1 29,00 - - -

1 (x 2)

1 32,00 - - -

10(x 2)

1 56,00 7 224,00 1 - 7 -

Cernusco Lombardone

I Gelsi

via S. Dionigi 11,
23870 Cernusco Lombardone (LC)
Tel. 0399902790 Fax 0399902790
Web: www.igelsi.com

'Farmhouse accommodation in a family environment' is the motto of this establishment located in the Montevecchia and Val Curone Nature Park, one of the most attractive areas of Brianza.

\-

1 - - - -

4 (x 1/4)

1 45,00 - 63,00 -

2 (x 2/5)

1 - 7 - 1 180,00 7 450,00

Codevilla

Montelio

via D. Mazza 1, 27050 Codevilla (PV)
Tel. 0383373090 Fax 0383373083
Web: www.itinerariverdi.it

In a peaceful village of wine growers, this farm has an arcaded courtyard and an 18th-century building reserved for guests, with wrought-iron beds and a fine view.

\-

1 - - - -

\-

1 - - - -

6 (x 2/3)

1 30,00 7 150,00 1 - 7 -

Consiglio di Rumo

La Sorgente

at Brenzio 24, 22010 Consiglio di Rumo (CO)
Tel. 034481859 Fax 034481859
E-mail: ciappa@interfree.it

Offering a splendid view of Lake Como, this authentic working farm, with its numerous animals and wholesome dishes served at table, is a reminder of a bygone age.

\-

1 - - - -

1 (x 4)

1 30,00 - - -

2(x 6)

1 - 7 - 1 - 7 350,00

Costa di Serina

La Peta

at Gazzo, via Peta 3, 24010 Costa di Serina (BG)
Tel. 034597955 Fax 034597955
E-mail: emanuele.nessi@tin.it

On the sunny slopes of Monte Alben (2015 m), a charming 15th-century inn with its outbuildings offers accommodation surrounded by meadows and woods.

6 (x 4)

35,00 17,50 46,00 -

-
- - - -

-
- - - -

FONTENO

COOP. AGRITURISTICA LA FLORA

at Monte 1, 24060 Fonteno (BG)
Tel. 035969115 Fax 035848047
E-mail: la-flora@libero.it

In the Fonteno Valley, between lakes Endine and Iseo, a mule track winds up through meadows and woods to the completely renovated building where the accommodation is situated.

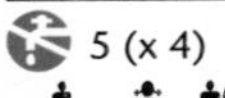

5 (x 4)
- - - 45,00

-
- - - -

1(x 6)
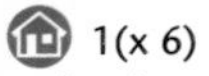

- - 70,00 -

FORTUNAGO

MACCARINI

at Gravanago, 27040 Fortunago (PV)
Tel. 0383875580 Fax 0383879000
Web: www.maccarini.it

In the area of the Comunità Montana dell'Oltrepò Pavese, amid vineyards, meadows and woods, this farmhouse has been renovated and furnished in a simple rustic style.

-
- - - -

4 (x 2/4)
31,00 - 44,00 -

1(x 4)
31,00 - - -

GONZAGA

CORTE VILLORESI

strada privata Pianone 1, 46023 Gonzaga (MN)
Tel. 0376550470 Fax 0376558090

In the Oltrepò Mantovano, accommodation is available in this rustic farmhouse dating from the early 20th century; it has horses and goats and serves local dishes.

-
- - - -

2 (x 2)
23,00 - - -

-
- - - -

GRANDOLA ED UNITI

LA VECCHIA CHIODERIA

at Codogna, via Mulini 3,
22010 Grandola ed Uniti (CO)
Tel. 034430152 Fax 034430152
E-mail: info@chioderia.com

The farm extends along the valley of the Sanagra River; descending from the Lepontine Alps to Lake Como, it is renowned for its trout farms.

- 1 - - -

10 (x 2)

1 30,00 - 39,00 -

-

1 - 7 - 1 - 7 -

Lenna

Ferdy

at Fienili, 24010 Lenna (BG)
Tel. 034582235 Fax 034582235
Web: www.agriturismoferdy.com

This is an excellent address in the upper Val Brembana, amid the peaks of the Orobie Alps, where the accommodation is in a stone cottage standing in a grassy glade.

-

1 - - -

4 (x 2/4)

1 40,00 - 55,00 -

-

1 - 7 - 1 - 7 -

Lonato

Arriga Alta

at Arriga Alta, 25017 Lonato (BS)
Tel. 0309913718 Fax 0309913718
Web: www.arrigaalta.it

On a hill with a view of Lake Garda, amid meadows and gardens, but near the village, the accommodation is situated in a complex dating from the 17th century.

-

1 - - -

11 (x 2/4)

1 40,00 - 65,00 -

-

1 - 7 - 1 - 7 -

Mantova

Corte San Girolamo

at Gambarara, strada San Girolamo 1,
46100 Mantova
Tel. 0376391018 Fax 0376391018

Not far from the lakes of Mantua, with herons and lotus flowers, this accommodation is located within the fluvial park extending along the River Mincio.

-

1 - - -

4 (x 2)

1 36,00 18,00 - -

1(x 2)

1 - 7 - 1 103,00 7 -

Montalto Pavese

Cella di Montalto

at Cella di Montalto, 27040 Montalto Pavese (PV)
Tel. 0383870519 Fax 0383870117

In the peaceful setting of the hills of the Oltrepò Pavese, this splendid house has large arcades and stables. The cuisine is particularly inviting.

-

1 - - - -

8 (x 2)

1 32,00 - 60,00 -

-

1 - 7 - 1 - 7 -

Monticelli Brusati

Villa Gradoni

via Villa, 25040 Monticelli Brusati (BS)
Tel. 030652329 Fax 0306852305
Web: www.villa-franciacorta.it

This renovated 18th-century building is located in a village in Franciacorta. The spacious, cool rooms are simply furnished.

-

1 - - - -

-

1 - - - -

13 (x 2/6)

1 - 7 - 1 - 7 728,00

Monzambano

Corte Fattori

at Castellaro Lagusello, strada Moscatello 131, 46040 Monzambano (MN)
Tel. 037688913 Fax 0376845007
Web: www.cortefattori.it

This old farmhouse has only recently started to provide accommodation: the rooms are attractive with the colours of the wood, terracotta tiles and bare stone, while the furnishings are romantic in style.

-

1 - - - -

5 (x 2)

1 55,00 - - -

2 (x 3/5)

1 23,00 7 - 1 - 7 -

Trebisonda

via Tononi 92, 46040 Monzambano (MN)
Tel. 0376809381 Fax 0376809381
E-mail: trebisonda@libero.it

The stone walls and the wood-lined interiors attest to Signora Valeria's excellent taste. Historic cities and the attractions of Lake Garda are close at hand.

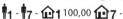

- - - -

1 (x 2)

35,00 - - -

2(x 2)

- - 1 90,00 7 630,00

Muscoline

Il Brolo

at Castrezzone, via Tese 9, 25080 Muscoline (BS)
Tel. 036531927 Fax 036531927
E-mail: erpontig@tin.it

The accommodation is on the hills separating Lake Garda from the Chiese Valley in renovated farmhouses, with modern conveniences, a grassy courtyard and a swimming pool.

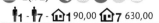

-

- - - -

-

- - - -

8 (x 2/6)

- - 1 100,00 7 -

Ome

Al Rocol

via Provinciale 79, 25050 Ome (BS)
Tel. 0306852542 Fax 0306852542
Web: www.alrocol.com

The pleasant atmosphere of the house, embellished with period furniture, is in harmony with the beautiful scenery surrounding it.

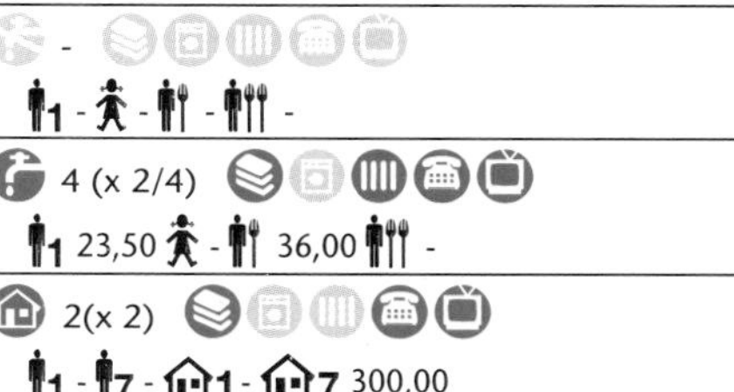

-

- - - -

4 (x 2/4)

23,50 - 36,00 -

2(x 2)

- - 1 - 7 300,00

Ostiglia

Arginino Piccolo

via Arginino 9, 46035 Ostiglia (MN)
Tel. 038631475 Fax 038631475
E-mail: argininopiccolo@libero.it

A peaceful holiday is possible in this rural complex comprising the 17th-century owners' house and the guests' rooms in the adjacent 19th-century building.

-

- - - -

3 (x 2/4)

20,66 - - -

-

- - 1 - 7 -

Palazzago

Cascina dei Brüder e La Roncalina

at Gromlongo, via Belvedere 16,
24030 Palazzago (BG)
Tel. 035611016 Fax 035258599
E-mail: agbruder@tin.it

The two farms are both at the mouth of the Valle San Martino, on the slopes of Monte Albenza. They comprise stone buildings and rustic cottages.

-

1 - - -

-

1 - - -

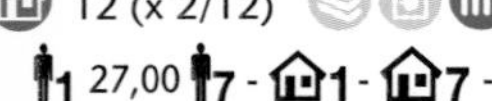

12 (x 2/12)

1 27,00 7 - 1 - 7 -

Piadena

Riviera D'Oglio

at San Paolo Ripa D'Oglio, via Maggiore 6, 26034 Piadena (CR)
Tel. 0375380282 Fax 0375380282
Web: www.rivieraoglio.com

A large farm round a courtyard, with high arcades and a park with a small lake, is the perfect setting for a thoroughly relaxing holiday.

-

1 - - -

4 (x 2/4)

1 25,00 - -

-

1 - 7 - 1 - 7 -

Pian Camuno

Oasi Camuna

via Fane 50, 25050 Pian Camuno (BS)
Tel. 0364590403

This centre for tourism on horseback caters for people of all ages: there's a friendly atmosphere and the sport gives guests a good appetite.

-

1 - - -

-

1 - - -

8 (x 2/4)

1 - 7 - 1 50,00 7 250,00

Piancogno

La Sognata

at Annunciata, via Ribalda 2, 25052 Piancogno (BS)
Tel. 0364361218 Fax 0364362112
Web: www.lasognata.it

Standing on a terrace overlooking the valley, the farm offers a holiday with the accent on the well-being of its guests, who will discover the wholesome flavours of yesteryear.

-

1 - - -

-

1 - - -

4(x 2)

1 46,50 7 - 1 - 7 -

Ponti sul Mincio

Ai Vigneti

strada Colombara 13,
46040 Ponti sul Mincio (MN)
Tel. 0376808065 Fax 0376808065

Passing under an arch of roses in flower, guests will find a charming cottage surrounded by plants and a lawn. The cuisine is excellent.

-

1 - - -

7 (x 2)

1 35,00 - 48,00 -

1(x 2)

1 35,00 7 - 1 - 7 -

La Montina

at Montina, via Monzambano 51,
46040 Ponti sul Mincio (MN)
Tel. **037688202** Fax **037688202**

Located in the northern part of Mantua, this is a modern building, but the food is first-rate; in addition to the surrounding countryside, various historic towns and villages are worth visiting.

-

1 - - -

4 (x 2/4)

1 31,00 - 44,00 -

-

1 - 7 - 1 - 7 -

Porto Mantovano

Corte Schiarino-Lena

at Sant'Antonio, strada Santa Maddalena 7/9,
46047 Porto Mantovano (MN)
Tel. **0376398238** Fax **0376393238**
Web: **www.villaschiarino.it**

The accommodation is in the annexe of a 16th-century villa formerly belonging to the Gonzaga. The apartments are spacious and elegant, the welcome is extremely warm.

-

1 - - -

-

1 - - -

3 (x 2/4)

1 - 7 - 1 100,00 7 -

Rodigo

Monte Perego

at Rivalta sul Mincio, strada Francesca Est 141,
46040 Rodigo (MN)
Tel. **0376653290** Fax **0376681299**
Web: **www.monteperego.it**

In the Mincio Regional Nature Park, where the river forms the lakes of Mantua, this typical Po Valley farmhouse, built round a courtyard and dating from the late 18th century, now provides accommodation.

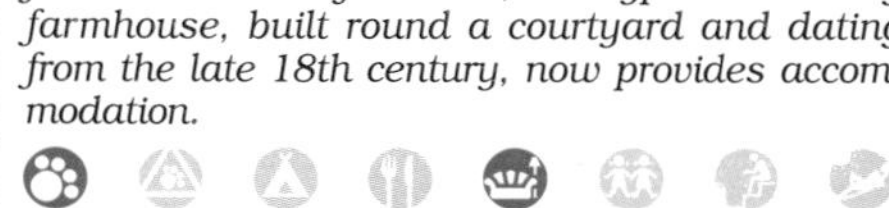

-

1 - - -

4 (x 1/4)

1 41,00 - - -

3(x 4)

1 - 7 - 1 104,00 7 -

Rovescala

Castello di Luzzano

E

at Luzzano, via Luzzano 5, 27040 Rovescala (PV)
Tel. **0523863277** Fax **0523865909**
Web: **www.castelloluzzano.it**

This village on the border with Emilia is surrounded by 80 hectares of vineyards. The accommodation is in 18th-century farmhouses offering modern comforts.

-

1 - - -

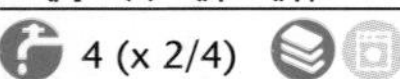

4 (x 2/4)

1 57,00 - 85,00 -

6 (x 2/4)

1 - 7 - 1 217,00 7 955,00

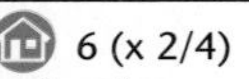

Ruino

Cai Mariangela

E D

at Pometo, via Diaz 2, 27040 Ruino (PV)
Tel. **038598813** Fax **038598813**
Web: **www.oltrepopavese.it**

In the Oltrepò Pavese, Signora Mariangela provides superb accommodation: in addition to walks, guests can engage in such activities as cookery, drawing, painting and sculpture.

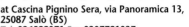

-

1 - - -

-

1 - - -

4 (x 2/5)

1 21,00 7 - 1 - 7 -

Salò

Conti Terzi

E

at Cascina Pignino Sera, via Panoramica 13, 25087 Salò (BS)
Tel. **036522071** Fax **0307721037**
Web: **www.contiterzi.it**

This picturesque farmhouse surrounded by terracing is ideal for a country holiday featuring both the lake and the mountains in the Alto Garda Bresciano Park.

-

1 - - -

-

1 - - -

1(x 6)

1 32,00 7 - 1 - 7 -

Il Bagnolo

E D

at Bagnolo di Serniga, 25087 Salò (BS)
Tel. **036520290** Fax **036521877**
Web: **www.gardalake.it/ilbagnolo**

Overlooking the Golfo di Salò, this large farm is an excellent base for visiting the Alto Garda Bresciano Park, with the towns on the west shore and the valleys behind them.

\-

9 (x 2)

1 48,00 - -

\-

1 - 7 - 1 - 7 -

San Benedetto Po

Amaterra

at Portiolo, strada Argine Zara 18,
46020 San Benedetto Po (MN)
Tel. 0376611306 Fax 0376611306

On the estate of the abbey of Polirone, this farm has adopted organic methods for growing its crops, while alternative medicine is an additional activity.

3 (x 4)  

1 23,00 - -

\-

1 - - -

\-

1 - 7 - 1 - 7 -

Corte Medaglie d'Oro

via Argine Secchia 63,
46027 San Benedetto Po (MN)
Tel. 0376618802 Fax 0376618802
Web:
http://digilander.libero.it/cortemedagliedoro

Amid willows and oaks, just a stone's throw from the river, this country house built round a courtyard is notable for its refined architecture, while the interior is comfortable and bright.

\-

5 (x 2/4) 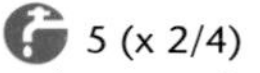 

1 32,00 - -

\-

1 - 7 - 1 - 7 -

San Felice del Benaco

La Breda

at Baia del Vento,
25010 San Felice del Benaco (BS)
Tel. 0365559443 Fax 0365557449
E-mail: cavazza@fornella.it

Located in an olive grove overlooking the lake, where bathing is possible, this farmhouse has been carefully renovated, with attention being paid to the details.

\-

1 - - -

\-

1 - - -

6 (x 2/6) 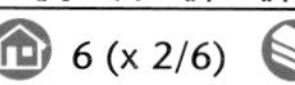 

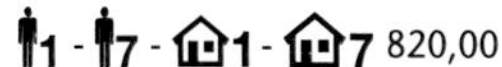

1 - 7 - 1 - 7 820,00

Le Chiusure

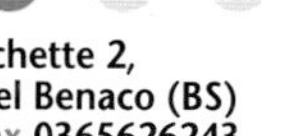

at Portese, via Boschette 2,
25010 San Felice del Benaco (BS)
Tel. 0365626243 Fax 0365626243
E-mail: info@lechiusure.net

Two ancient mulberry trees flank the entrance to the farmhouse, built in traditional style round a courtyard and adjacent to the brolo, a large vineyard surrounded by walls.

-
1 - - -
-
1 - - -
3(x 4)
1 - 7 - 1 - 7 750,00

San Giorgio di Mantova

Loghino Caselle

E D

via Caselle 40,
46030 San Giorgio di Mantova (MN)
Tel. **0376340699**
Web: **http://digilander.iol.it/agriturismocaselle**

This 19th-century farmhouse is ideal for a holiday focusing on art and nature, with the splendours of Mantua and Sabbioneta, and the attractions of the Mincio Regional Nature Park nearby.

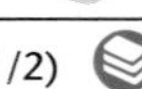

4 (x 1/2)
1 30,00 - 50,00 -
2 (x 2)
1 27,50 - 47,50 -
1(x 2)
1 - 7 - 1 70,00 7 -

Santa Giuletta

Marchesi

E D

at Castello, 27046 Santa Giuletta (PV)
Tel. **0383899733** Fax **0383814063**
Web: **www.aziendaagrariamarchesi.com**

In the hamlet of Castello, the old fortress of the Isimbardi has been converted to its present form, that of a 19th-century villa offering excellent accommodation.

AE VISA MC

3 (x 2/4)
1 34,00 20,00 52,00 -
1 (x 4)
1 34,00 20,00 52,00 -
-
1 - 7 - 1 - 7 -

Schignano

Al Marnich

E D

road for Marnico 8, 22020 Schignano (CO)
Tel. **031819242** Fax **031819814**
Web: **www.al-marnich.it**

Amid the woods of the Val d'Intelvi, dominated by Monte Generoso (1701 m), three stone farmhouses have a pleasant atmosphere, antique furniture and fireplaces in the rooms.

AE VISA MC

-
1 - - -
7 (x 2)

1 41,00 25,00 72,00 -

\-

1 - 7 - 1 - 7 -

Soiano del Lago

Il Ghetto

vicolo Ghetto 3/A, 25080 Soiano del Lago (BS)
Tel. **0365502986** Fax **0365674359**
Web: **www.ilghetto.it**

Standing on a hillock amid the olive groves and vineyards of the Valtenesi, this handsome stone building has loggias, balconies offering fine views and rustic furnishings.

\-

1 - - -

\-

1 - - -

12 (x 3/6)

1 36,00 7 - 1 - 7 -

Solferino

Le Sorgive e Le Volpi

via Piridello 6, 46040 Solferino (MN)
Tel. **0376854252** Fax **0376855256**
Web: **www.lesorgive.it**

The accommodation is in the handsome 19th-century farmhouse with its arcades and dovecot. There's a restaurant with a veranda, run by the same family, in the adjacent Cascina Le Volpi.

\-

1 - - -

8 (x 2/4)

1 50,00 16,00 - -

2(x 4)

1 - 7 - 1 - 7 850,00

Sormano

La Conca d'Oro

at Pian del Tivano, 22030 Sormano (CO)
Tel. **031677019** Fax **031677019**

In upper Valassina, at Pian del Tivano (1000 m), this vast estate with its meadows and woods is ideal for horse-riding and tours on mountain bikes.

\-

1 - - -

\-

1 74,40 - - -

4(x 4)

1 - 7 - 1 - 7 -

Sotto il Monte Giovanni XXIII

Casa Clelia

via Corna 1/3,
24039 Sotto il Monte Giovanni XXIII (BG)
Tel. **035799133** Fax **035791788**
Web: **www.casaclelia.com**

Standing on the slopes of Monte Canto, this complex forming part of an old monastery has been rebuilt in accordance with the principles of ecological architecture.

\-

1 - - -

10 (x 2)

1 46,50 - - -

Torlino Vimercati

Cascina Santa Maria

via Cascine 27, 26017 Torlino Vimercati (CR)
Tel. **0373288925** Fax **037371036**
Web: **www.cascina-santamaria.it**

Accommodation is available in this large Lombard farm built round a courtyard. Two fluvial parks are close at hand, one by the Adda, the other by the Serio.

2 (x 2/4)

31,00 - -

4 (x 2/4)

31,00 - -

1 - 7 - 1 - 7 -

Toscolano Maderno

Giulio Comboni

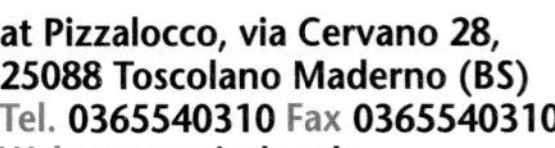

at Pizzalocco, via Cervano 28,
25088 Toscolano Maderno (BS)
Tel. **0365540310** Fax **0365540310**
Web: **www.pisaloc.de**

In this establishment located close to both the lake and the mountains, the pleasant surroundings and the warm welcome will probably encourage guests to take things easy.

1 - - -

1 (x 2)

1 25,00 - -

1(x 4)

1 35,00 7 - 1 - 7 -

Scuderia Castello

at Gaino, via Castello 10,
25088 Toscolano Maderno (BS)
Tel. **0365644101** Fax **0365541555**
E-mail: **sc.castello@ciaoweb.it**

The main activity offered by this establishment is horse-riding, but in this area sailing and rock-climbing are also possible.

\-

1 - - -

8 (x 2/4)

1 29,00 23,00 42,00 -

\-

1 - 7 - 1 - 7 -

VARESE

GOCCIA D'ORO RANCH

at Bizzozero, via dei Vignò 134, 21100 Varese
Tel. 0332265389 Fax 0332265389
Web: www.gocciadororanch.it

For a holiday comprising both art and nature, Brianza, the Campo dei Fiori Nature Park, the archaeological area at Castelseprio and the collegiate church of Castiglione Olona are all worth a visit.

\-

1 - - -

 4 (x 2/4)

1 26,00 - 39,00  -

\-

1 - 7 - 1 - 7 -

NICOLINI

via Pacinotti 99, 21100 Varese
Tel. 0332491118
Web: www.agri-varese.it

Located in the basin of the Olona Valley on the slopes of the Campo dei Fiori, this former stud farm is now renowned for its goat's milk cheese.

\-

1 - - -

 4 (x 2)

1 25,00 - 37,50 -

\-

1 - 7 - 1 - 7 -

VARZI

DELLAGIOVANNA MARIA

at Piane 1, 27057 Varzi (PV)
Tel. 038352704 Fax 038352704

Surrounded by meadows and woods, these simple rural buildings offer accommodation in close contact with nature; wholesome dishes are served at table.

\-

1 - - -

\-

1 - - -

 3(x 2) 

1 - 7 - 1 100,00 7 580,00

VIADANA

CORTE DONDA

at Salina, via Palazzo 35, 46030 Viadana (MN)
Tel. 0375785697 Fax 0375857006

This fine 18th-century farmhouse has been renovated and furnished without altering the original structure; it has an arcade, a winery with a wide range of wines, and stables.

\-

1 - - -

4 (x 2) 

1 29,00 - - -

\-

1 - 7 - 1 - 7 -

Corte Lavadera

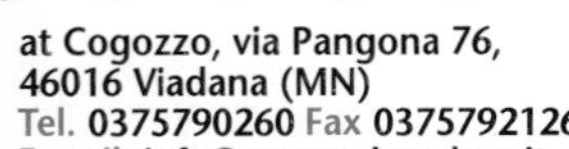

at Cogozzo, via Pangona 76,
46016 Viadana (MN)
Tel. 0375790260 Fax 0375792126
E-mail: info@countrylavadera.it

In the southern part of the province of Mantua, fields under cereals surround this accommodation located in a building with notably linear forms; the farm itself is about 4 km away.

\-

1 - - -

2 (x 2)

1 60,00 - - -

1(x 3)

1 - 7 - 1 140,00 7 775,00

Volta Mantovana

Corte Onida

at Lonida 3, 46049 Volta Mantovana (MN)
Tel. 0376838137 Fax 0376838137
Web: www.corteonida.it

Standing on the edge of the Mincio Regional Nature Park, this farm is surrounded by vineyards producing a surprisingly wide range of wines.

\-

1 - - -

6 (x 1/2)

1 40,00 15,00 48,00 -

2(x 4)

1 - 7 - 1 100,00 7 645,00

Gardenali

via XXV Aprile 8, 46049 Volta Mantovana (MN)
Tel. 037683487 Fax 037683487
Web: www.gardenali.it

In the pleasant setting of the morainic hills south of Lake Garda, this farm has vineyards and orchards cultivated with organic methods.

\-

1 - - -

\-

1 - - -

9(x 3)

1 31,00 7 - 1 - 7 -

Lucillo

at Bezzetti, 46049 Volta Mantovana (MN)
Tel. 0376838284 Fax 0376838284
Web: www.agriturismolucillo.it

In a panoramic position on the hills near Lake Garda, this restaurant is situated in the vaulted space of the former cowsheds; the guests' rooms are cosy and functional.

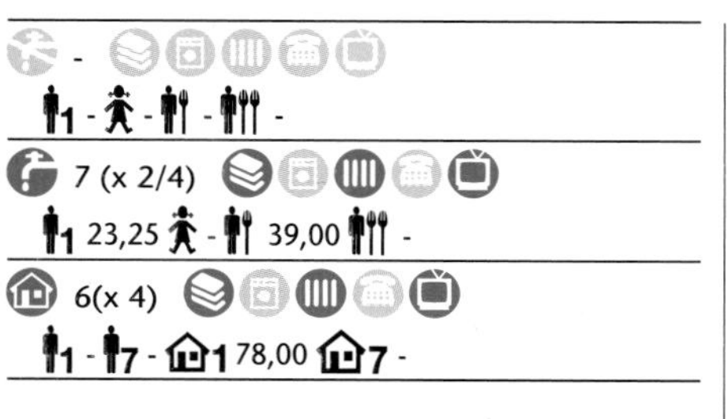

-

1 - - -

7 (x 2/4)

1 23,25 - 39,00 -

6(x 4)

1 - 7 - 1 78,00 7 -

ZANICA

CASCINA BUONA SPERANZA

via Pradone 17, 24050 Zanica (BG)
Tel. 035671301

This accommodation is in the high Bergamasque plain, on the old Francesca road, which leads through unexpectedly beautiful countryside to fortified villages.

-

1 - - -

-

1 - - -

1(x 5)

1 20,00 7 - 1 - 7 -

ZAVATTARELLO

VALTIDONE VERDE

at Casa Canevaro,
27059 Zavattarello (PV)
Tel. 0383589668 Fax 0383589668
Web: www.valtidoneverde.it

This farmhouse stands out on a hill in the upper Val Tidone amid vineyards and orchards. This beautiful area is ideal for peaceful holidays and the cuisine is excellent.

-

1 - - -

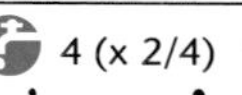 

4 (x 2/4)

1 62,00 - 82,00 -

-

1 - 7 - 1 - 7 -

Formai de Mut dell'Alta Valle Brembana

"Consorzio dei Produttori per la Tutela e la Valorizzazione del Formai de Mut" (Mut Cheese Promotion Producers Consortium) dell'Alta Val Brembana.

Registered Office: Largo Belotti, 16 - 24124 Bergamo (BG)
Base: Via P. Ruggeri, 12 - 24019 Zogno (BG) - Tel. 0345 93910, fax 0345 93804
Via Mangili, 21 - 24125 Bergamo (BG) - Tel. 035 4524123, fax 035 4524126
E-mail: formaidemutvb@tiscalinet.it - www.formaidemut.info

"realized with the contribution of the General Agricultural Office of the Lombardy Region"

FAUNAL PARK

LE CORNELLE

"THE WONDERFUL WORLD OF ANIMALS"

Respect, love and care for nature and its protection are just a few of the fundamental values that govern the relationship between man and his environment, the same values that the park has been constantly promoting for over twenty years in its activities. The well-established collaboration with Milan University, aiming at the development of scientific research and the participation to international projects for the protection of species threatened with extinction like the Macaw, the sabre horn Oryx, the Siamang, the variegated Lemur and the Cheetah confirm a will to continue the work started some time ago. Many are the animals living in the park: the Snow Leopard, the White Tiger, a most precious species only found in Italy at Le Cornelle Park, the White Rhino, the Otter, the Giraffe (with the largest group in Europe), and others still. The Park offers, moreover, up to date facilities for a more pleasant and easily planned visit. A large picnic area, with a wooden structure and wide, luminous glass windows, has been recently completed, to provide maximum comfort also for large parties. Special attention has always been given to disabled people, showing commitment and sensitivity to a type of visitors with very special requirements.

VILLA D'ALME'
VALBREMBO
BG
BS
A4
DALMINE
A4
MI

Valbrembo(Bg)•Tel.+39035527422•Fax+39035528285
Motorway, exit Dalmine

MARCHE

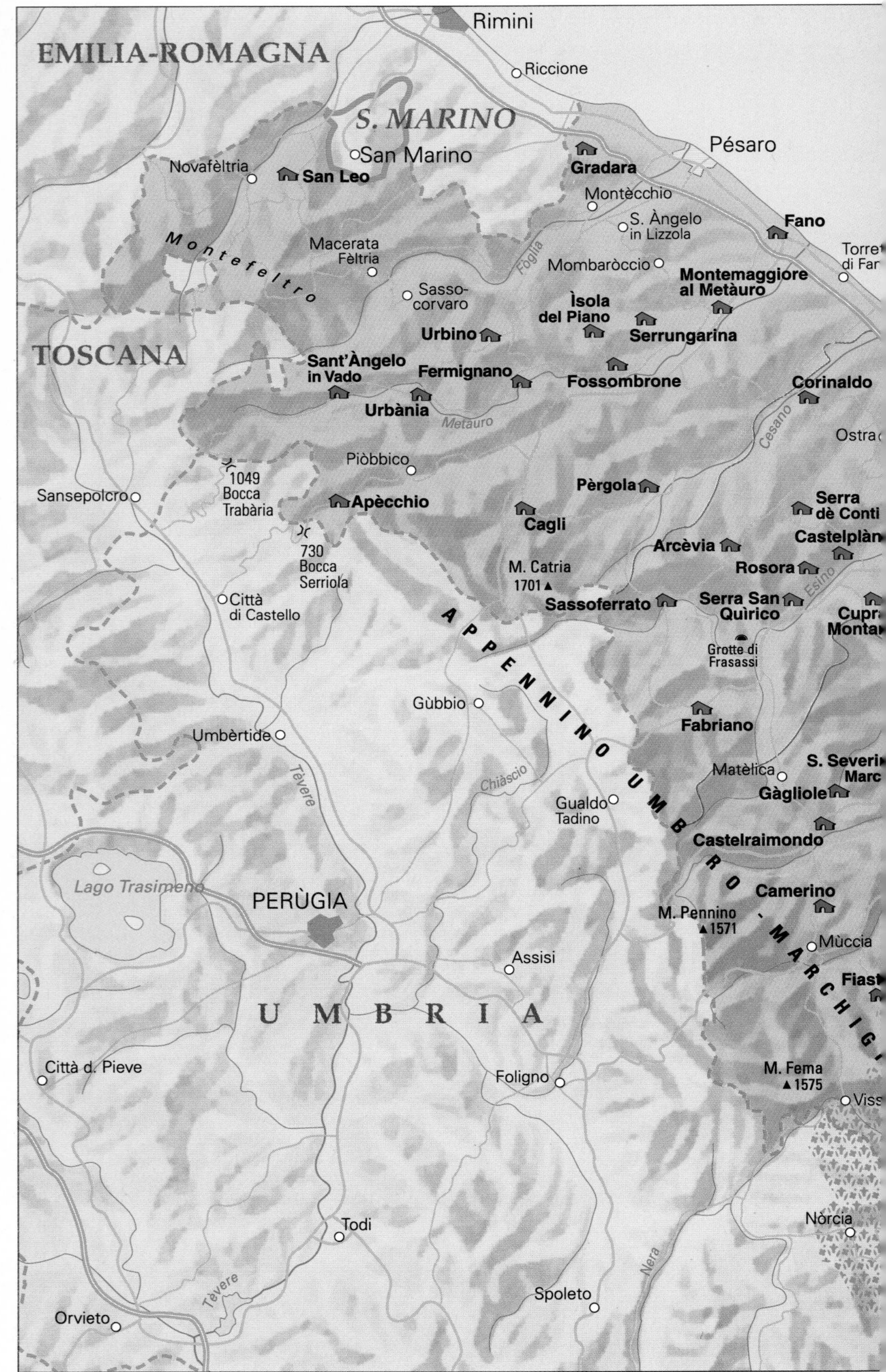
Rimini
EMILIA-ROMAGNA
Riccione
S. MARINO
San Marino
Pésaro
Novafèltria
San Leo
Gradara
Montècchio
S. Àngelo in Lizzola
Fano
Montefeltro
Macerata Fèltria
Fòglia
Mombaròccio
Montemaggiore al Metàuro
Sasso-corvaro
Ìsola del Piano
Urbino
Serrungarina
TOSCANA
Sant'Àngelo in Vado
Fermignano
Fossombrone
Corinaldo
Urbània
Metauro
Cesano
Pièbbico
1049 Bocca Trabària
Sansepolcro
Apècchio
Pèrgola
Serra dè Conti
Cagli
730 Bocca Serriola
Arcèvia
M. Catria 1701
Rosora
Esino
Città di Castello
Sassoferrato
Serra San Quìrico
APPENNINO UMBRO-MARCHIGIANO
Grotte di Frasassi
Gùbbio
Fabriano
Umbèrtide
Matèlica
Chiàscio
Tèvere
Gualdo Tadino
Gàgliole
Castelraimondo
Lago Trasimeno
PERÙGIA
Camerino
M. Pennino 1571
Mùccia
Assisi
UMBRIA
Città d. Pieve
Foligno
M. Fema 1575
Nòrcia
Todi
Nera
Tèvere
Spoleto
Orvieto

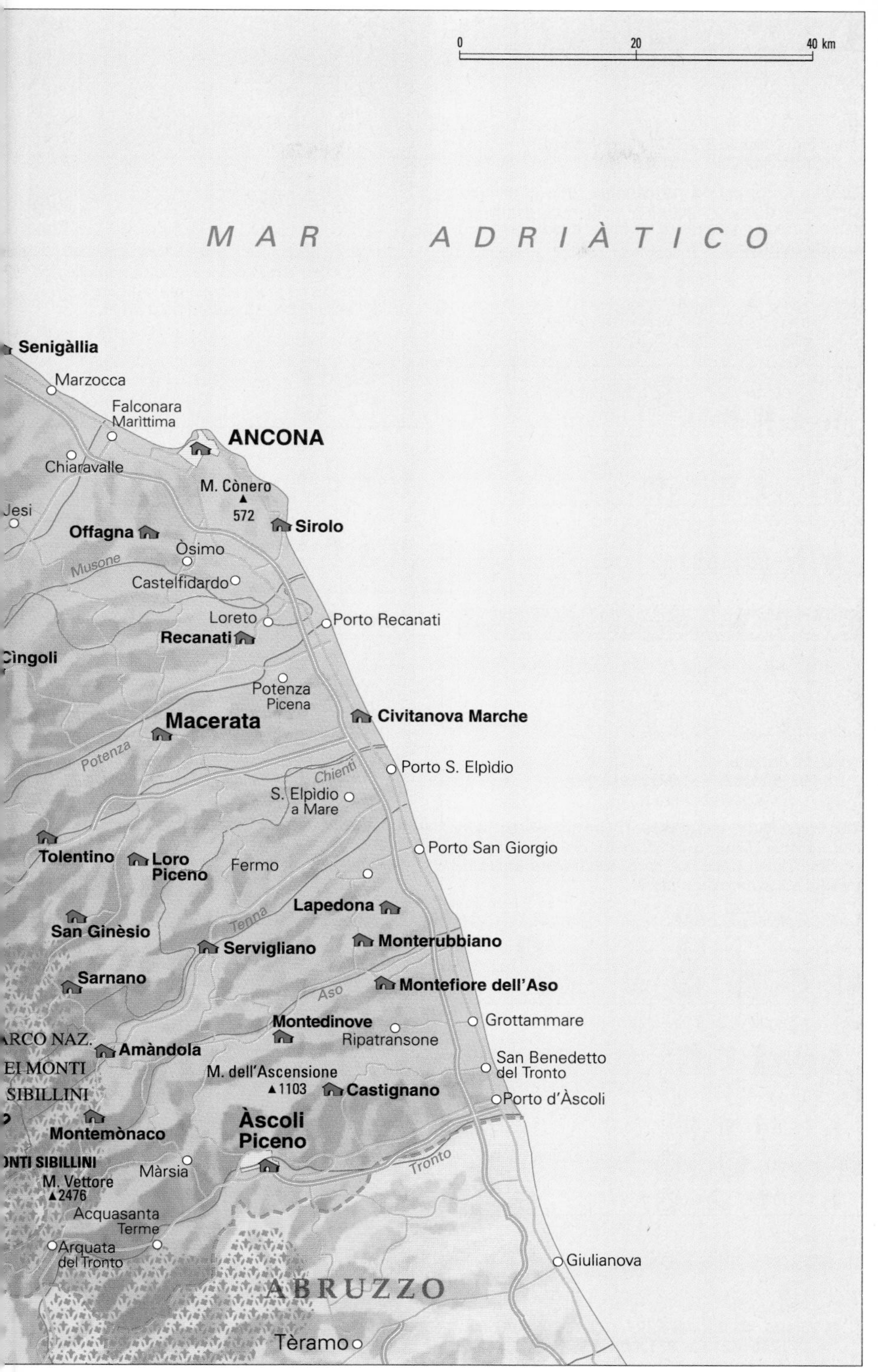
0
20
40 km
MAR ADRIÀTICO
Senigàllia
Marzocca
Falconara Marìttima
ANCONA
Chiaravalle
M. Cònero
572
Jesi
Sirolo
Offagna
Òsimo
Musone
Castelfidardo
Loreto
Porto Recanati
Recanati
Cìngoli
Potenza Picena
Civitanova Marche
Macerata
Potenza
Porto S. Elpìdio
Chienti
S. Elpìdio a Mare
Porto San Giorgio
Tolentino
Loro Piceno
Fermo
Lapedona
Tenna
San Ginèsio
Servigliano
Monterubbiano
Sarnano
Montefiore dell'Aso
Aso
Montedinove
Grottammare
Ripatransone
Amàndola
San Benedetto del Tronto
M. dell'Ascensione
1103
Castignano
SIBILLINI
Porto d'Àscoli
Àscoli Piceno
Montemònaco
Màrsia
Tronto
M. Vettore
2476
Acquasanta Terme
Arquata del Tronto
Giulianova
ABRUZZO
Tèramo

Amandola

San Lorenzo

via San Lorenzo 3, 63021 Amandola (AP)
Tel. 0736847535 Fax 0736847535

Thanks to its period furnishings, this renovated farmhouse dating from the late 19th century has preserved its original charm, and the guests get very special treatment.

-

1 - - -

7 (x 1/4)

1 25,00 - 40,00 -

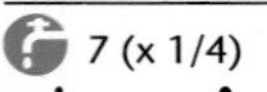

-

1 - 7 - 1 - 7 -

Ancona

Consorzio Parco del Conero-Centro visite

60100 Ancona
Tel. 0719331879 Fax 0719331879
Web: www.parcoconero.it

The consortium comprises 15 farms, some with restaurants. Holidays for all tastes are available, including those with activities relating to environmental education for children.

12 (x 1/4)

1 46,50 - - -

9 (x 4)

1 46,50 - - -

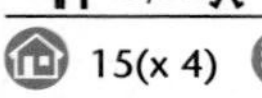

15(x 4)

1 51,00 7 - 1 - 7 -

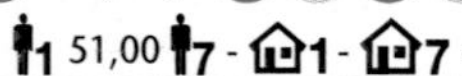

Il Rustico del Conero

at Varano, via Boranico 197/199, 60100 Ancona
Tel. 0712861821 Fax 0712083597
E-mail: la.primavera@libero.it

This is a horse-riding centre in the Conero Regional Park; the accommodation is in a cottage with its clean-cut volumes surrounded by a lawn.

-

1 - - -

-

1 - - -

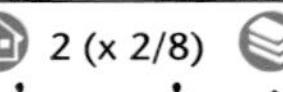

2 (x 2/8)

1 30,99 7 - 1 - 7 -

La Giuggiola

at Angeli di Varano, via Boranico 204/A, 60029 Ancona
Tel. 071804336

In the breezy hills just inland from the Adriatic, a handsome farmhouse has been renovated with simplicity and is kept in order in a pleasant manner.

-

1 - - -

8 (x 1/4)

1 26,00 - 40,00 -

1 - 7 - 1 - 7 -

APECCHIO

VAL DEL LAGO

at Acquapartita, 61042 Apecchio (PU)
Tel. **072299633** Fax **072299356**

This cottage, a splendid example of the vernacular architecture of the 17th century, has been completely renovated, but without altering its traditional features.

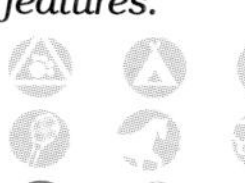

1 - - -

1 - - -

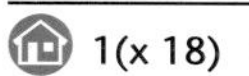

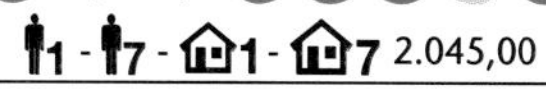

1(x 18)

1 - 7 - 1 - 7 2.045,00

ARCEVIA

IL PICCOLO RANCH

at San Pietro, S. Pietro in Musio castle 48/B, 60011 Arcevia (AN)
Tel. **0731982162** Fax **0731982902**
Web: **www.piccoloranch.com**

This group of buildings surrounding the castle of San Pietro in Musio resembles a country club, with restaurants and a swimming pool with a Jacuzzi.

1 - - -

6 (x 1/4)

1 35,00 - - -

1 - 7 - 1 - 7 -

SAN SETTIMIO

at Palazzo, 60010 Arcevia (AN)
Tel. **07319905** Fax **07319912**
Web: **www.sansettimio.com**

Arcevia is a small town with a medieval atmosphere. This vast estate offers accommodation of a hotel standard and first-rate sports facilities.

1 - - -

16 (x 2)

1 52,00 - 64,00 -

11(x 2)

1 - 7 - 1 - 7 1.350,00

ASCOLI PICENO

CONCA D'ORO

by the Rosara abbey, via Salaria Sup. 137, 63100 Ascoli Piceno
Tel. **0736252272**
Web: **www.villacicchi.it**

This is an 18th-century holiday villa with a chapel and a large cellar. The rooms, some of them with frescoed ceilings, are romantic and have period furniture.

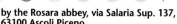

-

1 - - -

8 (x 2/4)

1 62,00 - 78,00 -

-

1 - 7 - 1 - 7 -

Cagli

Ca' Belvedere

at Smirra di Cagli, strada Pigno-Monte Martello 103, 61040 Cagli (PU)
Tel. **0721799204** Fax **0721799204**
Web: **www.flashnet.it/cabelvedere**

The farm, centring on an old house that has been carefully renovated, extends over a hilly area dotted with ancient oak trees.

-

1 - - -

4 (x 2)

1 30,00 - 55,00 -

-

1 - 7 - 1 - 7 -

Ca' le Suore

at Monte Peruzzo, via D. G. Celli 33, 61043 Cagli (PU)
Tel. **0721787425** Fax **0721787425**
Web: **www.calesuore.it**

This establishment has grown up by an old monastic residence, and has maintained all of its atmosphere; all around is the large farm, with cultivated land and woods.

-

1 - - -

-

1 - - -

14 (x 2/4)

1 - 7 - 1 60,00 7 790,00

Casale Torre del Sasso

strada Civita 12, 61043 Cagli (PU)
Tel. **0721782655** Fax **0721701336**
Web: **utenti.tripod.it/torresasso**

This farmhouse was built in the 15th century round a fortified tower. It has been splendidly restored to become the refined setting for quality rural holidays.

-

1 - - -

-

1 - - -

4 (x 4/6)

1 - 7 - 1 233,00 7 801,00

Camerino

La Cavallina

at Polverina, S.S. (state road) 77 at km 48.9, 63027 Camerino (MC)
Tel. **073746173** Fax **0737464500**
Web: **www.lacavallina.it**

Here, in the green and still unspoilt Chienti Valley, guests may enjoy 'a holiday focusing on relaxation, culture and good food'.

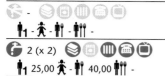

2 (x 2)

25,00 - 40,00 -

-

1 - 7 - 1 - 7 -

Castelplanio

Sant'Anna

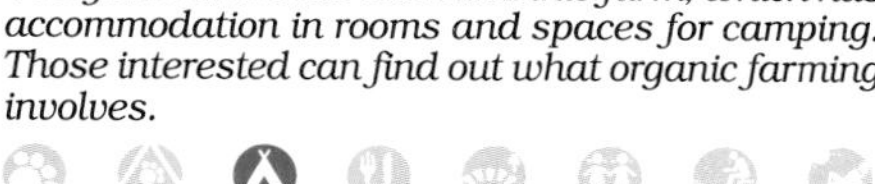

via S. Anna 11, 60031 Castelplanio (AN)
Tel. 0731814104 Fax 073156761
Web: www.campingagrituristsantanna.com

Vineyards and oaks surround this farm, which has accommodation in rooms and spaces for camping. Those interested can find out what organic farming involves.

-

1 - - -

-

1 - - -

5(x 3)

1 - 7 - 1 55,00 7 -

Castelraimondo

Il Giardino degli Ulivi

at Castel Sant'Angelo, via Crucianelli 54,
62022 Castelraimondo (MC)
Tel. 0737642600 Fax 0737640441

This is a journey back in time: the village is medieval, as is this splendidly restored building with its stone walls, huge beams and floors made of terracotta tiles.

-

1 - - -

5 (x 2/4)

1 55,00 - 75,00 -

1(x 4)

1 - 7 - 1 - 7 500,00

Castignano

Fiorenire

contrada Filette 9, 63032 Castignano (AP)
Tel. 0736821606 Fax 0736822117
Web: www.fiorenire.it

In the upper Tesino Valley, surrounded by extensive vineyards and eroded hillsides, this establishment has excellent facilities, including a park, a tennis court and a football field.

-

1 - - -

8 (x 1/2)

1 26,00 - 42,00 -

-

1 - 7 - 1 - 7 -

Cingoli

Fonte Pennici

at Coppo 17, 62011 Cingoli (MC)
Tel. 0733603355 Fax 0733603355

The view extends from the River Musone to Monte Vicino. the accommodation is in verdant surroundings in a modern house with arcades and a large space in front.

 3 (x 2)

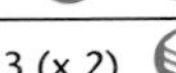  

16,00 - - -

\- - - -

\- - - - -

Civitanova Marche

Campolungo

contrada Migliarino 30,
62012 Civitanova Marche (MC)
Tel. 0733709504
E-mail: cescam@libero.it

Careful renovation has provided this interesting rural edifice with modern comforts without spoiling its previous appearance. Guests are warnly welcomed.

\- - - - -

\- - - - -

5(x 2)

\- - 88,00 -

Corinaldo

Villino Campagnolo

via Gasparini 4, 60013 Corinaldo (AN)
Tel. 0717975159 Fax 0717976389

Just a few minutes' drive from Senigallia's 'velvet beach', a farm road winding through the countryside skirts this attractive house.

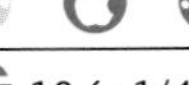 10 (x 1/4)   

22,00 11,00 - -

\- - - - -

\- - - - -

Cupra Montana

Colonnara

via Romita 8, 60034 Cupra Montana (AN)
Tel. 0731789979 Fax 0731789979
E-mail: fonti.romita@libero.it

In an area renowned its Verdicchio, the wine produced on this farm is particularly outstanding. The restaurant and accommodation are in a 14th-century monastery.

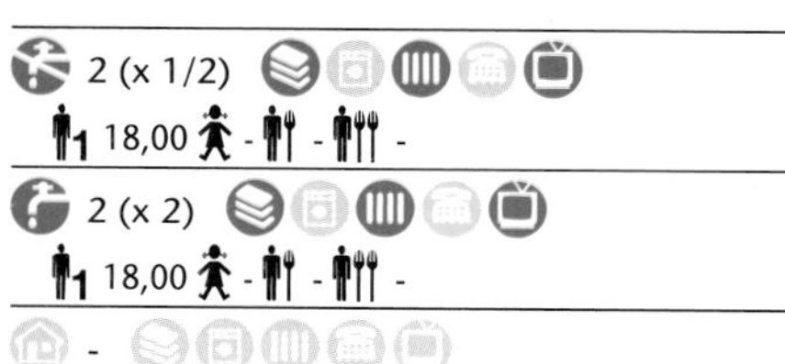

2 (x 1/2)

1 18,00 - - -

2 (x 2)

1 18,00 - - -

-

1 - 7 - 1 - 7 -

La Distesa

via Romita 28, 60034 Cupra Montana (AN)
Tel. 0731781230
Web: www.ladistesa.it

Amid the Verdicchio vineyards, it comes as no surprise that in this establishment devoted to quality rural tourism the main focus of interest is wine-making.

-

1 - - - -

-

1 - - - -

3 (x 3/4)

1 - 7 - 1 - 7 440,00

Fabriano

Gocce di Camarzano

at Moscano 70, 60044 Fabriano (AN)
Tel. 0732628172 Fax 0732628173
Web: www.youritaly.com

On the edge of the woods, in the Gola Rossa and Frasassi Regional Park, this large house surrounded by a park giving onto the countryside near Fabriano.

-

1 - - - -

6 (x 2)

1 65,00 - - -

-

1 - 7 - 1 - 7 -

La Casa di Campagna

at Bassano 32, 60044 Fabriano (AN)
Tel. 0732626519 Fax 07325720

The pink of the main house and its outbuildings, in the centre of a game reserve, recalls the atmosphere of a bygone age. The period furnishings are particularly attractive.

\-

1 - - -

\-

1 - - -

5 (x 2/6)

1 28,41 7 - 1 - 7 -

La Ginestra

via Serraloggia, 60044 Fabriano (AN)
Tel. **073224013**

Just a few kilometres from Fabriano, this farm has examples of ancient rural architecture and a fine collection of relics of the agricultural society.

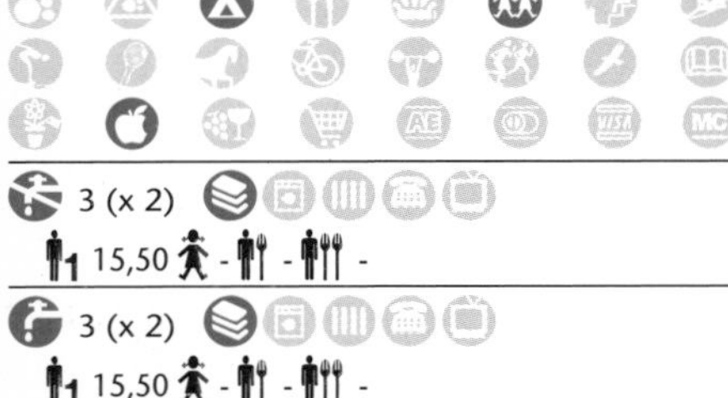

3 (x 2)

1 15,50 - -

3 (x 2)

1 15,50 - -

\-

1 - 7 - 1 - 7 -

Fano

Santa Cristina

at Rosciano 2, 61032 Fano (PU)
Tel. **0721862685**
Web: **www.agriturismosantacristina.it**

During the recent renovation work, this large 19th-century farmhouse was provided with a glass-fronted veranda, which is used as a communal space.

\-

1 - - -

6 (x 2)

1 35,00 25,00 - -

\-

1 - 7 - 1 - 7 -

Fermignano

Locanda della Valle Nuova

at Sagrata, La Cappella 14, 61033 Fermignano (PU)
Tel. **0722330303** Fax **0722330303**
Web: **www.vallenuova.it**

Set amid the woods and cultivated land of a large estate, this farmhouse provides numerous activities for its guests, including horse-riding, for which there are excellent facilities.

\-

1 - - -

6 (x 4)

1 45,00 - 62,00 -

\-

1 - 7 - 1 - 7 -

Fiastra

Le Casette

at Casette di Campobonomo 26,
62033 Fiastra (MC)
Tel. **073752571** Fax **073752208**

This farmhouse accommodation is located in the upper Fiastrone Valley, in the Monti Sibillini National Park. The lake beyond the village is ideal for bathing and fishing.

\-

1 - - -

6 (x 1/4)

1 23,24 - 38,73 -

\-

1 - 7 - 1 - 7 -

Fossombrone

El Gatarel

at Isola di Fano, via Pantaneto 10,
61034 Fossombrone (PU)
Tel. 0721727189 Fax 0721727189
Web: www.elgatarel.it

This late 18th-century farmhouse has been carefully converted into three self-contained apartments. Use of the swimming pool and mountain bikes is included in the price.

\-

1 - - -

\-

1 - - -

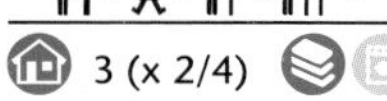

3 (x 2/4)

1 - 7 - 1 - 7 940,00

Gagliole

Locanda San Rocco

at Collaiello 2, 62020 Gagliole (MC)
Tel. 0737642324 Fax 0737642324

This 18th-century cottage has been converted to provide accommodation, but without spoiling its original appearance. The comfortable rooms have period furniture.

\-

1 - - -

6 (x 2/4)

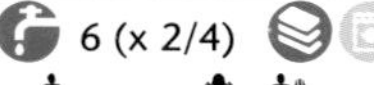

1 44,00 - 67,00 -

1(x 4)

1 - 7 - 1 - 7 465,00

Gradara

Agricola della Serra

at Fanano, via Serra 8, 61012 Gradara (PU)
Tel. 0541969856 Fax 0541969856
E-mail: dualsrl@libero.it

An ideal base for exploring the Montefeltro region, this renovated farmhouse provides accommodation in rooms with a rustic atmosphere and wallpaper in Provençal style.

\-

1 - - -

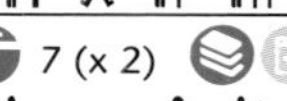

7 (x 2)

1 46,50 - 56,50 -

\-

1 - 7 - 1 - 7 -

Isola del Piano

Alce Nero

at Montebello, via Valli 21,
61030 Isola del Piano (PU)
Tel. 0721720126 Fax 0721720326
Web: www.alcenero.it

Renowned for its organic produce, this farmer's cooperative has accommodation with a restaurant. The rooms are small but well-kept and have period furniture.

4 (x 2/4)

1 28,50 - 41,50 -

4 (x 2)

1 31,00 - 46,50 -

2(x 4)

1 - 7 - 1 98,00 7 -

Lapedona

Casa Vecchia

via Aso 11, 63010 Lapedona (AP)
Tel. 0734933159 Fax 0734937539
Web: www.casavecchia.it

This large farmhouse, with its large rooms and traditional furnishings, offers its guests a warm welcome and dishes prepared with wholesome produce.

-

1 - - -

8 (x 1/4)

1 35,00 20,00 45,00 -

1(x 4)

1 - 7 - 1 75,00 7 500,00

Loro Piceno

Al Castelluccio

at Borgo San Lorenzo, contrada Appezzana, 62020 Loro Piceno (MC)
Tel. 0733510001

Located in the hills of the upper Fiastra Valley, this renovated country house of the late 18th century is not far from the SS 78 main road (known as the Picena).

4 (x 1/2)

1 20,70 - - -

6 (x 1/2)

1 20,70 - - -

-

1 - 7 - 1 - 7 -

Macerata

Floriani di Villamagna

contrada Montanello 3, 62100 Macerata
Tel. 0733492267 Fax 0733492267
Web: www.florianicompagnoni.it

In the centre of a farm growing olives, a number of romantic rooms with frescoed ceilings are in a villa; the other rooms and the apartments are in the adjacent farmhouse.

-

1 - - -

4 (x 2)

1 36,00 - - -

3 (x 2/4)

1 - 7 - 1 78,00 7 -

Virgilio Lucangeli

contrada Valle 27, 62100 Macerata
Tel. 0733270072 Fax 0733270072

The owners' house, dating from the late 17th century, is in the centre of the estate. This is where the farmhouse is, with the winery and various outbuildings; another nine farmhouses are located nearby.

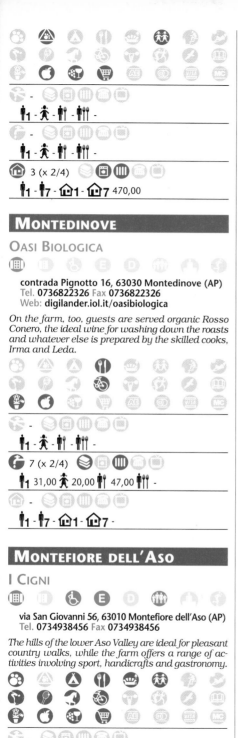

-
1 - - -

-
1 - - -

3 (x 2/4)
1 - 7 - 1 - 7 470,00

Montedinove

Oasi Biologica

contrada Pignotto 16, 63030 Montedinove (AP)
Tel. 0736822326 Fax 0736822326
Web: digilander.iol.it/oasibiologica

On the farm, too, guests are served organic Rosso Conero, the ideal wine for washing down the roasts and whatever else is prepared by the skilled cooks, Irma and Leda.

-
1 - - -

7 (x 2/4)
1 31,00 20,00 47,00 -

-
1 - 7 - 1 - 7 -

Montefiore dell'Aso

I Cigni

via San Giovanni 56, 63010 Montefiore dell'Aso (AP)
Tel. 0734938456 Fax 0734938456

The hills of the lower Aso Valley are ideal for pleasant country walks, while the farm offers a range of activities involving sport, handicrafts and gastronomy.

-
1 - - -

-
1 - - -

7 (x 4/5)
1 - 7 - 1 - 7 620,00

La Campana

contrada Menocchia 39,
63010 Montefiore dell'Aso (AP)
Tel. 0734939012 Fax 0734938229
Web: www.lacampana.it

Located on a large farm in the hills, this ancient building, which has vaulted rooms, balconies and terraces, has been carefully renovated.

-
1 - - -

11 (x 2/4)
1 67,50 - 76,50 -

-
1 - 7 - 1 - 7 -

La Favella

contrada Menocchia 54,
63010 Montefiore dell'Aso (AP)
Tel. 0734939017 Fax 0734939067
Web: www.biomarche.com/lafavella

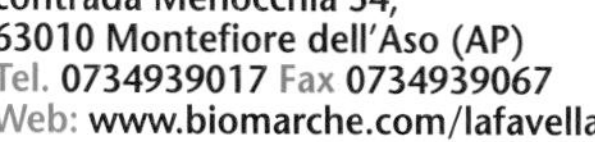

Various activities are organised by the farm, especially those relating to life on a working farm and English courses for all ages (especially young children).

2 (x 1/2)

1 31,00 - 55,00 -

4 (x 4)

1 31,00 - 55,00 -

\-

1 - 7 - 1 - 7 -

Montemaggiore al Metauro

La Carbonara

at San Liberio, via Carbonara 26,
61030 Montemaggiore al Metauro (PU)
Tel. 0721895028

Simple accommodation is available in this manor-house dating from the end of the 19th century.

\-

1 - - -

\-

1 - - -

1(x 2)

1 30,00 7 - 1 - 7 -

Montemonaco

La Cittadella

at Cittadella, 63048 Montemonaco (AP)
Tel. 0736856361 Fax 0736844262
Web: www.cittadeisibillini.it

Not far from the Monti Sibillini National Park, accommodation is available in a 16th-century farmhouse and rooms in the carefully converted hayloft.

\-

1 - - -

16 (x 1/4)

1 30,00 - 47,00 -

\-

1 - 7 - 1 - 7 -

Monterubbiano

Crosta

at Valdaso, contrada Pozzetto 2,
63026 Monterubbiano (AP)
Tel. 073459169 Fax 0734255151
Web: www.agriturismo-crosta.it

'A friendly atmosphere, tranquil and salubrious' is how the lady of the house puts it. The surroundings are simple and modern, but the hospitality is genuinely warm.

2 (x 2)

1 - - 58,00 -

7 (x 1/2)

1 - - 58,00 -

\-

1 - 7 - 1 - 7 -

Offagna

Arcobaleno

via Torre 10, 60020 Offagna (AN)
Tel. 0717107567

Located just 20 km from the Conero Regional Park, this farm, with its simple, warm welcome, gives its guests a new perspective on life.

7 (x 2/4)

1 20,00 - 36,00 -

-

1 - - -

-

1 - 7 - 1 - 7 -

Pergola

Calamello

at Cartoceto, 61045 Pergola (PU)
Tel. 0721772048 Fax 0721772048
Web: www.vacanzea.com/calamello

Located in the Cesano Valley, this establishment is not far from such old towns and villages as Mondolfo, Corinaldo, Mondavio, Pergola and the more isolated Cartoceto.

2 (x 2)

1 35,00 23,00 45,00 -

4 (x 2)

1 35,00 23,00 45,00 -

1(x 7)

1 - 7 - 1 130,00 7 -

Merlino

at Mezzanotte, via Mezzanotte 29,
61045 Pergola (PU)
Tel. 0721778222 Fax 0721778222
Web: www.agriturismomerlino.it

This farm run by a young family is in the hills; the rooms have their own bathrooms and the wholesome cuisine is based on traditional dishes.

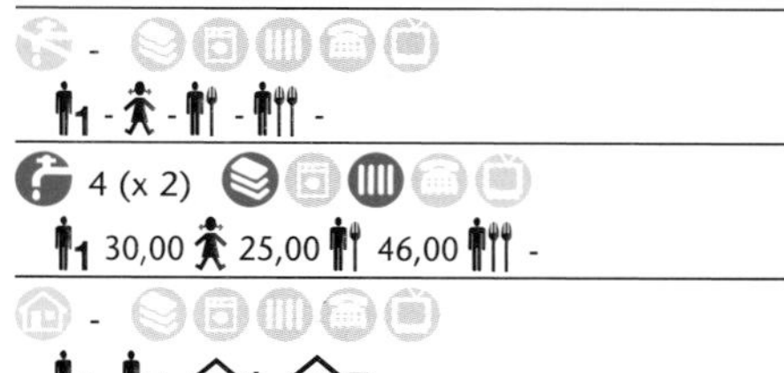

-

1 - - -

4 (x 2)

1 30,00 25,00 46,00 -

-

1 - 7 - 1 - 7 -

Recanati

Il Gelso

contrada S. Croce 46, 62019 Recanati (MC)
Tel. 071987002 Fax 0733263285

This farm, which adopts organic agricultural methods, is involved in a project for environmental improvement including the planting of hedges and distribution of artificial nests.

5 (x 1/2)

1 25,82 11,36 - -

-

1 - - -

-

1 - 7 - 1 - 7 -

Rosora

Croce del Moro

at Croce del Moro, via Tassanare 5,
60030 Rosora (AN)
Tel. 0731812112 Fax 0731814308
Web: www.crocedelmoro.it

This farm commands a splendid view ranging from the Apennines to the Adriatic Coast. The rooms are large and well-kept, with rustic furnishings, and there's an attractive large garden.

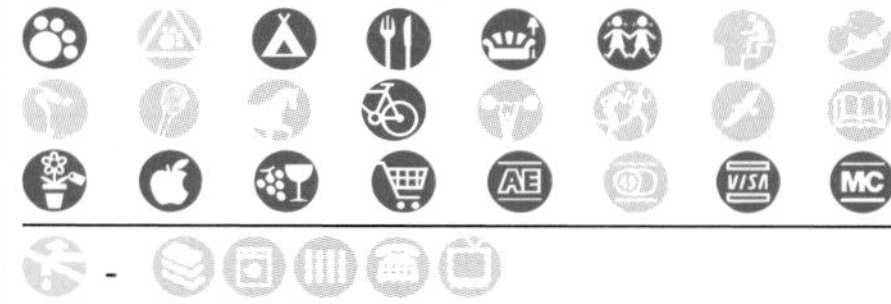

-

1 - - -

6 (x 2)

1 22,00 - 35,00 -

1(x 3)

1 - 7 - 1 50,00 7 -

Le Colline

at Tassanare, via Fondiglie 68, 60030 Rosora (AN)
Tel. **0731813844**
Web: **www.pasadena.it**

Solid yet comfortable, this stone cottage dating from the late 19th century is the ideal setting for those seeking rest and relaxation.

1 - - -

1 - - -

4 (x 2/4)

1 25,00 7 - 1 - 7 -

San Ginesio

Bellebuono

at Cesa Cappuccini 17, 62026 San Ginesio (MC)
Tel. **0733656296** Fax **0733652042**
Web: **www.bellebuono.it**

In the 19th century this building was the starting-point for walks and hunts. The view, which includes the magnificent medieval village, is superb.

1 - - -

4 (x 2)

1 18,00 - - -

4 (x 2/4)

1 - 7 - 1 60,00 7 400,00

Il Sambuco

contrada Necciano 29, 62026 San Ginesio (MC)
Tel. **0733656392**

This is location is ideal for a peaceful holiday amid the hydrangeas blooming under the tall trees; cultural interest is provided by Camerino and the other historic places in the province of Macerata.

1 - - -

  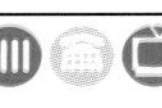

6 (x 1/2)

1 21,95 - - -

1 - 7 - 1 - 7 -

Silvia

contrada Santa Croce 86,
62026 San Ginesio (MC)
Tel. **0733656315**

The view has earned San Ginesio the title of 'balcony of the Sibillini', which may also be applied to this establishment standing close to its ancient walls.

1 - - -

-

1 - - -

57(x 2)

1 - 7 - 1 50,00 7 -

San Leo

La Lama

road for Pugliano 4, 61018 San Leo (PU)
Tel. 0541926928 Fax 0541926928

At the foot of the famous Rocca Feltresca, there's a relaxing atmosphere in this farmhouse that has been carefully converted to provide tourist accommodation.

3 (x 2)

1 27,50 - 43,00 -

4 (x 2)

1 32,50 - 43,00 -

1 - 7 - 1 - 7 -

Locanda San Leone

at Piega di San Leo, strada S. Antimo 102,
61018 San Leo (PU)
Tel. 0541912194 Fax 0541912348

In the Marecchia Valley, accommodation is available in a group of buildings incorporating the former mill of Piega, with its very special atmosphere.

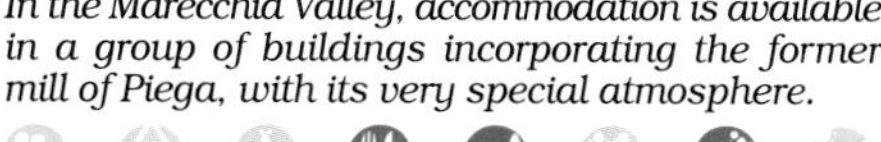

1 - - -

7 (x 2/4)

1 61,50 - - -

1 - 7 - 1 - 7 -

San Severino Marche

La Locanda dei Comacini

via San Francesco 2,
62027 San Severino Marche (MC)
Tel. 0733639691

On the slopes of Monte d'Aria, this rural complex has two new buildings, with period furniture, devoted to tourist accommodation.

1 - - -

5 (x 2)

1 20,00 - 38,00 -

1 - 7 - 1 - 7 -

Sant'Angelo in Vado

Villa dell'Agata

at Baciuccaro, 61048 Sant'Angelo in Vado (PU)
Tel. 072288768 Fax 0722819350
Web: www.villa-agata.de

Isolated amid the greenery of the upper Metauro Valley, this fine old house has accommodation, as well as a riding-school and swimming pool. In the vicinity, guests can hunt for truffles and visit medieval villages.

1 - - -

1 40,00 - - -

2 (x 2/4)

1 - 7 - 1 60,00 7 240,00

Sarnano

Il Jolly

at Case Rosse, 62028 Sarnano (MC)
Tel. 0733657571 Fax 0733657571

At the foot of the Monti Sibillini, accommodation is available in this modern but attractive rural building with an arcade, balconies and large open spaces.

-
1 - - - -

5 (x 1/4)
1 21,00 - 34,00 -

-
1 - 7 - 1 - 7 -

Sassoferrato

Colmerù

via Colmeroni 6, 60041 Sassoferrato (AN)
Tel. 07329277

In the centre of a vast farm growing cereals, this cottage is, in effect, a museum. Its ancient appearance has survived intact and it still has its original furniture.

3 (x 2)
1 20,00 - - -

-
1 - - - -

-
1 - 7 - 1 - 7 -

Senigallia

Beatrice

at Borgo Bicchia, via San Gaudenzio 1,
60019 Senigallia (AN)
Tel. 0717926807

This pleasant little country house is perfect for seaside holidays far from the madding crowd. The restaurant is run by a couple of wine-growers doubling as sommeliers.

4 (x 2)
1 27,50 - 40,00 -

6 (x 1/2)
1 27,50 - 40,00 -

2 (x 4/6)
1 - 7 - 1 100,00 7 -

Il Papavero

at Bettolelle, via Arceviese 98,
60019 Senigallia (AN)
Tel. 07166405 Fax 07165111
Web: www.agriturismoilpapavero.it

In the farmhouse, which dominates the land surrounding it, the accommodation is provided by large rooms with period furniture, and there's a well-equipped garden.

-
1 - - - -

3 (x 2)
1 35,00 20,00 - -

-
1 - 7 - 1 - 7 -

Serra de' Conti

La Giara

via San Paterniano 18, 60030 Serra de' Conti (AN)
Tel. 0731878090
E-mail: lagiara@infinito.it

This old complex of farm buildings has a large courtyard and park. The accommodation is in a brick cottage with traditional furniture, including pieces in wrought iron.

-

1 - - - -

4 (x 1/2)

1 30,00 - 45,00 -

-

1 - 7 - 1 - 7 -

Serra San Quirico

Chiaraluce

via Pergolesi 2, 60048 Serra San Quirico (AN)
Tel. 073186682 Fax 073186003

The farm, long renowned for its production of olive oil, has accommodation in excellently renovated rooms. In the medieval village there are remains of an old castle.

-

1 - - - -

-

1 - - - -

3(x 4)

1 - 7 - 1 46,00 7 -

La Tana del Lele

at Madonna delle Stelle 1,
60048 Serra San Quirico (AN)
Tel. 073186737 Fax 073186737
Web: www.pasadena.it

The accommodation is in the handsome stone farmhouse where the owners live. An arcade gives onto a large garden where hammocks hanging in the shade offer an opportunity to meditate on life.

-

1 - - - -

3 (x 2)

1 30,00 - 50,00 -

1(x 2)

1 - 7 - 1 60,00 7 450,00

Serrungarina

Il Mandorlo

via Tomba 57, 61030 Serrungarina (PU)
Tel. 0721891480 Fax 0721891480

Between Urbino and the sea, in the central part of the Metauro Valley, accommodation is available in the large rooms of an establishment where the main emphasis is on the restaurant.

-

1 - - - -

8 (x 2/4)

1 30,00 - 41,50 -

2(x 6)

1 25,00 7 - 1 - 7 -

SERVIGLIANO

CASCINA DEGLI ULIVI

   E D

contrada Commenda 4, 63029 Servigliano (AP)
Tel. 0734710235 Fax 0734710235

The old farmhouse is on a hill halfway between the sea and the mountains. The building has been carefully renovated, preserving its traditional appearance.

\-

1 - - -

5 (x 2/4) 

1 26,00 - 52,00 -

\-  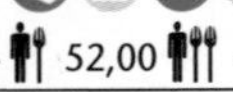

1 - 7 - 1 - 7 -

SIROLO

IL RITORNO

 E D

at Coppo, via Piani d'Aspio 12, 60020 Sirolo (AN)
Tel. 0719331544 Fax 0717360239
Web: www.ilritorno.com

This farm, which accommodates its guests in a traditional rural house, is a centre for tourism on horseback recognised by the FISE.

\-

1 - - -

6 (x 2/4) 

1 30,00 - 45,00 -

\- 

1 - 7 - 1 - 7 -

TOLENTINO

AGRIMAGNOLIA

   E D  

contrada Salcito 13, 62029 Tolentino (MC)
Tel. 0733967366
Web: www.terranostra.it

Of historical and cultural interest, this farmhouse, with its outbuildings, provides comfortable accommodation amid the trees and meadows of a peaceful hillside.

\-

1 - - -

4 (x 2)

1 30,99 - - -

7 (x 2/9) 

1 - 7 - 1 103,29 7 -

URBANIA

CA' BOSCARINI

  E D  

S.S. (state road) 73/bis at km 10,
61049 Urbania (PU)
Tel. 0722312127 Fax 0722319485
Web: www.caboscarini.it

Urbania is noted for its history and works of art. Thus holidays here focus on cultural visits, but without neglecting the pleasures of lazing in the countryside and good food.

\-

1 - - -

\-

1 - - -

4(x 2)  

1 - 7 - 1 75,00 7 -

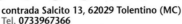

Cal Terrazzano

via dei Fangacci - San Giorgio 7,
61049 Urbania (PU)
Tel. 0722319529 Fax 068610247

This 19th-century farmhouse in the upper Metauro Valley, renovated with the accent on tradition and comfort. The rooms have furnishings belonging to the family.

-

1 - - -

4 (x 2)

1 41,31 - - -

1(x 2)

1 - 7 - 1 82,63 7 -

Candianaccio

via Candigliano 6, 61049 Urbania (PU)
Tel. 0722986246 Fax 0722981196
E-mail: gjm.mochi@libero.it

Golden grain and dark green woods surround the large farmhouse: the accommodation is suitable for families and large groups.

-

1 - - -

-

1 - - -

1(x 14)

1 - 7 - 1 - 7 2.000,00

Mulino della Ricavata

via Porta Celle 5, 61049 Urbania (PU)
Tel. 0722310326 Fax 0722310326
E-mail: mulinodellaricavata@libero.it

Located in the heart of the Montefeltro region, on a loop in the Metauro, this old building is now in the centre of a farm devoted to organic agriculture.

2 (x 2)

1 38,00 - 55,00 -

2 (x 2)

1 40,00 - 57,00 -

-

1 - 7 - 1 - 7 -

Urbino

Cà Andreana

via Gadana 119, 61029 Urbino (PU)
Tel. 0722327845 Fax 0722327845
Web: www.caandreana.it

In the heart of Montefeltro it is easy to feel that one has gone back in time: not only in Urbino, but also in the countryside, in this farmhouse offering holiday accommodation.

-

1 - - -

6 (x 2/4)

1 33,50 27,00 - -

-

1 - 7 - 1 - 7 -

Fosso del Lupo

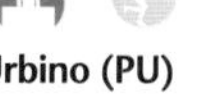

at Scotaneto, via Scotaneto 11, 61029 Urbino (PU)
Tel. 0722340233 Fax 0722340233
E-mail: d.garota@libero.it

In the woods, fallow deer and boar abound; in the sky, buzzards and harriers. Perhaps this is also thanks to the owners, who have adopted organic farming methods.

\-

1 - - - -

\-

1 - - - -

3 (x 2/6)

1 - 7 - 1 90,00 7 600,00

La Corte della Miniera

at Miniera, podere Pozzo Nuovo Miniera 74, 61029 Urbino (PU)
Tel. 0722345322 Fax 0722345322
E-mail: cortedellaminiera@abanet.it

The buildings of a former sulphur mine house this establishment with a 'cultural slant'; it organises pottery, lithography and etching workshops.

\-

1 - - - -

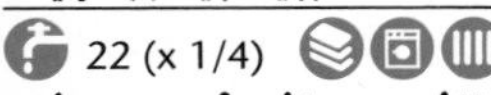

22 (x 1/4)

1 42,00 - 41,00 -

\-

1 - 7 - 1 - 7 -

Le Fontane

at Pallino 56, 61029 Urbino (PU)
Tel. 0722328281 Fax 07222883
Web: www.lefontaneurbino.it

The farm grows and processes hazelnuts. In wooded areas or sunnier ones, accommodation is available in three renovated farmhouses.

\-

1 - - - -

\-

1 - - - -

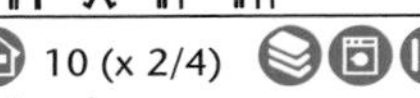

10 (x 2/4)

1 - 7 - 1 177,00 7 -

Valdinoce

via Monte Avorio 43, 61029 Urbino (PU)
Tel. 0722345180 Fax 0722345180
E-mail: valdinoce@katamail.com

Accommodation, for non-smokers only, is available in this brick and stone farmhouse, renovated in accordance with the principles of ecological architecture; the fruit and vegetables are grown organically.

\-

1 - - - -

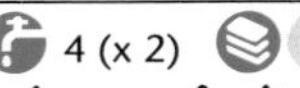

4 (x 2)

1 36,00 - 50,00 -

\-

1 - 7 - 1 - 7 -

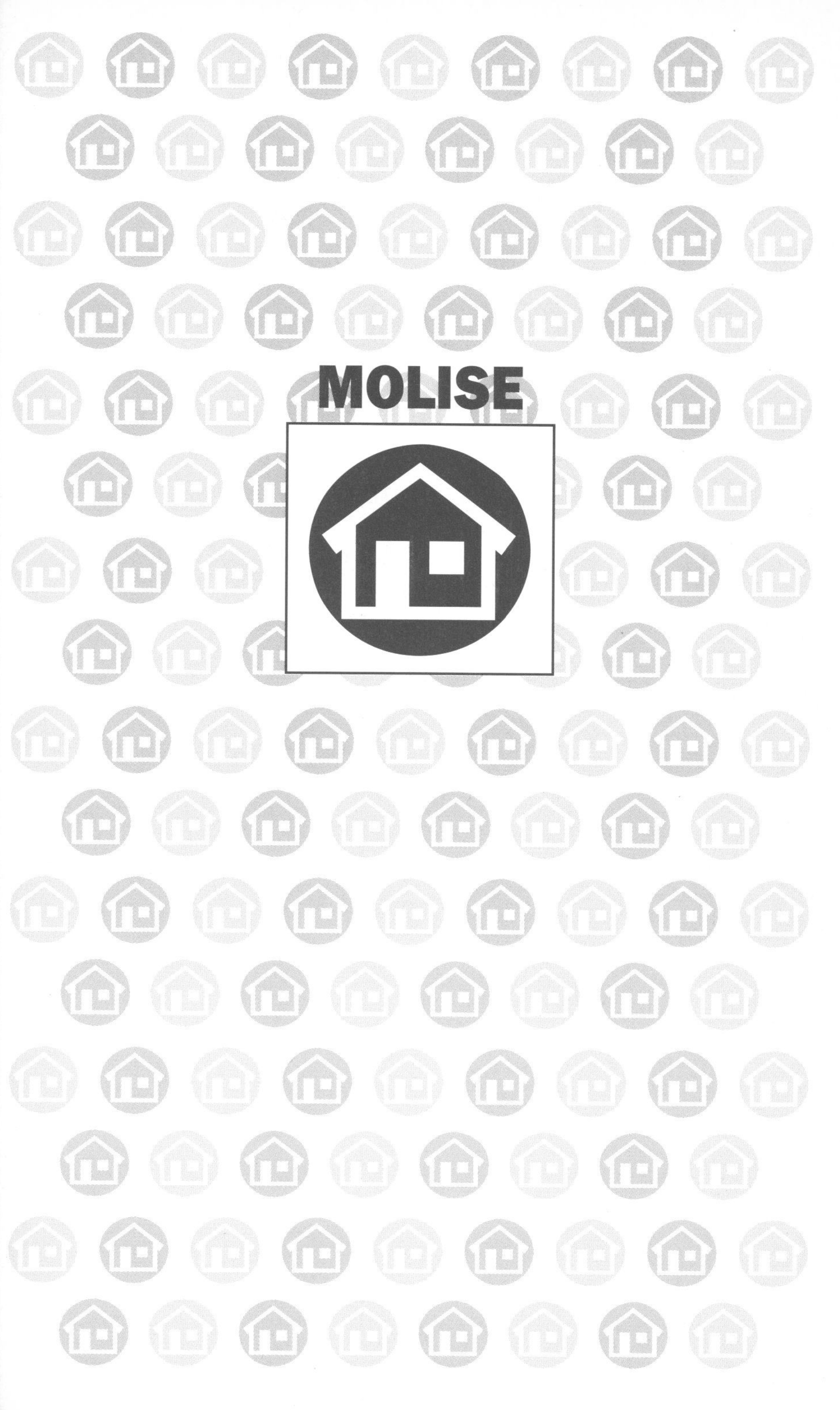

MOLISE

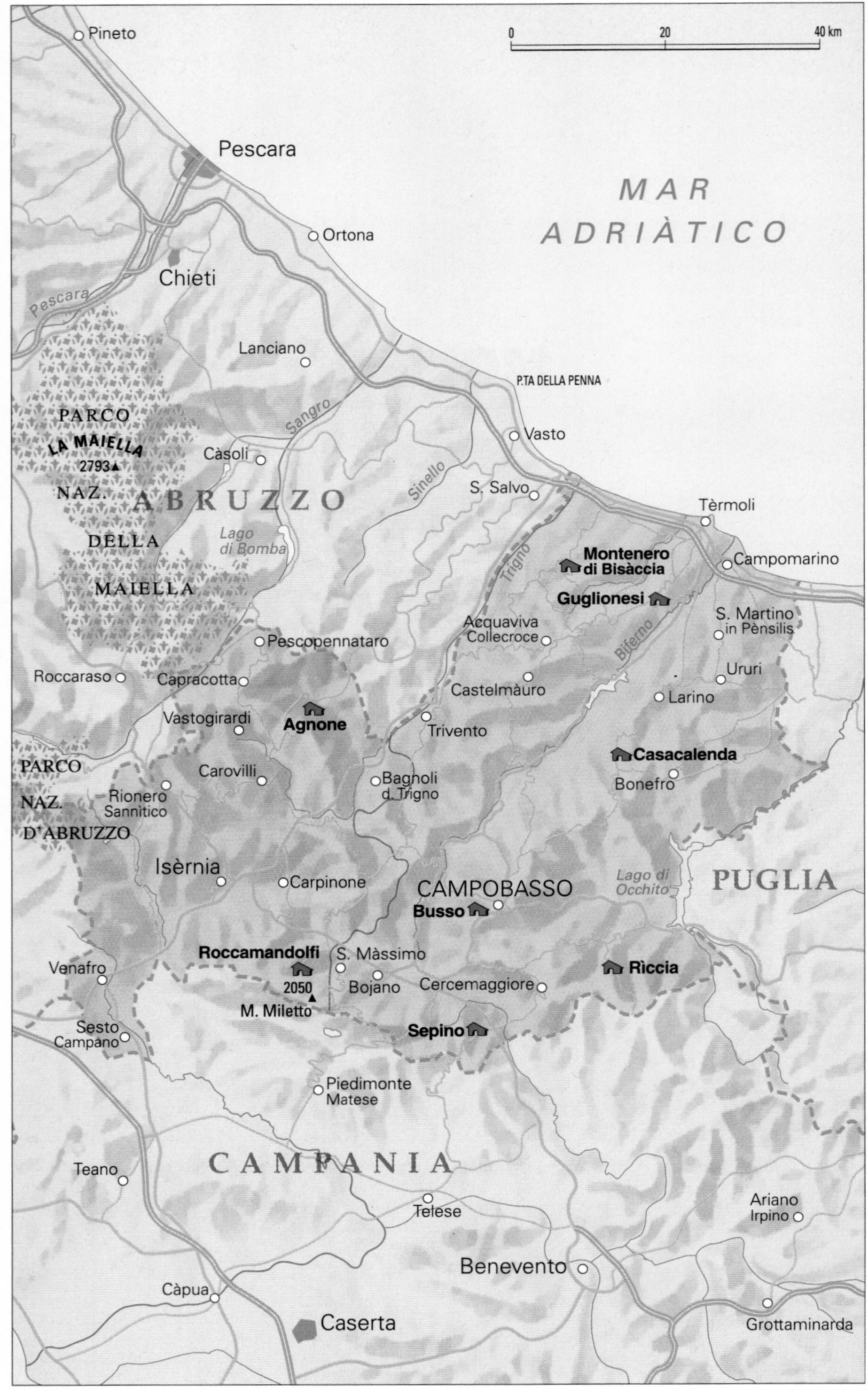

0
20
40 km
Pineto
Pescara
MAR
ADRIÀTICO
Ortona
Chieti
Pescara
Lanciano
P.TA DELLA PENNA
Sangro
PARCO
LA MAIELLA
2793
NAZ.
DELLA
MAIELLA
Càsoli
ABRUZZO
Sinello
Vasto
S. Salvo
Tèrmoli
Lago
di Bomba
Trigno
Montenero
di Bisàccia
Campomarino
Guglionesi
Biferno
S. Martino
in Pènsilis
Acquaviva
Collecroce
Pescopennataro
Roccaraso
Capracotta
Castelmàuro
Ururi
Larino
Vastogirardi
Agnone
Trivento
Casacalenda
PARCO
NAZ.
D'ABRUZZO
Carovilli
Rionero
Sannitico
Bagnoli
d. Trigno
Bonefro
Isèrnia
Carpinone
CAMPOBASSO
Lago di
Occhito
PUGLIA
Busso
Roccamandolfi
S. Màssimo
Venafro
Bojano
Cercemaggiore
Rìccia
2050
M. Miletto
Sesto
Campano
Sepino
Piedimonte
Matese
CAMPANIA
Teano
Telese
Ariano
Irpino
Benevento
Càpua
Caserta
Grottaminarda

Agnone

Selvaggi

at Staffoli, S.P. (provincial road) Montesangrina at km 1, 86081 Agnone (IS)
Tel. **086577177** Fax **086577177**

This farmhouse, which comprises an ancient fortified building and later extensions, is much appreciated by nature lovers.

\-

1 - - -

5 (x 4)

1 37,00 - - 68,00

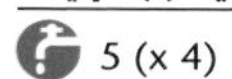

\-

1 - 7 - 1 - 7 -

Busso

Giovanni Di Niro

contrada Perito, 86010 Busso (CB)
Tel. **0874447210**
E-mail: **gdiniro@interfree.it**

In this recently renovated old stone building, guests may participate in the farm's activities, such as the making of bread, pasta and cheese.

\-

1 - - -

2 (x 2)

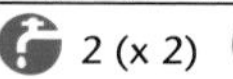

1 31,00 15,00 45,00 -

\-

1 - 7 - 1 - 7 -

Pesco la Corte

contrada Pesco la Corte, via Trento 67, 86010 Busso (CB)
Tel. **0874447285**
E-mail: **domenicocoladangelo@interfree.it**

This accommodation in a comfortable house in the upper Biferno Valley is ideal for those wishing to discover the beautiful landscape and cuisine of Sannio and the Matese.

3 (x 2/4)

1 23,50 - 33,50 -

\-

1 - - -

\-

1 - 7 - 1 - 7 -

Casacalenda

Fattoria La Quercia

contrada Convento, 86043 Casacalenda (CB)
Tel. **0874841146** Fax **0874841146**

Located in the valley of the Cigno, by an ancient oak tree, this handsome stone farmhouse has been renovated, with attention being paid to the original details.

6 (x 2/4)

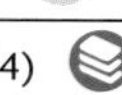

1 26,00 - 36,00 -

\-

1 - - - -

\-

1 - 7 - 1 - 7 -

Fontemazzocca

contrada Macchia Puzzo 1, 86043 Casacalenda (CB)
Tel. 0874841041

This farm, which looks out over beautiful rolling hills, stands on the edge of an oak-wood forming part of the Bosco Casale Nature Reserve.

2 (x 2)

1 18,00 - - 36,00

3 (x 2)

1 18,00 - - 36,00

\-

1 - 7 - 1 - 7 -

Guglionesi

La Masseria

contrada Petriglione 11, 86034 Guglionesi (CB)
Tel. 0875689827
E-mail: agridicesare@tibernet.it

In the splendid setting of the River Biferno and Lake Liscione, accommodation is available in a farmhouse with comfortable rooms in which special care has been taken over the details.

1 (x 2)

1 - - - -

5 (x 2)

1 23,00 - 39,00 -

\-

1 - 7 - 1 - 7 -

Montenero di Bisaccia

Masseria Bisaccia

contrada Piscone, 86036 Montenero di Bisaccia (CB)
Tel. 0875966972 Fax 0875968788
E-mail: agribisaccia@tin.it

Particularly suitable for families with children, this establishment has rooms with floors made of terracotta tiles and wooden furniture, creating a simple but homely atmosphere.

1 (x 2)

1 22,00 - - -

3 (x 2/4)

1 25,00 - - -

\-

1 - 7 - 1 - 7 -

Riccia

Manocchio

contrada Rio Secco 115, 86016 Riccia (CB)
Tel. 0874716259

Guests are accommodated in a two-storeyed farmhouse, with the stables and cowsheds on the lower floor, in a verdant area rich in springs.

1(x 6)

16,00

Notartomaso

contrada Escamare 335, 86016 Riccia (CB)
Tel. 0874712185

This accommodation is in the higher hills, in an open position between cultivated fields and orchards, in close contact with the world of agriculture.

2 (x 1/2)

16,00 31,00

Roccamandolfi

Zia Concetta

at Rio, 86098 Roccamandolfi (IS)
Tel. 0865816353

This accommodation is provided by a pleasant attic with simply furnished rooms as befits a real farmhouse; horse-riding facilities are available nearby.

2 (x 2)

18,00 25,00

Sepino

La Taverna

contrada Piana d'Olmo 6, 86017 Sepino (CB)
Tel. 087479626 Fax 0874790118
E-mail: parente@netpoint.it

This 18th-century farmhouse, with its adjacent water-mill, has been carefully converted to provide accommodation.

14 (x 1/4)

25,00 40,00

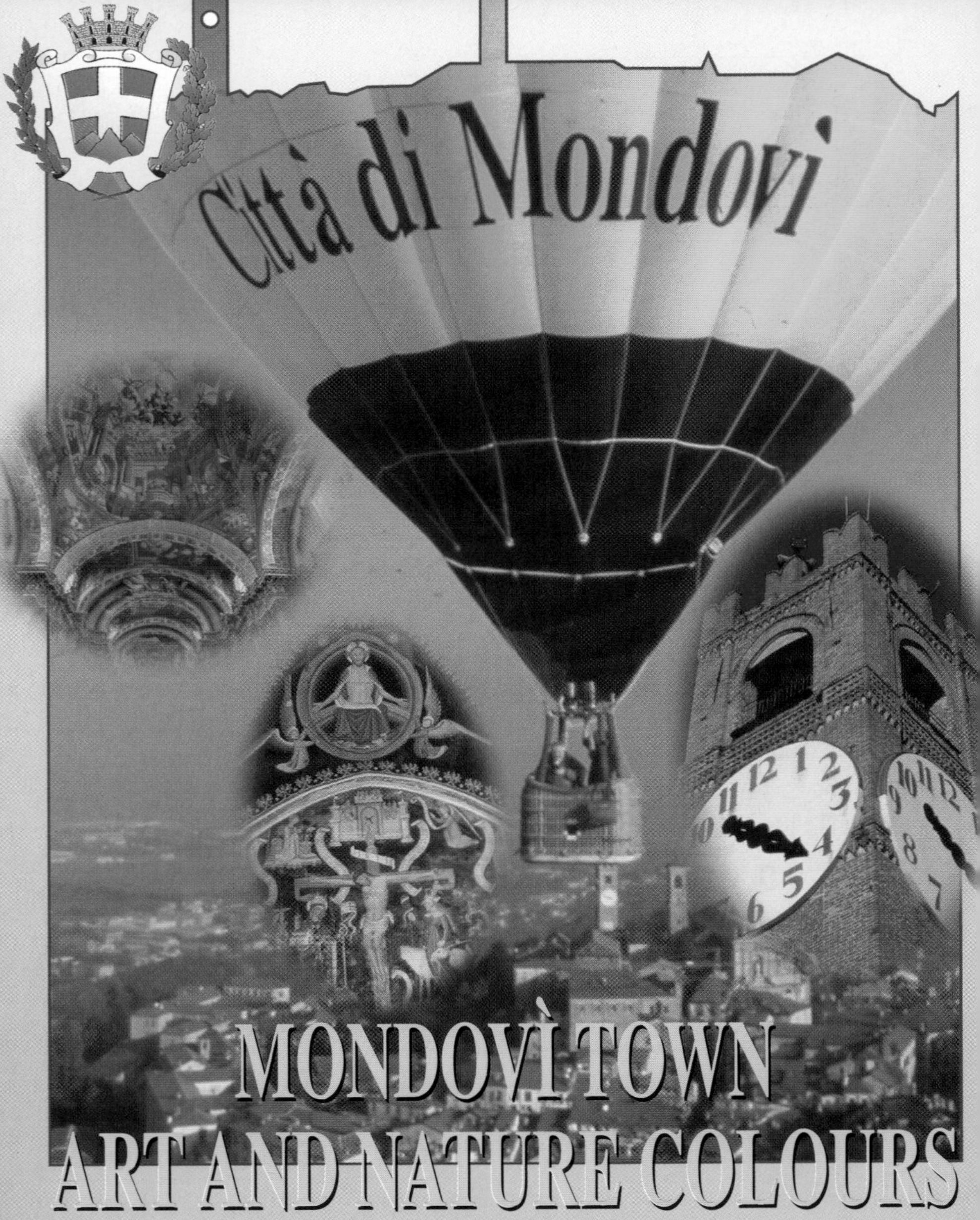
Città di Mondovì
MONDOVÌ TOWN
ART AND NATURE COLOURS

PIEMONTE

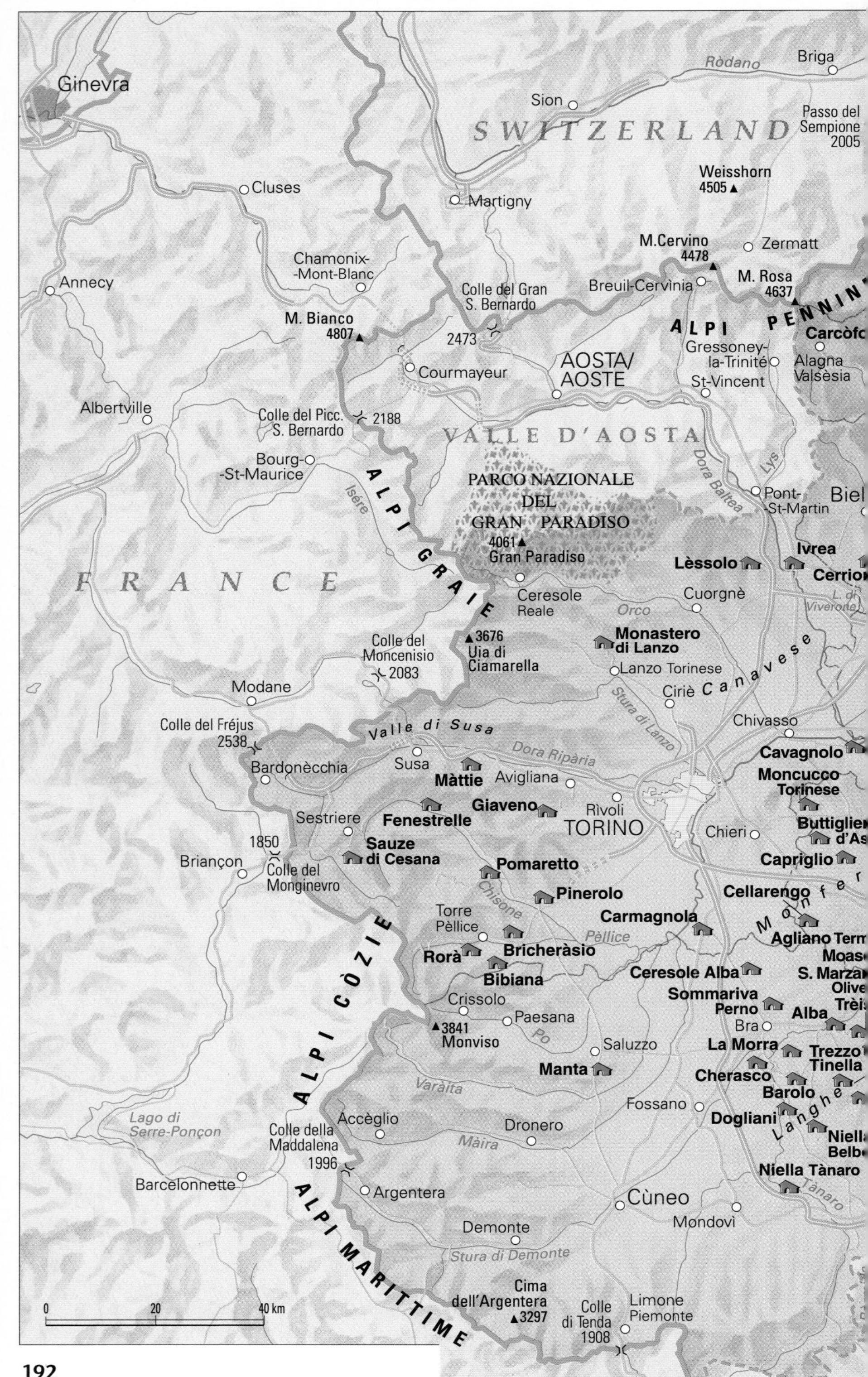

Ginevra
Ròdano
Briga
Sion
SWITZERLAND
Passo del Sempione 2005
Cluses
Martigny
Weisshorn 4505
M.Cervino 4478
Zermatt
Chamonix-Mont-Blanc
Annecy
Colle del Gran S. Bernardo
Breuil-Cervìnia
M. Rosa 4637
M. Bianco 4807
2473
ALPI PENNINE
Carcòfo
Gressoney-la-Trinité
Alagna Valsèsia
Courmayeur
AOSTA/ AOSTE
St-Vincent
Albertville
Colle del Picc. S. Bernardo
2188
VALLE D'AOSTA
Bourg-St-Maurice
Dora Baltea
Lys
ALPI GRAIE
Isère
PARCO NAZIONALE DEL GRAN PARADISO
Pont-St-Martin
Biel
4061 Gran Paradiso
Ivrea
Lèssolo
Cerrio
FRANCE
Ceresole Reale
Cuorgnè
L. di Viverone
Orco
Colle del Moncenisio
2083
3676 Uia di Ciamarella
Monastero di Lanzo
Lanzo Torinese
Canavese
Modane
Ciriè
Stura di Lanzo
Colle del Fréjus 2538
Valle di Susa
Chivasso
Bardonècchia
Susa
Dora Ripària
Cavagnolo
Màttie
Avigliana
Moncucco Torinese
Giaveno
Rivoli
Sestriere
Fenestrelle
TORINO
Chieri
Buttigliera d'Asti
1850
Sauze di Cesana
Briançon
Colle del Monginevro
Pomaretto
Capriglio
Chisone
Pinerolo
Cellarengo
Monferrato
Carmagnola
Torre Pèllice
Pèllice
Agliano Terme
Rorà
Bricheràsio
Moasca
Bibiana
Ceresole Alba
S. Marzano Oliveto
ALPI CÒZIE
Crissolo
Sommariva Perno
Alba
Trèiso
Paesana
Bra
3841 Monviso
Po
Saluzzo
La Morra
Trezzo Tinella
Manta
Cherasco
Varàita
Barolo
Lago di Serre-Ponçon
Fossano
Langhe
Accèglio
Colle della Maddalena 1996
Dronero
Dogliani
Niella Belbo
Màira
Niella Tànaro
Barcelonnette
Argentera
Cùneo
Tànaro
Mondovì
ALPI MARITTIME
Demonte
Stura di Demonte
Cima dell'Argentera 3297
Colle di Tenda 1908
Limone Piemonte
0
20
40 km

SWITZERLAND
Formazza
Varzo
Val d'Ossola
Toce
Locarno
Bellinzona
Chiavenna
Mera
Sòndrio
Adda
Morbegno
ALPI ORÒBIE
Fòppolo
Domodóssola
PARCO NAZ. D. VAL GRANDE
Verbània
Luino
Lugano
Lago di Lugano
Lago Maggiore
Omegna
Lago d'Orta
Varese
Lago di Como
Lecco
S. Pellegrino Terme
Serio
Como
Bèrgamo
Lago d'Iseo
Borgosèsia
Borgomanero
Borgo Ticino
Mezzomerico
Cossato
Oléggio
Busto Arsìzio
Monza
Treviglio
MILANO
Abbiategrasso
LOMBARDIA
Novara
Vercelli
Vigevano
Crema
Oglio
Sèsia
Mortara
Ticino
Lambro
Lodi
Lomellina
Pavia
Adda
Cremona
Ontestura
Casale Monferrato
Po
Serralunga Crea
Cella Monte
Lomello
Moncalvo
Vignale Monf.
Valenza
Piacenza
Castagnole Monf.
Voghera
Asti
Alessàndria
Tànaro
Tortona
Stàffora
Trèbbia
Costigliole d'Asti
Castelnuovo Calcéa
Avolasca
Fidenza
Nizza Monferrato
Novi Ligure
S. Sebastiano Curone
Bòbbio
EMILIA-ROMAGNA
Calamandrana
Stazzano
Canelli
Castel Boglione
Àcqui Terme
Bùbbio
Gavi
Ovada
Passo dei Giovi 472
Ravanzana
LIGURIA
Passo d. Cisa 1039
Càiro Montenotte
GÈNOVA
Nervi
Lavagna
Pontrèmoli
435
Colle di Cadibona
Savona
Rapallo
Chiàvari
MAR LÌGURE

Agliano Terme

La Mela Verde

via Noce 34, 14041 Agliano Terme (AT)
Tel. 0141954148 Fax 0141954148

On a hillside in the Barbera production area, the accommodation is in an old farmhouse with a patio and furnishings helping to create a pleasant atmosphere.

 -

1 - - -

-

1 - - -

 2(x 4)

1 22,00 7 - 1 - 7 -

Alba

Villa La Favorita

at Altavilla 12 bis, 12051 Alba (CN)
Tel. 3384715005 Fax 0173364746
Web: www.villalafavorita.it

In the hills surrounding Alba crowned by vineyards producing Grignolino and Nebbiolo, an early 20th-century villa that has been entirely renovated offers accommodation.

 -

1 - - -

 4 (x 2)  

1 93,00 - - -

-

1 - 7 - 1 - 7 -

Avolasca

La Vecchia Posta

via Montebello 2, 15050 Avolasca (AL)
Tel. 0131876254 Fax 0131876254

In the Colli Tortonesi - verdant, tranquil and off the beaten track - this accommodation is in a farmhose near a village of wine-growers and small stock-breeders. Simple food is available.

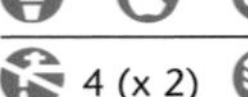 4 (x 2)   

1 - - 38,00 -

-

1 - - -

-

1 - 7 - 1 - 7 -

Barolo

Il Gioco dell'Oca

via Crosia 46, 12060 Barolo (CN)
Tel. 017356206 Fax 017356206
Web: www.gioco-delloca.it

In the hills where Barolo is produced, this farmhouse has preserved its traditional appearance, which is echoed by the rooms, with their simple furnishings.

7 (x 2)

30,00 - -

1(x 2)

- - 60,00 -

Bibiana

Il Frutto Permesso

via del Vernè 16, 10060 Bibiana (TO)
Tel. 012155383 Fax 012155383
Web: www.fruttopermesso.it

At the mouth of the Val Pellice, there are four buildings providing comfortable accommodation and two restaurant serving a theme dinner on Friday evenings.

12 (x 2)

36,00 - -

Borgo Ticino

Cascina Cesarina

at Gagnago, via Dei Cesari 32,
28040 Borgo Ticino (NO)
Tel. 032190491 Fax 032190491
E-mail: cascinacesarinamail@yahoo.com

The accommodation is in a pleasant farmhouse with long balconies that has been renovated without spoiling its original appearance, in accordance with the principles of ecological architecture. Simple country meals are served here.

2 (x 4)

44,00 - 58,00 -

Bricherasio

Turina

via Tagliarea 16, 10060 Bricherasio (TO)
Tel. 012159257 Fax 012159257
Web: www.agriturismo-turina.it

At the mouth of the Val Pellice, this establishment is just a stone's throw from Pinerolo and half an hour's drive from Turin, with a wide variety of trips to be made in the area.

4(x 2)

- - 75,00 -

Bubbio

La Dogliola

regione Infermiera 226, 14051 Bubbio (AT)
Tel. 014483557 Fax 0144852714
Web: www.ladogliola.it

On the Langa Astigiana, this is a farm belonging to the Movimento del Turismo del Vino. Guests will get a warm welcome in farmhouse where the young owner lives.

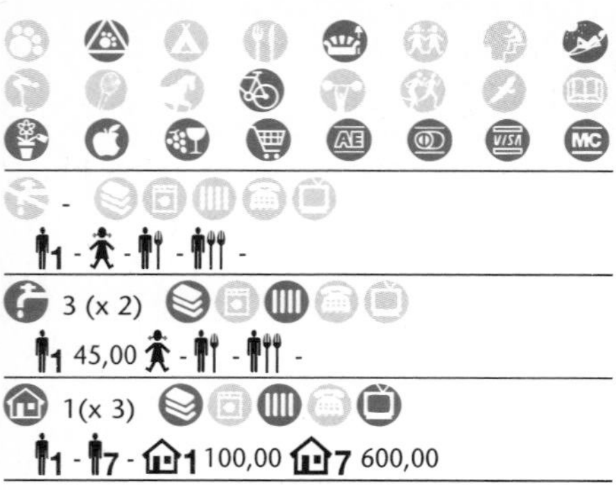

-

1 - - -

3 (x 2)

1 45,00 - -

1(x 3)

1 - 7 - 1 100,00 7 600,00

Buttigliera d'Asti

Cascina Campora

at Serra, 14021 Buttigliera d'Asti (AT)
Tel. 0119921821 Fax 0141901360
E-mail: novara@interfree.it

'Holidays amid the fragrance of nature' is a truly appropriate slogan for a farm firmly committed to organic methods of agriculture.

5 (x 1/2)

1 23,00 - 31,00 -

-

1 - - -

-

1 - 7 - 1 - 7 -

Calamandrana

La Corte

regione Quartino 6, 14042 Calamandrana (AT)
Tel. 0141769109 Fax 0141769991
Web: www.agrilacorte.com

Surrounded by seven hectares of vineyards in the area where the Monferrato meets the Langhe, this 18th-century group of farm buildings, has a courtyard closed on one side by the old winery.

-

1 - - -

9 (x 1/4)

1 52,00 - 68,00 -

-

1 - 7 - 1 - 7 -

Canelli

La Casa in Collina

regione S. Antonio 30, 14053 Canelli (AT)
Tel. 0141822827 Fax 0141823543
Web: www.casaincollina.com

In the hills near Asti, this old farmhouse is surrounded by vineyards producing Moscato and Barbera. This area dear to Cesare Pavese is ideal for leisurely walks.

-

1 - - -

6 (x 2)

1 70,00 - -

-

1 - 7 - 1 - 7 -

La Luna e i Falò

regione Aie 37, 14053 Canelli (AT)
Tel. 0141831643 Fax 0141831643
Web: www.initaly.com/hisres/lunafalo

The name (bisogna tradurlo in inglese!), deriving from a quotation from the writer Cesare Pavese, is particularly suitable for this place because when lazing in the arcade of the old farmhouse one really does lose oneself.

\-

1 - - -

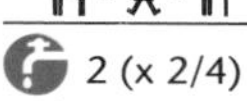
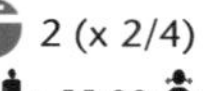

2 (x 2/4)

1 55,00 - 80,00 -

1(x 4)

1 55,00 7 - 1 - 7 -

Rupestr

regione Piancanelli 12, 14053 Canelli (AT)
Tel. 0141824799 Fax 0141824799
Web: www.rupestr.it

'Traditional hospitality', as the owner puts it, is available between the Monferrato and the Langhe, in the centre of an area renowned for its superb food and wine.

\-

1 - - -

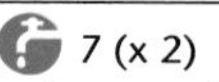

7 (x 2)

1 35,00 - 60,00 -

\-

1 - 7 - 1 - 7 -

Capriglio

Cascina Piola

at Serra, via Fontana 2, 14014 Capriglio (AT)
Tel. 0141997447 Fax 0141997447
E-mail: cascinapiola@inwind.it

This pink house stands out In the green hills between Turin and Asti; wisteria and geraniums bedeck the windows, the furnishings and atmosphere are those of a bygone age.

\-

1 - - -

2 (x 2)

1 27,50 - 46,00 -

\-

1 - 7 - 1 - 7 -

Carcoforo

Brüc

at Alpe Brüc, 13026 Carcoforo (VC)
Tel. 016395600

Brüc' is the heather growing between the larches. Close to the Alta Valsesia Nature Park, this establishment is on the route of the Grande Traversata delle Alpi (GTA).

3 (x 2/4)

1 16,00 - 37,00 -

-

1 - - -

-

1 - 7 - 1 - 7 -

Carmagnola

Cascina Montebarco

at Casanova, via Poirino 650,
10022 Carmagnola (TO)
Tel. 0119795051 Fax 0119795907
E-mail: cenapier@tiscali.it

This farmhouse, in accordance with the tradition of the Po Valley, is built round a large courtyard. A short distance away is the Cistercian abbey of Casanova.

-

1 - - -

-

1 - - -

4 (x 2/3)

1 26,00 7 - 1 - 7 -

Casale Monferrato

Cascina Pelizza

at Vialarda, 15033 Casale Monferrato (AL)
Tel. 0142408130 Fax 0142408177

Not far from the Po, on the first offshoots of the famous hills, guests are accommodated in a farmhouse surrounded by vineyards.

-

1 - - -

5 (x 2/4)

1 31,00 - 42,00 -

-

1 - 7 - 1 - 7 -

Castagnole Monferrato

Tenuta dei Re

regione Cascina Nuova 1,
14030 Castagnole Monferrato (AT)
Tel. 0141292147 Fax 0141292147
Web: www.tenutadeire.it

In the Grignolino production area, accommodation is available in a peaceful setting in this late 19th-century manor-house. The farm roads are ideal for long walks.

3 (x 1)

1 20,00 10,00 36,15 -

3 (x 2/4)

1 26,33 10,00 43,90 -

-

1 - 7 - 1 - 7 -

Castel Boglione

Cascina La Carlotta

at Gianola, strada Gianola 28,
14040 Castel Boglione (AT)
Tel. 0141762496 Fax 0141762496
Web: www.cascinalacarlotta.interfree.it

Located in the hills flanking the River Belbo, this wine-producing estate accommodates its guests in an old, carefully renovated farmhouse.

-

1 - - -

4 (x 2/4)

1 50,00 - - -

1(x 4)

1 - 7 - 1 74,29 7 -

Castelnuovo Calcea

La Mussia

regione Opessina 4, 14040 Castelnuovo Calcea (AT)
Tel. 0141957201 Fax 0141957402
Web: www.lamussia.it

This large group of buildings emerges from the sea of vineyards covering the hills; around the farmyard are two houses, an arcade, a hayloft and a cowshed.

-

1 - - -

11 (x 2)

1 28,50 - 45,00 -

2 (x 2/4)

1 - 7 - 1 - 7 593,00

Cavagnolo

Terra dei Profumi

via Maiaris 13, 10020 Cavagnolo (TO)
Tel. 0119152723 Fax 0119152723
E-mail: terradeiprofumi@virgilio.it

In the Basso Monferrato, not far from Turin, this mid-19th-century farmhouse, with rooms containing period furniture, is in the centre of an area rich in greenery.

-

1 - - -

3 (x 2)

1 20,00 - - 65,00

-

1 - 7 - 1 - 7 -

Cella Monte

Villa Perona

strada Perona 1, 15034 Cella Monte (AL)
Tel. 0142488280 Fax 0142488280

Standing amid the orderly vineyards of the Monferrato, this 19th-century house has, in its cellars, remains attesting to its much more ancient origins.

3 (x 2)

1 28,50 - - -

6 (x 2)

1 46,50 - - -

-

1 - 7 - 1 - 7 -

Cellarengo

Cascina Papa Mora

via Ferrere 16, 14010 Cellarengo (AT)
Tel. 0141935126
Web: www.cascinapapamora.it

This large farmhouse dating from the early 20th century offers accommodation in the peaceful hills around Asti. The rooms lend a special tone to the stay here.

-

1 - - -

5 (x 2/4)

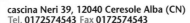

1 26,00 18,00 49,00 -

-

1 - 7 - 1 - 7 -

Ceresole Alba

Cascina Neri

cascina Neri 39, 12040 Ceresole Alba (CN)
Tel. 0172574543 Fax 0172574543

In the Roero, an area of castles and great wines, guests may indulge in gastronomic pleasures and go for walks. Educational activities are organised for schoolchildren.

-

1 - - - -

2 (x 2)

1 31,00 - 45,00 -

-

1 - 7 - 1 - 7 -

Cerrione

La Bessa - Ippica San Giorgio

at Cascina Pianone, 13882 Cerrione (BI)
Tel. 0152587916 Fax 015677156

This 19th-century farmhouse is a centre for tourism on horseback. Behind it rises the vast wooded area of the Serra, a morainic ridge extending towards the Valle d'Aosta.

4 (x 1/4)

1 19,00 12,00 38,00 -

2 (x 2)

1 21,00 14,00 41,00 -

-

1 - 7 - 1 - 7 -

Cessole

Zabaldano

regione Zabaldano, 14050 Cessole (AT)
Tel. 014480275 Fax 014480275
E-mail: zabaldano@libero.it

Located in the hills of the Alta Langa Astigiana, this farm is surrounded by unspoilt countryside where badgers, salamanders, truffles and wild orchids are to be found.

-

1 - - - -

-

1 - - - -

3(x 3)

1 - 7 - 1 - 7 550,00

Cherasco

Ca' dii Ghiru

at San Bartolomeo, via Meane 4,
12062 Cherasco(CN)
Tel. 0172488018

In the fascinating area known as the Langhe, Cherasco is renowned for its delicious snails and its antiques fairs.

-

1 - - - -

3 (x 2)

1 31,00 15,00 52,00 -

-

1 - 7 - 1 - 7 -

Cravanzana

La Collina degli Scoiattoli

via Dietro Langhe 12, 12050 Cravanzana (CN)
Tel. 0173855226 Fax 0173855226
Web: www.lantime.it/cds

The name itself refers to the verdant setting of this farm, a small group of buildings in the Langhe, in the middle of terraced land growing vegetables and fruit.

-

1 - - - -

5 (x 2)

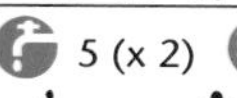 
1 20,50 - 39,00 -

-

1 - 7 - 1 - 7 -

Dogliani

Cascina Martina

borgata Martina III 12, 12063 Dogliani (CN)
Tel. 0173721239
Web: www.geocities.com/cascinamartina

This farmhouse in Langhe stone has flower-decked balconies and a courtyard that speaks of rural life. The attractive rooms have old woodwork, bare stone walls and fine fabrics.

2 (x 2)

1 28,00 - - -

2 (x 2)

1 28,00 - - -

1(x 3)

1 - 7 - 1 65,00 7 370,00

Fenestrelle

Meizoun Blancho

at Mentoulles, via Granges 10,
10060 Fenestrelle (TO)
Tel. 012183933 Fax 012183933

This farmhouse accommodation is at an altitude of over 1000 m. The name, which means 'The White House', is a reminder that this is a area where Provençal (closely related to French) is spoken.

2 (x 1/2)

1 20,75 - 33,60 -

3 (x 2)

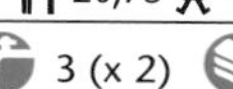 
1 20,75 - 33,60 -

-

1 - 7 - 1 - 7 -

Gavi

Valle del Sole

borgata Alice, cascina S. Martino 1,
15066 Gavi (AL)
Tel. 0143643102

In the basin in the hills crossed by the Leme, accommodation is available in a renovated farmhouse surrounded by meadows and close to a wood.

-

1 - - -

3 (x 2/4)

1 32,50 - 57,00 -

-

1 - 7 - 1 - 7 -

Giaveno

La Patuana

at Sala, via S. Francesco d'Assisi 178,
10094 Giaveno (TO)
Tel. 0119377182 Fax 0119377182

This accommodation is available in a renovated farmhouse in the hills, in the district of the Comunità Montana della Val Sangone.

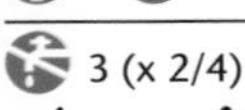 

3 (x 2/4)

1 25,00 - 37,00 -

-

1 - - -

-

1 - 7 - 1 - 7 -

Ivrea

La Perulina

via S. Pietro Martire 35, 10015 Ivrea (TO)
Tel. 012545222 Fax 012545222

Amid the chestnut trees of the Serra d'Ivrea, peaceful accommodation is available in a farm where bee-keeping, crop-growing and stock-raising are the main activities.

-

1 - - -

4 (x 2/4)

1 24,00 - 44,00 -

-

1 - 7 - 1 - 7 -

La Morra

Erbaluna

borgata Pozzo 43, 12064 La Morra (CN)
Tel. 017350800 Fax 0173509336
Web: www.erbaluna.it

In the setting of the Langhe, this renovated old farmhouse has very spacious rooms with early 20th-century furniture.

1 (x 2)

1 27,50 10,00 - -

4 (x 2/4)

1 27,50 10,00 - -

2(x 2)

1 - 7 - 1 85,00 7 -

La Ca' d'Olga

at Rivalta, borgata Caminali 46,
12064 La Morra (CN)
Tel. 0173509763 Fax 0173500854
Web: www.agriturismolacadolga.it

Ideal for a peaceful holiday, this group of farmhouses has been refurbished with a sense of tradition and the accent on comfort.

-
1 - - -

3 (x 2)
1 40,00 15,00 - -

1(x 4)
1 - 7 - 1 95,00 7 600,00

LESSOLO

LA MINIERA

at Calea, via Miniere 9, 10010 Lessolo (TO)
Tel. 012558618 Fax 0125561963
Web: www.laminiera.it

Close to the beginning of the Valle d'Aosta, between the Serra d'Ivrea and the Dora Baltea, this is very unusual accommodation, housed in the buildings of the former mine of Brosso.

2 (x 2)
1 23,50 - - -

-
1 - - -

2 (x 3/10)
1 23,50 7 - 1 - 7 -

MANTA

LE CAMELIE

via Collina 4, 12030 Manta (CN)
Tel. 017585422 Fax 017585422

Now the property of the Fondo Ambiente Italiano, the medieval castle at Manta upholds the traditions of an area noted for the beauty of its landscape.

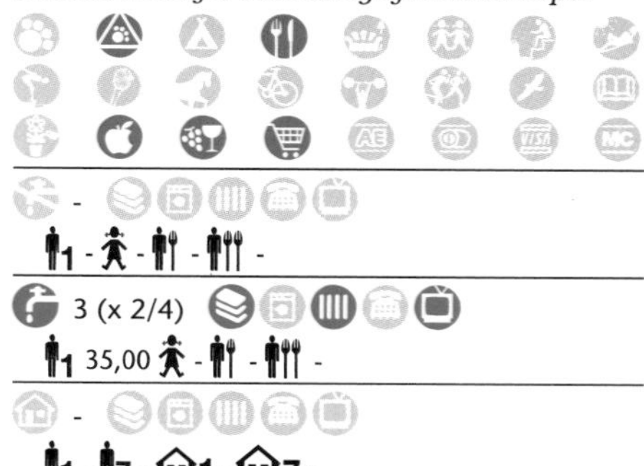

-
1 - - -

3 (x 2/4)
1 35,00 - - -

-
1 - 7 - 1 - 7 -

MATTIE

IL MULINO

at Giordani 52, 10050 Mattie (TO)
Tel. 012238132 Fax 012238132
Web: www.mulinomattie.it

Horse-riding is possible in the pleasant setting of the Val di Susa. Guests stay in this old mill, which has been converted to provide tourist accommodation.

10 (x 2)

1 25,00 20,00 - 60,00

3 (x 2)

1 31,00 20,00 - 65,00

\-

1 - 7 - 1 - 7 -

Occitania

E D

at Giordani, via La Losa 2, 10050 Mattie (TO)
Tel. 012238444 Fax 012238444
E-mail: agriturismoccitania@libero.it

This establishment is in the Val di Susa, just below the Orsiera Rocciavrè Nature Park, amid splendid mountains; just a few kilometres away are the Sacra di San Michele and Avigliana.

\-

1 - - - -

2 (x 2)

1 25,00 12,00 45,00 -

\-

1 - 7 - 1 - 7 -

Mezzomerico

Cargandino

E

road for Vaprio, 28040 Mezzomerico (NO)
Tel. 0321923008 Fax 0321923008

The farm has large rooms with balconies for its guests in an excellently renovated house; there's an airfield for ultralights and helicopters.

\-

1 - - - -

10 (x 2)

1 22,50 - - -

\-

1 - 7 - 1 - 7 -

Moasca

Il Rifugio

regione Ronco 4, 14050 Moasca (AT)
Tel. **0141856446** Fax **0141856569**
Web: **www.ilrifugio.com**

In the Monferrato, amid vineyards producing Moscato and Barbera, this 19th-century farmhouse, with a large garden and a homely atmosphere, is in a dominant position.

\-

1 - - - -

5 (x 1/2)

1 42,00 15,00 57,00 -

\-

1 - 7 - 1 - 7 -

Monastero di Lanzo

Salvin

borgata Mussa 40,
10070 Monastero di Lanzo (TO)
Tel. **012327205** Fax **01234325**
Web: **www.rifugiosalvin.com**

This accommodation is in a mountain hut amid the farm's cattle and the horses reserved for the guests. This is the ideal place for observing the natural phenomena and rock-climbing.

8 (x 2/4)

1 - - 40,00 -

-
1 - - -

1(x 2)

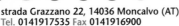

1 - 7 - 1 - 7 300,00

Moncalvo

La Quercia Rossa

strada Grazzano 22, 14036 Moncalvo (AT)
Tel. 0141917535 Fax 0141916900
Web: www.querciarossa.com

Amid vineyards and hazel groves in the first hills of the Monferrato, an 18th-century farmhouse provides accommodation in comfortable rooms and serves meals.

-
1 - - -

10 (x 2)
1 37,50 - 55,00 -

-
1 - 7 - 1 - 7 -

Moncucco Torinese

Graglia Roberto

via Bocchettino 6,
14024 Moncucco Torinese (AT)
Tel. 0119874621

Rooms with a view of the hills are available on a real working farm, where a traditional approach is also evident in the wholesome food served to guests.

-
1 - - -

1 (x 2)
1 20,00 - 31,00 -

1(x 4)
1 21,00 7 - 1 - 7 185,00

Niella Belbo

Mozzone Battista

at Pian Lea 2, 12050 Niella Belbo (CN)
Tel. 0173796108 Fax 01733796108

The upper Belbo Valley is the spectacular setting for a holiday that will be spent discovering the gastronomic delights and superb wines of the Langhe.

-
1 - - -

3 (x 2)
1 21,00 - 40,00 -

-
1 - 7 - 1 - 7 -

Niella Tanaro

Fornelli

at Fornello 1, 12060 Niella Tanaro (CN)
Tel. 0174226181 Fax 0174226181

In area surrounded by hills, guests are accommodated in the rustic rooms of an early 19th-century farmhouse that has been adapted to meet modern requirements.

-
1 - - -

3 (x 4)
1 25,00 - 38,00 -

5(x 2)
1 20,00 7 - 1 - 7 -

Nizza Monferrato

Monsignorotti

at San Nicolao 87, 14049 Nizza Monferrato (AT)
Tel. 0141721100 Fax 0141721100
Web: www.monsignorotti.it

Surrounded by the rolling hills of the Monferrato, this attractive renovated farmhouse built round a large courtyard has rooms with modern comforts.

\-

1 - - - -

9 (x 1/2) 

1 40,00 - - -

\-

1 - 7 - 1 - 7 -

Novi Ligure

Cascina degli Ulivi

strada della Mazzola 14, 15067 Novi Ligure (AL)
Tel. 0143744598 Fax 0143320898
E-mail: cascinadegliulivi@libero.it

In the hills flanking the Scrivia, surrounded by vineyards, old villages and castles, there are views of the Ligurian Apennines in one direction and the Monferrato in the other.

\-

1 - - - -

4 (x 4)

1 25,00 15,00 36,00 -

\-

1 - 7 - 1 - 7 -

Pinerolo

Fiorendo

at Talucco, via Talucco Alto 65, 10064 Pinerolo (TO)
Tel. 0121543481 Fax 0121543481
E-mail: fiorendo@libero.it

This mountain farm is in a panoramic position surrounded by chestnut woods. This peaceful place is the starting-point for hikes of special interest to nature lovers.

\-

1 - - - -

5 (x 2/4)

1 25,00 - 42,00 -

2 (x 4/5)

1 - 7 - 1 - 7 465,00

Pomaretto

Lâ Chabranda

via E. Long 28, 10063 Pomaretto (TO)
Tel. 012182018 Fax 012182018

This accommodation is at the bottom of the valley. The area is of interest not only for hiking and tours on mountain bikes, but also for visits to the talc mine and the fort of Fenestrelle.

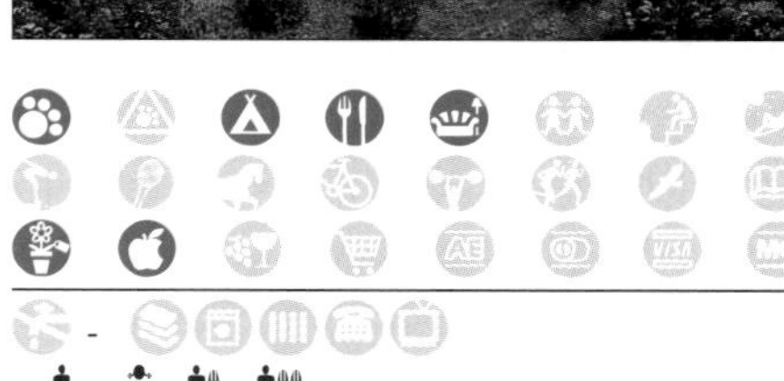

\-

1 - - - -

4 (x 4)

1 24,00 - 35,00 -

\-

1 - 7 - 1 - 7 -

Pontestura

Cascina Smeralda

strada Coniolo Vialarda 1, 15027 Pontestura (AL)
Tel. 0142466275 Fax 0142466275
Web: www.agriturismocascinasmeralda.it

In this late 17th-century manor-house, yellowing photos are a reminder of how the hard-working country folk used to live in the past; now farming is supplemented by rural tourism.

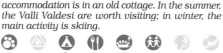

-
1 - - -

3 (x 2)

1 33,00 - 48,00 -

-

1 - 7 - 1 - 7 -

Rorà

Sibourgh

via Fornaci 4, 10060 Rorà (TO)
Tel. 012193105 Fax 012193105

In the mountain district of the Valle del Pellice, the accommodation is in an old cottage. In the summer, the Valli Valdesi are worth visiting; in winter, the main activity is skiing.

-
1 - - -

4 (x 2/4)

1 30,00 - 44,00 -

-

1 - 7 - 1 - 7 -

San Marzano Oliveto

La Viranda

regione Corte 68/69,
14050 San Marzano Oliveto (AT)
Tel. 0141856571 Fax 014175735
E-mail: laviranda@tin.it

This late 19th-century farmhouse is surrounded by vineyards producing Moscato d'Asti; it has a large restaurant and spacious rooms with traditional furnishings and fine views.

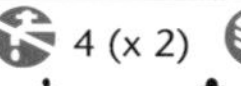

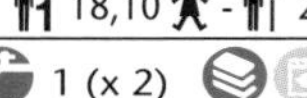

4 (x 2)

1 18,10 - 23,30 -

1 (x 2)

1 18,10 - 23,30 -

-

1 - 7 - 1 - 7 -

San Sebastiano Curone

La Battignana

15056 San Sebastiano Curone (AL)
Tel. 0131786252 Fax 0131786129

Located in the Curone Valley, this farmhouse dates from 1789, when this area, now frequented by gourmets, was infested by brigands.

-

1 - - -

7 (x 1/4)

29,00 13,00 42,00 -

1(x 2)

- - - 300,00

SAUZE DI CESANA

ALPE PLANE

at Valle Argentera, 10054 Sauze di Cesana (TO)
Tel. 330685278

This accommodation is located below the Colle di Sestriere. There's plenty to keep guests busy here: hiking and climbing, as well as trout-fishing in the Dora river.

4 (x 4)

- - 35,00 -

-

- - - -

-

- - - -

SERRALUNGA DI CREA

TENUTA GUAZZAURA

at La Madonnina, via Guazzaura 9,
15020 Serralunga di Crea (AL)
Tel. 0142940289 Fax 0142940289
E-mail: guazzaura@dada.it

This imposing 18th-century villa has outbuildings, a park and a spectacular tree-lined drive; courses on various aspects of the rural world are held here.

-

- - - -

-

- - - -

5 (x 2/3)

- - 57,00 341,00

SINIO

LE ARCATE

at Gabutto 2, 12050 Sinio (CN)
Tel. 0173613152 Fax 0173613152
Web: www.agriturismolearcate.it

Sinio is a medieval jewel not far from Alba, and the splendid view it offers will only increase the traveller's delight.

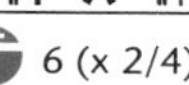 

-

- - - -

6 (x 2/4)

33,00 - 45,00 -

-

- - - -

SOMMARIVA PERNO

LA CIUENDA

at Ciura 23, 12040 Sommariva Perno (CN)
Tel. 017246286 Fax 017246286
Web: www.agripiu.it/ciuenda

The chestnut woods, vineyards, orchards and market gardens of this farm, which extends into three communes, are the first things that attract the guests' attention (and may involve them directly).

2 (x 2)

31,00 - - -

STAZZANO

LA TRAVERSINA

cascina Traversina 109, 15060 Stazzano (AL)
Tel. 014361377 Fax 014361377
Web: www.latraversina.com

This is rural tourism for romantic souls: the blaze of roses and mass of irises surrounding the house create a setting of uncommon beauty.

-

1 - - -

2 (x 2)

1 49,00 - 68,00 -

4 (x 2/4)

1 - 7 - 1 - 7 1.010,00

TREISO

IL CILIEGIO

via Meruzzano 21, 12050 Treiso (CN)
Tel. 0173630126 Fax 0173638970
Web: www.ilciliegio.it

In the countryside of the Bassa Langa, with its intense cultivation of the vine, accommodation is provided by two typical rural houses, recently renovated and surrounded by greenery.

-

1 - - -

3 (x 2/4)

1 23,50 - -

5 (x 4/6)

1 - 7 - 1 - 7 450,00

RIZZI

via Rizzi 15, 12050 Treiso (CN)
Tel. 0173638161 Fax 0173638935
Web: www.cantinarizzi.it

Set among vineyards producing Barbaresco, Barbera, Dolcetto and Moscato d'Asti, this attractively renovated farmhouse is ideal for a holiday focusing on wine.

3 (x 2)

1 26,00 - -

1 (x 2)

1 26,00 - -

-

1 - 7 - 1 - 7 -

TREZZO TINELLA

ANTICO BORGO DEL RIONDINO

via dei Fiori 13, 12050 Trezzo Tinella (CN)
Tel. 0173630313 Fax 0173630313

A medieval village, in the centre of an amphitheatre with vineyards, meadows and woods, is the setting for this beautifully refurbished house offering accommodation.

\-

1 - - -

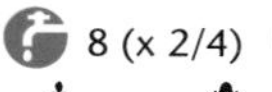 8 (x 2/4) 

 1 67,15 - -

\-

 1 - 7 - 1 - 7 -

VALENZA

CASCINA NUOVA

road for Pavia 2, 15048 Valenza (AL)
Tel. 0131954120 Fax 0131928553
E-mail: cascinanuova@tin.it

The poplars and willows lining the Po form the backdrop to the flight of the herons. To the delight of bird-watchers, the farm is located in a nature reserve.

\-

 1 - - -

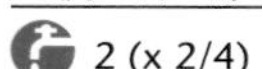 2 (x 2/4)

 1 30,00 - -

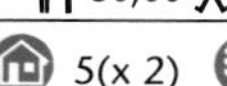 5(x 2) 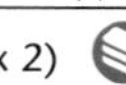   

 1 - 7 - 1 80,00 7 400,00

VILLA GROPELLA

road for Solero 8, 15048 Valenza (AL)
Tel. 0131951166 Fax 0131927255
Web: www.gropella.it

This 18th-century villa with an old park and private chapel is ideal for a holiday in style. The farm buildings are adjacent, surrounding a large courtyard.

\-

1 - - -

 7 (x 1/2)

1 36,00 20,00 - -

\-

1 - 7 - 1 - 7 -

VARZO

ALPE CORTIGGIO

at Alpe Cortiggio, 28868 Varzo (VB)
Tel. 032472436

The setting is that of the Val Divedro, through which the road to the Simplon Pass runs. The farm is on the high pastures of the confluent Val Cairasca.

 4 (x 2)

1 21,00 - - 46,00

\-

1 - - -

\-

1 - 7 - 1 - 7 -

VERBANIA

MONTEROSSO

at Cima Monterosso 30, 28048 Verbania
Tel. 0323556510 Fax 0323519706
Web: www.paginegialle.it/ristorovb

This accommodation is in a farmhouse surrounded by 25 hectares of woods crossed by marked paths that can be explored on foot, horseback or mountain bikes.

\-

1 - - -

9 (x 1/4)

1 36,00 20,50 52,00 -

1(x 4)

1 - 7 - 1 - 7 700,00

Vigliano d'Asti

Cascina del Tiglio

via Nalbissano 24, 14040 Vigliano d'Asti (AT)
Tel. 0141951204 Fax 0141953468
Web: www.tiglio.it

Between the Monferrato and the Langhe, accommodation is available in this farmhouse with splendid views, traditional furnishings and excellent food.

\-

1 - - -

2 (x 2)

1 35,00 - - -

3(x 4)

1 - 7 - 1 130,00 7 -

Vignale Monferrato

Ca' San Lorenzo

at Ca' San Lorenzo 24,
15049 Vignale Monferrato (AL)
Tel. 0142933314 Fax 0142933314

On one side is the Monferrato, on the other, towards the Po, Casale. The accommodation is in a building that was already a welcome stopping-place in the 18th century, when it was a post-house.

4 (x 2)

1 25,00 - - -

1 (x 4)

1 25,00 - - -

\-

1 - 7 - 1 - 7 -

Cascina Alberta

at Cascina Prano 14,
15049 Vignale Monferrato (AL)
Tel. 0142933313 Fax 0142933313
E-mail: cascinalberta@italnet.it

Surrounded on three sides by vineyards and market gardens, this complex offering accommodation dominates a pleasant rural scene, with cultivated fields and clumps of trees.

\-

1 - - -

5 (x 2)

1 26,00 - 42,00 -

\-

1 - 7 - 1 - 7 -

Il Mongetto

via Piave 2, 15049 Vignale Monferrato (AL)
Tel. 0142933442 Fax 0142933469
Web: www.mongetto.it

The Monferrato is noted for its beautiful landscape and excellent cuisine. Here there's the added pleasure of a holiday in a villa, with its frescoes and period furniture.

 2 (x 2)

1 25,00 - - -

 3 (x 2)

1 30,00 - - -

 -

1 - 7 - 1 - 7 -

La Pomera

at San Lorenzo, 15049 Vignale Monferrato (AL)
Tel. 0142933378
Web: www.lapomera.it

In the land where Barbera del Monferrato holds sway, the hills are also bountiful in other ways: for instance, fruit and vegetables, as at the Pomera, where old varieties of apples are grown.

-

1 - - - -

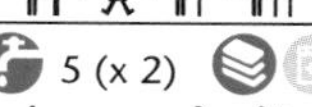 5 (x 2)

1 30,00 - - -

 -

1 - 7 - 1 - 7 -

PUGLIA

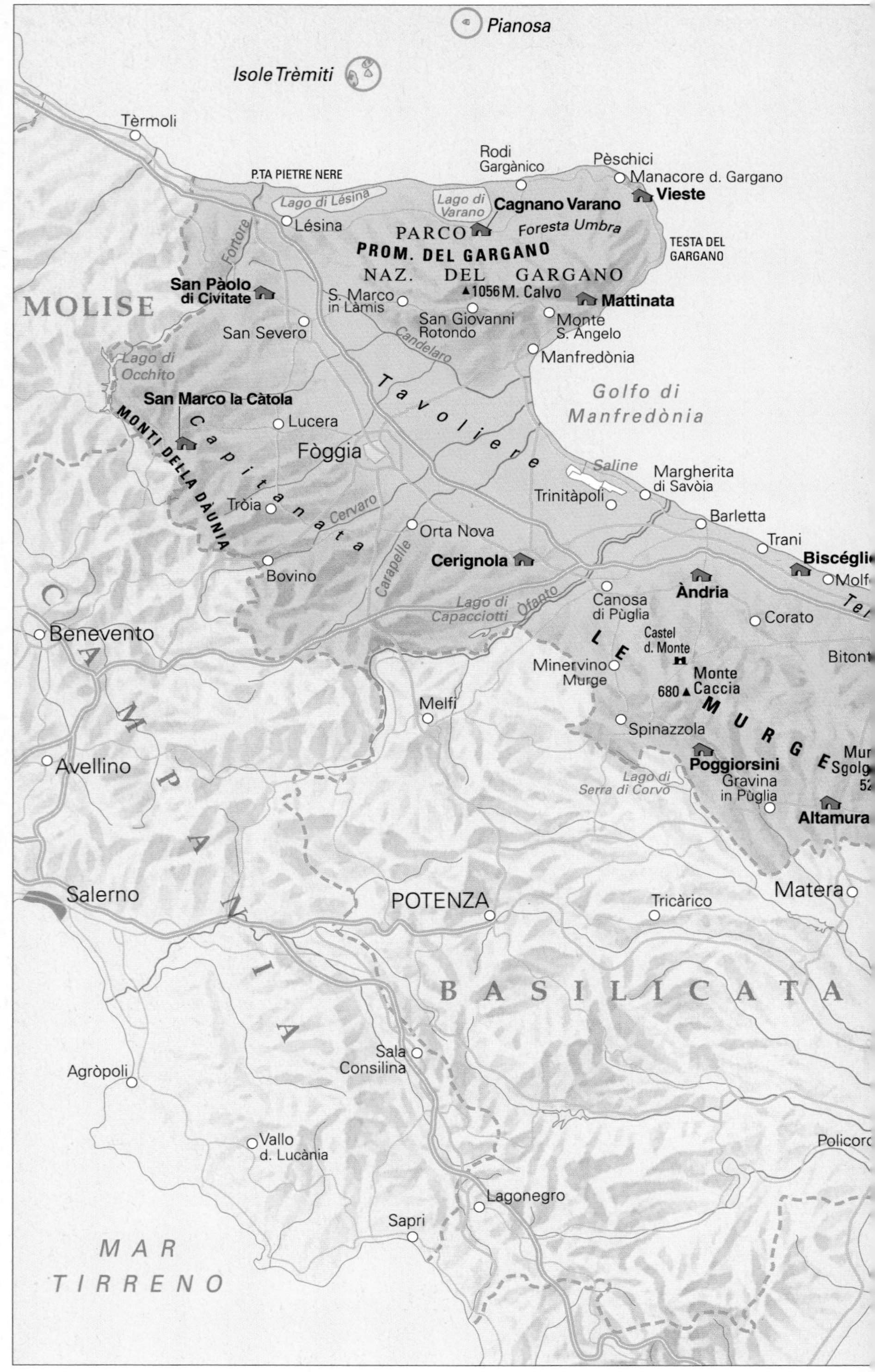
Pianosa
Isole Trèmiti
Tèrmoli
P.TA PIETRE NERE
Lago di Lésina
Lésina
Fortore
Rodi Gargànico
Pèschici
Manacore d. Gargano
Vieste
Lago di Varano
Cagnano Varano
PARCO
Foresta Umbra
PROM. DEL GARGANO
NAZ. DEL GARGANO
TESTA DEL GARGANO
MOLISE
San Pàolo di Civitate
S. Marco in Làmis
1056 M. Calvo
Mattinata
San Severo
San Giovanni Rotondo
Monte S. Angelo
Candelaro
Manfredònia
Lago di Occhito
Tavoliere
Golfo di Manfredònia
San Marco la Càtola
MONTI DELLA DÀUNIA
Capitanata
Lucera
Fòggia
Saline
Margherita di Savòia
Trinitàpoli
Tròia
Cervaro
Barletta
Orta Nova
Trani
Cerignola
Biscégli
Bovino
Carapelle
Àndria
Molf
Canosa di Pùglia
Lago di Capacciotti
Ofanto
Corato
Benevento
LE MURGE
Castel d. Monte
Bitont
Minervino Murge
Monte Caccia
680
CAMPANIA
Melfi
Spinazzola
Avellino
Poggiorsini
Lago di Serra di Corvo
Gravina in Pùglia
Altamura
Salerno
POTENZA
Tricàrico
Matera
BASILICATA
Sala Consilina
Agròpoli
Vallo d. Lucània
Policor
Lagonegro
Sapri
MAR TIRRENO

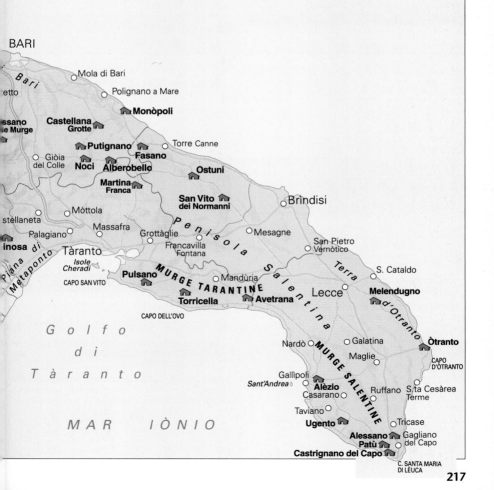

0
20
40
60 km
MAR ADRIÀTICO
BARI
Bari
etto
Mola di Bari
Polignano a Mare
Monòpoli
ssano
e Murge
Castellana
Grotte
Putignano
Fasano
Torre Canne
Giòia
del Colle
Noci
Alberobello
Ostuni
Martina
Franca
San Vito
dei Normanni
Brìndisi
Mòttola
stellaneta
Massafra
Palagiano
Grottàglie
Mesagne
Penisola Salentina
inosa
Francavilla
Fontana
San Pietro
Vernòtico
Tàranto
Isole
Cheradi
Piana di Metaponto
CAPO SAN VITO
Pulsano
MURGE TARANTINE
Mandùria
Terra d'Otranto
S. Cataldo
Torricella
Avetrana
Lecce
Melendugno
CAPO DELL'OVO
Golfo di Tàranto
Nardò
Galatina
Òtranto
Maglie
CAPO
D'ÒTRANTO
MURGE SALENTINE
Gallìpoli
Sant'Andrea
Alèzio
Casarano
Ruffano
S.ta Cesàrea
Terme
Taviano
Ugento
Tricase
MAR IÒNIO
Alessano
Gagliano
del Capo
Patù
Castrignano del Capo
C. SANTA MARIA
DI LÈUCA

Alberobello

Abbondanza

contrada Lama Colonna 5, 70011 Alberobello (BA)
Tel. 0804325762 Fax 0804325762
Web: www.abbondanzagriturismo.com

Just a few minutes' drive from the village, the farm is surrounded by olive groves and ancient oaks; it comprises a number of old buildings and a trullo (traditional Apulian inhabitation).

\-

1 - - -

3 (x 2)

1 33,57 15,50 - -

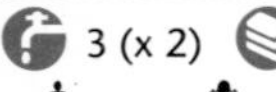 

3 (x 2/6)

1 33,57 7 222,08 1 - 7 -

Villa Raggio di Sole

contrada Villa Curri 5, 70011 Alberobello (BA)
Tel. 0804321248

This large farm has modern apartments on two floors, with a terrace and a barbecue area outside.

\-

1 - - -

\-

1 - - -

12(x 4)

1 - 7 - 1 100,00 7 -

Alessano

Masseria Macurano

contrada Macurano 1, 73031 Alessano (LE)
Tel. 0833524287
Web: www.masseriamacurano.com

In a fortified 16th-century farmhouse, accommodation is available in very large rooms, with ceilings formed by cross- or barrel-vaulting and rustic furniture.

\-

1 - - -

5 (x 2)

1 30,00 - - -

1(x 3)

1 30,00 7 - 1 - 7 440,00

Alezio

Santa Chiara

via Provinciale Parabita, 73011 Alezio (LE)
Tel. 0833281708 Fax 0833281290
E-mail: antcataldi@tin.it

In an old country house, formerly belonging to the Order of Poor Clares, there are large airy rooms with the atmosphere of a bygone age.

6 (x 2/4)

26,00 - 50,00 -

2 (x 2/4)

- - - 574,00

ALTAMURA

MADONNA DELL'ASSUNTA

S.S. (state road) 378 at km 45, 70022 Altamura (BA)
Tel. **0803103328** Fax **0803103328**

This establishment is housed in a fascinating 18th-century monastery that has a chapel and large spaces for the restaurant.

-

- - -

4 (x 2/4)

23,00 - 40,00 -

-

- - - -

ANDRIA

IACOVIELLO ANTONINO

contrada Lamacaminata, 70031 Andria (BA)
Tel. **330355354**

In the north-western Murgia, in a windy position, this is a rustic stone building that has recently been renovated and has large self-contained rooms.

-

- - -

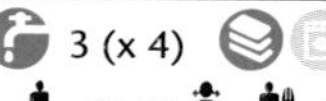

3 (x 4)

20,65 - 41,32 -

-

- - - -

AVETRANA

BOSCO DI MUDONATO

contrada Bosco Mudonato, 74020 Avetrana (TA)
Tel. **0999704597** Fax **0999704597**

Small but carefully furnished rooms and the airy forms of Mediterranean architecture characterise this building surrounded by an oak-wood.

-

- - -

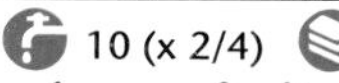

10 (x 2/4)  

50,00 - 70,00 -

-

- - - -

BISCEGLIE

LE VEDUTE

S.P. Corato-Molfetta at km 6.2, 70052 Bisceglie (BA)
Tel. **0803952416** Fax **0803952416**
Web: **www.geocities.com/hippospuglia**

Accommodation is available in modern buildings; there's a stud-farm with riding courses - it is a FISE (Italian Federation of Equestrian Sports) centre - and the food is also highly recommended.

1 - - -

7 (x 2/4)

1 28,40 - -

1 - 7 - 1 - 7 -

CAGNANO VARANO

FALCARE

contrada Falcare, 71010 Cagnano Varano (FG)
Tel. 08848238 Fax 08848232
Web: www.agriturismofalcare.it

There is a blend of old and new in the three buildings used as the family's house, the communal spaces and the guests' accommodation.

1 - - -

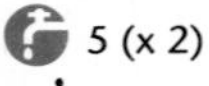

5 (x 2)

1 27,00 18,00 40,00 -

1 - 7 - 1 - 7 -

CASSANO DELLE MURGE

AMICIZIA

via Cristo Fasano 162,
70020 Cassano delle Murge (BA)
Tel. 080763393 Fax 080763393

An old farm in the Murgia Barese, with quiet self-contained rooms in the former sheepfolds, while food is served in the modern owners' house.

1 - - -

12 (x 1/2)

1 28,00 18,00 49,00 -

1 - 7 - 1 - 7 -

MASSERIA RUÒTOLO

contrada Ruòtolo, via Lago di Nuzzi,
70020 Cassano delle Murge (BA)
Tel. 080764511 Fax 080764511
Web: www.paginegialle.it/ruotolo-01

In the fascinating setting of the Murge, surrounded by olive groves and scrubland, guests are accommodated in the large rooms of this 19th-century farmhouse.

1 - - -

6 (x 1/4) 

1 42,00 - 52,00 -

1(x 6)

1 42,00 7 - 1 - 7 -

Castellana-Grotte

Serragambetta

via Conversano 204, 70013 Castellana-Grotte (BA)
Tel. 0804965487 Fax 0804962181
Web: www.serragambetta.it

This late 19th-century complex, the villa and a number of outbuildings belonging to the winery have been splendidly converted to provide accommodation.

-

1 - - - -

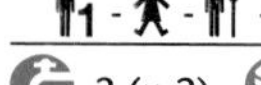

2 (x 2)

1 37,00 26,00 56,00 -

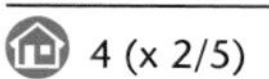 4 (x 2/5) 

1 - 7 - 1 210,00 7 -

Castrignano del Capo

Serine

contrada Serine, 73040 Castrignano del Capo (LE)
Tel. 0833751337 Fax 0833753521
Web: www.agriturismoserine.it

Only two kilometres from Santa Maria di Leuca, accommodation is available in small, carefully renovated apartments, furnished in a simple but tasteful manner.

-

1 - - - -

-

1 - - - -

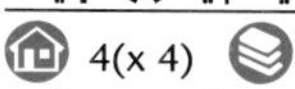 4(x 4) 

1 52,00 7 - 1 - 7 -

Cerignola

Masseria San Lorenzo

at Torre Quarto, 71042 Cerignola (FG)
Tel. 0885418436 Fax 0885418460
Web: www.masseriasanlorenzo.com

Comfortable self-contained rooms are available in the outbuildings of the main villa, which was originally a hunting-lodge surrounded by a private wood.

-

1 - - - -

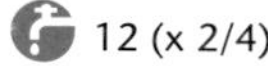 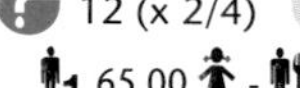

12 (x 2/4)

1 65,00 - - -

-

1 - 7 - 1 - 7 -

Fasano

Masseria Maccarone

contrada Carbonelli 29, 72015 Fasano (BR)
Tel. 0804829300 Fax 0804413085
Web: www.masseriamaccarone.it

This monumental complex of the 17th century comprises the owners' house and church, as well as the farmhouses where the guests' rooms are located.

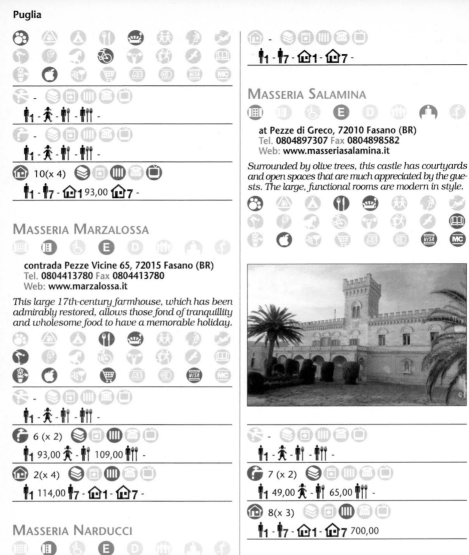

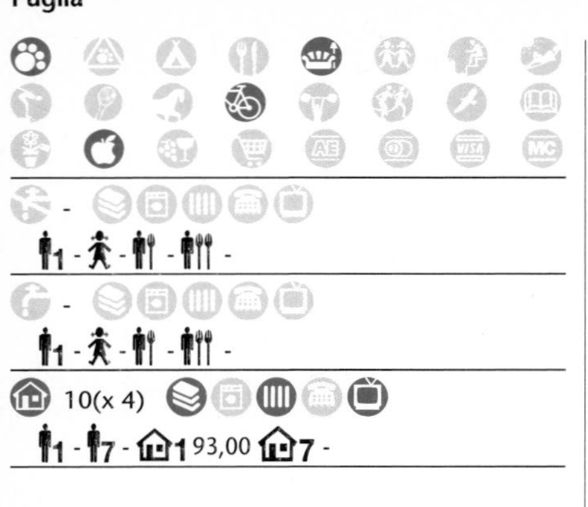

\-

1 - - - -

\-

1 - - - -

10(x 4)

1 - 7 - 1 93,00 7 -

Masseria Marzalossa

contrada Pezze Vicine 65, 72015 Fasano (BR)
Tel. 0804413780 Fax 0804413780
Web: www.marzalossa.it

This large 17th-century farmhouse, which has been admirably restored, allows those fond of tranquillity and wholesome food to have a memorable holiday.

\-

1 - - - -

6 (x 2)

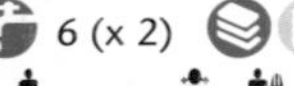

1 93,00 - 109,00 -

2(x 4)

1 114,00 7 - 1 - 7 -

Masseria Narducci

at Speziale, via Lecce 131, 72016 Fasano (BR)
Tel. 0804810185 Fax 0804810185
Web: www.agriturismonarducci.it

This complex surrounds an old post-house; the restaurant is particularly remarkable for its setting and the variety of farm produce it serves.

\-

1 - - - -

9 (x 2/4)

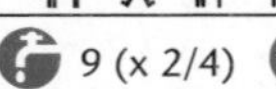

1 31,00 - 57,00 -

\-

1 - 7 - 1 - 7 -

Masseria Salamina

at Pezze di Greco, 72010 Fasano (BR)
Tel. 0804897307 Fax 0804898582
Web: www.masseriasalamina.it

Surrounded by olive trees, this castle has courtyards and open spaces that are much appreciated by the guests. The large, functional rooms are modern in style.

\-

1 - - - -

7 (x 2)

1 49,00 - 65,00 -

8(x 3)

1 - 7 - 1 - 7 700,00

Ottava Piccola

at Montalbano, 72016 Fasano (BR)
Tel. 0804810902 Fax 0804810902
Web: www.agriturist.it

This old farmhouse has carefully furnished rooms with vaulted ceilings. A boat equipped for fishing is also available.

\-

1 - - - -

5 (x 2/4)

1 - - 51,70 -

-

1 - 7 - 1 - 7 -

Parco di Castro

**at Speziale, S.S. (state road) 16 at km 868.4,
72016 Fasano (BR)**
Tel. **0804810944**

Surrounded by palms and bougainvillaea, this 17th-century farmhouse used to belong to the Knights of Malta; delicious Apulian dishes are served at table.

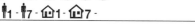

-

1 - - - -

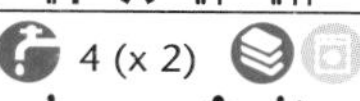

4 (x 2)

1 25,82 - 46,48 -

-

1 - 7 - 1 - 7 -

Ginosa

Valle Rita

contrada Girifalco, 74013 Ginosa (TA)
Tel. **0998271824** Fax **0998271824**
Web: **www.vallerita.it**

In the countryside round Ginosa, accommodation is available in a modern establishment that has functional, comfortable apartments of various types.

-

1 - - - -

-

1 - - - -

9 (x 2/4)

1 - 7 - 1 - 7 900,00

Martina Franca

Il Vignaletto

**via Minco di Tata 1 zona F,
74015 Martina Franca (TA)**
Tel. **0804490354** Fax **0804490387**
Web: **www.vignaletto.it**

In a white farmhouse surrounded by woods, accommodation is available in simple but pleasant rooms; meals are served in a dining-room with rustic furnishings.

Mattinata

Giorgio

contrada Giorgio, 71030 Mattinata (FG)
Tel. 0884551477 Fax 0884552070

The rooms looking out over the olive trees are tastefully furnished. There a museum of rural culture in the old olive-store, and a restaurant with a large, elegant dining-room.

Monte Sacro

contrada Stinco, 71030 Mattinata (FG)
Tel. 0884558941 Fax 0884558941
Web: www.montesacroagritur.it

This hill farm commands a superb view over the highlands of the Gargano and the sea; accommodation is also available in a number of bungalows.

- 7 (x 2/4) 31,00 - 46,50 -
- 14 (x 2/4) - - - 830,00

Melendugno

Masseria Malapezza

at Borgagne, 73020 Melendugno (LE)
Tel. 0832811402
Web: www.salentopoint.com/aziendaagrituristica malapezza

In the countryside of the Salento, self-contained apartments are available with verandas and terraces. Guests may freely consume the produce from the vegetable garden.

- 5(x 4) 22,00 - - -

Monopoli

Curatori

contrada Cristo delle Zolle 227,
70043 Monopoli (BA)
Tel. 080777472 Fax 080777472
E-mail: agricurcon@libero.it

There's a touch of pink in the countryside thanks to this 18th-century farmhouse about 1 km from the village and 3 km from the sea and hills.

\-

1 - - -

2 (x 2)

1 24,00 16,00 40,00 -

3 (x 4/6)

1 30,00 7 - 1 - 7 -

Noci

Le Casedde

at Giordanello, zona B/23, 70015 Noci (BA)
Tel. 0804978946 Fax 0804978946

Guests are accommodated in the curious setting of the Apulian 'trulli' inhabitations or in functional rooms in the converted cowsheds, with pleasant open spaces outside and well-arranged interiors.

\-

1 - - -

5 (x 2)

1 29,00 15,00 52,00 -

1(x 6)

1 - 7 - 1 170,00 7 -

Ostuni

Il Frantoio

S.S. (state road) 16 at km 874, 72017 Ostuni (BR)
Tel. 0831330276 Fax 0831330276
Web: www.trecolline.it

There's an excellent combination between history and quality accommodation in this fortified farmhouse, built in the 17th century over an ancient olive-press in a cave.

\-

1 - - -

8 (x 1/4)

1 88,00 52,00 126,00 -

\-

1 - 7 - 1 - 7 -

I Poderi del Sole

contrada Tamburroni, 72017 Ostuni (BR)
Tel. 0831991761 Fax 0831991761
Web: www.ipoderidelsole.it

The accommodation is in a number of charming cottages; guests may consume the fruit and vegetables produced on the farm free of charge.

\-

1 - - -

\-

1 - - -

1(x 4)

1 - 7 - 1 - 7 550,00

Masseria Salinola

contrada Salinola 134, 72017 Ostuni (BR)
Tel. 0831330683 Fax 0831308330
Web: www.agriturismo.com/salinola

This picturesque 18th-century farmhouse, surrounded by olive trees and flowers, has a swimming pool with a Jacuzzi, pergolas and terraces where guests can take things easy; there are large rooms for banquets.

\-

1 - - -

5 (x 2)

1 26,00 - 65,00 -

6 (x 2/4)

1 - 7 - 1 85,00 7 560,00

Sant'Andrea

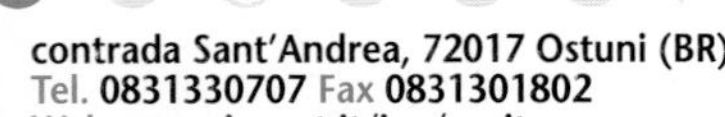

contrada Sant'Andrea, 72017 Ostuni (BR)
Tel. 0831330707 Fax 0831301802
Web: www.igsnet.it/ipa/agritour

This 19th-century farm with its outbuildings is surrounded by ancient olives and almond trees; it has a large restaurant serving hearty regional dishes.

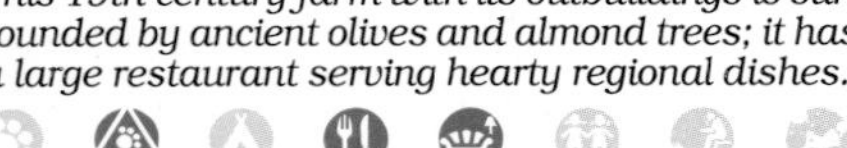

\-

1 - - -

\-

1 - - -

9(x 2)

1 - 7 - 1 98,00 7 -

Otranto

Il Piccolo Lago

at Fontanelle 137, 73028 Otranto (LE)
Tel. 0836805628
Web: www.ilpiccololago.it

Just inland from the coast, in sight of the Alimini lakes, two-room flats are available in terraced houses with front gardens and cultivated land all around.

\-

1 - - -

\-

1 - - -

5(x 4)

1 - 7 - 1 - 7 700,00

La Fattoria

S.S. (state road) Otranto-Uggiano,
73028 Otranto (LE)
Tel. 0836804651 Fax 0836804651
Web: www.lafattoria.otranto.it

This farm offers accommodation in large rooms, simply furnished but comfortable, and in well-equipped bungalows with kitchenettes.

1 - - -

7 (x 2/4)

1 - - 42,00 -

6 (x 2/4)

1 - 7 - 1 - 7 500,00

Torre Pinta

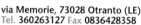

via Memorie, 73028 Otranto (LE)
Tel. 360263127 Fax 0836428358

This is a corner of paradise where, from the top of the tower, there's a splendid view of the valley with its rich colours and perfumes, while the blue sea lies beyond.

1 - - -

7 (x 2/4)

1 45,00 - 70,00 -

1(x 4)

1 50,00 7 - 1 - 7 -

Patù

Masseria San Nicola

at San Nicola, 73053 Patù (LE)
Tel. 0833752243 Fax 0833752243
Web: www.masseriasannicola.it

This 16th-century farmhouse offers accommodation in simple but comfortable rooms and in a number of apartments with vaulted ceilings and bare stone walls.

1 - - -

1 - - -

7 (x 2/3)

1 - 7 - 1 - 7 362,00

Poggiorsini

Il Cardinale

contrada Capoposta, 70020 Poggiorsini (BA)
Tel. 0803237279 Fax 0803237279
Web: www.ilcardinale.it

The accommodation is partly in the old house and partly in the outbuildings with their rustic tone; there are special offers for long weekends and public holidays.

1 - - -

10 (x 4)

1 27,00 - 46,00 -

5(x 5)

1 27,00 7 - 1 - 7 -

Pulsano

Tenuta del Barco

at Marina di Pulsano, contrada Porvica,
74026 Pulsano (TA)
Tel. 0995333051
Web: www.tenutadelbarco.com

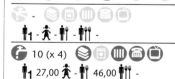

Accommodation is available in seven buildings in converted cowsheds and barns; well-furnished and comfortable, they have excellent bathrooms.

-

1 - - -

10 (x 2)

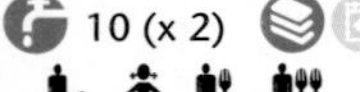

1 - - -

7(x 4)

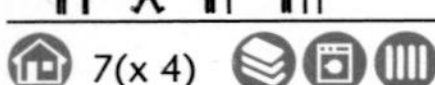

1 - 7 - 1 - 7 1.749,00

-

1 - - -

1 (x 2)

1 10,00 7,50 -

5 (x 2/4)

1 10,00 7 - 1 - 7 -

Putignano

Angiulli Nuova

contrada Conforti, 70017 Putignano (BA)
Tel. **0804057898**
E-mail: **olgatateo@media.it**

Tranquillity and a friendly welcome are guaranteed in this farm offering self-contained rooms with simple early 20th-century furniture.

6 (x 2)

1 21,00 - 33,50 -

-

1 - - -

-

1 - 7 - 1 - 7 -

San Marco la Catola

Casanatura Avellaneta

at San Cristoforo,
71030 San Marco la Catola (FG)
Tel. **0881556115** Fax **0881556115**

A holiday on this farm will be devoted to nature, as its name suggests; this is helped by its commitment to organic methods of agriculture.

San Paolo di Civitate

Difensola Ranch

contrada Difensola 976,
71010 San Paolo di Civitate (FG)
Tel. **330806352** Fax **0882551889**

As appears from its name, this establishment is oriented towards horse-riding; it serves dishes based on the area's traditional cuisine.

-

1 - - -

7 (x 2/4)

1 35,00 - 52,50 -

-

1 - 7 - 1 - 7 -

San Vito dei Normanni

Tenuta Deserto

72019 San Vito dei Normanni (BR)
Tel. **0831983062** Fax **0831983062**
Web: **www.tenutadeserto.it**

In a 17th-century farm complex with a small church and the owner's and steward's houses, accommodation is available in a number of functional apartments in the converted outbuildings.

\-

1 - - -

\-

1 - - -

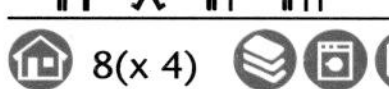

8(x 4)

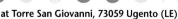

1 - 7 - 1 - 7 1.050,00

TORRICELLA

ANTICA MASSERIA JORCHE

contrada Jorche, 74020 Torricella (TA)
Tel. 0999573355 Fax 0999573053
Web: www.jorche.com

This fine 17th-century farmhouse has been restored without spoiling its original appearance. The rooms, with views over the Salento countryside, are large and airy.

\-

1 - - -

9 (x 2)

1 - - 65,00 -

6(x 4)

1 - 7 - 1 100,00 7 -

UGENTO

PALESE COSIMO

at Torre San Giovanni, 73059 Ugento (LE)
Tel. 0833931581
Web: www.agriturismopalese.8m.com

In a modern building, this small farm provides simple and inexpensive accommodation with a friendly welcome.

\-

1 - - -

8 (x 2)

1 20,00 13,00 42,00 -

\-

1 - 7 - 1 - 7 -

VIESTE

AZZARONE FRANCESCO

contrada Piano Grande, 71019 Vieste (FG)
Tel. 0884701332

Between the dazzling white cliffs and shady beechwoods, simple accommodation is available in a modern building with pleasant terraces and myriads of flowers.

\-

1 - - -

6 (x 2)

1 30,50 - 40,00 -

\-

1 - 7 - 1 - 7 -

PARCO CIMAGLIA

at Pian Piccolo, 71019 Vieste (FG)
Tel. 0884708050 Fax 0884706471
Web: www.garganoagriturismo.it

Accommodation is available in a large farm of 150 hectares extending from the sparkling sea of the Gargano to the beechwoods of the Foresta Umbra.

\-

1 - - -

\-

1 - - -

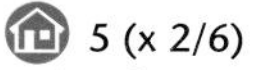

5 (x 2/6)

1 - 7 - 1 107,50 7 -

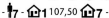

Sarra Balestra - Arzachena (SS) - Tel 0789 98969
www.italiaagriturismo.net/calasomara - calasomara@libero it

Immersed in a magical atmosphere a few minutes away from the Costa Smeralda it welcomes guests eager for a "full immersion" in nature in comfortable and welcoming rooms characterised by their individual style. The fittings are personally looked after by the owners; white washed walls, niches with rounded edges and hand painted ceramic baths. At evening you can sense something mysterious in the magic alternating with the light and shadows given by the many candles and old lanterns. You discover how enjoyable it can be to get away from formality and everyday life.

Azienda Agrituristica
Donna Lina
Orosei

The farm "Donna Lina", 2 Km. far from the sea, stretches for 10 hectares (25 acres) planted with vines (wine and table grapes), olive grove, fruit trees, whose products have been taken for preparing all the meals offered to the guests.
The farmhouse offers a half board service to families and small groups in some confortable lodgings and grants a natural and relaxing holiday.

Via Nazionale, 13
Loc Foiai - OROSEI
Tel. +39 0784 98698, fax +39 0784 997506
e-mail: donnalina@tiscalinet.it

SARDEGNA

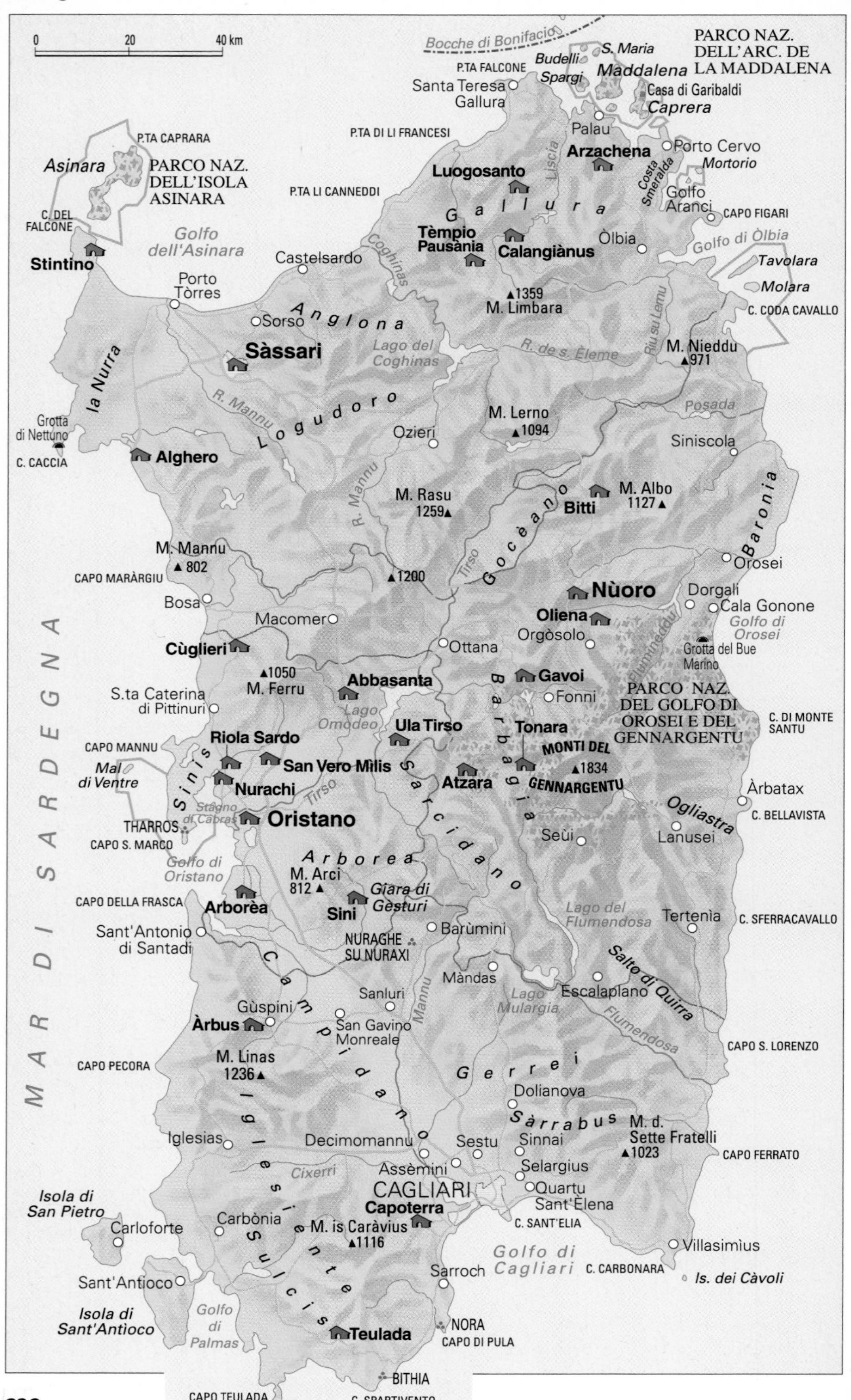

0 20 40 km
Bocche di Bonifacio
PARCO NAZ. DELL'ARC. DE LA MADDALENA
S. Maria
Budelli
Spargi
Maddalena
Casa di Garibaldi
Caprera
P.TA FALCONE
Santa Teresa Gallura
Palau
P.TA CAPRARA
Asinara
PARCO NAZ. DELL'ISOLA ASINARA
P.TA DI LI FRANCESI
Arzachena
Porto Cervo
Mortorio
Costa Smeralda
Luogosanto
Liscia
Golfo Aranci
CAPO FIGARI
P.TA LI CANNEDDI
G a l l u r a
C. DEL FALCONE
Golfo dell'Asinara
Stintino
Tèmpio Pausània
Calangiànus
Òlbia
Golfo di Òlbia
Tavolara
Molara
Castelsardo
Coghinas
Porto Tòrres
▲1359 M. Limbara
Riu su Lernu
C. CODA CAVALLO
Sorso
A n g l o n a
Sàssari
Lago del Coghinas
R. de s. Èleme
M. Nieddu ▲971
la Nurra
R. Mannu
L o g u d o r o
Posada
Grotta di Nettuno
C. CACCIA
M. Lerno ▲1094
Ozieri
Siniscola
Alghero
R. Mannu
M. Rasu 1259▲
G o c è a n o
M. Albo 1127▲
Bitti
B a r o n i a
M. Mannu ▲802
CAPO MARÀRGIU
▲1200
Tirso
Orosei
Bosa
Nùoro
Dorgali
Cala Gonone
Macomer
Oliena
Golfo di Orosei
Cùglieri
Ottana
Orgòsolo
Flumineddu
Grotta del Bue Marino
▲1050 M. Ferru
Abbasanta
Gavoi
B a r b a g i a
S.ta Caterina di Pittinuri
Fonni
PARCO NAZ. DEL GOLFO DI OROSEI E DEL GENNARGENTU
Lago Omodeo
C. DI MONTE SANTU
Ula Tirso
Riola Sardo
Tonara
CAPO MANNU
S i n i s
San Vero Milis
MONTI DEL
▲1834
GENNARGENTU
Mal di Ventre
Nurachi
Atzara
Àrbatax
Tirso
Stagno di Cabras
THARROS
Oristano
S a r c i d a n o
Ogliastra
C. BELLAVISTA
Lanusei
CAPO S. MARCO
Seùi
Golfo di Oristano
A r b o r e a
M. Arci 812▲
Giara di Gèsturi
CAPO DELLA FRASCA
Arborèa
Sini
Lago del Flumendosa
Tertenìa
C. SFERRACAVALLO
Sant'Antonio di Santadi
Barùmini
NURAGHE SU NURAXI
Salto di Quirra
Màndas
Escalaplano
C a m p i d a n o
Sanluri
Lago Mulargia
Gùspini
Àrbus
San Gavino Monreale
Mannu
Flumendosa
CAPO S. LORENZO
MAR DI SARDEGNA
CAPO PECORA
M. Linas 1236▲
G e r r e i
Dolianova
S à r r a b u s
M. d. Sette Fratelli ▲1023
Iglesias
Decimomannu
Sestu
Sinnai
CAPO FERRATO
I g l e s i e n t e
Assèmini
Selargius
Cixerri
CAGLIARI
Quartu Sant'Èlena
Isola di San Pietro
Capoterra
C. SANT'ELIA
Carbònia
Carloforte
M. is Caràvius ▲1116
S u l c i s
Villasimìus
Golfo di Cagliari
Sarroch
C. CARBONARA
Is. dei Càvoli
Sant'Antioco
Isola di Sant'Antioco
Golfo di Palmas
NORA
CAPO DI PULA
Teulada
BITHIA
CAPO TEULADA
C. SPARTIVENTO

ABBASANTA

MANDRA EDERA

via Dante 20, 09071 Abbasanta (OR)
Tel. 078552710 Fax 078552710
Web: www.mandraedera.it

The remarkable quality of the environment is reflected in the agricultural produce, which forms the basis of the dishes served to the guests. The rooms are comfortable and well-arranged.

-

1 - - -

8 (x 2/4)

1 30,00 20,00 45,00 -

-

1 - 7 - 1 - 7 -

ALGHERO

CONSORZIO AGRITURISMO DI SARDEGNA

at Santa Maria La Palma, 07041 Alghero (SS)
Tel. 0783411660 Fax 0783411660
E-mail: cas.agriturismo@tiscali.it

This recently refurbished farmhouse with modern comforts is the ideal base for exploring the surrounding area.

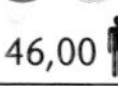

-

1 - - -

4 (x 2)

1 - - 46,00 -

3 (x 2/6)

1 46,00 7 - 1 - 7 -

COOP. AGRITURISTICA DULCAMARA

at Santa Maria La Palma, piazza Olbia 7,
07041 Alghero (SS)
Tel. 079999197 Fax 079999250
Web: www.dulcamarasardegna.org

An enterprising group of farms just inland from the Riviera del Corallo offer accommodation in houses on reclaimed land around Alghero.

7 (x 2)

1 34,00 - 44,00 -

16 (x 2)

1 31,00 - 44,00 -

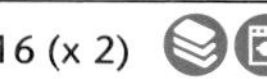

9(x 2)

1 26,00 7 - 1 - 7 -

ARBOREA

LE MIMOSE

strada 24 Ovest, 09092 Arborea (OR)
Tel. 0783800587

The accommodation, surrounding a large farmyard, is two kilometres from the village. The busy restaurant uses, above all, the farm's own produce.

6 (x 2/4)

1 26,00 - 39,00 -

7 (x 2)

1 26,00 - 39,00 -

-

1 - 7 - 1 - 7 -

Arbus

La Quercia

at Riu Martini-Sibiri, 09031 Arbus (CA)
Tel. 0709756035 Fax 0709756035
E-mail: saba@mail.omnitel.it

Close to a splendid wood, this establishment has large, airy communal rooms, while the accommodation is located in small stone buildings.

-

1 - - -

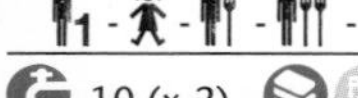

10 (x 2)

1 - - 43,40 -

-

1 - 7 - 1 - 7 -

Arzachena

Ca' la Somara

at Sarra Balestra, 07021 Arzachena (SS)
Tel. 078998969 Fax 078998969
E-mail: calasomara@libero.it

This rural accommodation is located just inland from the Costa Smeralda. In addition to lazing on Sardinia's finest beaches, guests can participate in a variety of sporting and social activities.

4 (x 2)

1 41,00 - - -

6 (x 2)

1 42,00 - - -

-

1 - 7 - 1 - 7 -

Atzara

Zeminariu

at Zeminariu, 08030 Atzara (NU)
Tel. 078465235

This farm offering accommodation is close to the village and comprises the owner's house with communal rooms separated by cowsheds and storehouses.

1 - - - -

3 (x 2)

1 23,00 - 40,00 -

1(x 6)

1 23,00 7 - 1 - 7 -

Bitti

Ertila

at Ertila, S.P. (provincial road) 50 at km 31, 08021 Bitti (NU)
Tel. 0784414558 Fax 0784414558

Accommodation and food is provided here in the traditional Sardinian manner. Courses for visitors focus on the making of dairy products, bread and pasta.

-

1 - - - -

4 (x 2)

1 21,00 - 36,00 -

-

1 - 7 - 1 - 7 -

Calangianus

Li Licci

at Valentino, 07023 Calangianus (SS)
Tel. 079665114 Fax 079665114

Ilexes, cork-oaks and Mediterranean scrub are the setting for this farm focusing on stock-raising and the making of dairy products, which also offers tourist accommodation.

-

1 - - - -

4 (x 2/4)

1 - - 67,00 -

-

1 - 7 - 1 - 7 -

Capoterra

Fratelli Piga

at Baccalamanza, 09012 Capoterra (CA)
Tel. 070728131

The accommodation is in self-contained apartments, which are large and airy. For nature lovers, the lagoons of Cagliari and the WWF nature reserve of Monte Arcosu are within easy reach.

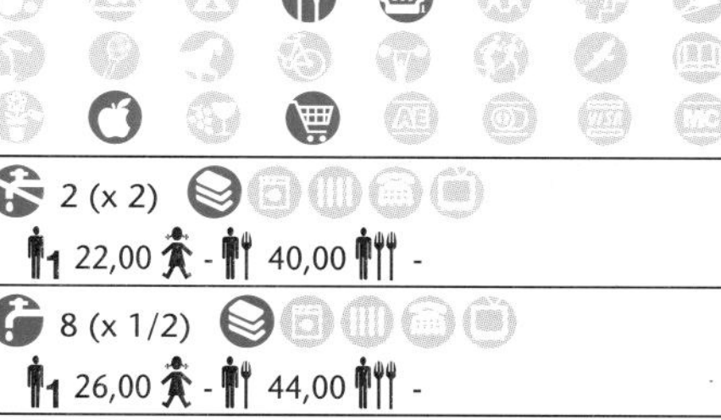

2 (x 2)

1 22,00 - 40,00 -

8 (x 1/2)

1 26,00 - 44,00 -

-

1 - 7 - 1 - 7 -

Cuglieri

Pittinuri

at Corconeddu, 09073 Cuglieri (OR)
Tel. 078538314
E-mail: agriturismopittinuri@libero.it

A very warm welcome is assured in this vast farm 15 kilometres from Cuglieri, with well-maintained and functional facilities for the guests.

-

1 - - - -

11 (x 2/4)

24,00 - 46,00 -

-

Gavoi

Antichi Sapori da Speranza

via Cagliari 192, 08020 Gavoi (NU)
Tel. 078452021 Fax 078452021
E-mail: saporiantichi@tiscali.it

This accommodation is in the village, with its granite houses forming an amphitheatre in a wooded basin. There are numerous activities available, both of a sporting nature and otherwise.

3 (x 1/2)

23,24 - 40,80 -

5 (x 1/2)

28,41 - 45,97 -

-

Luogosanto

Sole e Terra

at Funtana d'Alzi, 07020 Luogosanto (SS)
Tel. 079659773 Fax 079659773

This rural accommodation couldn't be better situated: everything is close at hand, while the surrounding landscape of hills and streams is superb.

-

- - -

7 (x 2/4)

36,15 - 49,00 -

-

Nuoro

Costiolu

at Costiolu, 08100 Nuoro
Tel. 0784260088 Fax 0784260088
E-mail: agriturismocostiolu@lycos.it

Guests are accommodated on the upper floor of a large farmhouse that is built around a courtyard and comprises various workrooms, a winery and a large dining-room.

6 (x 2)

32,00 - 50,00 -

4 (x 2)

32,00 - 50,00 -

-

Testone

via Verdi, 08100 Nuoro
Tel. 0784230539 Fax 0784230539
E-mail: matteo.secchi@tiscali.it

This accommodation is ideal for those fond of country holidays; the way the old granite farmhouses have been renovated is admirable, as is the provision of courses for visitors.

\-

1 - - -

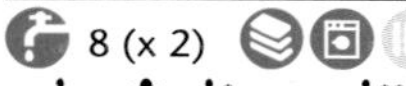

8 (x 2)

1 - - 39,00 -

\-

1 - 7 - 1 - 7 -

Nurachi

S'Ungroni

at S'Ungroni, via Case Sparse 25, 09070 Nurachi (OR)
Tel. 0783411398 Fax 0783411398
Web: www.agriturismosungroni.it

Particularly suitable for families, this accommodation offers a variety of activities: sea bathing, visits to archaeological sites (from Tharros to San Giovanni in Sinis) and country walks.

\-

1 - - -

6 (x 2/4)

1 30,00 - 40,00 -

\-

1 - 7 - 1 - 7 -

Oliena

Camisadu

at Logheri, 08025 Oliena (NU)
Tel. 3683479502

This modern building is in a valley abounding in broom, myrtle, cork-oaks and ilex; guided tours of the area are organised for visitors.

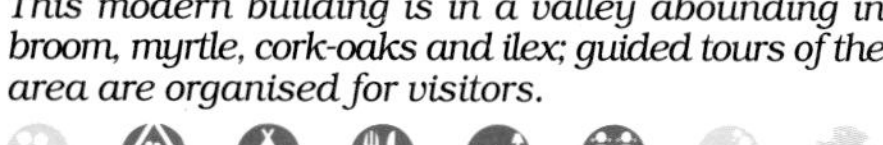

4 (x 2)

1 31,00 - 49,00 -

2 (x 2)

1 33,00 - 51,00 -

\-

1 - 7 - 1 - 7 -

Oristano

Consorzio Agriturismo di Sardegna-Posidonia

via Umberto I 66, 09170 Oristano
Tel. 0783411660 Fax 0783411660
Web: www.agriturismodisardegna.it

These establishments offering tourist accommodation in the Oristano district have joined forces; beautiful white beaches and areas of outstanding natural beauty are nearby.

95 (x 1/2)

1 - - 34,00 -

20 (x 2/4)

1 - - 39,00 -

\-

1 - 7 - 1 - 7 -

Riola Sardo

Casa Bellu

via Roma 15, 09070 Riola Sardo (OR)
Fax 0783411660
Web: www.sardegnaturismo.net

This farm accommodates its guests in an excellently renovated building, tastefully furnished, with some antique pieces.

4 (x 2)

1 - - 34,00 -

5 (x 2)

1 - - 39,00 -

-

1 - 7 - 1 - 7 -

Su Lau

via Luigino Bellu 24, 09070 Riola Sardo (OR)
Tel. 0783410897 Fax 0783410897
Web: www.tribu.it/sulau

Located on the edge of the village, this small house with a garden and orchard has a friendly atmosphere and comfortable rooms.

-

1 - - - -

6 (x 1/2)

1 31,00 22,00 46,00 -

-

1 - 7 - 1 - 7 -

San Vero Milis

Il Ginepro

at Putzu Idu, 09070 San Vero Milis (OR)
Fax 0783411660
Web: www.sardegnaturismo.net

This recently built accommodation is in a landscape rich in lagoons and sand-dunes. The sea, where beaches and cliffs alternate, is just 300 metres away.

9 (x 2)

1 - - 45,00 -

3 (x 2)

1 - - 50,00 -

-

1 - 7 - 1 - 7 -

Sassari

Finagliosu

at Palmadula, 07100 Sassari
Tel. 336777141 Fax 079530474
Web: web.tiscali.it/finagliosu

Amid the colours and odours of the Mediterranean scrub, with its vineyards and animals out to pasture, this family-run establishment serves Sardinian dishes, prepared with home-grown produce.

-

1 - - - -

8 (x 2/4)

1 32,00 22,40 45,00 -

-

1 - 7 - 1 - 7 -

L'AGLIASTRU

at Campanedda, via Monte Casteddu-Podere 75, 07040 Sassari
Tel. 079306070

This farm stands on the top of a hill with other similar buildings and, in the summer months, is an excellent alternative to the crowded coast.

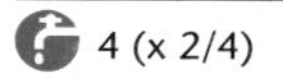

-

1 - - - -

4 (x 2/4)

1 23,34 - 40,80 -

-

1 - 7 - 1 - 7 -

SINI

SA SCRUSSURA

at Su Padrosu, 09090 Sini (OR)
Tel. 0783936167 Fax 0783936167

This is very simple accommodation that puts the accent on the use of natural materials; the busy restaurant with its tasty cuisine specialises in local dishes.

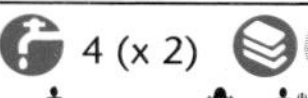

-

1 - - - -

4 (x 2)

1 23,24 - 36,15 -

1(x 4)

1 - 7 170,00 1 - 7 -

STINTINO

CALA SCOGLIETTI

07040 Stintino (SS)
Fax 0783411660
Web: www.sardegnaturismo.net

This farm is off the beaten track, in the peace and quiet of the countryside. The coast may also be explored on horseback, starting from the nearby riding-school.

6 (x 2)

1 22,00 - - -

3 (x 2)

1 28,00 - - -

-

1 - 7 - 1 - 7 -

TEMPIO PAUSANIA

STAZZO LA CERRA

07029 Tempio Pausania (SS)
Tel. 079670972
Web: www.agriturismolacerra.it

This farm has workshops equipped for the study of biology; the nearby restaurant features both the local cuisine and vegetarian dishes.

-

1 - - - -

5 (x 2/4)

25,00 13,00 43,00 -

1(x 3)

- - - 260,00

Teulada

Coop. Agrituristica Matteu

at Matteu, 09019 Teulada (CA)
Tel. 0709270003 Fax 0709270003

With their rustic furnishings, the charming rooms give onto a terrace with a gazebo and pergola where guests are served wholesome local fare.

\-

\- - - -

10 (x 2)

23,22 11,61 41,30 54,23

\-

\- - - -

Tonara

Mattalé

at Mattalé, 08039 Tonara (NU)
Tel. 078463319
Web: www.labarbagia.com

Accommodation is available in a panoramic farmhouse renovated with care, where Signora Miriam prepares tasty local dishes.

\-

\- - - -

7 (x 1/2)

24,00 - 40,00 -

\-

\- - - -

Ula Tirso

Sa Tanchitta

09089 Ula Tirso (OR)
Fax 0783411660
Web: www.sardegnaturismo.net

This farm, in the depths of the countryside, is ideal for relaxing walks in the mountains or along the shores of Lake Omodeo.

2 (x 2)

\- - 34,00 -

3 (x 2)

\- - 39,00 -

\-

\- - - -

SICILIA

MAR TIRRENO
Ùstica
(Palermo)
CAPO GALLO
M. Pellegrino
606
PALERMO
CAPO SAN VITO
PUNTA RAISI
Golfo di Castellammare
Golfo di Tèrmini Imerese
Conca d'Oro
Monreale
Bagheria
Castellammare del Golfo
Partinico
Misilmeri
Tèrmini Imerese
Isole Ègadi
Èrice
Tràpani
Lèvanzo
Marettimo
Favignana
Paceco
Buseto Palizzolo
SEGESTA
Freddo
Alcamo
Piana degli Albanesi
L. di Piana degli Albanesi
Santa Cristina Gela
Ventimiglia di Sicilia
S. Leonardo
Bordino
Isole dello Stagnone
Salemi
1613
Rocca Busambra
Corleone
Sclàfani Bagni
C. BOEO O LILIBEO
Marsala
Val di Mazara
1457
Pzo. Cangialoso
Lercara Friddi
Partanna
Castelvetrano
Bèlice
L. Aràncio
Mazara del Vallo
Campobello di Mazara
Menfi
SELINUNTE
1578
M. Cammarata
Mussom
CAPO GRANÌTOLA
Verdura
Ribera
Sciacca
CAPO S. MARCO
Platani
Aragona
ERACLEA MINOA
Agrigento
Porto Empèdocle
Favara
VALLE DEI TEMPI
MAR DI SICILIA
MAR MEDITERRANEO
0
20
40
60 km

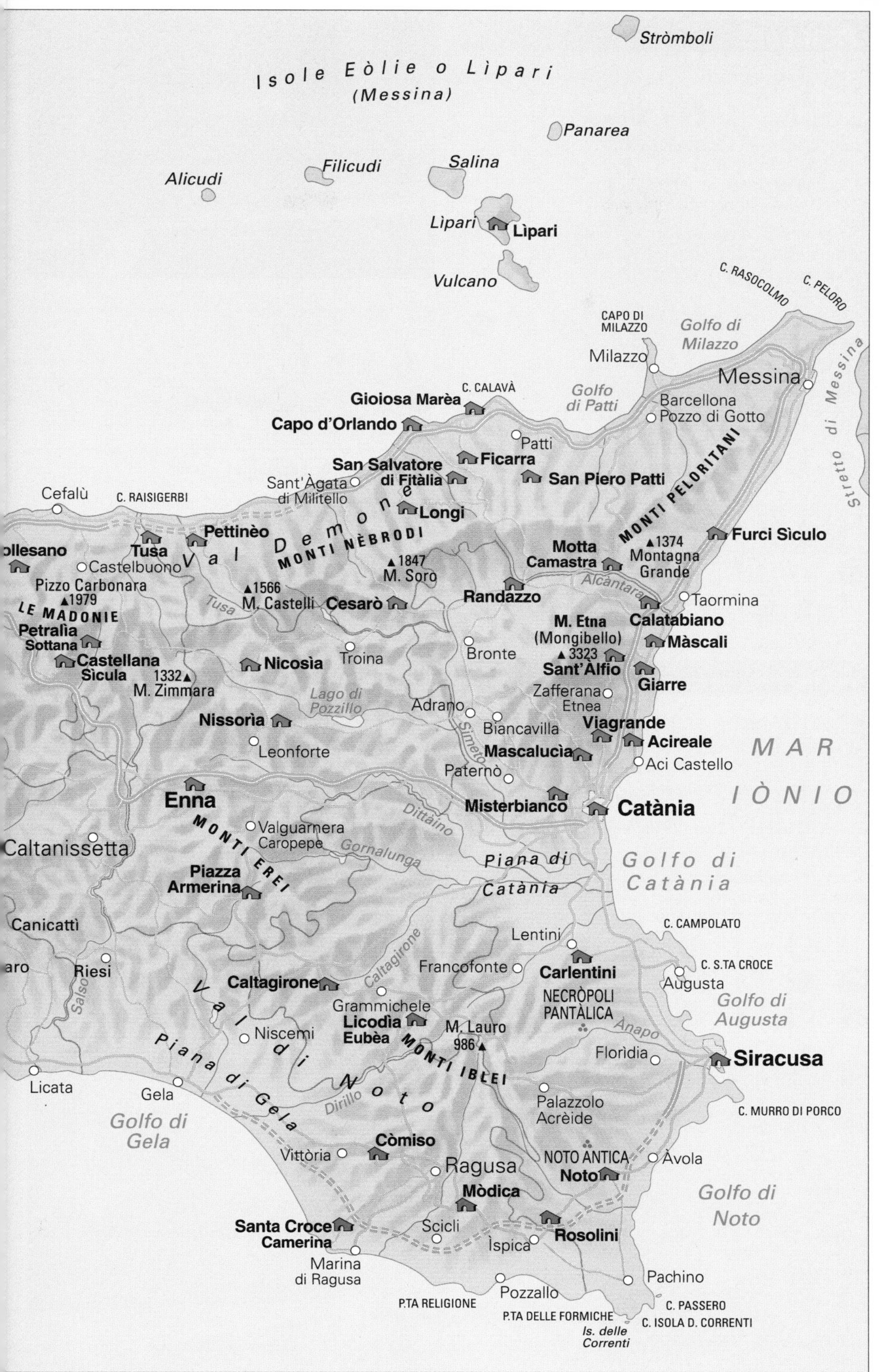
Stròmboli
Isole Eòlie o Lìpari
(Messina)
Panarea
Alicudi
Filicudi
Salina
Lìpari
Lìpari
Vulcano
C. RASOCOLMO
C. PELORO
CAPO DI MILAZZO
Golfo di Milazzo
Milazzo
Messina
Stretto di Messina
C. CALAVÀ
Gioiosa Marèa
Golfo di Patti
Barcellona Pozzo di Gotto
Capo d'Orlando
Patti
Ficarra
San Salvatore di Fitàlia
San Piero Patti
Sant'Àgata di Militello
MONTI PELORITANI
Cefalù
C. RAISIGERBI
Longi
Val Demone
MONTI NÈBRODI
Pettinèo
Motta Camastra
▲1374 Montagna Grande
Furci Sìculo
Tusa
Collesano
Castelbuono
▲1847 M. Soro
Alcàntara
Randazzo
Taormina
Pizzo Carbonara
▲1979
▲1566 M. Castelli
Cesarò
Tusa
LE MADONIE
M. Etna (Mongibello)
Calatabiano
Petralìa Sottana
Màscali
▲3323
Bronte
Troina
Castellana Sìcula
Nicosìa
Sant'Alfio
1332▲ M. Zimmara
Giarre
Zafferana Etnea
Lago di Pozzillo
Adrano
Nissorìa
Biancavilla
Viagrande
Simeto
Leonforte
Acireale
Mascalucìa
MAR IÒNIO
Aci Castello
Paternò
Enna
Misterbianco
Catània
MONTI EREI
Dittàino
Valguarnera Caropepe
Caltanissetta
Gornalunga
Piana di Catània
Golfo di Catània
Piazza Armerina
C. CAMPOLATO
Canicattì
Lentini
Riesi
Francofonte
Carlentini
C. S.TA CROCE
Caltagirone
Salso
Augusta
Caltagirone
Grammichele
NECRÒPOLI PANTÀLICA
Golfo di Augusta
Val di Noto
Licodìa Eubèa
M. Lauro 986▲
Anapo
Niscemi
MONTI IBLEI
Floridia
Siracusa
Piana di Gela
Licata
Gela
Palazzolo Acrèide
C. MURRO DI PORCO
Golfo di Gela
Dirillo
Còmiso
Vittòria
NOTO ANTICA
Àvola
Ragusa
Noto
Golfo di Noto
Mòdica
Santa Croce Camerina
Scicli
Rosolini
Ìspica
Marina di Ragusa
Pachino
Pozzallo
P.TA RELIGIONE
C. PASSERO
P.TA DELLE FORMICHE
C. ISOLA D. CORRENTI
Is. delle Correnti

Acireale

Il Limoneto

at Scillichenti, via D'Amico 41,
95020 Acireale (CT)
Tel. 095886568 Fax 095886568
Web: www.illimoneto.it

The accommodation is in an old house with a terrace and a delightful pergola with views of the sea and Etna; guests get to enjoy citrus and other fruit free of charge.

\-

1 - - -

\-

1 - - -

3(x 4)

1 - 7 - 1 88,00 7 -

Alia

Villa Dafne

contrada Cozzo di Cicero,
90021 Alia (PA)
Tel. 0918219174 Fax 0918219928
Web: www.villadafne.com

This old farmhouse has recently been excellently refurbished. Exhibitions and concerts are often held in the rooms of the large restaurant.

\-

1 - - -

10 (x 2/4)

1 34,00 - 55,00 -

2(x 4)

1 - 7 - 1 - 7 550,00

Buseto Palizzolo

Baglio Case Colomba

at Pianoneve, via Toselli 185,
91012 Buseto Palizzolo (TP)
Tel. 3472116470
Web: www.casecolomba.com

This accommodation is situated in a renovated baglio (the traditional winery of the area), dating from the late 19th century; located amid the luxuriant greenery of an orchard, it has large, cool rooms.

\-

1 - - - -

4 (x 2/4)

1 31,00 - - -

\-

1 - 7 - 1 - 7 -

Pianoneve

at Pianoneve, via Agrigento 112,
91012 Buseto Palizzolo (TP)
Tel. 0923851227 Fax 0923533158
E-mail: trapani@coldiretti.it

This farm, a pioneer in rural tourism, offers accommodation in self-contained cottages with large verandas and a fine view of the surrounding valleys.

\-

1 - - - -

\-

1 - - - -

5 (x 2/6)

1 25,00 7 - 1 - 7 -

Calatabiano

Galimi

at Pasteria, via Pasteria 19/E,
95011 Calatabiano (CT)
Tel. 095641756 Fax 095641756
Web: www.galimi.it

This modern country house has apartments giving onto a garden full of flowers; nearby are facilities for sports and other recreational activities.

\-

1 - - - -

2 (x 2/4)

1 21,50 - - -

2 (x 2/4)

1 - 7 - 1 80,00 7 -

Caltagirone

Il Casale delle Rose

contrada Croce Vicario, 95041 Caltagirone (CT)
Tel. 093325064 Fax 093325064
E-mail: casalerose@tiscali.it

A friendly welcome is assured in this tastefully refurbished 19th-century farmhouse with a courtyard and large restaurant.

\-

1 - - - -

9 (x 2/4)

1 34,00 24,00 47,00 -

\-

1 - 7 - 1 - 7 -

La Casa degli Angeli

at Angeli, S.P. (provincial road) 39 at km 9,
95041 Caltagirone (CT)
Tel. 093325317 Fax 093325317
Web: www.comune.caltagirone.ct.it/alberghi

Amid carefully tended vineyards and citrus groves, this typical two-storeyed rural building has a large terrace and views over the Valle degli Angeli.

6 (x 2)

25,82 - 45,00 -

13 (x 2)

40,00 - 56,00 -

12(x 2)

50,00 -

Capo d'Orlando

Milio

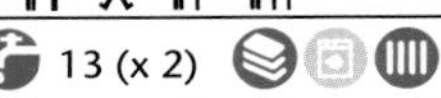

at San Gregorio, 98071 Capo d'Orlando (ME)
Tel. 0941955008 Fax 0941955281
E-mail: pmilio@enterprisenet.it

The accommodation is in small one-family houses in a peaceful olive grove just 500 metres from the sea. The Aeolian Islands are just 40 minutes away by hydrofoil.

4(x 4)

35,00 -

Tenuta di Roccadia

contrada Roccadia, 96013 Carlentini (SR)
Tel. 095990362 Fax 095990362
Web: www.roccadia.com

In the hills, less than 10 kilometres from the sea, accommodation is available in large 19th-century buildings; the busy restaurant is recommended.

10 (x 2)

49,00 - 57,00 -

Carlentini

Casa dello Scirocco

contrada Piscitello, 96013 Carlentini (SR)
Tel. 0957836120 Fax 0957139257
Web: www.casadelloscirocco.it

Curiously enough, in an orange grove, large rooms have been built inside caves inhabited in prehistoric times and now a protected archaeological site.

Terias

at Corridore del Pero, 96013 Carlentini (SR)
Tel. 095997212 Fax 095445787
Web: www.terias.it

Simple accommodation is available in a renovated 19th-century farmhouse surrounded by the wide expanses of the farm's citrus groves and cornfields.

-

1 - - -

-

1 - - -

7 (x 4/6)

1 - 7 - 1 120,00 7 600,00

Castellammare del Golfo

Camillo Finazzo

contrada Baida,
91014 Castellammare del Golfo (TP)
Tel. 092438051 Fax 092438051
Web: www.camillofinazzo.com

This accommodation is located in the hills, cheek by jowl with the splendid Zingaro Nature Reserve (crystal-clear waters, stacks rising out of the sea and rare birds).

-

1 - - -

-

1 - - -

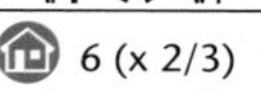  

6 (x 2/3)

1 30,00 7 - 1 - 7 -

Castellana Sicula

Feudo Tudia

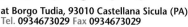

at Borgo Tudia, 93010 Castellana Sicula (PA)
Tel. 0934673029 Fax 0934673029
Web: www.tudia.net

Amid the rolling hills on the southern edge of the Madonie Regional Park, this farmhouse offers accommodation with all modern comforts.

-

1 - - -

-

1 - - -

6(x 2)

1 39,00 7 - 1 - 7 -

Villa Padura

at Calcarelli, via Matteotti,
90020 Castellana Sicula (PA)
Tel. 0921562180 Fax 091304951

The furnishings of this 18th-century house are particularly attractive. It's also a good base for excursions to the Madonie Mountains and villages rich in history.

-

1 - - -

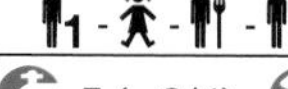 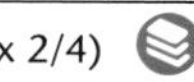 

7 (x 2/4)

1 36,00 18,00 57,00 -

-

1 - 7 - 1 - 7 -

Catania

Bagnara

contrada Cardinale, 95129 Catania
Tel. 095336407 Fax 095451239
Web: www.agribagnara.it

The accommodation is in recently renovated houses, with large spaces for children and the possibility of using the outside oven and barbecue.

\-
1 - - -

\-
1 - - -

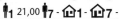

 14 (x 2/4)

1 21,00 7 - 1 - 7 -

Fondo 23

via San Giuseppe la Rena - fondo 23, 95100 Catania
Tel. **095592521** Fax **095592521**
Web: **www.fondo23.it**

Flowering bougainvillaea and oleanders are a pleasant setting for this 19th-century farmhouse built of lava, with self-contained apartments.

\-
1 - - -

\-
1 - - -

 5 (x 2/4)

1 32,00 7 - 1 - 7 -

Cesarò

Destro Pastizzaro Sergio

contrada Scalonazzo, 98033 Cesarò (ME)
Tel. **095697331**

In the area of the Monti Erei, near the interesting villages around Etna, this accommodation is an ideal base for tours of the district.

 4 (x 1/2)

1 21,00 - 31,00 -

\-
1 - - -

\-
1 - 7 - 1 - 7 -

Collesano

Guarnera

contrada Gargi di Cenere, 90016 Collesano (PA)
Tel. **0921428431** Fax **0921428431**
Web: **www.gargidicenere.it**

Everything in this cottage reflects the owners' care and good taste, from the choice of the furnishings to the cuisine based entirely on the farm's organic produce.

\-
1 - - -

5 (x 2)

1 41,00 - 58,00 -

\-
1 - 7 - 1 - 7 -

Comiso

Torre di Canicarao

contrada Canicarao, 97013 Comiso (RG)
Tel. **0932731167** Fax **0932683309**
Web: **www.canicarao.it**

This large house, which grew up over the centuries around a 15th-century tower, has courtyards shaded by mulberry trees and gardens with palms and cypresses.

\-
1 - - -

11 (x 1/4)

1 31,00 22,00 41,50 -

\-
1 - 7 - 1 - 7 -

Enna

Il Mandorleto

contrada Gerace, 94100 Enna
Tel. 0935541389
Web: www.agriturismo-sicilia.com/ilmandorleto

This farmhouse is located in a pleasant position on Monte Gerace. A nearby farm offers excellent food at special rates.

       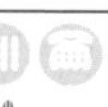

1 - - -

3 (x 2/4) 

1 26,00 13,00 - -

1 - 7 - 1 - 7 -

Erice

Pizzolungo

at Pizzolungo, contrada San Cusumano,
91016 Erice (TP)
Tel. 0923563710 Fax 0923569780
Web: www.pizzolungo.it

Located in the early 20th-century owner's villa and its outbuildings, this accommodation is close to both the sea and the mountains, and is within easy reach of the city.

1 - - -

1 - - -

45 (x 2/6)

1 40,00 7 - 1 - 7 -

Ficarra

Fattoria di Grenne

at Grenne 27, 98062 Ficarra (ME)
Tel. 0941582757 Fax 0941583107
Web: www.grenne.it

This ancient house is just 4 kilometres from the sea, and has links with Tomasi Di Lampedusa, who wrote part of Il Gattopardo (The Leopard) here.

1 - - -

6 (x 2) 

1 35,00 - 50,00 -

1 - 7 - 1 - 7 -

Furci Siculo

Nasita

at Grotte, via Cesare Battisti 272,
98023 Furci Siculo (ME)
Tel. 0942794461 Fax 0942794461

The accommodation is in a renovated farmhouse that has preserved - thanks also to its period furnishings - a delightful 19th-century atmosphere.

1 - - -

5 (x 1/4)  

1 25,82 - - -

1 - 7 - 1 - 7 -

Giarre

Codavolpe

at Trepunti, strada 87 n. 35, 95010 Giarre (CT)
Tel. 095939802 Fax 095939802
Web: www.codavolpe.it

Four kilometres from the sea, apartments are available in an old cottage; guests can get together at the palmento, the large vat where, in the past, grapes were pressed and fermented.

-
1 - - -

-
1 - - -

5 (x 2/3)
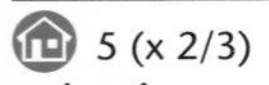 
1 - 7 - 1 67,00 7 -

San Leonardello

at San Leonardello, via Madonna della Libertà 165, 95014 Giarre (CT)
Tel. 095964020 Fax 095946020
Web: www.sanleonardello.it

This accommodation is in the shadow of the vulcano, in renovated rural houses on a farm where citrus fruit (lemons and kumquats) is organically grown, as are the vegetables.

-
1 - - -

4 (x 1/4)
1 30,00 - - -

-
1 - 7 - 1 - 7 -

Gioiosa Marea

Santa Margherita

contrada S. Margherita 89,
98063 Gioiosa Marea (ME)
Tel. 094139703 Fax 1782223223
Web: www.agriturismosantamargherita.com

Between the Nebrodi Regional Park and the coast facing the Aeolian Islands (just half an hour away by hydrofoil), this establishment offers courses on cookery, handicrafts and health disciplines.

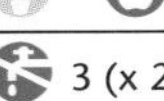 3 (x 2)
1 31,00 - 55,00 -

 8 (x 2)
1 31,00 - 55,00 -

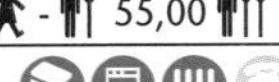 3(x 4)
1 - 7 - 1 - 7 670,00

Licodia Eubea

Dain

contrada Alia, S.S. (state road) 194 at km 52,
95040 Licodia Eubea (CT)
Tel. 0933965682

In the centre of a vast estate, a number of farmhouses have been converted into comfortable tourist accommodation.

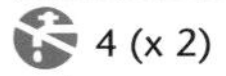 4 (x 2)

1 35,00 - 50,00 -

 6 (x 2)  
1 35,00 - 50,00 -

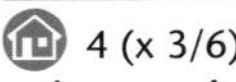 4 (x 3/6)  
1 35,00 7 - 1 - 7 -

Lipari

U Zu Peppino

at Pianoconte, via Quattropani 21,
98050 Lipari (ME)
Tel. 0909822330 Fax 0909822330
Web: www.wel.it/uzupeppino

Far from the madding crowd of summer holiday-makers, this accommodation is, however, within easy reach of some of the island's finest beaches.

 -

1 - - -

 5 (x 2) 

1 31,00 - 47,00 -

 2 (x 3/4) 

1 25,00 7 - 1 - 7 -

Longi

Il Vignale

contrada Pado, piazza Gen. Moriondo 6,
98070 Longi (ME)
Tel. 0941485015 Fax 0941485015
Web: web.tiscali.it/vignale

Extremely tranquil holidays are possible in this 19th-century silk-mill surrounded by the woods at the foot of the spectacular Rocche del Crasto.

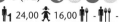

3 (x 2)

1 24,00 16,00 - -

1 (x 2)

1 24,00 16,00 - -

-

1 - 7 - 1 - 7 -

Marsala

Baglio Vajarassa

at Spagnola, via Vajarassa 176,
91025 Marsala (TP)
Tel. 0923968628 Fax 0923968628

The Art Nouveau style of this attractive late 19th-century house, with an agricultural museum attached, makes it ideal for holiday accommodation: the sea is just a stone's throw away.

1 (x 2)

1 37,50 - 50,00 -

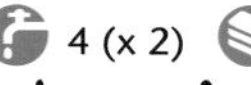 4 (x 2) 

1 37,50 - 50,00 -

-

1 - 7 - 1 - 7 -

Mascali

Russo Rocca

at Artale Marina, 95016 Mascali (CT)
Tel. 095931259 Fax 0957794765
Web: www.agriturismorussorocca.it

This fine late 19th-century building stands in a large garden with citrus and other fruit trees. The sea is within walking distance, at Riposto, or just a few minutes' drive away.

\-
1 - - -

\-
1 - - -

4 (x 2/4)
1 25,00 7 - 1 - 7 -

Mascalucia

Trinità

via Trinità 34, 95030 Mascalucia (CT)
Tel. 0957272156 Fax 0957272156
Web: www.aziendatrinita.it

On the slopes of Etna, accommodation is available in 17th-century buildings set in a botanical garden over a hectare in size, with Mediterranean and exotic plants.

\-
1 - - -

\-
1 - - -

5 (x 2/5)
1 31,00 7 - 1 - 7 -

Misterbianco

Alcalà

contrada Terrebianche, S.S. (state road) 192 at km 78, 95045 Misterbianco (CT)
Tel. 0957130029 Fax 0957130029
Web: www.omnia.it/alcala

This early 20th-century rural complex is shaded by large ornamental trees; in the middle of it are the palmento (the vat where grapes were pressed) and vinery, where guests often eat together.

\-
1 - - -

\-
1 - - -

5 (x 2/4)
1 44,00 7 - 1 - 7 -

Modica

Villa Teresa

contrada Bugilfezza, via Crocevia Cava d'Ispica, 97015 Modica (RG)
Tel. 0932771690 Fax 0932771690
Web: www.villateresaweb.it

This is a 17th-century farmhouse with comfortable, well-equipped rooms giving onto a small veranda overlooking the kitchen garden shaded with trees.

\-
1 - - -

8 (x 1/4)

1 40,00 - 53,00 -

\-

1 - 7 - 1 - 7 -

Motta Camastra

Gole Alcantara

via Nazionale 5, 98030 Motta Camastra (ME)
Tel. 0942985010 Fax 0942985264
Web: www.golealcantara.it

The accommodation is in a recent building, as well as two old buildings, Il Poggio and La Casa delle Monache, that have been renovated in order to increase capacity.

 4 (x 2)  

 1 30,00 - -

 4 (x 2)

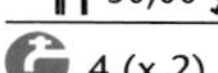 1 30,00 - -

 -

 1 - 7 - 1 - 7 -

Nicosia

Masseria Mercadante

contrada Mercadante, 94014 Nicosia (EN)
Tel. 0935640771 Fax 0935640771
E-mail: agrimerc@blu.it

In the open countryside, this farm building dates from the 17th century; the rooms devoted to tourist accommodation are simple but functional.

 -

1 - - -

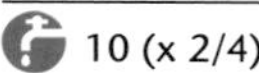 10 (x 2/4)  

 1 28,00 - 45,00 -

-

1 - 7 - 1 - 7 -

Nissoria

Isola Felice

contrada Favara, 94010 Nissoria (EN)
Tel. 0935640390

Surrounded by an oak-wood, this farm comprises two renovated buildings and offers rooms with beams furnished in a functional manner.

-

1 - - -

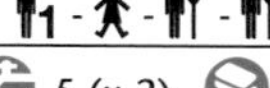 5 (x 2)   

1 - - 35,00 -

-

1 - 7 - 1 - 7 -

Noto

Il Roveto

at Roveto-Vendicari, 96017 Noto (SR)
Tel. 093166024 Fax 093136946
Web: www.roveto.it

This 18th-century fortified farmhouse is close to the coast, where it's possible to see birds such as the flamingo, the pride of the Pantani di Vendicari Nature Reserve.

\-

1 - - -

\-

1 - - -

4(x 4)

1 - 7 - 1 124,00 7 -

Terra di Solimano

contrada Busulmone, 96017 Noto (SR)
Tel. 0931836606 Fax 0931836606
Web: www.terradisolimano.it

In a beautiful natural setting, accommodation is available in this 19th-century villa, surrounded by a large organic farm.

\-

1 - - -

6 (x 2)

1 30,00 15,00 45,00 -

\-

1 - 7 - 1 - 7 -

Paceco

Baglio Costa di Mandorla

via Verderame 37, 91027 Paceco (TP)
Tel. 0923409100
Web: www.costadimandorla.it

This rural complex, with rooms that have recently been excellently refurbished, is near the monumental Villa Serraino. A swimming pool is under construction.

\-

1 - - -

1 (x 2)

1 36,00 - - -

3(x 6)

1 36,00 7 - 1 - 7 -

Partinico

Fattoria Manostalla Villa Chiarelli

contrada Manostalla, 90047 Partinico (PA)
Tel. 0918787033 Fax 0924508742
Web: www.wel.it

This old farmhouse has a courtyard shaded by three large mulberry trees and a dairy where cow's and goat's milk cheeses are made in the traditional way.

\-

1 - - -

10 (x 2/4)

1 35,00 - 48,00 -

\-

1 - 7 - 1 - 7 -

Petralia Sottana

Monaco di Mezzo

contrada Monaco, 90027 Petralia Sottana (PA)
Tel. 0934673949 Fax 0934676114
Web: www.monacodimezzo.com

The accommodation is in the large farmhouse that was at the centre of the old Monaco estate; as far as the eye can see, are the wide expanses of wheat-fields ruffled by the wind.

\-

1 - - -

5 (x 2)

1 44,00 - 58,00 -

6(x 4)

1 - 7 - 1 - 7 935,00

Pettineo

Bosco

contrada Bosco, 98070 Pettineo (ME)
Tel. 0921336056 Fax 0921336056
Web: www.agrituristbosco.it

Near a wood of chestnuts and hazelnuts, a stone cottage dating from 1888 stands in the centre of 10 hectares of cultivated land, mainly planted with fruit trees.

\-

1 - - -

4 (x 1/4)

1 32,00 - 50,00 -

1(x 5)

1 32,00 7 - 1 - 7 -

Casa Migliaca

contrada Migliaca, 98070 Pettineo (ME)
Tel. 0921336722 Fax 0921391107
Web: www.casamigliaca.com

Olive groves surround the handsome 19th-century house used for tourist accommodation and the 18th-century building where the oil-press was sited, which now contains a number of old artefacts.

\-

1 - - -

8 (x 2/4)

1 - - 65,00 -

\-

1 - 7 - 1 - 7 -

Piana degli Albanesi

Masseria Rossella

contrada Rossella, S.P. (provincial road) 5 at km 28.9, 90037 Piana degli Albanesi (PA)
Tel. 0918460012 Fax 0918460012
Web: www.masseria-rossella.com

This fascinating 18th-century farmhouse, which has been carefully renovated, has recently started to provide accommodation and serve local dishes.

\-

1 - - -

9 (x 2/4)

1 50,00 30,00 73,00 -

\-

1 - 7 - 1 - 7 -

Piazza Armerina

Gigliotto

contrada Gigliotto, 94015 Piazza Armerina (EN)
Tel. 0933970898 Fax 0933970898
Web: www.gigliotto.com

This old farmhouse has been excellently converted into tourist accommodation; in addition to practising sports, guests may explore the area on foot, bicycle or horseback.

-
$_1$ - - -

15 (x 2)
$_1$ 35,00 - 55,00 -

-
$_1$ - $_7$ - $_1$ - $_7$ -

Il Glicine

contrada Vallegrande C.P. 187,
94015 Piazza Armerina (EN)
Tel. 0935684119 Fax 0935684119
E-mail: atishaserlingpa@yahoo.com

This farm produces organic crops (it grows olives, hazelnuts, almonds, fruit and vegetables) that are used in the exclusively vegetarian dishes.

-
$_1$ - - -

-
$_1$ - - -

2(x 4)
$_1$ 35,00 $_7$ - $_1$ - $_7$ -

Randazzo

L'Antica Vigna

at Montelaguardia, 95036 Randazzo (CT)
Tel. 095924003 Fax 095923324

This tourist accommodation is on the edge of the Etna Regional Park, and close to the Nebrodi Regional Park and the Valle dell'Alcantra Nature Reserve.

-
$_1$ - - -

10 (x 2/4)
$_1$ 31,50 - 46,50 -

-
$_1$ - $_7$ - $_1$ - $_7$ -

Rosolini

Pirainito

contrada Pirainito, via Manzoni 156,
96019 Rosolini (SR)
Tel. 0931857475 Fax 0931857475

Among its merits of this farm, situated in a late 19th-century complex, is its country cuisine, with its wholesome traditional dishes.

-
$_1$ - - -

6 (x 2/4)
$_1$ 22,00 11,00 40,00 -

1(x 5)
$_1$ 22,00 $_7$ - $_1$ - $_7$ -

San Piero Patti

Il Daino

contrada Manganello 2, 98068 San Piero Patti (ME)
Tel. 0941660362 Fax 0941660362
Web: www.ildaino.com

In the Nebrodi district, accommodation is available in this 19th-century farm cottage; new rooms, suites and sports facilities are being added.

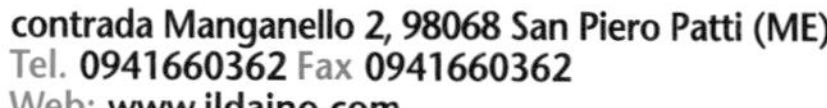

-
$_1$ - - -

10 (x 4)

1 40,00 - 50,00 -

\-

1 - 7 - 1 - 7 -

SAN SALVATORE DI FITALIA

LA VEDETTA DEI NEBRODI

contrada Bufana Alta,
98070 San Salvatore di Fitalia (ME)
Tel. **0941421977**
Web: **www.vedettadeinebrodi.it**

This rustic building has been completely renovated; it's surrounded by a wood that is particularly rich in mushrooms.

\-

1 - - -

3 (x 2)

1 25,00 20,00 42,00 -

\-

1 - 7 - 1 - 7 -

SANTA CRISTINA GELA

AL POGGETTO

contrada Pianetto, via Spagna 3,
90030 Santa Cristina Gela (PA)
Tel. **0918570213** Fax **0917302718**
Web: **www.alpoggetto.it**

Near the Bosco della Ficuzza and pleasantly surrounded by hills, accommodation is available in a large house renovated in rustic style.

\-

1 - - -

10 (x 2/4)

1 60,00 - 80,00 -

\-

1 - 7 - 1 - 7 -

SANTA CROCE CAMERINA

CAPO SCALAMBRI

at Palmento, contrada Punta Secca,
97010 Santa Croce Camerina (RG)
Tel. **0932239928** Fax **0932616263**
Web: **www.caposcalambri.com**

Just behind the long beach of Punta Secca, this farm offers simple but functional accommodation, mainly in buildings scattered in the pinewood.

\-

1 - - -

\-

1 - - -

7 (x 2/5)

1 31,00 7 - 1 - 7 -

Sant'Alfio

La Cirasella

contrada Petralia Finaita, via Trisciala 13,
95010 Sant'Alfio (CT)
Tel. **095968000** Fax **095968000**
E-mail: **laurabillitteri@tiscali.it**

'Accommodation on organic farms, a new approach to holidays', is the motto of this farm, which also provides accommodation in a number of old lava cottages.

\-

1 - - -

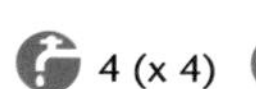 4 (x 4)  

1 35,00 - 43,00 -

\-

1 - 7 - 1 - 7 -

Sciacca

Montalbano

at Scunchipani, 92019 Sciacca (AG)
Tel. **092580154** Fax **092580154**
E-mail: **smontalb@freemail.it**

This attractive modern house is located in the Piana Piccola di Misilifurme; from the terrace there's a magnificent view extending from the sea to the mountains.

\-

1 - - -

2 (x 2)

1 26,00 - - -

5(x 2)

1 26,00 7 - 1 - 7 -

Sclafani Bagni

Antica Masseria Fontana Murata

contrada Fontana Murata,
90020 Sclafani Bagni (PA)
Tel. **0921542018** Fax **0921543553**
Web: **www.tuscanyfarmholidays.it**

In the heart of the Madonie Mountains, in a area of thermal springs, this typical Sicilian building houses a well-known restaurant. Palermo is just an hour's drive away.

\-

1 - - -

\-

1 - - -

 3(x 4)  

1 37,00 7 - 1 - 7 520,00

Siracusa

Case Damma

contrada Damma, S.P. (provincial road) 14 at km 9, 96100 Siracusa
Tel. **0931705273** Fax **0931463131**
Web: **www.casedamma.it**

The storerooms and hayloft of an old farmhouse have been converted to provide rooms with modern comforts; meals are served in the building formerly containing the oil-press.

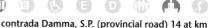

-

1 - - - -

4 (x 2/4)

1 39,00 27,30 57,00 -

-

1 - 7 - 1 - 7 -

La Perciata

via Spinagallo 77, 96100 Siracusa
Tel. 0931717366 Fax 0931717366
Web: www.perciata.it

This tourist complex is well equipped with sports facilities and modern comforts. The main town is ten kilometres away.

-

1 - - - -

9 (x 1/2)

1 41,00 - - -

2(x 4)

1 - 7 - 1 151,00 7 -

Limoneto

S.P. (provincial road) 14 for Canicattini Bagni, 96100 Siracusa
Tel. 0931717352 Fax 0931717352
Web: www.emmeti.it/limoneto

Significantly, the road leading to this attractive farm is called Mare Monti (Sea and Mountains). On one side is Syracuse, on the other the interior, which is well worth exploring.

-

1 - - - -

8 (x 2/4)

1 38,00 28,00 54,00 -

-

1 - 7 - 1 - 7 -

Terrauzza sul Mare

via Blanco 8, 96100 Siracusa
Tel. 0931714362 Fax 093166395
Web: www.terramar.it

This farm has small air-conditioned apartments with direct access to the sea. Of particular interest are its production of ornamental pottery and the courses on decoration held here.

-

1 - - - -

-

1 - - - -

9(x 2)

1 45,00 7 - 1 - 7 -

Villa Lucia

contrada Isola, traversa Mondello 1, 96100 Siracusa
Tel. 0931721007 Fax 0931721587
E-mail: villaluciavinfo@sistemia.it

In the owner's house, the rooms are of hotel standard; the rustic annexe opening onto the countryside is, however, more typical of farmhouse accommodation.

-

1 - - - -

5 (x 2)

1 77,50 - - -

3 (x 2/4)
1 - 7 - 1 105,00 7 -

Tusa

Borgo degli Olivi

contrada Aielli, 98079 Tusa (ME)
Tel. 090712430 Fax 090719081
E-mail: borgodegliolivi@katamail.com

The large rooms in this 18th-century farmhouse, containing traditional rural furniture, have balconies and terraces overlooking the Tusa Valley.

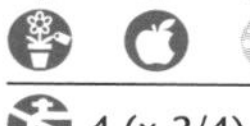

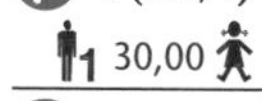
4 (x 2/4)

1 30,00 - 45,00 -

1 (x 4)
1 30,00 - 45,00 -

\-
1 - 7 - 1 - 7 -

Ventimiglia di Sicilia

Crapa Licca

contrada Traversa, S.P. (provincial road) 16 at km 15.6, 90020 Ventimiglia di Sicilia (PA)
Tel. 0918202144 Fax 0918202878
Web: www.crapalicca.it

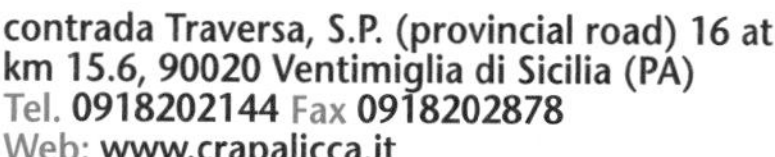

This is a 17th-century farmhouse that has been well preserved, and the additions blend well with the building's external features. The restaurant is excellent.

\-
1 - - -

6 (x 2)
1 52,00 20,00 62,00 -

\-
1 - 7 - 1 - 7 -

Viagrande

Blandano

contrada Blandano, via Garibaldi 441,
95029 Viagrande (CT)
Tel. 0957893704 Fax 0957893704
Web: www.blandano.com

This family-run farm accommodates its guests in old rural houses that have been carefully renovated and furnished; wines produced on the farm are served with the meals.

\-
1 - - -

1 (x 2)
1 48,00 - - -

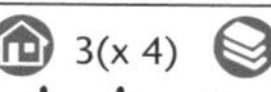

3(x 4)
1 - 7 - 1 104,00 7 -

Catania University Botanical Garden

One of the few green areas in Catania's old town, the Botanical Garden, created in 1858 by Francesco Tornabene, is a veritable living museum, still to this day with the original structure, as shown by the neoclassical building with a double colonnade front, and the near geometric layout of the garden. The thick tangle of exotic plants makes it look like a tropical garden, a cool oasis in the heart of the city, offering a number of remarkable collections. Surely the richest one (with about 2,000 species) is the succulent plants collection, one of the garden's main attractions thanks to the original forms and structures on display. Just as interesting is the palms collection, numbering about a hundred trees.
In the Sicilian Garden are kept plants growing spontaneously all over Sicily.

Entry: via A. Longo, 19 95125 Catania
Telephone 095.430901 - Fax 095.441209
e-mail: dipbot@mbox.dipbot.unict.it
Internet: http://www.dipbot.unict.it
Opening times: weekdays from 9.00 a.m. to 1.00 p.m.

Farm Holiday Villa dei Papiri

Farm Holidays in Sicily Syracuse "Villa dei Papiri".
When one thinks of a protected natural area, one is imagining immediately natural areas far away from the populated city centers,you are picturing mountains, forests and swamps designed and costructed from the slow rhythms of the nature, more than from the achievements of the history of men. Instead, just at the doors of Syracuse, Sicily (Italy), a natural reserve is guarding a site at which the passing of the centuries is intimately interlaced with the history of a city, with its ancient legends and cultural traditions.
It is directly in this vast natural reserve where one finds the Villa dei Papiri, the Villa of the Papyrus. Embedded in the green, equipped with every comfort, it offers its visitors the possibility to relax and savour in tranquillity the beauties of the place, either at the sea or with a diversity of activities like horseback-riding, mountainbiking, excursions etc. But only to the visitor these places will unveil the countless sensations of well-being that associated with them.

Farm Holiday Villa dei Papiri

Contrada Cozzo Pantano - Fonte Ciane - 96100 Siracusa
Mail: info@villadeipapiri.it - Web Site: www.villadeipapiri.it
Tel/Fax +39 0931 721321 - Mobile +39 335 6064735

TOSCANA

LIGURIA
EMILIA
APPENNINO TO
Rapallo
Chiàvari
Sestri Levante
Lèvanto
La Spèzia
Pontrèmoli
Mulazzo
Villafranca in Lunigiana
Tresana
Lunigiana
Magra
Licciana Nardi
Castelnuovo di Garfagnana
Fivizzano
Aulla
Sarzana
Carrara
Massa
ALPI APUANE
Garfagnana
Serchio
Abetone
Gallicano
Barga
Marina di Carrara
Marina di Massa
Montignoso
Forte dei Marmi
Serraval Pistoiese
Pieve a Nièvole
Péscia
Viareggio
Lucca
Montecarlo
Montecat Terme
Lago di Massaciùccoli
MAR LÌGURE
Capànnori
Lamporécch
S. Giuliano Terme
Pisa
Calci
Arno
San Miniato
Pontedera
Ponsacco
Palàia
Lari
Livorno
Montaio
Santa Luce
Lajàtico
Era
Gorgona (Livorno)
Rosignano Marìttimo
Volte
Montecatini Val di Cècina
Vada
Guardistallo
Cècina
Riparbella
Pomarance
Cècina
Bibbona
Castelnuov di Val di Cècin
Larderello
Castagneto Carducci
Monteverdi Marìttimo
Sassetta
Monteroton Marìtti
San Vincenzo
Capràia (Livorno)
Campìglia Marìttima
Suvereto
Massa Marìttim
Populònia
Scarlino
Piombino
Follònica
Golfo di Follònica
Gavorra
Portoferràio
Marciana
PUNTA ALA
Isola d'Elba (Livorno)
Porto Azzurro
Capolìveri
Castiglione della Pescài
CORSICA (France)
PARCO NAZIONALE DELL' ARCIPELAGO TOSCANO
Pianosa (Livorno)
MAR TIRRENO
0
20
40 km
Montecristo (Livorno)
Giglio (Grosseto)

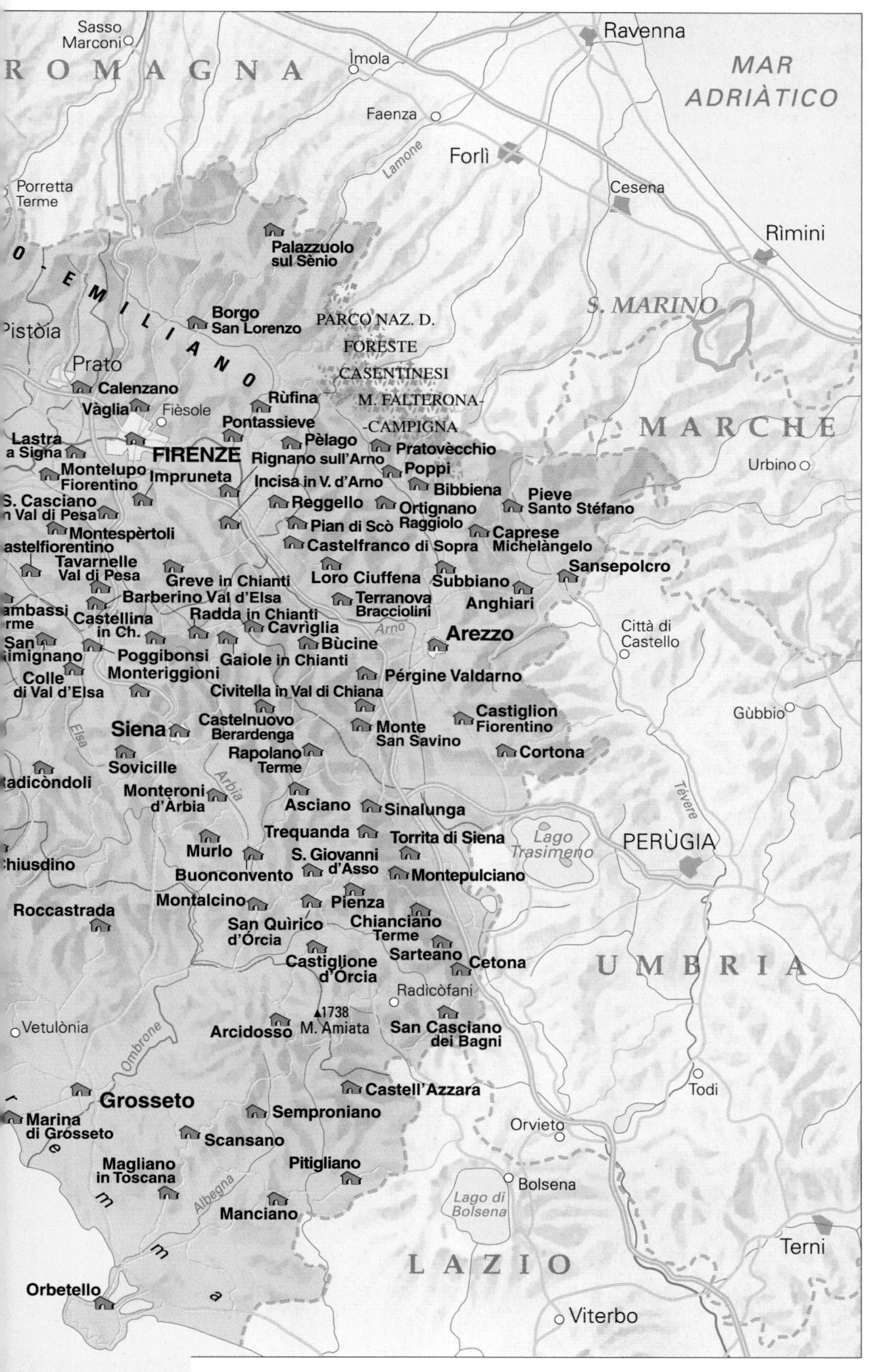

Giannutri
(Grosseto)

Anghiari

Ca' del Viva

at Scheggia, via Ca' del Viva 63,
52031 Anghiari (AR)
Tel. **0575749171** Fax **0575749171**
Web: **www.go.to/cadelviva**

From the ridge there are views of both the Arno and the Tiber valleys. The complex consists of the owner's house and two stone cottages reserved for the guests.

 -

1 - - -

 -

1 - - -

 4(x 4)

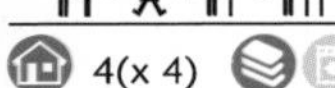 1 - 7 - 1 - 7 600,00

Ca' Faggio

at Toppole 42, 52031 Anghiari (AR)
Tel. **0575749025**
Web: **www.cafaggio.it**

There's a timeless atmosphere in the countryside around Anghiari, with its woods, olive groves and vineyards. This is the ideal setting for the courses in organic agriculture held on this farm.

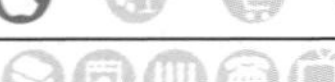 -

1 - - -

-

1 - - -

 5(x 4)

1 - 7 - 1 85,00 7 -

Arcidosso

I Rondinelli

at Rondinelli, 58031 Arcidosso (GR)
Tel. **0564968168** Fax **0564968168**

In the shade of chestnut trees on the slopes of Monte Amiata, a 19th-century farmhouse has recently been converted into tourist accommodation. The rooms are large, with period furniture.

-

1 - - -

 8 (x 2/4)

 1 34,00  26,00 52,00  -

-

1 - 7 - 1 - 7 -

Arezzo

Badia Ficarolo

at Palazzo del Pero 57, 52030 Arezzo
Tel. **0575369320** Fax **0575369320**
Web: **users.iol.it/la-badia**

The ruins of a Benedictine abbey give a romantic touch to a panoramic hill surrounded by woods. The accommodation is in a very well renovated farmhouse.

 -

 1 - - -

6 (x 3/4)

1 - 7 - 1 120,00 7 1.200,00

Barone Albergotti

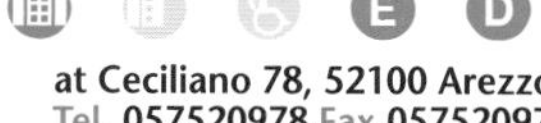

at Ceciliano 78, 52100 Arezzo
Tel. 057520978 Fax 057520978
Web: www.villaalbergotti.com

Accommodation is available in the renovated farmhouses built around a magnificent villa dating from the late 16th-century.

-

1 - - -

-

1 - - -

4(x 4)

1 - 7 - 1 140,00 7 650,00

La Fabbrica

at Santa Maria alla Rassinata, 52100 Arezzo
Tel. 0575319012

In the hills, amid oaks and chestnuts, accommodation is available in a large 18th-century house with floors of terracotta tiles, wooden beams and traditional furniture.

-

1 - - -

-

1 - - -

2 (x 4/6)

1 - 7 - 1 62,00 7 -

Magnanini Massimo

via Fontebranda 47, 52100 Arezzo
Tel. 057527627 Fax 057527627
Web: www.retetoscana.it

At the foot of the Alpe di Poti, amid oaks and pines, apartments are available in a group of converted farmhouses. The terracotta floors and beams recall the buildings' origins.

-

1 - - -

-

1 - - -

3 (x 2/4)

1 - 7 - 1 105,00 7 620,00

Asciano

Podere Scurcoli

at Case Sparse, 53041 Asciano (SI)
Tel. 3483039576 Fax 0444695209
Web: www.scurcoli.it

Two stone cottages stand with their outbuildings on a hillock. Both recently renovated, they have large spaces for relaxing in the open air.

-

1 - - -

-

1 - - -

3(x 3)

1 - 7 - 1 258,00 7 1.518,00

Tenuta di Monte Sante Marie

at Monte Sante Marie, 53041 Asciano (SI)
Tel. 0577700020 Fax 0577700020
Web: www.montesantemarie.it

This accommodation is in renovated farmhouses in a medieval village. There's a children's pool and courses on photography, the technique of fresco painting and cookery.

-

1 - - -

-

1 - - -

6 (x 2/6)

1 - 7 - 1 - 7 950,00

-

1 - - -

9 (x 2/4)

1 90,00 - 120,00 -

-

1 - 7 - 1 - 7 -

Barberino Val d'Elsa

La Spinosa

via Le Masse 8, 50021 Barberino Val d'Elsa (FI)
Tel. 0558075413 Fax 0558066214
Web: www.laspinosa.it

The accommodation is in two 17th-century farmhouses. The interiors have been excellently refurbished and there's a large garden with lawns.

Bibbiena

Casale Camalda

at Serravalle-Castagnoli 33, 52010 Bibbiena (AR)
Tel. 0575519104 Fax 0575519104
Web: www.agriturismocamalda.it

This old rural complex amid the woods and streams of the Foreste Casentinesi National Park is just a short distance away from the monastery of Camaldoli.

-

1 - - -

-

1 - - -

3(x 3)

1 43,90 7 - 1 - 7 -

Bibbona

Villa Caprareccia

via Bolgherese 4, 57020 Bibbona (LI)
Tel. 0586670128 Fax 0586671942
Web: www.villacaprareccia.it

This family-run farm is only 6 km from the coast. As an alternative to the beach, guests may visit the nearby Macchia della Magona Nature Reserve.

-

1 - - -

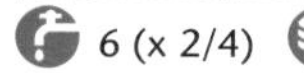

6 (x 2/4)

1 31,00 - 46,48 -

-

1 - 7 - 1 - 7 -

Borgo San Lorenzo

Collefertile

at La Sughera-Montegiovi, via Arliano 37,
50032 Borgo San Lorenzo (FI)
Tel. 0558495201 Fax 0558490154
Web: www.collefertile.com

In the heart of the Mugello, this large hill farm offers accommodation in a notable group of buildings combining a rustic atmosphere with modern comforts.

-

1 - - -

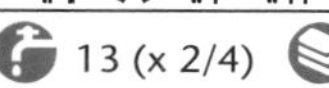

13 (x 2/4)

1 - - 116,50 -

-

1 - 7 - 1 - 7 -

La Topaia

via S. Giovanni Maggiore 57,
50032 Borgo San Lorenzo (FI)
Tel. 0558408741 Fax 0558408741
Web: www.wel.it/latopaia

The name is hardly suitable for an establishment that is notable for its order and cleanliness: in front of the house there's a lawn and its windows are decked with geraniums.

-

1 - - -

2 (x 2)

1 26,00 - - -

2(x 4)

1 - 7 - 1 140,00 7 840,00

Sanvitale

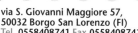

at Luco Mugello, via Campagna 20,
50030 Borgo San Lorenzo (FI)
Tel. 0558401158 Fax 0558401158
Web: www.wel.it/AAsanvitale

This farm grows a wide variety of crops. Next to the farmhouse is a low stone building used to accommodate the guests.

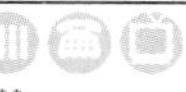

-

1 - - -

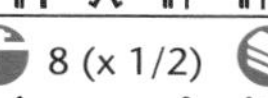

8 (x 1/2)

1 44,00 - 67,00 -

-

1 - 7 - 1 - 7 -

Bucine

Borgo Iesolana

at Iesolana, 52021 Bucine (AR)
Tel. 055992988 Fax 055992879
Web: www.iesolana.it

In this hamlet surrounded by greenery there are rustic stone houses with gardens and apartments, splendidly renovated with all modern comforts and antique furniture.

 -

1 - - -

 -

1 - - -

 8 (x 2/4)

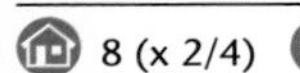 1 - 7 - 1 358,00 7 -

Fattoria le Ginestre

at Greti 56, 52021 Bucine (AR)
Tel. 0559918032 Fax 0559918032
E-mail: fattorialeginestre@tiscali.it

Located in the hills of the upper Arno Valley, the accommodation is in a modern building with balconies overlooking the garden and swimming pool.

-

1 - - -

-

1 - - -

 3 (x 2/6) 

1 - 7 350,00 1 - 7 - 

Buonconvento

La Ripolina

at Pieve di Piana, 53022 Buonconvento (SI)
Tel. 0577282280 Fax 0577282280
Web: www.laripolina.it

The accommodation is in the medieval setting of Pieve di Piana. Apartments and rooms, with furnishings in Tuscan style, are available in renovated farmhouses.

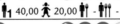

-

1 - - -

 8 (x 2/4)

 1 40,00 20,00 - -

6 (x 2/4)

1 45,00 7 - 1 - 7 -

Poggio alle Rose

at Piana, 53022 Buonconvento (SI)
Tel. 0577270219 Fax 0577223910
E-mail: elicrest@tin.it

There is plenty of atmosphere here: floors of terracotta tiles, fireplaces, carpets and flowered fabrics help to create a setting of rustic elegance.

4 (x 1/4)

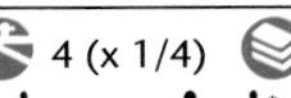 1 35,00 - - -

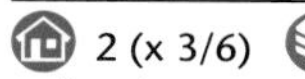

2 (x 3/6)

1 - 7 - 1 200,00 7 -

Calci

Villa Rosselmini

via Rosselmini 10, 56011 Calci (PI)
Tel. 050934226 Fax 050934226
Web: www.villarosselmini.com

This vast farm at the foot of the Colline Pisane has comfortable apartments available in the outbuildings adjacent to the 17th-century villa.

7 (x 2/4)

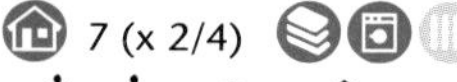

1 - 7 - 1 - 7 1.000,00

Calenzano

Fattoria di Sommaia

via delle Cantine 118, 50041 Calenzano (FI)
Tel. 0558825358 Fax 0558825358

Just outside Florence, this establishment is set amid olives and cypresses. An group of old rural buildings has been converted into the apartments.

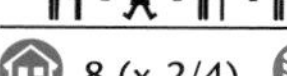

8 (x 2/4)

1 - 7 - 1 - 7 700,00

Campiglia Marittima

La Ranocchiaia

at Venturina, via Aurelia Sud 44,
57029 Campiglia Marittima (LI)
Tel. 0565852048 Fax 0565852048
Web: www.ranocchiaia.com

An alternative to the countryside, the Costa degli Etruschi extends from Cecina to Piombino. Accommodation is available in the main villa or the adjacent farmhouse.

5(x 6)

1 - 7 - 1 - 7 878,00

Villa Toscana

at Granai, 57029 Campiglia Marittima (LI)
Tel. 3356911674 Fax 0565853462
Web: www.wel.it/VillaToscana

The old rose of the farmhouse contrasts with the green lawn and blue swimming pool; there's even a small vegetable garden at the guests' disposal.

7(x 2)

1 - 7 - 1 120,00 7 -

CAPANNORI

ALLE CAMELIE

at Pieve di Compito, 55065 Capannori (LU)
Tel. 058355505 Fax 0583977001
Web: www.linketto.it/allecamelie

With its renovated outbuildings, this 19th-century villa is ideal for holidays where the accent is on physical fitness and the exploration of the surrounding countryside.

-

1 - - -

4 (x 2)

1 38,75 - - -

2 (x 4/6)

1 - 7 - 1 - 7 880,00

FATTORIA DI FUBBIANO

road for Fubbiano 6, 55012 Capannori (LU)
Tel. 0583978011 Fax 0583978344
Web: www.fattoriadifubbiano.it

An 18th-century villa with its own chapel, a garden and copse of ilexes, farm workers' cottages, cellars and stables: this is the Fubbiano farm.

-

1 - - -

-

1 - - -

2(x 4)

1 - 7 - 1 - 7 4.600,00

FATTORIA DI PETROGNANO

at Petrognano, via Comunale 13,
55010 Capannori (LU)
Tel. 0583978038 Fax 0118190908
Web: www.fattoriadipetrognano.it

Amid the vineyards and olive groves of the Colline Lucchesi, a 17th-century villa and farmhouses with a beautiful garden and splendid views are the ideal setting for an 'old-style' holiday.

-

1 - - -

6 (x 2)

1 40,00 - - -

3(x 4)

1 - 7 - 1 150,00 7 880,00

FATTORIA MAIONCHI

at Tofori, 55012 Capannori (LU)
Tel. 0583978194 Fax 0583978345
Web: www.fattoriamaionchi.it

Surrounded by walls, this beautiful villa gives onto its Italian garden in the Colline Lucchesi. The accommodation is in the outbuildings surrounding it.

1 - - -

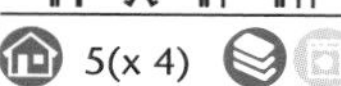
1 - - -

5(x 4)

1 - 7 - 1 - 7 981,27

Capoliveri

Bioelba

via Straccoligno 1, 57031 Capoliveri (LI)
Tel. 0565939072 Fax 0565939072
Web: www.bioelba.it

An organic farm that offers four self-contained apartments facing the sea in one of the remotest parts of the island of Elba.

1 - - -

-

1 - - -

4(x 2)

1 - 7 - 1 - 7 1.290,00

Caprese Michelangelo

Selvadonica

at Selvadonica,
52033 Caprese Michelangelo (AR)
Tel. 0575791051 Fax 0575791051
Web: www.selvadonica.it

On the slopes of the Alpe di Catenaia, the accommodation is in the cottages scattered over the farm; self-contained and excellently renovated, they are ideal for a relaxing holiday.

-

1 - - -

1 (x 2)

1 20,00 - - -

7 (x 2/4)

1 - 7 - 1 - 7 720,00

Castagneto Carducci

Grattamacco - Podere Santa Maria

at Grattamacco 130,
57022 Castagneto Carducci (LI)
Tel. 0565763933 Fax 0565763933
Web: www.agriturismo-grattamacco.com

Grattamacco is 'an oasis of peace': the olive oil produced by this farm is itself worth the trip here.

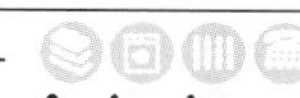
1 - - -

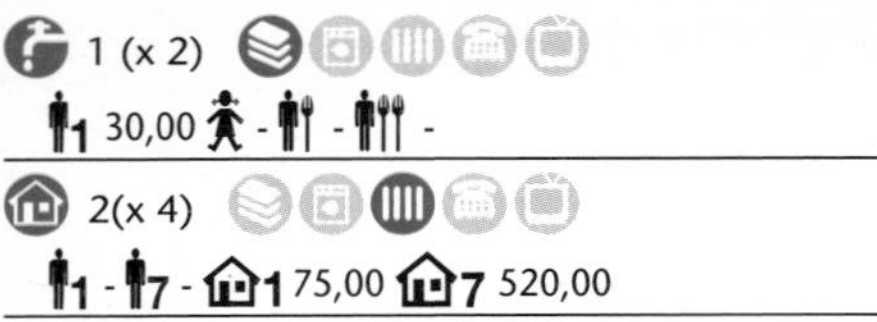

1 (x 2)

30,00 - - -

2(x 4)

- - 1 75,00 7 520,00

Greppo all'Olivo

at Donoratico, via Greppo all'Olivo 49,
57024 Castagneto Carducci (LI)
Tel. 0565775366 Fax 0565775366
Web: www.agritourism.net/greppoallolivo

There's a warm welcome from the farmer's family for guests staying in these well-equipped apartments, just 4 km from the sea, with a garden, barbecue and parking space.

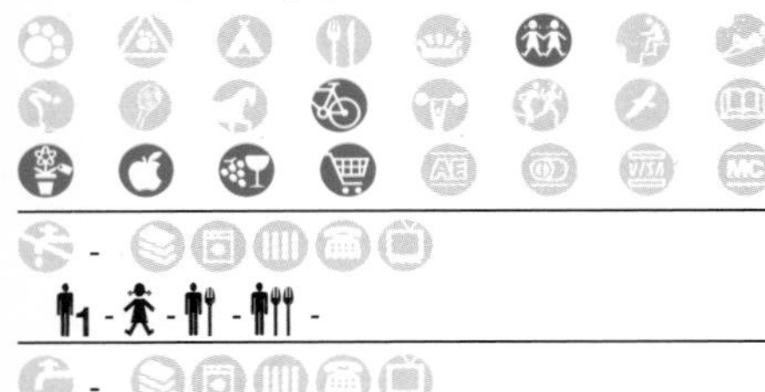

\- - - -

\- - - -

4 (x 3/7)

- - 1 100,00 7 -

Sughericcio

at Sughericcio 253,
57022 Castagneto Carducci (LI)
Tel. 0564415359 Fax 0564415359
Web: www.sughericcio.it

The recent conversion has provided three self-contained apartments, opening onto the garden through a veranda covered with canes.

\- - - -

\- - - -

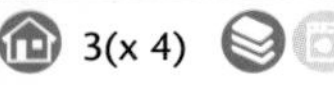

3(x 4)

- - 1 95,00 7 590,00

Castelfiorentino

Monteolivo

at Petrazzi, via Monteolivo 28,
50051 Castelfiorentino (FI)
Tel. 057164924 Fax 057164924
Web: www.monteolivo.com

This farm in the Elsa Valley has comfortable apartments in buildings that have been converted without spoiling their appearance. Amid the olives, there's a large garden and a swimming pool.

\- - - -

\- - - -

4 (x 2/4)

- - 1 135,00 7 -

Sorbigliana

via O. Bacci 59, 50051 Castelfiorentino (FI)
Tel. 0571629951 Fax 0571629951
Web: www.aracne.com/sorbigliana

At Castelfiorentino this farmhouse, which was built round a medieval tower-house, is an excellent base for visiting the historic towns and cities of Tuscany.

\- - - -

\- - - -

7 (x 2/3)

1 - 7 - 1 120,00 7 820,00

Castelfranco di Sopra

Borgo Mocale

at Mocale, via Lama 26,
52020 Castelfranco di Sopra (AR)
Tel. **0559149302** Fax **0559149932**
Web: **www.borgomocale.it**

A number of farmhouses clustered around a 12th-century tower-house accommodate their guests with good taste and discretion in very well renovated rooms and apartments.

\-

1 - - -

3 (x 2)

1 45,00 - -

5(x 4)

1 - 7 - 1 140,00 7 -

La Capraia

at Pulicciano, 52020 Castelfranco di Sopra (AR)
Tel. **0559149500** Fax **0559148991**
Web: **www.borgolacapraia.com**

Amid the olive groves and scrub of the Pratomagno - ideal for hiking and tours on mountain bikes - this refined country house is located in an ancient village.

\-

1 - - -

\-

1 - - -

12 (x 2/4)

1 45,00 7 - 1 - 7 1.150,00

La Casella

at La Casella, via Lama 24,
52020 Castelfranco di Sopra (AR)
Tel. **0559149440** Fax **0559149440**
Web: **www.agriturismolacasella.com**

Overlooking the Arno Valley from the slopes of the Pratomagno, this charming cottage is embellished with beautiful displays of geraniums and hydrangeas.

\-

1 - - -

8 (x 2/4)

1 52,00 - -

3(x 4)

1 - 7 - 1 - 7 832,00

Castell'Azzara

Il Cornacchino

at Cornacchino, 58034 Castell'Azzara (GR)
Tel. **0564951582** Fax **0564951655**
Web: **www.cornacchino.it**

From the River Fiora to the sea, Lake Bolsena, the beechwoods of Monte Amiata... these are but a few of the places within easy reach of this unusual establishment with stables.

12 (x 1/2)

1 47,00 23,50 - 74,00

\-

1 - - -

1 - 7 - 1 - 7 -

Castellina in Chianti

Casavecchia alla Piazza

at La Piazza 37, 53011 Castellina in Chianti (SI)
Tel. 0577749754 Fax 0577733662
Web: www.chianticlassico.com/buondonno

This farmhouse dating from the 16th century once belonged to Michelangelo's family: it produces a highly-rated Chianti Classico and olive oil to match.

1 - - -

1 - - -

2 (x 3/4)

1 - 7 - 1 110,00 7 -

Castello di Fonterutoli

at Fonterutoli, via Rossini 5,
53011 Castellina in Chianti (SI)
Tel. 057773571 Fax 0577735757
Web: www.stagionidelchianti.com

This farmhouse is in a hamlet on a hill in the heart of the Chianti Classico zone, where there are the apartments accommodating the guests.

1 - - -

1 - - -

6 (x 2/3)

1 - 7 - 1 - 7 2.685,00

Castelnuovo Berardenga

Casalgallo

at Quercegrossa, via del Chianti Classico 5,
53010 Castelnuovo Berardenga (SI)
Tel. 0577328008 Fax 0577328008

There's a very warm welcome in this family-run farm. The accommodation, with a pleasant atmosphere, is in renovated cottages.

1 - - -

4 (x 2)

1 30,00 - - -

6 (x 2/6)

1 - 7 - 1 68,00 7 460,00

Castello di Montalto

at Montalto 16,
53019 Castelnuovo Berardenga (SI)
Tel. 0577355675 Fax 0577355682
Web: www.montalto.it

This is a complex of rare beauty, consisting of a medieval castle, a tiny hamlet and a farmhouse a short distance away that is, however, still part of the farm.

-
1 - - -

-
1 - - -

5 (x 2/4)
1 - 7 - 1 - 7 2.000,00

Fattoria di Selvole

at Selvole, 53019 Castelnuovo Berardenga (SI)
Tel. 0577322662 Fax 0577322718
Web: www.selvole.com

A number of farm buildings have been converted into apartments with period furniture; each has its own open space with recreational facilities.

-
1 - - -

-
1 - - -

14 (x 4/6)
1 - 7 - 1 - 7 665,00

Podere Le Boncie

at San Felice,
53019 Castelnuovo Berardenga (SI)
Tel. 0577359383 Fax 0577359383
E-mail: leboncie@libero.it

Le Boncie offers accommodation with a difference: beautiful and romantic, it's a real home. The owner, a well-known wine expert, holds courses on wine-tasting at weekends.

-
1 - - -

-
1 - - -

1(x 8)
1 - 7 - 1 281,00 7 -

Poderi di Miscianello

at Ponte a Bozzone,
53010 Castelnuovo Berardenga (SI)
Tel. 0577356840 Fax 0577356604
Web: www.miscianello.it

The setting is Chianti, and that speaks for itself. A recent conversion has made comfortable, well-furnished rooms available for tourists.

-
1 - - -

1 (x 2)
1 40,00 - - -

3(x 3)
1 - 7 - 1 180,00 7 -

Castelnuovo di Garfagnana

La Palazzina

at Antisciana,
55032 Castelnuovo di Garfagnana (LU)
Tel. 058362631 Fax 058362631
Web: www.agriturismolapalazzina.com

For nature lovers and hikers, the Apuan Alps Regional Park is ideal, and for those seeking a holiday in verdant surroundings, there's a warm welcome from the Marchi family.

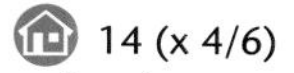

 -    

1 - - -

-

1 - - -

7 (x 4/5)

1 - 7 - 1 - 7 574,00

Castelnuovo di Val di Cecina

Il Pavone

at Valle del Pavone,
56041 Castelnuovo di Val di Cecina (PI)
Tel. 058820965 Fax 058820306
E-mail: eiughetti@tiscali.it

This renovated farmhouse is divided into four spacious self-contained apartments. They share the living-room with a fireplace and the wood-fired oven outside.

-

1 - - -

-

1 - - -

4 (x 4/5)

1 - 7 - 1 77,00 7 -

Castiglione della Pescaia

Podere Zuccherini

at Paesetto di Buriano,
58023 Castiglione della Pescaia (GR)
Tel. 0564424191 Fax 0564424191
Web: www.agriturismoalba.com

A farmhouse faced with pink stucco stands just below the village of Buriano. Apartments are also available in the Podere Calabria, belonging to the same owners.

-

1 - - -

-

1 - - -

6 (x 2/4)

1 - 7 - 1 44,00 7 1.033,00

Castiglione d'Orcia

Grossola

via Grossola 4, 53023 Castiglione d'Orcia (SI)
Tel. 0577887537 Fax 0577887537

In the varied landscape of the Val d'Orcia, this 16th-century stone farmhouse, which has been carefully restored, is ideal for holidays in close contact with nature.

 -

 1 - - -

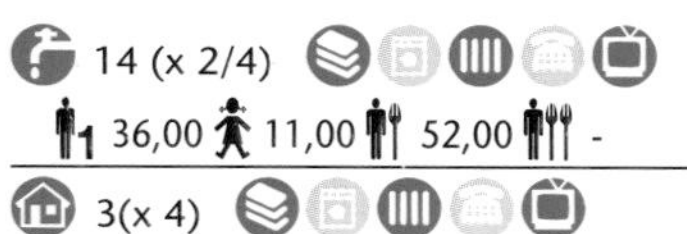

14 (x 2/4)

1 36,00 11,00 52,00 -

 3(x 4)

 36,00  7 - 1 - 7 -

Poggio Istiano

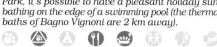

via Cassia at km 177, 53023 Castiglione d'Orcia (SI)
Tel. 0577887046 Fax 0577887046
Web: www.poggioistiano.it

In the middle of the Val d'Orcia Nature and Culture Park, it's possible to have a pleasant holiday sunbathing on the edge of a swimming pool (the thermal baths of Bagno Vignoni are 2 km away).

 -

1 - - - -

 -

1 - - - -

 3(x 2)

 50,00  7 - 1 -  7 -

Sant'Alberto

at Campiglia d'Orcia, via Cassia at km 167,
53029 Castiglione d'Orcia (SI)
Tel. 0577897227 Fax 0577897227
Web: www.agriturismo.com/santalberto

A reminder of the history of long ago, the Via Francigena, an old pilgrim route, crosses the farm. The accommodation is in a cottage with its Tuscan terracotta, wood and old furnishings.

 -

1 - - - -

1 (x 2)

1 35,00 - - -

2 (x 4/7)

 1 - 7 -  1 - 7 780,00

Castiglion Fiorentino

Casali in Val di Chio

via S. Cristina 16, 52043 Castiglion Fiorentino (AR)
Tel. 0575650179 Fax 0575650179
Web: www.buccelletti.it

Surrounded by olives and oaks, these three stone farmhouses are lavishly furnished, with a garden full of flowers and the inviting blue rectangle of the swimming pool.

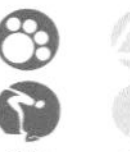

-

1 - - - -

-

1 - - - -

5(x 4)

 1 - 7 -  1 - 7 2.660,00

La Pievuccia

at Santa Lucia 118, 52043 Castiglion Fiorentino (AR)
Tel. 0575651007 Fax 0575651007
Web: www.lapievuccia.it

This farm in the Valdichiana consists of the main house with wine cellars and a restaurant, and two adjacent outbuildings converted into tourist accommodation.

-

1 - - -

-

1 - - -

4 (x 2/6)

1 - 7 - 1 150,00 7 980,00

Le Capanne

at Pieve di Chio 106,
52043 Castiglion Fiorentino (AR)
Tel. 0575656500 Fax 0575656500
Web: www.lecapanne.com

The Valdichiana and Casentino, Lake Trasimene, the Crete Senesi and Chianti: these are the main attractions of a holiday that will certainly be immensely rewarding.

-

1 - - -

-

1 - - -

4(x 4)

1 - 7 - 1 - 7 880,00

Lodolazzo

at Brolio 69, 52043 Castiglion Fiorentino (AR)
Tel. 0575652220 Fax 0575652900
Web: www.agriturismo.com/lodolazzo

The large arcade facing the rooms are a distinctive feature of this establishment, which is notable for its functional structure and the attention paid to the furnishings.

-

1 - - -

-

1 - - -

4 (x 2/6)

1 - 7 - 1 120,00 7 750,00

Cavriglia

Fattoria di Barberino

at Meleto, viale Barberino 19,
52020 Cavriglia (AR)
Tel. 055961321 Fax 055961071
Web: www.villabarberino.it

The original complex, renovated without altering its original appearance, has been converted into tourist accommodation full of atmosphere.

-

1 - - -

4 (x 1/2)

1 65,00 - 75,00 -

4 (x 2/6)

1 70,00 7 - 1 - 7 -

Cetona

Casa Vecchia

S.S. (state road) 321 Est 49, 53040 Cetona (SI)
Tel. **0578238383** Fax **0578238383**
Web: **www.agriturismocasavecchia.it**

Close to the border between Tuscany and Umbria are, in one direction, San Casciano dei Bagni, a small spa, Montepulciano and the Valdichiana, and, in the other, Città della Pieve and Lake Trasimene.

 -

1 - - -

 -

1 - - -

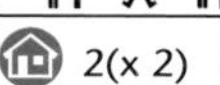 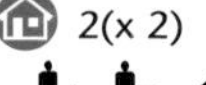 2(x 2)  

1 - 7 - 1 188,00 7 -

Chianciano Terme

Palazzo Bandino

at Palazzo Bandino, via Stiglianesi 3,
53042 Chianciano Terme (SI)
Tel. **057861199** Fax **057862021**
Web: **www.valerianigroup.com**

In the immediate vicinity of the spa, a 17th-century farmhouse has been converted into refined tourist accommodation after careful restoration.

 -

1 - - -

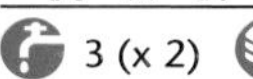 3 (x 2) 

1 39,00 - - -

 6 (x 2/6)   

1 - 7 - 1 250,00 7 800,00

Chiusdino

Il Mulino delle Pile

at Mulino delle Pile, 53012 Chiusdino (SI)
Tel. **0577750688** Fax **0577750686**
Web: **www.agriturismoilmulino.com**

With its millstones and fulling-mills, Il Mulino (The Mill) used to serve the monks of a nearby abbey; today guests are accommodated in the small, enchanting rooms in the tower.

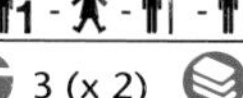 -

1 - - -

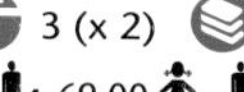 3 (x 2) 

1 69,00 - 89,00 -

-

1 - 7 - 1 - 7 -

Civitella in Val di Chiana

La Loccaia

at Ciggiano, via di Loccaia 23,
52040 Civitella in Val di Chiana (AR)
Tel. **0575440098** Fax **0575440098**
Web: **www.laloccaia.it**

This excellently renovated cottage, with a view over the Valdichiana, is located on a family-run farm with woods, olive groves, vineyards and fruit trees.

-

1 - - -

1 (x 2)
1 28,00 - - -

2 (x 2/4)
1 - 7 - 1 115,71 7 -

Colle di Val d'Elsa

Fattoria Belvedere

at Belvedere, 53034 Colle di Val d'Elsa (SI)
Tel. 0577920009 Fax 0577923500
Web: www.fattoriabelvedere.com

This 18th-century villa, with a large park, is now a hotel and restaurant. The accommodation is partly in the main house and partly in a farmhouse.

-
1 - - - -

-
1 - - - -

7 (x 2/4)
1 - 7 - 1 - 7 570,00

La Pieve

at Campiglia di Foci,
53034 Colle di Val d'Elsa (SI)
Tel. 0577920130 Fax 0577920130

Set in a small wood on a hill, this stone farmhouse offers rooms in traditional style and, when it gets cool, the pleasure of sitting in front of the fireplace.

-
1 - - - -

-
1 - - - -

4(x 3)
1 - 7 - 1 114,00 7 -

Tenuta di Mensanello

at Mensanello 34, 53034 Colle di Val d'Elsa (SI)
Tel. 0577971080 Fax 0577971080
Web: www.mensanello.com

This large farm is an excellent base for visiting San Gimignano, Volterra and Siena; renovated farmhouses have been converted to provide accommodation.

-
1 - - - -

-
1 - - - -

6(x 4)
1 - 7 - 1 170,00 7 825,00

Cortona

Borgo Elena

at Cegliolo, via Manzoni 18, 52042 Cortona (AR)
Tel. 0575604773 Fax 0575604773

This small hamlet has been converted into holiday accommodation. The care taken over the preservation of the rural buildings makes this an outstanding example of restoration for tourist purposes.

-
1 - - -

-
1 - - -

7 (x 2/4)
1 40,00 7 - 1 - 7 -

Da Domenico

via Teverina c.s. 24, 52044 Cortona (AR)
Tel. 0575616024 Fax 0575616011
Web: www.agriturismodadomenico.com

The stone of the farmhouse warmed by the sun and the cascade of roses framing the entrance are the first impressions visitors get of this delightful establishment.

-
1 - - -

5 (x 2)
1 60,00 30,00 - -

-
1 - 7 - 1 - 7 -

Fattoria Fabbri

at San Marco in Villa 2, 52044 Cortona (AR)
Tel. 0575630502 Fax 0575630502
Web: www.fattoriafabbri.com

Bare stone walls, ceilings with wooden beams, terracotta tiles on the floors: this is truly the traditional Tuscan farmhouse, as may be seen in this attractive renovated 17th-century building.

-
1 - - -

-
1 - - -

3 (x 2/4)
1 - 7 - 1 - 7 400,00

Fattoria Le Giare

at Fratticciola, via Ronzano 14,
52040 Cortona (AR)
Tel. 0575638063 Fax 0575638063
Web: www.fattorialegiare.com

This old farmhouse in a tranquil, panoramic position has been converted into seven apartments; there's also a swimming pool.

-
1 - - -

-
1 - - -

7 (x 3/4)

1 - 7 - 1 93,00 7 670,00

I Pagliai

at Montalla 23, 52044 Cortona (AR)
Tel. 0575605220 Fax 0575603676
Web: www.ipagliai.it

Located in a small hamlet, this farm provides accommodation in two self-contained cottages that have been renovated, closely adhering to their original state.

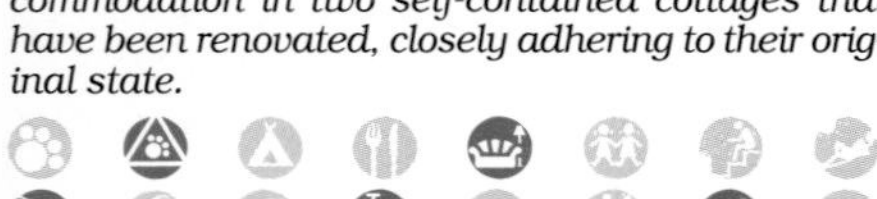

1 - - -

8 (x 2)

1 40,00 - -

4(x 8)

1 - 7 - 1 - 7 850,00

La Renaia

at Case Sparse 760, 52044 Cortona (AR)
Tel. 057562787 Fax 057562787
Web: www.larenaia.it

The original nucleus was a water-mill; around this was built the farmhouse, which has now been restored to its original appearance. The large rooms have period furniture.

1 - - -

1 - - -

3(x 4)

1 - 7 - 1 154,90 7 830,00

Rosa dei Venti

at Creti, via Quaratola 71,
52044 Cortona (AR)
Tel. 0575638085 Fax 0575638085
Web: www.rosadeiventi.net

The Micheli family have run their farm on a hill overlooking the Valdichiana for four generations, and today, with care and good taste, they also provide tourist accommodation.

1 - - -

1 - - -

5 (x 2/4)

1 - 7 - 1 185,00 7 1.200,00

Fiesole

Poggio al Sole

at Torre di Buiano, via Torre di Buiano 4,
50014 Fiesole (FI)
Tel. 055548839 Fax 055548839
Web: www.poggioalsole.net

This establishment is in an excellent position in the splendid setting of the Colli Fiorentini. The farm has revived the cultivation of saffron in this area.

1 - - -
5 (x 2)
1 50,00 - -
-
1 - 7 - 1 - 7 -

Firenze

La Fattoressa

at Galluzzo, via Volterrana 58, 50124 Firenze
Tel. 0552048418 Fax 0552048418

An 18th-century farmhouse below the Certosa di Firenze, with a garden, orchard and cultivated fields, offers accommodation in rooms in a converted hayloft.

-
1 - - -
6 (x 2/4)
1 45,00 - -
-
1 - 7 - 1 - 7 -

Le Macine

viuzzo del Pozzetto 1, 50126 Firenze
Tel. 0556531089 Fax 0556531089
Web: www.agriturismolemacine.com

Accommodation is available in the Piana di Ripoli in a building of 17th-century origin: it comprises tastefully furnished rooms and small apartments with separate entrances.

-
1 - - -
3 (x 2)
1 50,00 - 77,47 -
2(x 2)
1 50,00 7 - 1 - 7 -

Fivizzano

Il Bardellino

at Soliera Apuana, 54018 Fivizzano (MS)
Tel. 058593304 Fax 058593304
Web: www.ilbardellino.it

The road climbing up to the Passo del Cerreto passes this early 18th-century farmhouse where there's a warm, friendly welcome.

-
1 - - -
6 (x 2/4)
1 30,00 28,00 39,00 -
-
1 - 7 - 1 - 7 -

Gaiole in Chianti

Borgo Casa al Vento

at Casa al Vento, 53013 Gaiole in Chianti (SI)
Tel. 0577749068 Fax 022640754
Web: www.borgocasaalvento.com

There's the atmosphere of a bygone age in this medieval village. Guests are accommodated in well-preserved cottages that have been comfortably furnished.

 -

1 - - -

2 (x 2)

1 35,00 - 63,00 -

10(x 2)

1 - 7 - 1 180,00 7 1.550,00

Castello di Tornano

at Tornano, 53013 Gaiole in Chianti (SI)
Tel. 0577746067 Fax 0577746067
Web: www.castelloditornano.it

The majestic tower is a reminder of past conflicts. An apartment has been constructed in the tower, others in the houses in the village and a separate cottage.

-

1 - - -

7 (x 2/4)

1 120,00 - 145,00 -

9 (x 2/4)

1 - 7 - 1 400,00 7 2.500,00

Villa Vistarenni

at Vistarenni, 53013 Gaiole in Chianti (SI)
Tel. 0577738476 Fax 0577738754
Web: www.vistarenni.com

This accommodation is either in a Renaissance villa with elegant furnishings, or in the farmhouse in rustic style behind it. There's a swimming pool with a marvellous view.

 -

1 - - -

-

1 - - -

5 (x 2/4)

1 - 7 - 1 - 7 2.840,00

Gallicano

La Capannella

at Capannella 5, 55027 Gallicano (LU)
Tel. 058374401 Fax 058362058
E-mail: andrea.gua@libero.it

On the edge of the Garfagnana, the accommodation in a 'hut' to which the owners refer is, in fact, a charming converted loft, with a swimming pool.

-

1 - - -

-

1 - - -

2(x 4)

1 - 7 - 1 100,00 7 -

Gambassi Terme

Poggio ai Grilli

  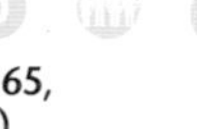

at Varna, via Vecchiarelle 165,
50050 Gambassi Terme (FI)
Tel. 0571631767 Fax 0571631767
E-mail: info@poggioaigrilli.it

Amid roses in full bloom, this romantic farmhouse has three rustic apartments with views over the Elsa Valley and the historic towns and villages dotted around it.

-

1 - - -

 -

1 - - -

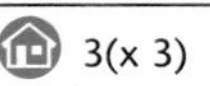 3(x 3) 

1 - 7 - 1 100,00 7 -

Gavorrano

Montebelli

at Molinetto, 58020 Gavorrano (GR)
Tel. 0566887100 Fax 056681439
Web: www.montebelli.com

This accommodation is in a tastefully renovated farmhouse with facilities for horse-riding. The rooms, with period furniture and modern comforts, overlook the park.

-

1 - - -

21 (x 1/4)

1 - - 100,00 -

-

1 - 7 - 1 - 7 -

Greve in Chianti

Castello Vicchiomaggio

via Vicchiomaggio 4, 50022 Greve in Chianti (FI)
Tel. 055854078 Fax 055853911
Web: www.vicchiomaggio.it

Accommodation is available in the hills around Greve in a turreted castle in Renaissance style. The apartments are simply furnished; a swimming pool will open soon.

-

1 - - -

-

1 - - -

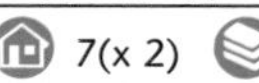 7(x 2) 

1 - 7 - 1 180,00 7 -

Fattoria Castello di Verrazzano

at Greti, 50022 Greve in Chianti (FI)
Tel. 055853211 Fax 055853211
Web: www.verrazzano.com

A fascinating holiday is assured in the guest-house of the castle that used to belong to the great navigator Giovanni da Verrazzano. On the farm, dishes typical of the Chianti district are served.

-

1 - - -

7 (x 2/4) 

1 50,00 - - -

2 (x 2/4)

1 - 7 - 1 - 7 900,00

Fattoria La Sala

at La Panca, via di Cintoia Alta 47,
50022 Greve in Chianti (FI)
Tel. 0558547962 Fax 0558547962
Web: www.agriturismolasala.it

Amid the wooded hills of the Chianti Classico production zone, this farm provides accommodation in comfortable apartments located in old buildings.

-

1 - - -

-

1 - - -

3(x 2)

1 - 7 - 1 - 7 700,00

Villa Vignamaggio

at Vignamaggio, via Petriolo 5,
50022 Greve in Chianti (FI)
Tel. 055854661 Fax 0558544468
Web: www.vignamaggio.com

It's said that the mysterious Mona Lisa, immortalised by Leonardo da Vinci, was born here. This is quality accommodation, with sports facilities and a fitness centre.

-

1 - - -

4 (x 2)

1 75,00 - - -

16 (x 2/4)

1 - 7 - 1 235,00 7 1.480,00

Grosseto

Il Duchesco

at Alberese, 58010 Grosseto
Tel. 0564407323 Fax 0564407323
Web: www.ilduchesco.it

From the coastal dunes to the Monti dell'Uccellina, the Maremma Regional Park is a patchwork of different environments, including cultivated areas and those devoted to pasturage.

-

1 - - -

10 (x 2)

1 35,00 - - -

-

1 - 7 - 1 - 7 -

La Fata

at Alberese, podere Ermada, 58010 Grosseto
Tel. 0564407162 Fax 0564407162

This is a recent building, with rooms giving onto arcades or loggias. There are numerous places of interest in the area, especially the Maremma Regional Park.

-

1 - - -

10 (x 1/2)
1 26,00 - - -

-
1 - 7 - 1 - 7 -

La Pulledraia del Podere Montegrappa

at Alberese, via del Molinaccio 10,
58010 Grosseto
Tel. 0564407237 Fax 0564407237
Web: www.pulledraia.it

The Maremma Regional Park is ideal for holidays focusing on nature: but in addition to the beautiful hills, rivers and beaches, there's comfortable accommodation and organic produce.

-

1 - - -

6 (x 2)
1 45,00 - 65,00 -

-
1 - 7 - 1 - 7 -

Lillastro

at Roselle, 58040 Grosseto
Tel. 0564401171 Fax 0564401171
Web: www.lillastro.com

This farm, which has many animals roaming freely, is ideal for lovers of tourism on horseback and is in an area of great interest for its natural environment and archaeological sites.

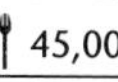

3 (x 1)
1 24,00 - 45,00 -

4 (x 2)
1 30,00 - 45,00 -

-
1 - 7 - 1 - 7 -

Podere Isonzo

at Alberese, via Strada Aurelia Antica 91,
58010 Grosseto
Tel. 0564405393 Fax 056648805
Web: www.agriturismo.net/isonzo

This is where the boatman who ferried people and goods across the Ombrone used to live. Today the house accommodates those seeking a holiday in the open air.

-
1 - - -

-
1 - - -

4 (x 2/4)

1 - 7 - 1 80,00 7 -

Guardistallo

Le Casette

via del Poggetto 13, 56040 Guardistallo (PI)
Tel. 0586794404 Fax 0586655040

On the slopes of the Colline Metallifere, this farm, which practises integrated agriculture, overlooks the valley of the River Cecina and has views of Volterra.

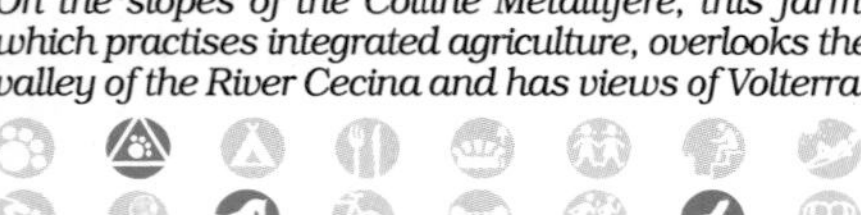

\-

1 - - - -

1 (x 2)

1 25,80 - - -

2(x 4)

1 - 7 - 1 82,63 7 -

Impruneta

Inalbi

E D

via Terre Bianche 32, 50023 Impruneta (FI)
Tel. 0552011797 Fax 0552312347
Web: www.inalbi.it

This fine farmhouse is set at the end of a country lane; all around are the other low buildings of a hamlet now totally devoted to tourist accommodation.

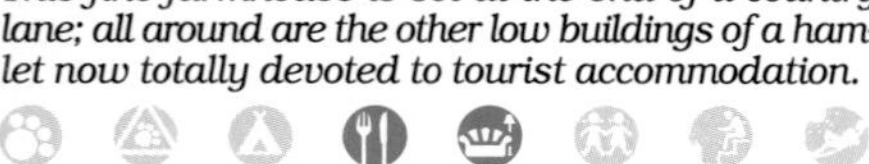

\-

1 - - - -

2 (x 2)

1 41,00 - - -

10 (x 2/4)

1 - 7 - 1 135,00 7 827,00

Incisa in Val d'Arno

Bellavista

E D

at Loppiano, via Montelfi 1,
50064 Incisa in Val d'Arno (FI)
Tel. 0558335768 Fax 0558335143
Web: www.agriturismobellavista.com

The farm offers accommodation in charming apartments that have been completely renovated; there's a panoramic view of the Arno Valley.

\-

1 - - - -

\-

1 - - - -

11 (x 2/3)

1 - 7 - 1 109,00 7 775,00

Fattoria Castello di Pratelli

E D

via di Pratelli 1/A, 50064 Incisa in Val d'Arno (FI)
Tel. 0558335986 Fax 0558336615
Web: www.castellodipratelli.it

As one might expect, this turreted fortress dating from the Lombard period is in a commanding position and from it there's a splendid view of the countryside round Florence.

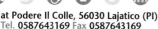

\-

1 - - -

\-

1 - - -

8 (x 2/4)

1 - 7 - 1 - 7 1.500,00

Lajatico

Trieste

at Podere Il Colle, 56030 Lajatico (PI)
Tel. 0587643169 Fax 0587643169

On the verdant hillside, the various stone buildings, renovated without spoiling the vernacular architecture, form a small, peaceful village.

\-

1 - - -

2 (x 4)

1 60,00 - -

10 (x 2/3)

1 - 7 - 1 - 7 700,00

Lamporecchio

Rinascita Agricola

at San Baronto, via Giugnano 85,
51030 Lamporecchio (PT)
Tel. 057388097 Fax 057388097
Web: utenti.lycos.it/cooria

At San Baronto there's a farm with a demanding name, confirmed by its adoption of organic methods and, above all, by the cheese made with the milk of the rare Massese sheep.

\-

1 - - -

\-

1 - - -

2(x 6)

1 - 7 - 1 210,00 7 -

Lari

Poggio di Mezzo

at Perignano, via Sottobosco 21,
56035 Lari (PI)
Tel. 0587617591 Fax 0587617591

On a hilltop, the accommodation is in comfortable rooms that have been tastefully furnished. The farm, which is under vines, is surrounded by woods.

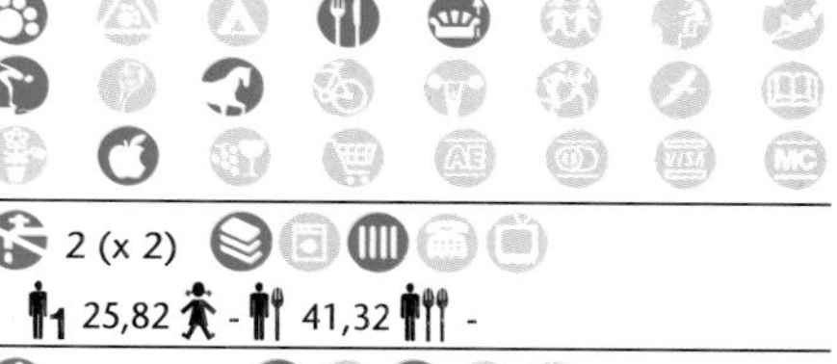

2 (x 2)

1 25,82 - 41,32 -

4 (x 1/2)

1 25,82 - 41,32 -

\-

1 - 7 - 1 - 7 -

Lastra a Signa

I Mori

at Ginestra Fiorentina,
via Maremmana 22,
50020 Lastra a Signa (FI)
Tel. 0558784452 Fax 0558784651
Web: www.i-mori.it

In the heart of the Colli Fiorentini, an area favoured by the Medici for their country residences, peaceful accommodation is available in the renovated rooms of old farmhouses.

\-

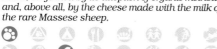

1 - - -

\-

1 - - -

4 (x 2/6)

1 - 7 - 1 155,00 7 -

Licciana Nardi

Montagna Verde

via Apella 1, 54016 Licciana Nardi (MS)
Tel. **0187421203** Fax **0187471450**
Web: **www.agriturismo.montagna.verde.it**

In the Lunigiana the holiday is always divided between the woods of the Apennines and the attractions of the Tyrrhenian coast. It is possible to spend a magnificent holiday on this game farm.

 -

 - - -

6 (x 1/4)

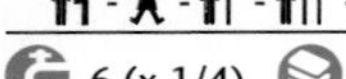 35,00 - 50,00 -

7 (x 2/6)

 31,00 - 70,00 -

Livorno

I Cinque Lecci

at Montenero, via di Quercianella 168, 57128 Livorno
Tel. **0586578111** Fax **0586578111**

This new complex looks out over the Costa degli Etruschi, an area ideal for lovers of horse-riding, with the sea just four kilometres away.

 -

- - -

-

- - -

7 (x 3/4)

 - - - 620,00

Loro Ciuffenna

Odina

at Odina, 52024 Loro Ciuffenna (AR)
Tel. **055969304** Fax **055969305**
Web: **www.odina.it**

A medieval village on the slopes of the Pratomagno, with a splendid view of the Arno Valley and the Chianti Hills - what more could you desire for a holiday in the true sense of the word?.

 -

 - - -

 -

- - -

5 (x 2/5)

 - - 92,00 2.580,00

Lucca

Villa Latmiral

at Cerasomma, via di Cerasomma 615, 55050 Lucca
Tel. **0583510286** Fax **0583512359**
Web: **www.lumet.it/aziende/carlottagori**

This large 18th-century villa has, in its park, a comfortable annexe used for the tourist accommodation, with a space for recreational activities.

\-

\-

1(x 4)

1 - 7 - 1 110,00 7 600,00

Villa Lenzi

at San Concordio di Moriano, via della Maolina 3644, 55050 Lucca
Tel. **0583395187** Fax **0583395919**

This impressive Neo-classical villa has a splendid dining-room and one of the guests' rooms in a frescoed salon. The other rooms are in well-kept cottages dotted round the farm.

2 (x 1/2)

1 43,00 - 64,00 -

5 (x 1/2)

1 54,00 - 75,00 -

2(x 4)

1 60,00 7 - 1 - 7 -

Magliano in Toscana

Da Remo

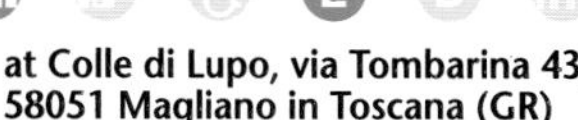

at Colle di Lupo, via Tombarina 43, 58051 Magliano in Toscana (GR)
Tel. **0564592408**
E-mail: **sonnini@tiscali.it**

Surrounded by walls and commanding fine views, the medieval village is 5 km away. The area includes the Maremma coast and important Etruscan cemeteries.

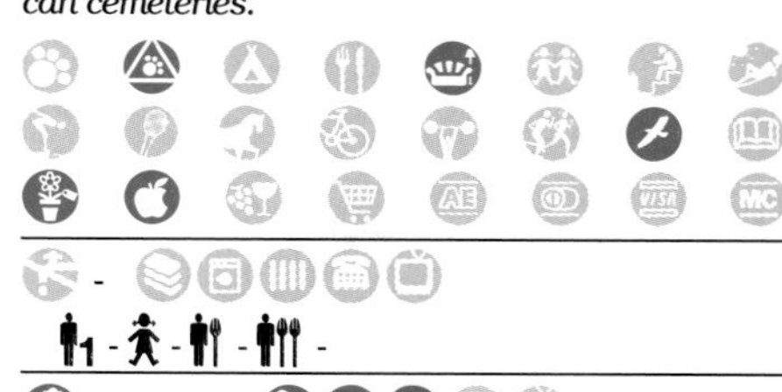

\-

5 (x 1/4)

1 31,00 - - -

\-

1 - 7 - 1 - 7 -

Pian del Noce

at Pereta, 58050 Magliano in Toscana (GR)
Tel. **0564505100** Fax **0564505100**
Web: **www.letsgotuscany.com/piandelnoce.html**

The medieval village stands on the top of a hill covered with olive trees. This excellently renovated farmhouse is not far away, amid the hills.

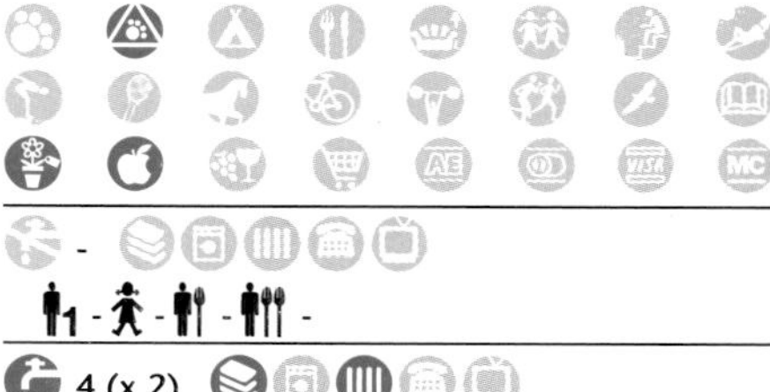

\-

4 (x 2)

1 35,00 - - -

\-

1 - 7 - 1 - 7 -

Tenuta Poggio Alto

at Cupi di Montiano, via Aurelia at km 169, 58052 Magliano in Toscana (GR)
Tel. **0564589696** Fax **0564589696**
Web: **www.arca.net/tourism/poggioalto**

There's a warm welcome at this establishment, which has stables for ten horses and a huge estate, largely covered with Mediterranean scrub; the sea is only 12 km away.

6 (x 2)

1 50,00 30,00 60,00 -

9 (x 2)

1 50,00 30,00 60,00 -

1(x 4)

1 - 7 - 1 - 7 1.050,00

Manciano

Da Lorena

at Marsiliana, 58010 Manciano (GR)
Tel. 0564606595 Fax 0564606807
Web: www.agriturismodalorena.com

The Argentario and the island of Giglio are just off the coast of the Maremma Grossetana. Inland, there's an area of great natural beauty, with thermal springs and Etruscan remains.

\-

1 - - - -

8 (x 2)

1 35,00 - 58,00 -

\-

1 - 7 - 1 - 7 -

Galeazzi

at Marsiliana, via Spinicci 250,
58010 Manciano (GR)
Tel. 0564605017 Fax 0564605017
Web: www.agriturismogaleazzi.com

This modern rural complex is in the hills, with views extending from Monte Amiata to the sea and the island of Montecristo. The accommodation is in self-contained rooms.

\-

1 - - - -

7 (x 1/2)

1 33,00 10,00 - -

\-

1 - 7 - 1 - 7 -

Le Fontanelle

at Poderi di Montemerano,
58050 Manciano (GR)
Tel. 0564602762 Fax 0564602762
Web: www.lefontanelle.net

The village, with its 15th-century fort, stands out against the green of the Mediterranean scrub. A charming stone house has rooms that are rustic yet elegant.

\-

1 - - - -

10 (x 2)

1 39,00 - 59,00 -

\-

1 - 7 - 1 - 7 -

Le Ginestre

at Saturnia, Poggio alle Calle,
58050 Manciano (GR)
Tel. 0564629513

On a hill, this excellently renovated cottage is just a few minutes' drive from the well-known spa of Saturnia and a large archaeological area with Etruscan remains.

\-

1 - - -

10 (x 1/4)

1 38,00 - -

\-

1 - 7 - 1 - 7 -

\-

1 - - -

\-

1 - - -

6 (x 2/4)

1 - 7 - 1 300,00 7 1.875,00

Le Macchie Alte

at Poderi di Montemerano, 58050 Manciano (GR)
Tel. **0564620470** Fax **0564629878**
Web: **www.lemacchiealte.it**

This farm has over 400 hectares of land on the hills behind Grosseto, which may be explored along nature trails; Maremma cattle roam freely on the uncultivated land.

\-

1 - - -

12 (x 1/4)

1 41,00 - 57,00 -

\-

1 - 7 - 1 - 7 -

Poggio Foco

at Poggio Foco, 58014 Manciano (GR)
Tel. **0564620970** Fax **0564620977**
Web: **www.poggiofoco.com**

The countryside is beautiful, with cultivated fields, hedges and tree plantations, large oaks and woods. On a hillock, a group of buildings is at the centre of a large farm.

Marciana

Casa Fèlici

via Costarella 32, 57030 Marciana (LI)
Tel. **0565901297**
Web: **www.infoelba.it**

In front are the low vines of Elba, behind a verdant valley. The comfortable apartments have terraces facing the sea, barbecues and parking spaces.

\-

1 - - -

\-

1 - - -

2 (x 3/5)

1 - 7 - 1 85,00 7 -

Marina di Grosseto

Femminella

at Principina a Mare, via S. Carlo 334, 58046 Marina di Grosseto (GR)
Tel. **056431179** Fax **056432628**
Web: **www.ombrone.it**

In the Maremma Regional Park, near the Ombrone, accommodation is available in modern, self-contained apartments, with a private garden.

-
1 - - - -

5 (x 2)
1 50,00 - - -

12 (x 2/6)
1 - 7 - 1 120,00 7 -

Quercesecca

at Tombolo, 58046 Marina di Grosseto (GR)
Tel. 0564425404 Fax 0564418859
Web: www.it-maremma.com

Amid maritime pines and sunflowers, this farm, typical of the plain of Grosseto, offers accommodation in comfortable rooms, just two kilometres from the beach.

-
1 - - - -

-
1 - - - -

7 (x 2/4)
1 - 7 - 1 - 7 929,00

Massa Marittima

Podere Riparbella

at Sopra Pian di Mucini, 58024 Massa Marittima (GR)
Tel. 0566915557 Fax 0566915558
Web: www.riparbella.com

'Dolce far niente' ("It's nice not to do anything"), as Christian and Veronica say. 'Riparbella is a place where you can just wander about, read, have a chat...'.

2 (x 1)
1 50,00 - 65,00 -

9 (x 1/4)
1 53,00 22,00 68,00 -

-
1 - 7 - 1 - 7 -

Montaione

Pistolese Ranch-Trail Horses

at Pistolese Samminiatese 34/117,
50050 Montaione (FI)
Tel. 057169196 Fax 057169196
Web: www.pistoleseranch.it

As the name suggests, this farm specialises in raising horses for riding Western-style and, consequently, for touring on horseback.

-
1 - - - -

3 (x 2)
1 - - - 134,00

-
1 - 7 - 1 - 7 -

Montalcino

Fattoria dei Barbi

at Podernuovi 170, 53024 Montalcino (SI)
Tel. 0577841111 Fax 0577841112
Web: www.fattoriadeibarbi.it

This Tuscan farmhouse, built in stone, is set amid vineyards and olive groves, and the famous Brunello is aged in its cellars. The accommodation is in separate buildings with well-arranged interiors.

\-
1 - - - -

\-
1 - - - -

3(x 3)
1 - 7 - 1 110,00 7 -

La Crociona

at La Croce 15, 53024 Montalcino (SI)
Tel. 0577848007 Fax 0577848007
Web: www.lacrociona.com

Of 15th-century origin, this farmhouse was later extended. The apartments are in the main building and the former hayloft, which was recently renovated.

\-
1 - - - -

\-
1 - - - -

7 (x 2/4)
1 - 7 - 1 - 7 773,00

La Verbena

at I Verbi, 53024 Montalcino (SI)
Tel. 0577848432 Fax 0577846687

The rural complex has been restored in an exemplary manner; it's of particular interest for its setting and the unusual way the volumes and levels are arranged.

\-
1 - - - -

\-
1 - - - -

2(x 3)
1 - 7 - 1 124,00 7 -

Podere Salicutti

podere Salicutti 174, 53024 Montalcino (SI)
Tel. 0577847003 Fax 0577847003
Web: www.poderesalicutti.it

There's quality all round here: the estate's wines are Rosso di Montalcino DOC and Rosso Dopoteatro IGT, made mainly from Cabernet grapes. Outstanding olive oil is also produced.

\-
1 - - - -

1 (x 2)
1 40,00 - - -

1(x 3)
1 - 7 - 1 - 7 660,00

Poderuccio

at Poderuccio, 53020 Montalcino (SI)
Tel. 0577844052 Fax 0577844150

This accommodation is full of atmosphere, starting with the stone farmhouse, which contains all the rooms, each with its own entrance and modern comforts.

\-
1 - - - -

7 (x 2/4)
1 42,50 - - -

\-
1 - 7 - 1 - 7 -

Montecarlo

Fattoria Michi

via S. Martino 34, 55015 Montecarlo (LU)
Tel. 058322011 Fax 058322011
Web: www.fattoriamichi.it

This accommodation is in a villa in an old converted building and isolated cottages on a hill overlooking the Valdinievole. All around are vineyards and olive groves.

\-
1 - - -

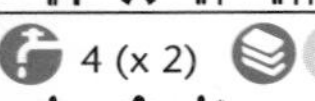

4 (x 2)
1 - - 55,00 -

2(x 6)
1 - 7 - 1 - 7 830,00

Montecatini Val di Cecina

Frassinello

at La Miniera 22,
56040 Montecatini Val di Cecina (PI)
Tel. 058830080 Fax 058830080
Web: www.ilfrassinello.com

Amid woods and pastures, this 19th-century farmhouse is the starting-point for a thousand and one excursions. The cosy, well-kept rooms are ideal for a really relaxing holiday.

\-
1 - - -

3 (x 2)
1 55,00 - 73,00 -

4 (x 2/4)
1 - 7 - 1 150,00 7 670,00

Montelupo Fiorentino

Fattoria Petrognano

via Bottinaccio 116,
50056 Montelupo Fiorentino (FI)
Tel. 0571913795 Fax 0571913796
Web: www.petrognano.it

In the lower Arno Valley, amid olive groves and vineyards, accommodation is available in renovated 18th-century farmhouses surrounded by a large, well-kept garden.

\-
1 - - -

\-
1 - - -

11 (x 2/4)
1 - 7 - 1 145,00 7 1.035,00

Tenuta San Vito in Fior di Selva

via S. Vito 32,
50056 Montelupo Fiorentino (FI)
Tel. 057151411 Fax 057151405
Web: www.san-vito.com

The accommodation is in three cottages close to the farmhouse, which stands in a panoramic position amid vineyards, olive groves and Mediterranean scrub.

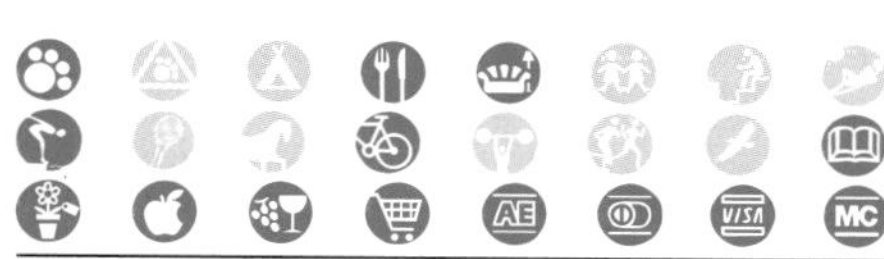

\-

1 - - - -

7 (x 2)

1 111,00 - - -

14 (x 2/4)

1 - 7 - 1 - 7 4.390,00

Montepulciano

Il Greppo

at Abbadia, via dei Greppi 47,
53040 Montepulciano (SI)
Tel. 0578707112 Fax 0578707528
Web: www.ilgreppo.it

This recently renovated 15th-century farmhouse contains six apartments with attractive furnishings in traditional style; there's also a living-room and garden.

\-

1 - - - -

\-

1 - - - -

6 (x 2/4)

1 - 7 - 1 - 7 1.140,00

Monteriggioni

Castel Pietraio

strada di Strove 33, 53035 Monteriggioni (SI)
Tel. 0577300020 Fax 0577300977
Web: www.castelpietraio.it

The farm comprises vineyards, fields under crops and large wooded areas. The rooms are particularly comfortable, while the apartments have period furniture and well-equipped kitchens.

\-

1 - - - -

8 (x 2/4)

1 86,00 - - -

2(x 4)

1 - 7 - 1 - 7 931,00

Fattoria Gavina di Sopra

at Gavina, strada di Casabocci 34,
53100 Monteriggioni (SI)
Tel. 0577317046 Fax 0577317046
E-mail: lagavina@libero.it

This distinctive building stands on a low hill. Not only is the place enchanting, but the owners are extremely friendly and the rooms comfortable, with traditional furnishings.

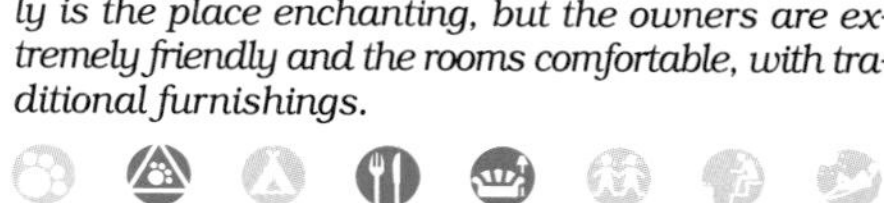

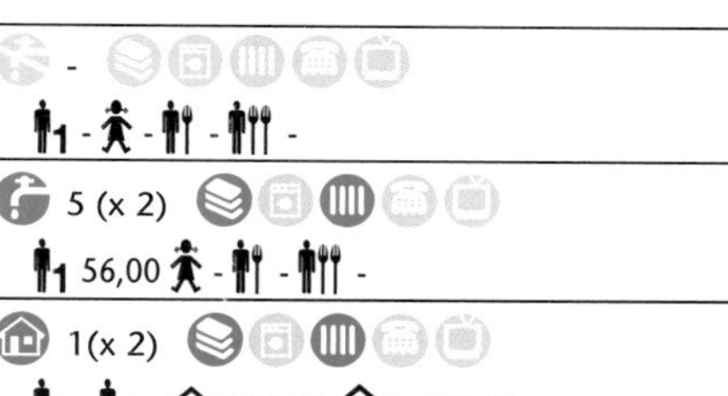

\-

1 - - - -

5 (x 2)

1 56,00 - - -

1(x 2)

1 - 7 - 1 80,00 7 550,00

Monteroni d'Arbia

Il Poggiarello

at Ville di Corsano, podere Poggiarello,
53010 Monteroni d'Arbia (SI)
Tel. 0577377117 Fax 0577377117
E-mail: monica.andreini@libero.it

Siena is not far away (15 km); known as the Crete, these bare clay hills, which change their appearance according to the light and the season, are dotted with cypresses and broom, and isolated farmhouses.

 3 (x 1/2)

1 30,00 - 50,00 -

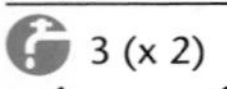   3 (x 2)

1 30,00 - 50,00 -

 1(x 8)

 1 - 7 - 1 310,00 7 -

Tenuta della Selva

at Ville di Corsano, 53010 Monteroni d'Arbia (SI)
Tel. 0577377063 Fax 0577377842
Web: www.tenutadellaselva.com

The accommodation is in the open countryside, 4 km from the main farmhouse, in old buildings divided into apartments of various sizes, available throughout the year.

 -

1 - - - -

-

1 - - - -

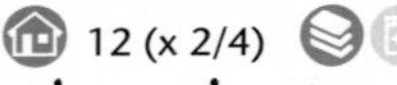   12 (x 2/4)

1 37,00 7 - 1 - 7 826,00

Monterotondo Marittimo

Podere Risecco

at Frassine,
58025 Monterotondo Marittimo (GR)
Tel. 0566910007 Fax 0566910007

With land under crops and uncultivated, pasture, scrub and woodland, this estate, located in a nature reserve in the Val di Cornia, has accommodation in an attractive stone farmhouse.

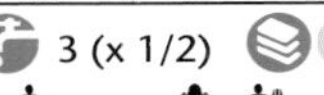 -

 1 - - - -

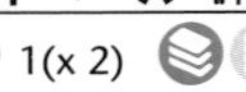  3 (x 1/2)

1 28,00 - 41,00 -

1(x 2)

1 - 7 - 1 - 7 500,00

Monte San Savino

Casa Contessa Francesca

at Gargonza, 52048 Monte San Savino (AR)
Tel. 0575847021 Fax 0575847054
Web: www.gargonza.it

The building where the accommodation is located is part of the medieval hamlet once incorporated in the castle of Gargonza - an excellent example of restoration.

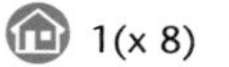  

1(x 8)

1.715,00

Villa Bugiana

via Bugiana 12,
52048 Monte San Savino (AR)
Tel. 0575844564 Fax 0575844564
E-mail: tecchim@techne.it

Accommodation is available in two renovated cottages, which, inside, have preserved a style consistent with their exteriors.

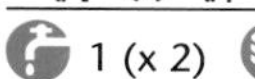 

1 (x 2)

26,00

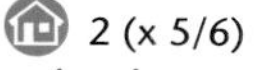 

2 (x 5/6)

500,00

Montespertoli

Le Fonti a San Giorgio

via Colle San Lorenzo 16,
50025 Montespertoli (FI)
Tel. 0571609298 Fax 0571608347
Web: www.lefontiasangiorgio.it

There's a friendly welcome in the pleasant setting of the farm's olive groves and vineyards. The spacious apartments all have a fireplace in the large living-room.

7 (x 2/3)

815,00

Monteverdi Marittimo

Podere Pratella

via della Badia 19,
56040 Monteverdi Marittimo (PI)
Tel. 0565784325 Fax 0565784325
Web: www.etruscan.li.it/pratella

In the Val di Cornia, between the Maremma and the Colline Metallifere - thus close to both the coast and the wooded hills - there's accommodation in an old farmhouse.

6 (x 2)

33,57 23,50 50,57

Villetta di Monterufoli

at Canneto, via Volterrana 20,
56040 Monteverdi Marittimo (PI)
Tel. 0565784251 Fax 0565784162
Web: www.villettadimonterufoli.it

This accommodation is in the former railway station of a lignite mine. The natural environment and cultural aspects make this a particularly interesting holiday.

-

1 - - -

11 (x 2/4)

1 39,00 - 114,00 -

1(x 4)

1 - 7 - 1 104,00 7 600,00

Montignoso

Karma

at Castello Aghinolfi, via Guadagni 1,
54038 Montignoso (MS)
Tel. 0585821237 Fax 0585821935
Web: www.agrikarma.it

The name heralds this lifestyle of this establishment in the hills, where they make good use of holistic health treatment and natural therapies.

-

1 - - -

3 (x 2/4)

1 31,00 - 65,00 -

-

1 - 7 - 1 - 7 -

Mulazzo

Ca' di Rossi

at Ca' di Rossi 2, 54026 Mulazzo (MS)
Tel. 0187439477 Fax 0187439936
Web: www.cadirossi.it

Ideal for holidays in the green hills, this 19th-century stone cottage has accommodation in rooms with period furniture and lace trimmings.

-

1 - - -

8 (x 2)

1 38,00 - 56,00 -

-

1 - 7 - 1 - 7 -

Eremo di San Matteo

at Lusuolo, 54026 Mulazzo (MS)
Tel. 0187494567 Fax 0187493102
Web: www.geocities.com/eremodisanmatteo

This is an interesting idea for a rural holiday, with accommodation in the charming medieval village of Lusuolo and numerous recreational activities on the farm.

-

1 - - -

-

1 - - -

3(x 4)

1 - 7 - 1 120,00 7 -

Murlo

I Pianelli

at I Pianelli, 53016 Murlo (SI)
Tel. 0577374496 Fax 0577374496
Web: www.ipianelli.com

Accommodation is available in 19th-century farmhouses set amid the fields, olive groves and woods of the huge estate, the ideal setting for walks suitable for everyone.

-
1 - - -

-
1 - - -

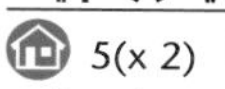
5(x 2)
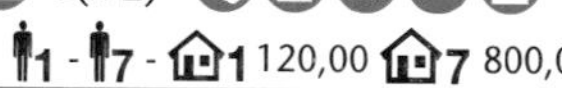
1 - 7 - 1 120,00 7 800,00

Podere Montorgialino

at Montorgialino, 53016 Murlo (SI)
Tel. 0577814373 Fax 0577814373
Web: www.montorgialino.com

The olive groves and woods are the ideal setting for a peaceful holiday. An old farmhouse has been converted to provide accommodation in rooms and apartments.

-
1 - - -

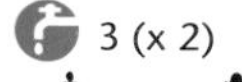

3 (x 2)
1 70,00 - -

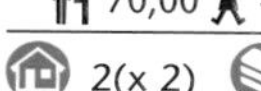

2(x 2)

1 - 7 - 1 200,00 7 1.200,00

Podere Vignali

at Vignali, road for Buonconvento 8,
53016 Murlo (SI)
Tel. 0577814368 Fax 0577814368
Web: www.geocities.com/poderevignali

An unsurfaced road running between meadows and clumps of broom climbs up the low hill to the two farmhouses offering accommodation. The rustic interiors have modern comforts.

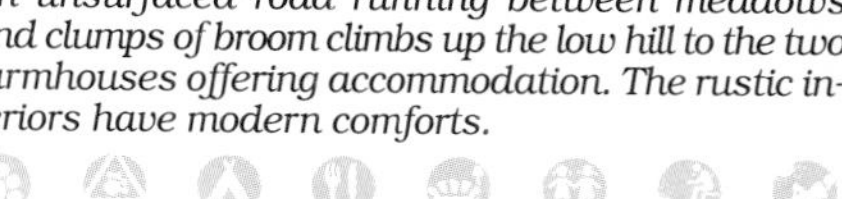

-
1 - - -

2 (x 2)
1 49,00 - -

3 (x 4/6)
1 - 7 - 1 - 7 1.250,00

Orbetello

Fattoria il Casalone

at Orbetello Scalo, Pitorsino, via Aurelia Sud
at km 140.5, 58016 Orbetello (GR)
Tel. 0564862160 Fax 0564866308
Web: www.agriturismocasalone.com

There's a beautiful view from under the pergola leading to the well-furnished rooms: the lagoon of Orbetello, expanses of wheat and sunflowers, and pastures.

-
1 - - -

-
1 - - -

7(x 4)

1 - 7 - 1 - 7 1.200,00

Grazia

at Provincaccia 110, 58016 Orbetello (GR)
Tel. 0564881182 Fax 0564881182
E-mail: m.graziacantore@tin.it

This large 19th-century farmhouse has an arcade and rooms full of atmosphere. Nearby are the paddocks and facilities of the stables.

 -

1 - - -

 -

1 - - -

 6 (x 2/4)

1 - 7 - 1 140,00 7 830,00

Peretti

at Fonteblanda, via Melosella 124,
58010 Orbetello (GR)
Tel. 0564885467 Fax 0564885467
Web: www.agriturismoperetti.it

There's a friendly welcome in this completely renovated cottage, with simple but comfortable rooms.

 -

1 - - -

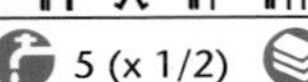 5 (x 1/2)

1 31,00 - -

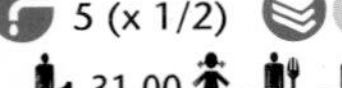 3 (x 3/4)

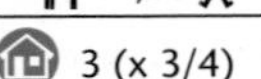  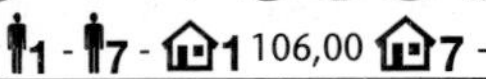

1 - 7 - 1 106,00 7 -

Ortignano Raggiolo

Caccialupi

at Villa, 52010 Ortignano Raggiolo (AR)
Tel. 0575594963 Fax 0575594963
Web: www.asia.it/agri-toscana/casentino/caccialupi

This fine stone farmhouse has a traditional atmosphere in the interior, where there's also a fireplace, and such modern conveniences as satellite television.

 -

1 - - -

-

1 - - -

4(x 4)

1 - 7 - 1 - 7 700,00

Palaia

Podere della Collina

at Toiano, S.P. (provincial road) delle Colline,
56036 Palaia (PI)
Tel. 0587632020
Web: www.poderedellacollina.it

In the Alta Valdera Park, this farm overlooks the village of Toiano; the accommodation is in apartments in the farmhouse and the two renovated adjacent outbuildings.

-

1 - - -

-

1 - - -

  5 (x 3/5)

1 - 7 - 1 - 7 750,00

San Gervasio

at San Gervasio, via Palaiese, 56036 Palaia (PI)
Tel. 0587483360 Fax 0587484361
Web: www.sangervasio.com

In the hamlet where the farm is located, a 17th-century farmhouse and its outbuildings have been converted to provide accommodation with furnishings in a genuinely Tuscan style.

\-

1 - - - -

\-

1 - - - -

16 (x 2/6)

1 - 7 - 1 - 7 628,00

Tenuta la Cerbana

at Montefoscoli, via Colline 35, 56036 Palaia (PI)
Tel. 0587632058 Fax 0587632058
Web: www.lacerbana.com

This accommodation is in the comfortable rooms of converted early 20th-century farmhouses in pleasant, typically Tuscan surroundings.

\-

1 - - - -

12 (x 2/4)

1 39,00 19,50 - 75,00

4(x 2)

1 - 7 - 1 105,00 7 -

Palazzuolo sul Senio

Fantino

at Fantino 29, 50035 Palazzuolo sul Senio (FI)
Tel. 0558046708 Fax 0558043928
Web: www.tuscanyrental.com/fantino

This 14th-century farmhouse is located in the area known as the Tuscan Romagna. It's an ideal base for trips to both the museums of Florence and the mosaics of Ravenna.

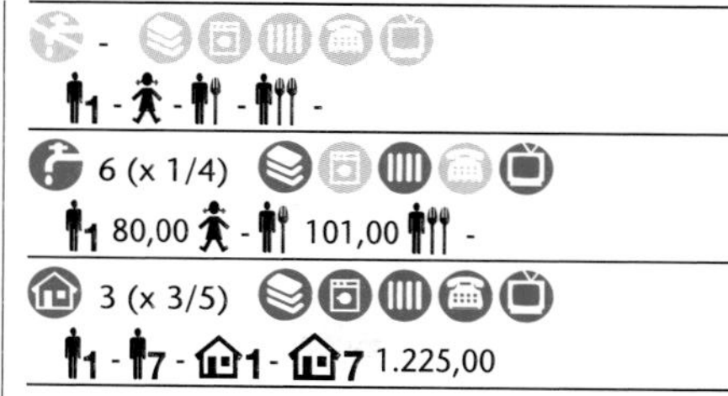

\-

1 - - - -

6 (x 1/4)

1 80,00 - 101,00 -

3 (x 3/5)

1 - 7 - 1 - 7 1.225,00

Pelago

La Pieve

at La Pieve, 50060 Pelago (FI)
Tel. 0558326030 Fax 0558326030
Web: www.lapieveagriturismo.it

There's a warm welcome on this farm on the slopes of the Pratomagno amid woods, olive groves and vineyards; the farmhouse is of 14th-century origin.

\-

1 - - - -

2 (x 2)

1 39,50 - 54,00 -

3 (x 2/6)

1 - 7 - 1 129,00 7 873,00

Pergine Valdarno

Castello di Montozzi

at Montozzi, 52020 Pergine Valdarno (AR)
Tel. 055574410 Fax 055580149
Web: www.bartolinibaldelli.it

In the hills of the Arno Valley, the accommodation is in a fortified hamlet dominating the farm and a vast game reserve.

4(x 4)

813,00

Montelucci

via Montelucci 10,
52020 Pergine Valdarno (AR)
Tel. 0575896525 Fax 0575896315
E-mail: montelucci@val.it

In the upper Arno Valley, this 17th-century villa and the farmhouses surrounding it offer accommodation full of atmosphere.

9 (x 2/4)

83,00

5(x 4)

450,00

Pescia

Fattoria di Pietrabuona

at Pietrabuona, road for Medicina 2,
51010 Pescia (PT)
Tel. 0572408115 Fax 0572408150
Web: www.pietrabuona.com

This little-known part of Tuscany is known as the 'Svizzera Pesciatina'. The accommodation is in farmhouses scattered over a vast farm.

5 (x 2/4)

1.000,00

Il Frantoio

at San Quirico, via del Frantoio 9,
51017 Pescia (PT)
Tel. 0572400294 Fax 0572453365
Web: www.guardatoie/frantoio/index.htm

In the hills, on a wooded slope where two streams converge, renovated rooms are available in an 18th-century oil-press with its adjacent outbuildings.

5 (x 2/6)

860,00

Le Colonne

at Monte a Pescia, via E. Berlinguer 19-21-23,
51017 Pescia (PT)
Tel. 0572477242 Fax 0572499598
Web: www.lecolonne.com

Well-situated for visiting the places of artistic interest in Tuscany, these seven villas stand amid vines and olives or on the edge of a wood. The area offers pleasant walks, good food and thermal baths.

-

1 - - -

-

1 - - -

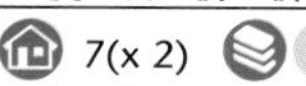 7(x 2)

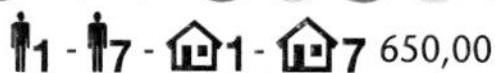

1 - 7 - 1 - 7 650,00

Marzalla

via di Collecchio 1, 51017 Pescia (PT)
Tel. 0572490751 Fax 0572478332
Web: www.guardatoie.it/marzalla

In the centre of a vast estate growing olives and vines stands the elegant Villa Guardatoia. A number of the surrounding farmhouses have been converted into delightful accommodation for guests.

-

1 - - -

 3 (x 2)

1 65,00 - - -

 5 (x 2/4)

1 - 7 - 1 - 7 1.030,00

Pian di Scò

Treggiano

at Treggiano, via di Casellina 81,
52026 Pian di Scò (AR)
Tel. 055960071 Fax 0554627014
E-mail: mau.serena@tiscali.it

In a panoramic position in the Arno Valley, the farm is wholly devoted to organic olive-growing; in addition to the beautiful natural surroundings, there are historic towns and villages to visit.

-

1 - - -

-

1 - - -

2(x 4)

1 - 7 - 1 - 7 1.680,00

Pienza

Barbi

at Monticchiello, podere Montello 26,
53020 Pienza (SI)
Tel. 0578755149 Fax 0578755149
E-mail: barbivilmo@libero.it

Located in the Val d'Orcia, one of the farmhouses dates from the early 20th century, the other is more recent, but in traditional style; the rooms are comfortable and well-furnished.

-

1 - - -

-

1 - - -

2 (x 4/6)

1 - 7 - 1 165,00 7 -

Le Macchie

at Monticchiello, via della Montagna,
53020 Pienza (SI)
Tel. 0578755182 Fax 0578755182
Web: www.lemacchie.it

The setting is the Val d'Orcia: the accommodation is in elegant apartments, some of them on two storeys in a 17th-century farmhouse furnished with sober tastefulness.

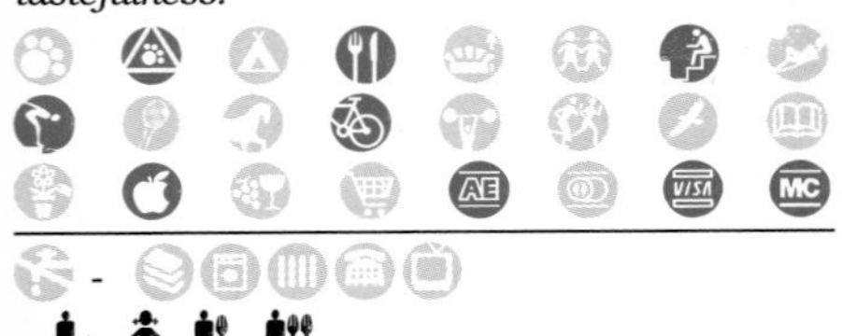

\-

1 - - -

\-

1 - - -

3 (x 2/6)

1 - 7 - 1 185,00 7 1.200,00

Podere Cretaiole

via S. Gregorio 14, 53026 Pienza (SI)
Tel. 0578748083 Fax 0578748378
Web: www.cretaiole.it

This 14th-century farmhouse is located in an area of great archaeological interest. The accommodation is in apartments with fireplaces and original mid-19th-century furnishings.

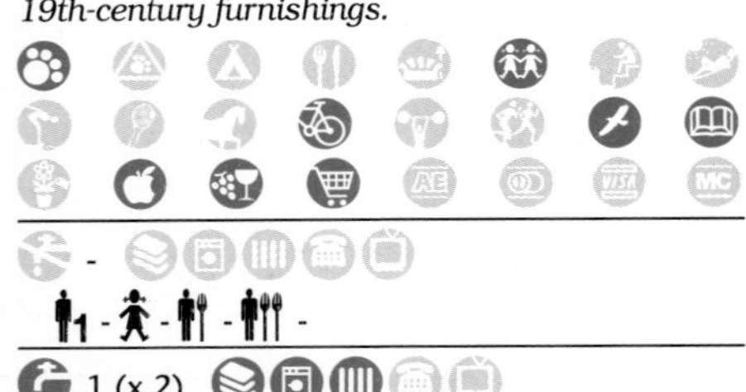

\-

1 - - -

1 (x 2)

1 32,00 - -

6 (x 2/4)

1 - 7 - 1 195,00 7 -

Pieve a Nievole

Il Bottaccino

via Ponte Monsummano 94,
51018 Pieve a Nievole (PT)
Tel. 0572952968 Fax 0572952968
Web: www.ilbottaccino.com

Between Florence, Pisa and Pistoia, in the triangle of art and nature of the Valdinievole, this refined accommodation has stables where guests may ride Western-style.

\-

1 - - -

2 (x 2)

1 50,00 - -

3(x 2)

1 - 7 - 1 - 7 1.200,00

Pieve Santo Stefano

Fattoria Sant'Apollinare

at Sant'Apollinare, 52036 Pieve Santo Stefano (AR)
Tel. 0575799112 Fax 0575796742

In a hamlet huddled round a manor-house and small church, accommodation is available in a wing of the main residence, which has been completely renovated.

2 (x 2)

1 40,00 - 50,00 -

9 (x 2/4)

1 40,00 - 50,00 -

\-

1 - 7 - 1 - 7 -

Piombino

Podere Santa Giulia

at Riotorto-Santa Giulia,
57020 Piombino (LI)
Tel. 056520830 Fax 056520830
E-mail: 2001dido@jumpy.it

The accommodation is in two buildings: one is a small house on the edge of a pinewood, the other a cottage in open country, suitable for groups or large families.

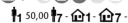

\-

 -

\-

 -

 9

 50,00 - -

Santa Trice

at Santa Trice, 57020 Piombino (LI)
Tel. 056520618 Fax 056520618

This vast farm, where the Chianina cattle are allowed to wander freely, offers accommodation in the huge rooms of two imposing farmhouses.

\-

 -

\-

\- - -

5 (x 4/8)

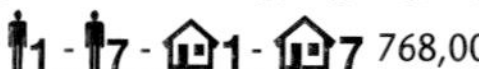 768,00

Tenuta di Vignale

at Vignale 5, 57025 Piombino (LI)
Tel. 056520846 Fax 056520846
Web: www.tenutadivignale.it

Amid olive groves and vineyards, this early 19th-century villa has apartments with rustic elegance. Other rooms are available in an old hunting-lodge at Bronzivalle.

\-

 -

8 (x 2)

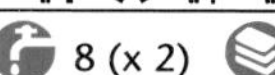 45,00 22,50 63,00 -

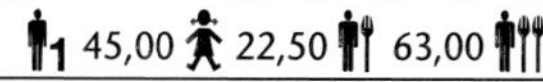 7 (x 3/4)

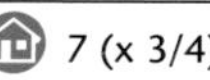  210,00 -

Pitigliano

Poggio del Castagno

via Pantano Basso, 58017 Pitigliano (GR)
Tel. 0564615545

Pitigliano is a fascinating town standing on a rocky spur; all around, the beautiful woods seem to be assuring visitors that they will have an enjoyable holiday.

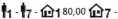

 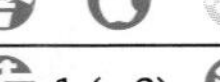  

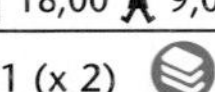  1 (x 2)

1 18,00 9,00 - -

 1 (x 2)

1 20,00 10,00 - -

 1(x 4)

1 - 7 - 1 80,00 7 -

Poggibonsi

Fattoria di Piecorto

at Piecorto, 53036 Poggibonsi (SI)
Tel. 0558072915 Fax 0558072238
E-mail: filippo.stefanelli@inwind.it

This splendid estate produces Chianti Classico Gallo Nero. A short distance from the farmhouse, the outbuildings have been carefully converted into five apartments.

 -

1 - - -

-

1 - - -

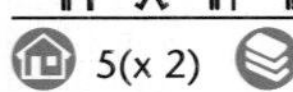  5(x 2)

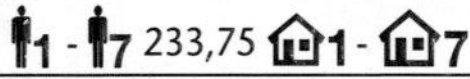 1 - 7 233,75 1 - 7 -

Pomarance

Fattoria il Cerreto

56045 Pomarance (PI)
Tel. 058864213 Fax 058864213
Web: www.ilcerreto.it

Roads and lanes allow guests to explore the huge farm on foot or by bicycle - there's something for everybody here. It's a truly relaxing holiday.

-

1 - - -

  5 (x 2)

1 33,00 - 57,00 -

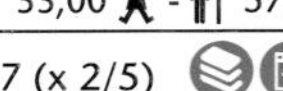 7 (x 2/5)

 1 - 7 - 1 - 7 825,00

Le Selvole

at Micciano, 56045 Pomarance (PI)
Tel. 058861033 Fax 058861033
E-mail: leselvole@sirt.pisa.it

This is the ideal holiday for those seeking peace and the pleasure of wandering around as they wish, especially by bicycle or on horseback.

 -

1 - - -

 -

1 - - -

4(x 4) - 1 - 7 - 1 - 7 750,00

Podere l'Apparita

at San Dalmazio, podere Apparita,
56040 Pomarance (PI)
Tel. 058866085 Fax 058866085
Web: www.apparita.it

The farm is surrounded by the countryside throbbing with life along the 'Itinerario dei ruderi' (Tour of the Ruins); there's a friendly welcome with large communal spaces.

-

1 - - -

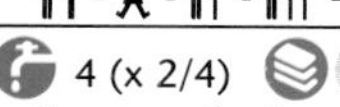 

4 (x 2/4)

1 39,00 - 59,00 -

-

1 - 7 - 1 - 7 -

Santa Lina

podere Santa Lina, 56045 Pomarance (PI)
Tel. 058865234 Fax 058865234
Web: www.santalina.com

A peaceful holiday is assured near the Berignone Nature Reserve. The house, in the centre of a large farm, offers apartments in rustic style and a swimming pool.

-

1 - - -

-

1 - - -

3 (x 2/5)

1 - 7 - 1 120,00 7 675,00

Ponsacco

San Martino

via Poggino 15, 56038 Ponsacco (PI)
Tel. 0587732949 Fax 0587732949

The Colline Pisane have numerous attractions; apart from the swimming pool amid the olives, a holiday at San Martino allows you to appreciate them all.

-

1 - - -

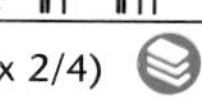 

12 (x 2/4)

1 26,00 - 44,00 -

1(x 4)

1 - 7 - 1 105,00 7 -

Pontassieve

Casabella

at Monterifrassine, via di Grignano 38,
50065 Pontassieve (FI)
Tel. 0558396168 Fax 0558399331
Web: www.fattorialavacchio.com

Between the Colli Fiorentini and the Mugello, accommodation is available in this farmhouse, which has its own windmill and is part of the old Lavacchio farm.

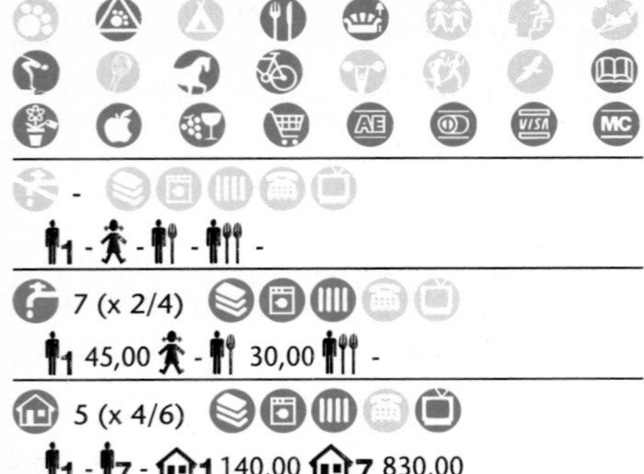

7 (x 2/4)

45,00 - 30,00 -

5 (x 4/6)

- - 140,00 830,00

Castello del Trebbio

at Santa Brigida, via S. Brigida 9,
50060 Pontassieve (FI)
Tel. 0558304900 Fax 0558304003
Web: www.vinoturismo.it

This farm, with its 400 hectares of land in the hills just north of Florence, has accommodation in apartments located in old farmhouses, with a garden.

5(x 4)

- - 1 - 1.135,00

La Querce

at Montefiesole, via dello Stracchino 46,
50065 Pontassieve (FI)
Tel. 0558364106 Fax 0558364106
Web: www.laquercefirenze.it

The massive walls are a reminder that a fortified tower formerly stood here. A farmhouse grew up around its remains, and has now been carefully restored.

3 (x 2/3)

- - 1 98,00 7 -

Pontremoli

Costa d'Orsola

at Orsola, 54027 Pontremoli (MS)
Tel. 0187833332 Fax 0187833332
Web: www.costadorsola.it

It's too good to be true: a whole village with stone houses huddled together on the grassy slope of a hill. And it's all been admirably restored.

15 (x 2/4)

46,50 31,00 62,00 -

Podere Rottigliana

at Rottigliana, 54027 Pontremoli (MS)
Tel. 0187833480 Fax 0187833480
Web: www.benderottigliana.com

The Lunigiana is the valley where Tuscany borders on both Liguria and Emilia. The chestnut trees are the setting for a holiday with access to both the hills and the sea, and not far from historic towns and cities.

$1 - 7 - 1 - 7$ 730,00

3 (x 2/6)

Poppi

Podere Fonte dei Serri

at San Martino a Monte 6, 52014 Poppi (AR)
Tel. 0575509231 Fax 0575509231
Web: www.carne-biologica.it

In a sunny, panoramic position, accommodation is available in a charming stone cottage with a terrace, adjacent to the farmhouse.

1(x 4)

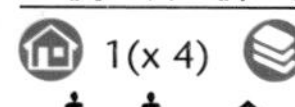

1 - 7 - 1 - 7 600,00

Porto Azzurro

Sapere

at Mola, via Provinciale Ovest 75,
57036 Porto Azzurro (LI)
Tel. 056595033 Fax 056595064
Web: www.sapereonline.it

Located amid olive trees and palms, in a flat area of the island of Elba, this old farmhouse has been converted into a modern complex for rural tourism.

14 (x 3/6)

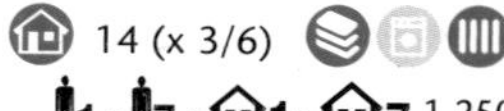

1 - 7 - 1 - 7 1.250,00

Portoferraio

Casa Marisa

at Schiopparello 12, 57037 Portoferraio (LI)
Tel. 0565933074 Fax 0565933074
E-mail: euanselmi@elbalink.it

Guests are accommodated in apartments with modern comforts that have terraces overlooking the large garden and the surrounding countryside.

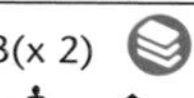

3(x 2)

1 - 7 - 1 103,29 7 -

Monte Fabbrello

at Schiopparello 30, 57037 Portoferraio (LI)
Tel. 0565933324 Fax 0565940020
Web: www.montefabbrello.it

This farm is located in the agricultural land near the main town. The accommodation is in the farmhouse, in attics with a rustic appearance.

2 (x 2)

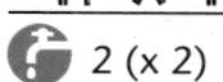

1 47,00 - - -

3(x 4)

1 - 7 - 1 55,00 7 -

Tenuta il Fortino

at Buraccio 6, 57037 Portoferraio (LI)
Tel. 0565940245 Fax 0565940245

Inland, but just 5 minutes from the sea, the rooms have terraces overlooking a deep valley covered with olives and scrub. In a sunny position, this building is sheltered from the prevailing winds.

\-

1 - - -

\-

1 - - -

2(x 4)

1 26,00 7 - 1 - 7 -

Pratovecchio

Maura Lucatello

at San Donato, via S. Donato 24,
52015 Pratovecchio (AR)
Tel. 0575582231 Fax 0575582231
E-mail: mauralucatello@technet.it

A castle, a church and a small village: this was Pratovecchio in a bygone age; now it's the ideal destination for those wishing to tour on horseback and for families with children.

\-

1 - - -

\-

1 - - -

1(x 6)

1 - 7 - 1 80,00 7 364,00

Radda in Chianti

Castello di Volpaia

at Volpaia, 53017 Radda in Chianti (SI)
Tel. 0577738066 Fax 0577738619
Web: www.volpaia.com

This remarkable farmhouse manages to perfectly combine technology and history. A stay here will be an unforgettable experience.

\-

1 - - -

\-

1 - - -

5(x 2)

1 73,00 7 465,00 1 - 7 -

Fattoria Castelvecchi

at Castelvecchi 17, 53017 Radda in Chianti (SI)
Tel. 0577738050 Fax 0577738608

The main villa, with the rooms, was built in the 19th century; the outbuildings with the apartments date from the 15th or 16th centuries. The complex is surrounded by the park with two swimming pools.

\-

1 - - -

9 (x 2)

1 72,30 - - -

13(x 2)

1 - 7 - 1 - 7 1.000,00

Podere Terreno alla via della Volpaia

at Volpaia, 53017 Radda in Chianti (SI)
Tel. **0577738312** Fax **0577738400**
Web: **www.chiantinet.it**

In the heart of the Chianti Classico zone, within sight of Volpaia Castle, this establishment is remarkable for its friendly atmosphere and cosmopolitan spirit.

 -

\- - - -

 7 (x 1/2)

\- - 90,00 -

 -

1 - 7 - 1 - 7 -

Radicondoli

Fattoria di Solaio

at Solaio, 53030 Radicondoli (SI)
Tel. **0577791029** Fax **0577791015**
Web: **www.fattoriasolaio.it**

This splendid Renaissance villa and its imposing annexes have been carefully restored to provide fascinating tourist accommodation.

 -

\- - - -

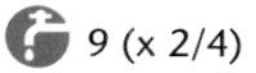 9 (x 2/4) 

42,50 - - -

 3(x 4)

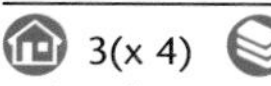 1 - 7 - 1 - 7 697,00

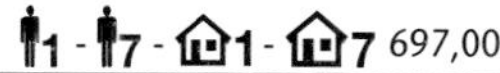

Il Tesoro

at Il Tesoro 83, 53030 Radicondoli (SI)
Tel. **0577790693** Fax **0577790693**
E-mail: **agriltesoro@tin.it**

This is real farmhouse accommodation: the guests mix with the owner's family and are in close contact with life on a working farm.

 7 (x 1/2)

 40,00 - 60,00 -

\- - - -

1 - 7 - 1 - 7 -

Rapolano Terme

Castello di Modanella

at Modanella, 53040 Rapolano Terme (SI)
Tel. **0577704604** Fax **0577704740**
Web: **www.modanella.com**

A vineyard surrounds the farmhouses containing the accommodation; there are no less than four swimming pools at the guests' disposal. Cultivated fields and over 400 hectares of woodland are close by.

\-

\- - - -

-

1 - - -

46 (x 3/6)

1 - 7 - 1 281,00 7 1.405,00

Villa Buoninsegna

E D

at Buoninsegna, 53040 Rapolano Terme (SI)
Tel. **0577724380** Fax **0577724380**
Web: **www.buoninsegna.it**

This vast farm alternates fields, vines and olives, while the beautiful 17th-century villa offers outstanding accommodation for a rural holiday.

-

1 - - -

-

1 - - -

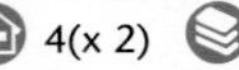 4(x 2)  

1 - 7 - 1 100,00 7 -

Reggello

Fattoria Montalbano

    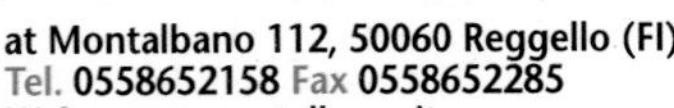

E D

at Montalbano 112, 50060 Reggello (FI)
Tel. **0558652158** Fax **0558652285**
Web: **www.montalbano.it**

'O wayfarer coming from afar, pause and sip the good wine of Montalbano' is the adage adopted by the family of wine-growers who run the farm.

-

1 - - -

1 (x 2) 

1 46,50 - - -

6 (x 2/6)

1 - 7 - 1 196,00 7 1.188,00

Torre del Castellano

 E 

via Torre del Castellano 59, 50066 Reggello (FI)
Tel. **055863300** Fax **055473308**
E-mail: **ommetg@tin.it**

Like every self-respecting castle, this one dominates the surrounding countryside; the three farmhouses share the same favourable position with its splendid views.

-

1 - - -

-

1 - - -

3(x 5)

1 - 7 - 1 - 7 2.110,00

Villa il Crocicchio

E D

at Cascia, via S. Siro 133, 50066 Reggello (FI)
Tel. **0558667262** Fax **055869102**
Web: **www.crocicchio.com**

On a hillside in rural surroundings, this old group of farm buildings, now completely renovated, has different types of accommodation with modern comforts.

The symbols
When a symbol is "lit up" ( ), this signifies that the corresponding characteristic or facility is present; if the symbol is not "lit up" ( ), this means that it is not provided.

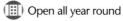

Main characteristics

- Open all year round
- Seasonal opening (closed for a period of at least three months)
- Wheelchair facilities for the disabled
- English spoken
- German spoken
- Suitable for families with children
- Suitable for smart holidays
- Suitable for sporty holidays

Services and key facilities offered

- Dogs allowed
- Dogs allowed by pre-arranged agreement
- Areas equipped for tents and/or caravans
- Restaurant
- Communal areas
- Play areas and/or equipment for children
- Sauna
- Solarium
- Swimming pool
- Tennis court(s)
- Riding-school or facilities for horse-riding
- Bicycle hire
- Sports' facilities

- Organised sports activities
- Naturalistic activities/courses
- Cultural activities/courses
- Certified organic crops
- Farm cultivation (vegetable crops, fruit, cereals)
- Wine production
- Farm produce sold directly
- American Express accepted
- Diner's card accepted
- Visa card accepted
- Mastercard accepted

Accommodation and prices

- Rooms without bathrooms (number of people)
- Rooms with bathrooms (number of people)
- Apartments (number of people)
- Laundry available
- Washing machine
- Central heating
- Telephone in the room
- Television in the room
- 1 Price per person per day
- Price per child per day
- Half board price per day
- Full board price per day
- 7 Price per person per week
- 1 Apartment hire per day
- 7 Apartment hire per week

4 (x 2)

48,00 - 73,00 -

10(x 2)

- 160,00 910,00

Rignano sull'Arno

Poggio Tre Lune

via Poggio 60, 50067 Rignano sull'Arno (FI)
Tel. 0558348346 Fax 0558348562
Web: www.poggiotrelune.com

The tower soaring over the park signals the presence of the country house and the adjacent farmhouse; all around, there's a large farm, animated with colours and sounds.

3 (x 2/4)

- - - 775,00

Riparbella

Le Serre

at Le Serre 72, 56046 Riparbella (PI)
Tel. 0586699100 Fax 0586699100

This is an excellent choice for those seeking a completely free holiday. Not only is the place beautiful and well-kept, with organic produce served at table, but it's also ideal for families with children.

4(x 2)

- 60,00 -

Roccastrada

Fattoria di Caminino

at Roccatederighi, via Provinciale direction Peruzzo, 58028 Roccastrada (GR)
Tel. 0564569737 Fax 0552675819
Web: www.caminino.com

In a area of ancient beauty, there are large spaces with recreational facilities in the verdant park with its small lake; the activities available range from hiking in the Maremma to food and wine tourism.

4 (x 2/4)

- 250,00 1.200,00

Rosignano Marittimo

Casale del Mare

at Castiglioncello, strada Vicinale delle Spianate, 57012 Rosignano Marittimo (LI)
Tel. 0586759007 Fax 0586759921
Web: www.casaledelmare.it

This is exceptional accommodation: although the external appearance of the farmhouse has been preserved, the interior has modern furnishings, with the predominance of white.

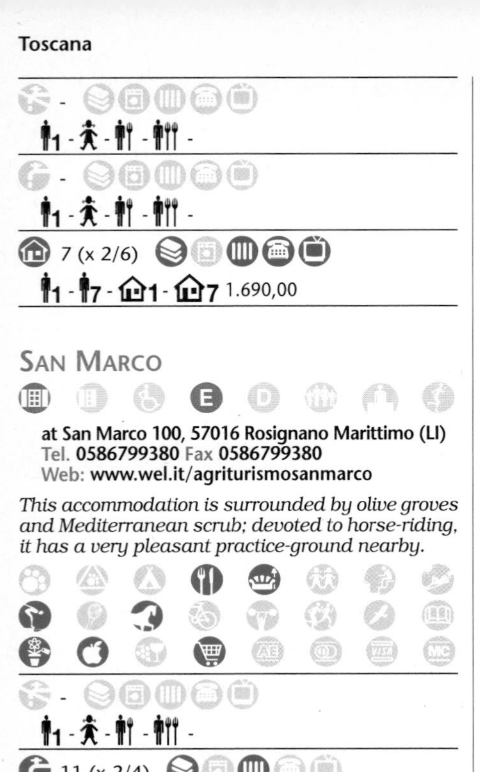

7 (x 2/6)

1.690,00

San Marco

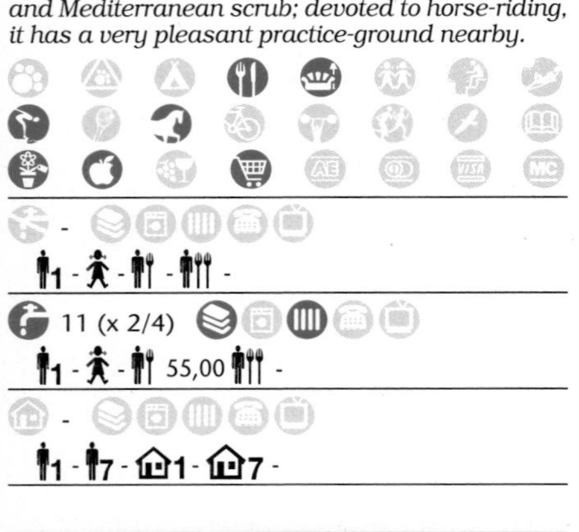

at San Marco 100, 57016 Rosignano Marittimo (LI)
Tel. 0586799380 Fax 0586799380
Web: www.wel.it/agriturismosanmarco

This accommodation is surrounded by olive groves and Mediterranean scrub; devoted to horse-riding, it has a very pleasant practice-ground nearby.

11 (x 2/4)

55,00

Rufina

Fattoria i Busini

at Scopeti 28, 50068 Rufina (FI)
Tel. 0558397809 Fax 0558397004
Web: www.ibusini.com

This accommodation of a hotel standard consists of apartments in the renovated farmhouses surrounding a 15th-century Medicean villa.

5 (x 4/6)

723,00

San Casciano dei Bagni

Il Poggio

at Il Poggio, 53040 San Casciano dei Bagni (SI)
Tel. 057853748 Fax 057853587
Web: www.ilpoggio.net

Riding in the Crete Senesi: this is the offer of an establishment that boasts a splendid position and surroundings that are perfect for horseback tours.

5 (x 4)

105,00 130,00

25 (x 4/6)

310,00 1.140,00

La Crocetta

at La Crocetta,
53040 San Casciano dei Bagni (SI)
Tel. 057858360 Fax 057858353
Web: www.agriturismolacrocetta.it

The exterior of this building has the sober appearance of a farmhouse; inside, instead, there are elegant rooms, with echoes of the Anglo-Saxon world.

8 (x 1/2)

54,00 30,00 76,00

Le Radici Natura & Benessere

at Le Radici, 53040 San Casciano dei Bagni (SI)
Tel. 057856038 Fax 057856038
Web: www.leradici.it

The farm's name reflects the philosophy of life of the owners, Alfredo and Marcello: the revival of old equilibria and the pleasures of a refined country 'relais'.

\-

1 - - -

10 (x 2/4)

1 93,00 - 123,00 -

2 (x 2/5)

1 - 7 - 1 - 7 1.281,00

San Casciano in Val di Pesa

Castello di Bibbione

at Montefiridolfi, via Collina 66,
50026 San Casciano in Val di Pesa (FI)
Tel. 0558249231 Fax 0558249231
Web: www.castellodibibbione.com

What used to be Niccolò Machiavelli's hunting lodge is located in the Florentine Chianti. Accommodation is available for today's tourists in the hamlet's cottages, with their stone, wood and terracotta tiles.

\-

1 - - -

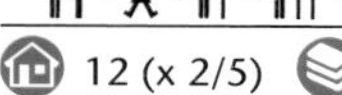

\-

1 - - -

12 (x 2/5)

1 - 7 - 1 1.000,00 7 4.700,00

Fattoria le Corti

via S. Pietro di Sotto 1,
50026 San Casciano in Val di Pesa (FI)
Tel. 055820123 Fax 0558290089
Web: www.principecorsini.com

This accommodation, centring on an imposing country house, has two self-contained apartments available in a wing of a farm.

\-

1 - - -

\-

1 - - -

2(x 4)

1 - 7 - 1 - 7 4.700,00

La Ginestra

at San Pancrazio, via Pergolato 3,
50020 San Casciano in Val di Pesa (FI)
Tel. 0558248196 Fax 0558248196
Web: www.laginestra.toscana.it

Broom symbolises an 'organic' choice of great respect for nature in this farm with its model piggery.

\-

1 - - -

15 (x 1/4)

1 38,00 26,60 58,00 -

6 (x 2/13)

1 - 7 - 1 - 7 2.080,00

Tenuta Castello il Corno

at San Pancrazio, via Malafrasca 64,
50026 San Casciano in Val di Pesa (FI)
Tel. 0558248009 Fax 0558248035

These apartments have been obtained by the conversion of old farmhouses and furnished in traditional rural style.

\-

1 - - -

\-

1 - - -

14 (x 2/4)

1 - 7 - 1 200,00 7 1.096,44

San Gimignano

Casanova di Pescille

at Pescille, 53037 San Gimignano (SI)
Tel. 0577941902 Fax 0577941902
Web: www.casanovadipescille.com

This 19th-century farmhouse has a fully-equipped farmyard, gazebo, large fireplaces, period furnishings and rustic finishings recalling the good old days.

\-

1 - - -

9 (x 1/4)

1 55,00 - - -

1(x 2)

1 - 7 - 1 105,00 7 -

Fattoria di Pietrafitta

at Cortennano 54, 53037 San Gimignano (SI)
Tel. 0577943200 Fax 0577943150
Web: www.pietrafitta.com

In the 19th century, after it had passed to the Savoy family, this villa, which is of 15th-century origin, became a model farm. The accommodation is in an early 18th-century farmhouses.

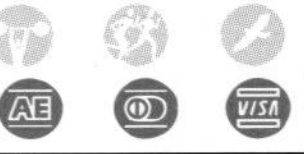

\-

1 - - -

9 (x 2)

1 57,00 - - -

4 (x 2/4)

1 - 7 - 1 - 7 1.195,00

Fattoria Poggio Alloro

at Sant'Andrea 23, 53037 San Gimignano (SI)
Tel. 0577950276 Fax 0577950290
Web: www.fattoriapoggioalloro.com

On this organic farm, where Chianina cattle are raised, a house has been converted to provide accommodation with a rustic appearance.

\-

1 - - -

8 (x 2)

1 42,50 - 75,00 -

2(x 2)

1 - 7 - 1 123,00 7 -

Fattoria San Donato

at San Donato 6, 53037 San Gimignano (SI)
Tel. **0577941616** Fax **0577906712**
Web: **www.sandonato.it**

The accommodation, located in the village clustered around a small church, has period furniture and gives the impression that one has gone back in time to an earlier age.

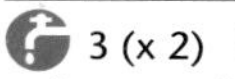 -

 1 - - -
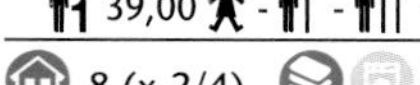 3 (x 2)
1 39,00 - - -
 8 (x 2/4)
1 39,00 7 - 1 - 7 -

Fattoria Voltrona

at San Donato, 53037 San Gimignano (SI)
Tel. **0577943152** Fax **0577906077**
Web: **www.voltrona.com**

Just 4 kilometres from the enchanting walled town of San Gimignano, accommodation is available in a villa with a large terrace and garden.

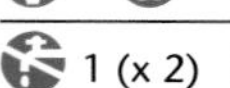 1 (x 2)
 1 - - -
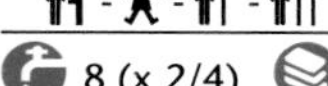 8 (x 2/4)
1 34,00 34,00 52,50 -
 -
 1 - 7 - 1 - 7 -

Podere Arcangelo

at Capezzano 26, via S. Benedetto 26,
53037 San Gimignano (SI)
Tel. **0577944404** Fax **0577945628**
Web: **www.poderearcangelo.it**

This is accommodation in a monastery, or rather in the 17th-century buildings where the monks used to pray and work.

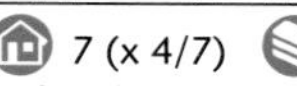 -
1 - - -
 6 (x 2/4)
1 40,00 - 63,00 -
7 (x 4/7)
1 - 7 - 1 - 7 1.084,00

Podere Cappella

at Lignite 20, 53037 San Gimignano (SI)
Tel. **0577941615** Fax **0577941615**

The surviving towers of San Gimignano are visible from here. The natural world plays a major role, as this the farm is located in a nature reserve.

-
1 - - -
3 (x 2)
1 22,00 - - -
-
1 - 7 - 1 - 7 -

Podere Villuzza

at Strada 25/26, 53037 San Gimignano (SI)
Tel. 0577940585 Fax 0577942247
Web: www.poderevilluzza.it

Two rows of cypresses line the road leading to this attractive farmhouse. The rooms are notable for their freshness and the attention paid to the details.

\-

1 - - -

4 (x 2)

1 50,00 - - -

3(x 2)

1 - 7 - 1 - 7 730,00

Tenuta Torciano

at Ulignano, via Crocetta 18,
53030 San Gimignano (SI)
Tel. 0577950055 Fax 0577950161
Web: www.torciano.com

This 'historic' estate has a renovated farmhouse with comfortable rooms and self-contained apartments with period furniture.

\-

1 - - -

8 (x 1/4)

1 49,00 13,00 - -

3 (x 2/4)

1 - 7 - 1 156,00 7 -

San Giovanni d'Asso

La Canonica

at Podere La Canonica,
53020 San Giovanni d'Asso (SI)
Tel. 0577834338 Fax 0577834338
Web: www.dama.it

The setting is that of the Crete Senesi. The farmhouse, in travertine, looks out over a landscape that seems to have emerged from a medieval fresco.

\-

1 - - -

\-

1 - - -

6 (x 2/3)

1 - 7 - 1 155,00 7 -

San Giuliano Terme

Green Farm

at Madonna dell'Acqua, via Vecchia Pietrasantina 11, 56010 San Giuliano Terme (PI)
Tel. 050890671 Fax 050890671
Web: www.pisaonline.it/greenfarm

Pisa, the San Rossore Regional Park and the sea are all within easy reach. But the main attraction of this place is the peace and quiet of the 18th-century villa.

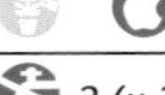

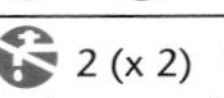

2 (x 2)

1 40,00 - 60,00 -

6 (x 1/4)

40,00 - 60,00 -

3(x 4)

185,00 750,00

San Miniato

Podere Canova

at Corazzano, via Zara 186,
56020 San Miniato (PI)
Tel. **0571460120** Fax **0571460013**
Web: **www.agriturismocanova.com**

This renovated 17th-century farmhouse has all modern comforts; the rooms are large and well-equipped, with a separate entrance.

8 (x 2/4)

42,00 - 60,00 -

San Quirico d'Orcia

Bagnaia

podere Bagnaia 47,
53027 San Quirico d'Orcia (SI)
Tel. **0577898272** Fax **0577898272**
Web: **www.terranostra.it**

In the heart of the Val d'Orcia Nature and Culture Park, a renovated stone farmhouse offers first-rate accommodation.

3(x 2)

96,00 450,00

Il Rigo

at Casabianca, 53027 San Quirico d'Orcia (SI)
Tel. **0577897291** Fax **0577898236**
Web: **www.agriturismoilrigo.com**

The farmhouse stands out on a hill in the Crete of the Val d'Orcia, within easy reach of the Renaissance town of Pienza and the medieval San Quirico and Bagno Vignoni.

12 (x 2/4)

44,00 22,00 64,50 -

La Buca

at La Buca, 53027 San Quirico d'Orcia (SI)
Tel. **0577897078** Fax **0577897078**
E-mail: **agriturismolabuca@libero.it**

This farmhouse in the Val d'Orcia has the ideal accommodation for an authentic rural holiday. The pleasures of country life are amplified by the domestic comforts.

1 (x 2)

28,50 - 53,00 -

1(x 2)

104,00 -

Sansepolcro

Calcinaia sul Lago

at Calcinaia, 52037 Sansepolcro (AR)
Tel. **0575742777** Fax **0575742777**
Web: **www.wel.it/calcinaia**

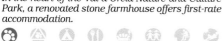

Surrounded by the green countryside of the Tiber Valley, this complex is 10 km from Sansepolcro, the

birthplace of Piero della Francesca; there are large open spaces and nicely furnished apartments.

\-

1 - - -

\-

1 - - -

5 (x 2/4)

1 38,00 7 - 1 - 7 -

La Conca

at Paradiso 16, 52037 Sansepolcro (AR)
Tel. 0575733301 Fax 0575733301
Web: www.laconca.it

In the Tiber Valley, accommodation is available in old stone farmhouses with rustic furnishings, fireplaces, wood-fired ovens and barbecues.

\-

1 - - -

3 (x 1/4)

1 35,00 - - -

6 (x 2/4)

1 35,00 7 - 1 - 7 -

Podere Violino

at Gricignano 99, 52037 Sansepolcro (AR)
Tel. 0575720174 Fax 0575720174
Web: www.podereviolino.it

This refined accommodation, with local cuisine, is ideal for those fond of horse-riding (and those who aren't): it's adjacent to stables belonging to the FISE and CONI.

\-

1 - - -

8 (x 2/4)

1 41,00 - 56,00 -

\-

1 - 7 - 1 - 7 -

Santa Luce

La Mariola

via della Serra 1, 56040 Santa Luce (PI)
Tel. 0586752583 Fax 0586752583
Web: www.primitaly.it/agriturismo/lamariola

A large meadow, an orchard and a clump of oaks in the background: beyond the green of the olives, there's the sea and the Apuan Alps. The accommodation is in a recently renovated farmhouse.

\-

1 - - -

\-

1 - - -

4 (x 3/6)

1 - 7 - 1 156,00 7 727,00

San Vincenzo

Costa Etrusca

via Castelluccio 127, 57027 San Vincenzo (LI)
Tel. 0565798019 Fax 0565798140
Web: www.agriturismocostaetrusca.it

Set on a hill, with splendid views, the accommodation is located in well-exposed apartments opening though arcades onto the garden.

-

1 - - - -

-

1 - - - -

10 (x 2/4)

1 - 7 - 1 173,00 7 -

Poggio ai Santi

at San Bartolo 100, 57027 San Vincenzo (LI)
Tel. 0565798032 Fax 0565798607
Web: www.terra-toscana.com/poggioaisanti

Beaches and pinewoods, Etruscan settlements and woods, mines and ancient metallurgic plant: all this is within easy reach of the farmhouse, set in the hills, with its friendly welcome.

-

1 - - - -

-

1 - - - -

4(x 3)

1 79,50 7 - 1 - 7 -

Sarteano

Moggiano

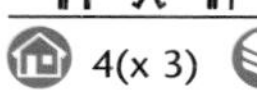  

via Moggiano 3, 53047 Sarteano (SI)
Tel. 0578265349 Fax 0578265349
Web: spazioweb.inwind.it/moggiano

The magnificent setting, swimming pool and domestic comforts will tempt many guests to take things easy in this establishment that is almost on the border with Umbria.

-

1 - - - -

-

1 - - - -

4 (x 3/4)

1 - 7 - 1 100,00 7 -

Sassetta

La Bandita

via Campagna Nord 30, 57020 Sassetta (LI)
Tel. 0565794224 Fax 0565794350
Web: www.labandita.com

This large farm comprises areas of Mediterranean scrub and, in the centre of it, a 17th-century villa, converted, with its outbuildings, into tourist accommodation.

-

1 - - - -

24 (x 2) 

1 80,00 - 105,00 - 

-

1 - 7 - 1 - 7 -

Podere la Cerreta

at Pian delle Vigne, 57020 Sassetta (LI)
Tel. 0565794352 Fax 0565794352
Web: www.lacerreta.it

Surrounded by scrub and chestnut trees at an altitude of 250 m and 15 km from the sea, this farm uses organic agricultural methods; the accommodation is in old stone houses.

\-

1 - - -

12 (x 1/4)

1 - - - 71,00

\-

1 - 7 - 1 - 7 -

Santa Lorica

via Campagna Nord,
57020 Sassetta (LI)
Tel. 0565794335 Fax 0565794335
Web: www.etruscan.li.it/lorica

Recent renovation work has added arcades to the original farmhouse, thus giving guests more opportunities for socialising.

\-

1 - - -

11 (x 2)

1 50,00 - 65,00 -

\-

1 - 7 - 1 - 7 -

Scansano

Borgo de' Salaioli

at Salaioli 181, 58054 Scansano (GR)
Tel. 0564599205 Fax 0564599735
Web: web.tiscali.it/salaioli

Just inland from the coast near Grosseto, ancient olives frame stone cottages where tourist accommodation is available.

\-

1 - - -

3 (x 2)

1 33,00 - - -

1(x 4)

1 - 7 - 1 100,00 7 -

Casa Nova

at Montepò 42/43, 58050 Scansano (GR)
Tel. 0564580317 Fax 0564580317
Web: www.agriturismocasanova.it

Amid oak-woods and vineyards, this farmhouse, a mixture of rusticity and elegance, offers accommodation; there's a large living-room with a fireplace, riding courses and tours on horseback.

\-

1 - - -

5 (x 2/4)

1 42,50 - - -

1(x 4)

1 - 7 - 1 105,00 7 670,00

Perucci di Sotto

at Montorgiali, 58050 Scansano (GR)
Tel. 0564580306 Fax 0564580306
E-mail: peruccisotto@interfree.it

Not far from Scansano, this farm is in a commanding position, with a view extending as far as the island of Elba. With its rustic atmosphere, this is a real farmhouse.

4 (x 1/2)

1 25,82 - -

-

1 - - -

3(x 3)

1 - 7 - 1 83,00 7 -

SCARLINO

CAMPO VALERIO

at Campo Valerio, 58020 Scarlino (GR)
Tel. 056637439 Fax 056638749
Web: www.campovalerio.com

This old farmhouse stands alone on a hill surrounded by olive trees. The recent renovation has added a large arcade and a paved area around the swimming pool.

-

1 - - -

7 (x 1/2)

1 45,00 - 62,00 -

-

1 - 7 - 1 - 7 -

SEMPRONIANO

POGGIO DELL'AIONE

at Catabbio, via Turati 2,
58050 Semproniano (GR)
Tel. 0564986389 Fax 0564987721
Web: www.laltramaremma.it/poggiodellaione

The accommodation is in old cottages surrounded by greenery, just a few minutes' drive from the thermal baths at Saturnia (guests are entitled to reductions here).

-

1 - - -

-

1 - - -

8 (x 2/4)

1 30,00 7 - 1 - 7 -

SERRAVALLE PISTOIESE

FATTORIA LE PÒGGIOLA

at Ponte di Serravalle, via Treggiaia 13,
51030 Serravalle Pistoiese (PT)
Tel. 057351071 Fax 057351071
Web: www.lepoggiola.com

A bright display of oleanders adorns the entrance to this estate comprising five holdings under vines and olives. The area is ideal for walking or riding.

2 (x 2)

1 40,00 - 60,00 -

7 (x 2/4)

1 50,00 - 65,00 -

2(x 4)

1 - 7 - 1 130,00 7 750,00

SIENA

BAGNO A SORRA

strada degli Agostoli 65, 53100 Siena
Tel. 0577393252 Fax 0577393252
Web: www.bagnassorra.com

'Olive-growers of the 15th century' is the slogan of this organic farm, excellently located just outside Siena.

\-

1 - - -

13 (x 1/2)

1 100,00 - - -

5 (x 4/5)

1 - 7 - 1 200,00 7 -

SINALUNGA

LA FRATTA

E

at La Fratta, 53048 Sinalunga (SI)
Tel. 0577679472 Fax 0577679685
Web: www.fratta.net

This is a large farm with a villa, garden and outbuildings converted into tourist accommodation, where it is also possible to go to Mass in the little church.

\-

1 - - -

2 (x 2)

1 25,00 - 48,00 -

11(x 2)

1 20,00 7 - 1 - 7 -

VILLA IL POGGIO

E

via del Poggio 316, 53048 Sinalunga (SI)
Tel. 0577630461 Fax 0577630461
Web: www.villailpoggio.ware.it

'People come to the Villa il Poggio, proud and secular as the cypresses surrounding it, as guests and leave as friends': this is Elisabetta Perez's pledge.

\-

1 - - -

5 (x 2)

1 41,05 - - -

3 (x 3/4)

1 - 7 - 1 104,00 7 725,00

SOVICILLE

MONTESTIGLIANO

E

at Montestigliano, 53010 Sovicille (SI)
Tel. 0577342189 Fax 0577342100
Web: www.montestigliano.it

On the offshoots of the Montagnola Senese stands this hamlet consisting of the owner's villa and the surrounding cottages.

-

1 - - -

-

1 - - -

11(x 3)

1 - 7 - 1 - 7 3.358,00

Montioni

at San Rocco a Pilli, 53010 Sovicille (SI)
Tel. 0577342016 Fax 0577342191
Web: www.montioni.it

On the hills around the Merse Valley, a farmhouse and the adjacent buildings have been converted into a number of apartments with different layouts and sizes.

-

1 - - -

-

1 - - -

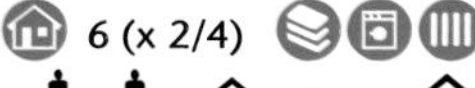

6 (x 2/4)

1 - 7 - 1 100,00 7 -

Subbiano

Le Gret

at Santa Mama, 52010 Subbiano (AR)
Tel. 0575487090 Fax 0575487090
Web: www.legrettuscany.com

'Le Gret for a carefree holiday' is the slogan of this elegant establishment with tourist accommodation overlooking a large park in the hills of the Casentino.

-

1 - - -

-

1 - - -

11 (x 2/4)

1 40,00 7 - 1 - 7 -

Suvereto

Poggetto Masino

via Poggetto Masino 169, 57028 Suvereto (LI)
Tel. 0565828176 Fax 0565828176
Web: www.agriturist.it/masino

A group of ancient cypresses screens a farmhouse with its complex structure. The interior has been carefully refurbished with materials traditionally used in Tuscany.

-

1 - - -

-

1 - - -

5 (x 2/4)

1 - 7 - 1 - 7 697,00

Tavarnelle Val di Pesa

Fattoria Villa Spoiano

at Spoiano, 50028 Tavarnelle Val di Pesa (FI)
Tel. 0558077313 Fax 0558061369
Web: www.toscanaholidays.com

The villa of Spoiano, with its adjacent farmhouse, recalls the age of the Medici, but also the age-old tradition of wine- and olive oil-making.

\-
1 - - -

7 (x 1/2)
1 45,00 - - -

7 (x 2/3)
1 - 7 - 1 90,00 7 -

Il Bacio

at Bonazza 35, 50028 Tavarnelle Val di Pesa (FI)
Tel. 0558076437 Fax 0558076437
Web: ilbacio.e12.it

Florence, Siena and San Gimignano are about 30 to 35 km away. But here the surroundings are so attractive that one just wants to stay put.

\-
1 - - -

\-
1 - - -

6 (x 2/5)
1 - 7 - 1 - 7 500,00

Sovigliano

via Magliano 9, 50028 Tavarnelle Val di Pesa (FI)
Tel. 0558076217 Fax 0558050770
Web: www.sovigliano.com

One tries to pick out the towers of San Gimignano, but the whole area is dotted with castles, churches and old villages. The accommodation is in a large renovated farmhouse.

\-
1 - - -

4 (x 2)
1 56,00 - 98,00 -

4 (x 2/4)
1 - 7 - 1 - 7 850,00

Terranuova Bracciolini

Valdarnese

at Paterna, 52028 Terranuova Bracciolini (AR)
Tel. 055977052 Fax 055977052
Web: www.paterna.it

At the foot of the Pratomagno, this farm has the best organic produce of the Colli Aretini and an osteria serving traditional dishes.

\-
1 - - -

\-
1 - - -

3(x 2)
1 - 7 - 1 52,00 7 -

Torrita di Siena

Le Capanne di Sopra

at Montefollonico, via Capanne 80,
53049 Torrita di Siena (SI)
Fax 0635341578
Web: www.toskana.net/lecapanne

Montepulciano is of particular interest to art lovers. The farm, with its olive groves and vineyards, comprises two stone houses that have been carefully restored.

-

1 - - -

-

1 - - -

2(x 6)

1 - 7 - 1 - 7 950,00

TREQUANDA

FATTORIA DEL COLLE

at Il Colle, 53020 Trequanda (SI)
Tel. 0577662108 Fax 0577662202
Web: www.cinellicolombini.it

Originally a rendezvous for hunters (and lovers), this villa is frequented today by tourists from many different countries who stay in the converted farm buildings of the huge estate.

-

1 - - -

2 (x 2)

1 46,50 - 66,50 -

19 (x 2/3)

1 - 7 - 1 645,57 7 2.685,58

TORRENIERI

E

at Sant'Anna in Camprena, 53020 Trequanda (SI)
Tel. 0578748112 Fax 0578748112
Web: www.nautilus-mp.com/torrenieri

The Torrenieri farmhouse, set amid tall oaks, promises holidays in the open air, but, when the temperature drops, guests can warm themselves in front of the large fireplace.

-

1 - - -

-

1 - - -

1(x 6)

1 - 7 - 1 135,00 7 -

TRESANA

ANTONIOTTI

E D

at Giovagallo, via Tavella 13, 54012 Tresana (MS)
Tel. 0187477070 Fax 058572897
E-mail: manlioan@tiscali.it

The setting for this holiday is the castles and churches of the Lunigiana, with the peaceful rhythm of days spent lazing amid meadows and chestnut trees.

-

1 - - -

-

1 - - -

4 (x 3/5)

1 23,00 7 - 1 - 7 -

VADA

LE BIRICOCCOLE

E D

via Vecchia Aurelia 200, 57018 Vada (LI)
Tel. 0586788394 Fax 0586786347
Web: www.biricoccole.it

The sea, pinewoods and the countryside are the main attractions of this comfortable accommodation in a renovated farmhouse with its wooden beams and arches.

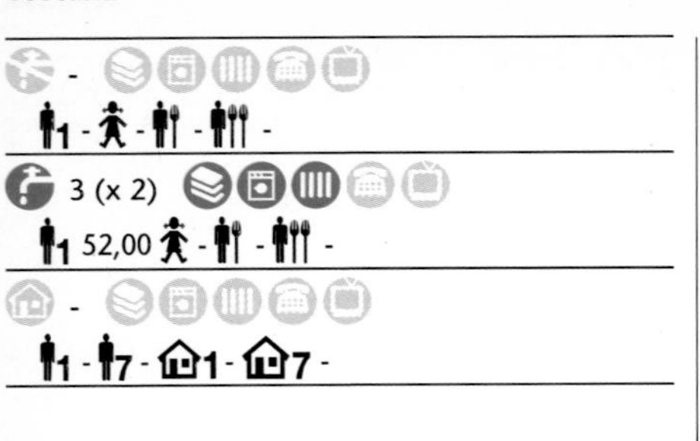

VILLA GRAZIANI

road for Rosignano 14,
57018 Vada (LI)
Tel. 0586788244 Fax 0586785998
Web: www.villagraziani.com

This is an imposing house of the mid-19th century. In addition to its ancient ilexes and cork oaks, the park contains sculptures, while the rooms have period furniture.

8 (x 2)
70,00 45,00 95,00 -

2(x 2)
900,00

VAGLIA

PODERI DI COIANO

via di Coiano 1476, 50030 Vaglia (FI)
Tel. 055407680 Fax 055407772
E-mail: coiano@dada.it

This farmhouse has preserved its original forms and spaces almost intact. It's not by chance that organic farming is practised here and the animals raised include the Cinta Senese pig.

2 (x 4/6)
115,00 550,00

VILLAFRANCA IN LUNIGIANA

CA' SOLA

at Mocrone, 54028 Villafranca in Lunigiana (MS)
Tel. 0187429892 Fax 0187429892
Web: www.seaol.com/agricasola

Overlooking the Magra Valley, this stone farmhouse, which employs organic methods, has romantic furnishings and offers opportunities for horse-riding.

2 (x 4/7)
198,00 1.100,00

Vinci

Podere Zollaio

via Pistoiese 25, 50059 Vinci (FI)
Tel. 057156439 Fax 057156439
Web: www.yacc.it/spazioweb/poderezollaio

The old farmhouses, with their beams and terracotta arches and floors, have been converted into tourist accommodation; the white walls and the furnishings give a touch of modernity.

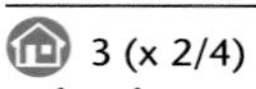 3 (x 2/4)   542,00

Tenuta le Colonie

via Valinardi 80, 50059 Vinci (FI)
Tel. 0571729154 Fax 0571568500
Web: www.tenutalecolonie.it

This is the village where Leonardo da Vinci was born. Surrounded by olive groves and vineyards, the farm offers charming, tasteful rooms with period furniture.

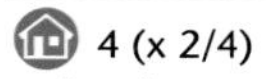 4 (x 2/4)   150,00 827,00

Volterra

Fattoria Lischeto

at San Giusto, 56048 Volterra (PI)
Tel. 058830403 Fax 058830403
Web: www.agrilischeto.com

This fine stone cottage has been renovated and equipped with wooden furniture. From the windows and the swimming pool there are views of the Balze and gullies of Volterra.

4 (x 2) 38,00 60,00 

7 (x 2/4) 616,00 

Mirandola

at Villamagna, S.P. (provincial road) 15 at km 10, 56040 Volterra (PI)
Tel. 058833058 Fax 058833058
Web: www.inyourlife.it

Between Volterra and San Gimignano, in the land of the Etruscans, this farmhouse stands on top of a low hill, with accommodation in a converted hayloft nearby.

 3 (x 3/6)  465,00

Tenuta Orgiaglia

at Ponsano, 56048 Volterra (PI)
Tel. 058835029 Fax 058835029
Web: www.orgiaglia.it

This organic oasis offers a relaxing holiday in the guesthouse of the 17th-century Castello di Luppiano, within easy reach of Volterra, San Gimignano and Siena.

-

1 - - -

6 (x 4)

1 25,00 - 49,00 -

3(x 4)

1 - 7 - 1 - 7 580,00

VILLA MONTAPERTI

at Montaperti, S.S. (state road) 439dir at km 11, 56048 Volterra (PI)
Tel. **058842038** Fax **058885240**
Web: **www.montaperti.com**

For a breathtaking holiday, this villa has huge rooms with terracotta tiles on the floors and period furniture, and, on the ground floor, a big kitchen with a fireplace and pantry.

-

1 - - -

12 (x 2)

1 93,00 32,00 - -

-

1 - 7 - 1 - 7 -

TUSCANY

IN THE MAREMMA NATURE PARK

PERCHED ON THE EDGE OF A SHEER CLIFF TO SEA, IN THE MAREMMA NATURE PARK, STANDS AN HISTORICAL OBSERVATION TOWER WHICH AFFORDS A PANORAMIC VIEW OVER THE TWO HUNDRED HECTARES OF WOODS, SPECKLED WITH BROOM.

THE VIEW RANGES FROM THE MAREMMA HILLS TO THE SEA AND RIGHT OUT TO THE ISLAND OF MONTECRISTO.

BE OUR GUEST FOR A STAY IN OUR COMFORTABLE ROOMS OVER-LOOKING THE SEA, IN MODERN FLATS, CHARMING WOODEN CHALETS OR IN OLD WEST-STYLE COACHES.

TOSCANA
LAZIO

GITAV BOOKING CENTER P.O. BOX 67 - I - 58010 ALBINIA (GR)
TEL 0039 - 0564 870068 FAX 0039 - 0564 870470
www.gitav.com E-MAIL: info@gitav.com

Farm Holidays in MUGELLO

The Mugello countryside is splendid in all seasons: the old farmhouses - finely restored by the farmers - offer hospitality in flats that generally include a kitchen, bedrooms and bathrooms, or in rooms which do not usually offer kitchen facilities. Some offer meals and the sale of home-grown produce, or numerous activities such as archery, walks, and horseback riding, mountain biking, swimming in panoramic swimming pools, and cooking courses, etc.

BARBERINO MUGELLO
✉ postal code 50031

■ **IL PALAZZACCIO**
Via Rezzano, 9 - 50030 Galliano M.llo
Tel. and Fax +390558428110
www.villailpalazzaccio.com
ilpalazzaccio@inwind.it
Flats: 4, (central heating); sleeping accommodations:11; bathrooms: 4. Production and sale of honey, extra virgin olive oil and asparagus. Swimming pool.

■ **PANZANO**
Via Panzano, 13 - guasconi@tin.it
Tel. and Fax +390558418231
Flat: 1; sleeping accommodations: 8; bathrooms 4. Excursions on foot and by mountain bike.

■ **POGGIO DI SOTTO**
Via di Galliano, 17 - 50030 Galliano M.llo
Tel. +390558428447/8
Fax +390558428449
www.wel.it/poggiodisotto
agriturismopoggiodisotto@virgilio.it
Rooms: 9; sleeping accommodations: 14; bathrooms: 9. Guided tours inside the farm, sale of honey, excursions on foot and by mountain bike.

BORGO SAN LORENZO
✉ postal code 50032

■ **COLLEFERTILE**
Via Arliano, 37
Loc. La Sughera - Montegiovi
Tel. +390558495201; +390558490074; +390558495207 - Fax +390558490154
www.collefertile.com - info@collefertile.com
Rooms: 15; sleeping accommodations: 30; bathrooms 15, (of which 2 outdoor). Restaurant, heated pool, 2 tennis courts, five-a-side football field, excursions on the estate on foot and by jeep, as well as fishing, baby sitting, and cooking lessons.

■ **IL POGGIO ALLE VILLE**
Loc. Le Ville - Mucciano
Tel. +390558408752 - Fax +39055599828
www.poggioalleville.it
raffaele@poggioalleville.it
Flat: 1 (central heating); sleeping accommodations: 16; bathrooms: 7. Swimming pool, five-a-side football field, bowls, sale of oil, excursions on foot and by mountain bike, as well as washing machine and Internet point.

■ **IL POGGIOLO**
Via delle Salaiole, 21 - Loc. Poggiolo
Tel. +390558495545 - Fax +390558409616
www.ilpoggioloagriturism.com
ilpoggiolagriturism@tiscalinet.it
Flats: 3 (central heating); sleeping accommodations: 13; bathrooms: 9. Excursions on foot and by mountain bike, swimming pool.

■ **LA FONTANA**
Loc. Canaglia - Tel. +390558042320
info@lafontana.org
Rooms: 5; sleeping accommodations 6; bathrooms: 2. Visits to the organically grown food farm holiday, and the dairy cattle breeding farm; restaurant, sale of farm products such as jam, tomato sauce, canned vegetables and liqueurs. Excursions on foot (with a nature guide), by mountain bike (rent available) and on horseback (with riding guide), stables for horses, dogs are welcome.

■ **LA TOPAIA**
Via San Giovanni Maggiore, 57
Tel. and Fax +390558408741
www.wel.it/latopaia - salsedo@tin.it
Flats: 2 (central heating); sleeping accommodations: 12; bathrooms: 3. Rooms: 3; sleeping accommodations: 6; bathrooms: 2. Excursions on foot, and sale of season fruit (peaches and pears).

■ **LE BUCHE**
Via Battiloro, 1 - Loc. Battiloro
Tel. +390558458279; +393280257226
Fax +390558453568
Flat: 1 (central heating); sleeping accommodations: 10, bathrooms: 3.

■ **LE SELVE**
Via San Giovanni Maggiore, 50
Tel. and Fax +390558408989
selveagriturismo@tin.it
Flats: 3 (central heating), sleeping accommodations: 6; bathrooms: 3. Excursions on foot and by mountain bike, and sale of season produce (apples, plums, cherries, pears).

■ **PALAZZO VECCHIO**
Via Piazzano, 41 - sgrossi@libero.it
Tel. +390558495235; +393339978977
Fax +390558495235
Flat: 1 (central heating); sleeping accom-

modations: 7; bathrooms: 2. Excursions on foot and by mountain bike. Visits to the dairy cattle breeding farm, sale of vegetables and courtyard animals.

■ **SANVITALE**
Via Campagna, 20 - Loc. San Giorgio
50030 Luco M.llo - sanvitale@dada.it
Tel. and Fax +390558401158
www.sottobosco.it/s.vitale.html
Rooms: 8; sleeping accommodations: 14; bathrooms: 8. Meals (breakfast, dinner), guided excursions on foot and by mountain bike, as well as the sale of honey, jam, chestnuts, and organically grown produce, reading rooms, and cooking courses.

FIRENZUOLA
postal code 50033

■ **BADIA DI MOSCHETA**
Via di Moscheta, 898
Tel. and Fax +390558144015
www.badiadimoscheta.com
badiadimoscheta@tiscalinet.it
Flat: 1; sleeping accommodations: 4; bathroom: 1. Rooms: 6; sleeping accommodations: 24; bathrooms: 6. Meals, chestnut harvest, centre for tourism on horseback, and excursions on foot.

■ **CAMAGGIANICA**
Covigliaio - Loc. Camaggianica
tel +39055812224
Rooms: 3; sleeping accommodations: 7.

■ **CROCETTI MASSIMO**
Fraz. Le Valli - Loc. Citerna, 35
Tel. +39055812115; +393385329637
Flats: 3; sleeping accommodations: 7; bathrooms: 3. Visits to the organically grown food farm, stables for horses; excursions on foot, on horseback and by mountain bike.

■ **I CONFIENTI**
Via I Confidenti, 640/a - Fraz. Bruscoli
Tel. and Fax +39055818159;
+393487633669.
Rooms: 5; sleeping accommodations: 12; bathrooms: 2. Meals, excursions on foot and on horseback.

■ **LA CASETTA**
Covigliaio - Loc. Casetta
Tel. +39055812038 - f.galeotti@inwind.it
Rooms: 4; sleeping accommodations: 6; bathrooms: 2. Meals, and sale of spelt.

■ **LA CHIESA**
Via Caburraccia, 2
Tel. and Fax +390558101035
Rooms: 4; sleeping accommodations: 5; bathroom: 1. Meals, sale of chestnuts, truffles, and mushrooms, excursions on foot and on horseback, and hunting near the estate.

■ **ROVIGNALE**
Loc. Capanna - Castro San Martino
Tel. +390558149297; +39055819782;
+39055819031 - Fax +39055819031
Rooms: 5; sleeping accommodations: 9; bathrooms: 3. Flat: 1 (central heating); sleeping accommodations: 4; bathrooms: 2. Meals, excursions on foot and by mountain bike, lake fishing for sport, and hunting.

■ **SCARPELLI EGIDIO**
Loc. Molinuccio - Casanova
tel. +390558144169
Rooms: 3; sleeping accommodations: 6; bathrooms: 2. Excursions on foot and by mountain bike, visits to the dairy cattle breeding farm.

MARRADI
postal code 50034

■ **CASALUCCIO DI GAMOGNA**
Via Est Gamogna, 2 - Lutirano
Tel. and Fax +3905580482O
Flats: 2 (central heating); sleeping accommodations: 7; bathrooms: 3.

■ **GALLIANA**
Casa Padronale e Podere Galliana di Sopra - Galliana
Tel. +390558044344
Flat: 1; sleeping accommodations: 17; bathrooms: 5.

■ **IL QUERCETO**
Via Case Sparse, 10 - Abeto di Lutirano
Tel. and Fax +390558049900
www.italiaabc.it/a/querceto
querceto@yahoo.it
Rooms: 3; sleeping accommodations: 6; bathrooms: 4. Meals, excursions on foot, on horseback, by mountain bike, lake fishing for sport, sale of mushrooms, truffles, jam, bread and pasta.

■ **LA SERRA**
Via Bulbana - tel +39055804836/2
Rooms: 14; sleeping accommodations: 30; bathrooms: 8. Visit to the organically grown food farm, excursions on foot and by mountain bike, archery, and sale of chestnuts.

■ **MOLINO DI CAMPIGNO**
Podere Gattoleto - Campigno
Tel. + 390554626629; +393482613697
Fax +390554626630 - info@foco.it
www.foco.it/agriturismo
Flat: 1 ; sleeping accommodations: 7; bathroom: 1. Excursions on foot and by mountain bike.

■ **MONTE DI SOTTO**
Via Monte di Sotto - Galliana
Tel. and Fax +390558045061
App. 5; P.L. 14. Escursioni a piedi e in mountain bike.

■ **PIANO ROSSO**
Via Piano Rosso - Biforco
Tel. +390558045345
Fax +390558042807; +390546621061
Flats: 3 (no heating); sleeping accommodations: 7; bathrooms: 3. Excursions on foot, on horseback, and by mountain bike, swimming pool, chestnut and vegetable harvest, games for children.

■ **VOLO DEL NIBBIO**
Loc. Popolano Vonibbio
Tel. and Fax +390558044225
Tel. and Fax +39055489694
agrivonibbio@hotmail.com
Flat: 2; sleeping accommodations: 6; bathrooms: 3. Excursions on foot and by mountain bike, chestnut harvest and mushroom picking, swimming pool and billiards.

PALAZZUOLO SUL SENIO
postal code 50035

■ **BADIA DI SUSINANA**
Via Badia di Susinana, 36
Tel. +390558046630/1 - Fax +390558046660
Rooms: 5; sleeping accommodations: 16; bathrooms: 5. Flats: 4 (central heating); sleeping accommodations: 6; bathrooms: 4. Meals, swimming pool, excursions on foot, on horseback and by mountain bike, lake fishing, sale of organically grown apples, chestnuts, and products of the under wood.

■ **CA' DI SCHETA**
Via Ca' di Scheta, 7
Loc. Lozzole
Hardy +393383484387
vittoriomonari@virgilio.it
Flat: 3; sleeping accommodations: 6; bathrooms: 3. Excursions on foot and by mountain bike.

■ **CA' NOVA**
Via Bibbiana, 21
Tel. and Fax +390558046569
www.agriturismocanova.it
info@agriturismocanova.it
Rooms: 3, sleeping accommodations: 6; bathrooms: 2. Meals, excursions on foot and by mountain bike, chestnut harvest, sale of honey, bread and flat cake.

■ **FANTINO**
Loc. Fantino, 29 di Piedimonte
Tel. +390558046708 - Fax +390558043928
www.tuscanyrental.com/fantino
bevett@tin.it
Excursions on foot and by mountain bike, archery, sale of honey and organically grown pears, picking and sale of chestnuts, production of jams and honey, painting courses on wood, vases, and cloth. Restoring of old and antique furniture, cooking courses using aromatic herbs.

■ **LE PANARE**
Via Lozzole - Piedimonte
Tel. +390558046346
Hardy +393384794222
www.lepanare.it - lepanare@tin.it
Rooms: 4; sleeping accommodations: 12; bathrooms: 4. Small museum with an exhibition of mediaeval armours, and the naturalistic, historical and educational evolution through the ages, courses in mediaeval and local cooking - mediaeval fencing - legends and symbolisms regarding animals. Breeding of animals in danger of extinction.

SAN PIERO A SIEVE
postal code 50037

■ **TREBBIO & CO**
Via del Trebbio, 1
Tel. +390558498777; +390558487196
Fax +390558498470 - info@y-knot.net
www.y-knot.net/trebbio.html
Flat: 1 (no heating); sleeping accommodations: 5; bathrooms 2. Excursions on foot, on horseback and by mountain bike, 2 swimming pools, and sale of extra virgin olive oil.

SCARPERIA
✉ postal code 50038

■ CATELACCIO
Via Montepoli, 34 - Loc. Sant'Agata
Tel. +390558406624 - catelaccio@libero.it
Flats: 2; sleeping accommodations: 8; bathrooms: 4. Sale of season fruit and vegetables, excursions on foot.

VAGLIA
✉ postal code 50030

■ LE CORTI
Via del Vico, 925 - 50036 Pratolino
Tel. and Fax +39055409222
www.lecorti.com - le.corti@tiscalinet.it
Flat: 1 (central heating); sleeping accommodations: 6; bathrooms: 2. Excursions on foot and by mountain bike, games for children, ceramics workshop, small library and video-library, board games, and swimming pool.

■ PODERI DI COIANO
Via di Paterno, 17 - Coiano
Tel. +39055407680 - Fax +39055407772
coiano@dada.it
Flats: 2 (central heating); sleeping accommodations: 10; bathrooms: 3. Walks around the farm, sale of fruit, vegetables and honey.

VICCHIO
✉ postal code 50039

■ ATTULAIO
Via di Paterno, 12
Tel. and Fax +390558493125
Flats: 3; sleeping accommodations: 8; bathrooms: 3. Harvest and sale of Mugello chestnuts, sale of vegetables and potatoes.

■ BONCIANI
Via Campestri, 44
Tel. and Fax +390558449983; +390552670275 - barbonci@tin.it
www.tuscanyrental.com/bonciani
Flats: 4 (central heating); sleeping accommodations: 12; bathrooms: 4. Excursions on foot and on horseback, or by mountain bike (rent available), sale of season fruit (walnuts, apples, hazelnuts, figs), as well as sheep, goats and horses.

■ FARNETINO
Via Pilarciano, 53
Tel. and Fax +390558497372
www.farnetino.com
farnetino@tiscalinet.it
Rooms: 4; sleeping accommodations: 8; bathrooms: 2. Meals with typical Tuscan cuisine, playgroups for children, excursions on foot and by mountain bike (rent available), harvest of chestnuts, sale of organically grown fruit and vegetables.

■ FATTORIA DI CASOLE
Via Casole, 30
Tel. and Fax +390558497383
Flats: 6 (central heating); sleeping accommodations: 17; bathrooms: 7. Swimming pool, excursions on foot, sale of peaches and extra virgin olive oil.

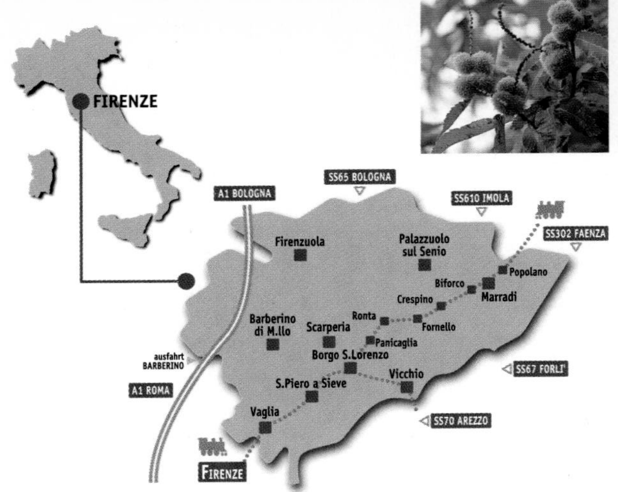

■ FATTORIA LE CASE
Via Pimaggiore, 20
Tel. +39055844090 - Fax +390558497847
Hardy +393489046497
www.fattorialecase.it - info@fattorialecase.it
Flats: 9 (central heating); sleeping accommodations: 18; bathrooms: 9. Excursions on foot and by mountain bike, as well as swimming pool, tennis court, and canoe rental.

■ IL PONTE
Via Gattaia, 88 - Fax +390558407690
Tel. +390558407690; +390558407671
www.agrivendolo.com/terranostra
rocco-trotta@libero.it
Flats: 3 (central heating); sleeping accommodations: 6; bathrooms: 3. Meals made with own farm produce (breakfast, dinner), excursions on foot and on horseback, and sale of chestnuts.

■ LA COLOMBAIA
Via Vespignano, 123 - Loc. Pesciola
Tel. and Fax +390558448028
www.wel.it/lacolombaia
claudiogalluzzi@inwind.it
Flats: 4 (central heating); sleeping accommodations: 17; bathrooms: 7. Excursions on foot and by mountain bike.

■ LA COMMENDA
Via Padule, 107 - Tel. +390558407924
Flat: 1 (central heating); sleeping accommodations: 6; bathrooms: 2. Restaurant, excursions on foot and on horseback, riding school (and issue of certificate), western and English style riding lessons, fence jump, stables for horses, and riding ground.

■ LA MATTERAIA
Via Cuccino, 10 - lamatteraia@virgilio.it
Tel. and Fax +39055844688
Flat: 1 (central heating); sleeping accommodations: 5; bathrooms: 2. Excursions on foot and by mountain bike, archery, and sale of the farm products: wine, oil and apples.

■ MARRANI MARIA
Padule, 125 - silviacellini@tiscali.it
Tel. and Fax +390558407886
Flats: 2 (central heating); sleeping accommodations: 5; bathrooms: 2. Excursions on foot and by mountain bike (rent available), embroidery lessons, and sale of vegetables.

■ MUCCIANELLO
Via Piazzano, 66 - Loc. Vespignano
Tel. and Fax +390558448017
Tel. and Fax +39055242713
www.blubus.com - cateni@iol.it
Flats: 3 (1 with central heating); sleeping accommodations: 23; bathrooms: 6. Sale of oil, wine, jams, and season fruit, cooking courses, and Italian and German courses.

■ PODERE LA MADONNA
Via Zuffolana, 42
tel. +390558448249; + 39063244996
Flats: 3 (no heating); sleeping accommodations: 7; bathrooms: 3. Sale of fruits and vegetables, Italian language courses, guided tours to Florence, and courses of botanical painting.

■ SEGONI
Via Villore, 201 - Segoni
Tel. +390558493123 - Fax +390558493060
0558493060@iol.it
Meals (breakfast only), excursions on foot and by mountain bike, cooking courses, painting courses, and sale of chestnuts.

For more information on Mugello:
COMUNITÁ MONTANA MUGELLO
MUGELLO TOURIST OFFICE
Via Palmiro Togliatti, 45
50032 Borgo San Lorenzo (Firenze) Italia
Tel. +39 055 845271
Fax. +39 055 8456288
Web site: http://turismo.mugello.toscana.
E-mail: turismo@cm-mugello.fi.it
Free tourist guidebooks are provided on request. nal data will be kept strictly confidential.

TRENTINO-ALTO ADIGE

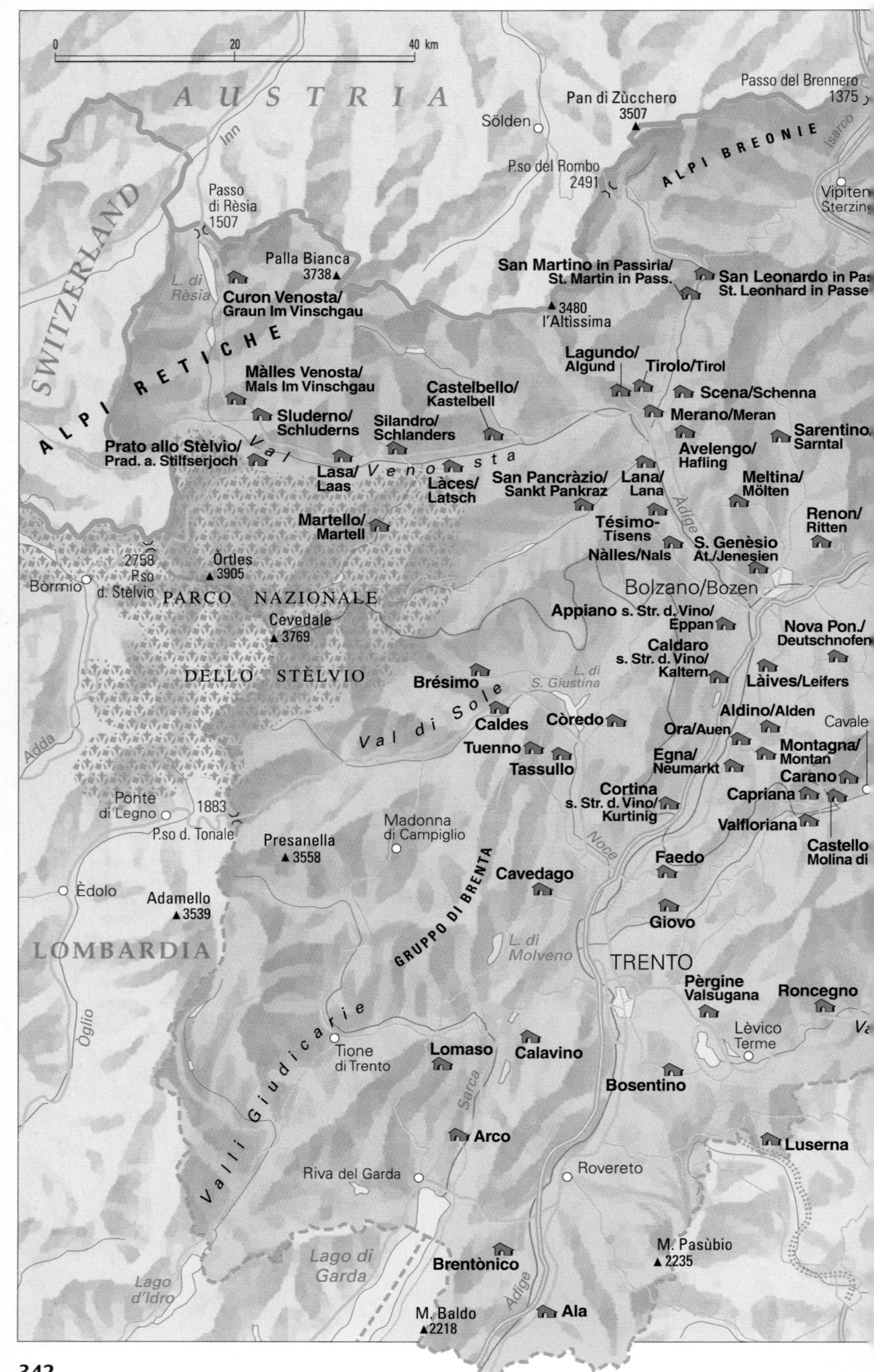
0
20
40 km
AUSTRIA
SWITZERLAND
LOMBARDIA
Passo del Brennero
1375
Pan di Zùcchero
3507
Sölden
P.so del Rombo
2491
ALPI BREONIE
Passo
di Rèsia
1507
Palla Bianca
3738
L. di
Rèsia
Curon Venosta/
Graun Im Vinschgau
San Martino in Passìria/
St. Martin in Pass.
San Leonardo in Pas
St. Leonhard in Passe
3480
l'Altìssima
ALPI RETICHE
Màlles Venosta/
Mals Im Vinschgau
Lagundo/
Algund
Tirolo/Tirol
Castelbello/
Kastelbell
Scena/Schenna
Sluderno/
Schluderns
Silandro/
Schlanders
Merano/Meran
Sarentino/
Sarntal
Prato allo Stèlvio/
Prad. a. Stilfserjoch
Val Venosta
Avelengo/
Hafling
Lasa/
Laas
Làces/
Latsch
San Pancràzio/
Sankt Pankraz
Lana/
Lana
Meltina/
Mölten
Martello/
Martell
Tésimo-
Tisens
Renon/
Ritten
Nàlles/Nals
S. Genèsio
At./Jenesien
2758
P.so
d. Stèlvio
Òrtles
3905
Bormio
PARCO NAZIONALE
DELLO STÈLVIO
Bolzano/Bozen
Appiano s. Str. d. Vino/
Eppan
Cevedale
3769
Caldaro
s. Str. d. Vino/
Kaltern
Nova Pon./
Deutschnofen
L. di
S. Giustina
Brésimo
Làives/Leifers
Val di Sole
Caldes
Còredo
Aldino/Alden
Cavale
Adda
Ora/Auen
Tuenno
Tassullo
Egna/
Neumarkt
Montagna/
Montan
Carano
Capriana
Ponte
di Legno
1883
P.so d. Tonale
Cortina
s. Str. d. Vino/
Kurtinig
Valfloriana
Madonna
di Campiglio
Presanella
3558
Noce
Castello
Molina di
Faedo
Èdolo
Cavedago
Adamello
3539
GRUPPO DI BRENTA
Giovo
L. di
Molveno
TRENTO
Pèrgine
Valsugana
Roncegno
Òglio
Valli Giudicarie
Lèvico
Terme
Tione
di Trento
Lomaso
Calavino
Bosentino
Sarca
Arco
Luserna
Riva del Garda
Rovereto
M. Pasùbio
2235
Lago di
Garda
Brentònico
Lago
d'Idro
Adige
M. Baldo
2218
Ala

2912
Vetta d'Itàlia
Matrei in Osttirol
Valle Aurina/ Ahrntal
Val di Vizze/ Pfitsch
Selva dei Molini/ Mühlwald
Campo Tùres/ Sand in Taufers
Passo Stalle 2052
AUSTRIA
Vandòies/ Vintl
Chiènes/ Kiens
Rio di Pusterìa/ Mühlbach
Terento/ Terenten
Brùnico/ Bruneck
Valle di Casìes/ Gsies
Rienza
Val Pusteria
Monguelfo/ Welsberg
Villabassa/ Niederdorf
Dobbiaco/ Toblach
S. Lorenzo di S./ St. Lorenzen
Valdàora/ Olang
Drava
S. Càndido/ Innichen
Val Badia
S. Vigilio di Marebbe/ St. Vigil in Enneberg
Bràies/Prags
Sesto/Sexten
Bressanone/ Brixen
San Martino in B./ St. Martin in Thurn
Tre Cime di Lavaredo
2999
1636
Passo di M. Croce di Comèlico
Fùnes/Villnöss
La Valle/Wengen
Laion/Lajen
Badìa/Abtei
3221 M. Cristallo
Sappada
Selva di V. Gardena/ Wolkenstein in Gr.
Castelrotto/ Kastelruth
Le Tofane 3244
Cortina d'Ampezzo
Fiè allo Sciliar/ Völs am Schlern
DOLOMITI
3152 Gruppo di Sella
2105 P.so di Falzàrego
2239 P.so Pordoi
Canazei
V. di Fassa
3343 Marmolada
Pieve di Cadore
1918 P.so di S. Pellegrino
Moena
Val di Fiemme
T. Avisio
FRIULI-
Passo di Rolle 1970
Predazzo
Pale di San Martino
Àgordo
Ziano di Fiemme
San Martino di Castrozza
2743
-VENEZIA
Canal San Bovo
Ponte nelle Alpi
Tonadico
Belluno
Passo del Brocon 1615
M. Pavione 2334
-GIULIA
Feltre
Vittòrio Vèneto
Pordenone
Livenza
Conegliano
VENETO
Oderzo
Bassano del Grappa

Ala

Maso Rocca

at Maso Rocca, 38061 Ala (TN)
Tel. **0464670173** Fax **0464670173**

This village stands on the east bank of the Adige in the Val Lagarina. The accommodation is in an old but renovated maso, with a terrace and grassy area on the edge of a wood.

-

1 - - -

-

1 - - -

3 (x 2/5)

1 - 7 - 1 - 7 360,00

Aldino/Aldein

Woeserhof

 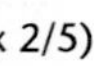 

at Lerch 29, 39040 Aldino/Aldein (BZ)
Tel. **0471886890**

On one side is the famous Strada del Vino, on the other the Strada delle Dolomiti heads towards the Val di Fiemme: a holiday in a peaceful maso farmhouse is certainly a pleasant prospect.

  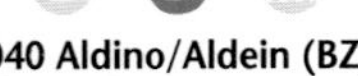

-

1 - - -

4 (x 2)

1 21,00 - - -

-

1 - 7 - 1 - 7 -

Appiano sulla Strada del Vino Eppan an der Weinstrasse

Federerhof

at San Michele/Sankt Michael, via Monticolo 29, 39057 Appiano sulla Strada del Vino/Eppan an der Weinstrasse (BZ)
Tel. **0471662048** Fax **0471662048**

The accommodation is 10 km from Bolzano in a new maso surrounded by meadows and woods not far from the lakes of Monticolo.

-

1 - - -

5 (x 2)

1 20,70 - - -

-

1 - 7 - 1 - 7 -

Rautscherhof

via Missiano 35/A, 39057 Appiano sulla Strada del Vino/Eppan an der Weinstrasse (BZ)
Tel. **0471636018**

San Michele is a village with the typical Gothic architecture of the west bank of the Adige; Missiano is a peaceful village of wine-growers and fruit-farmers.

-

1 - - -

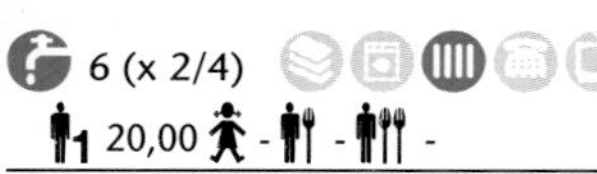

6 (x 2/4)

1 20,00 - - -

-

1 - 7 - 1 - 7 -

ARCO

MICHELOTTI

at Bolognano, via Soccesure 2, 38062 Arco (TN)
Tel. 0464516272 Fax 0464516272

The accommodation is in an attractive building with large balconies and rustic fittings. In the summer, fruit is provided free of charge; during the grape-harvest, guests can try the "grape cure".

-

1 - - - -

-

1 - - - -

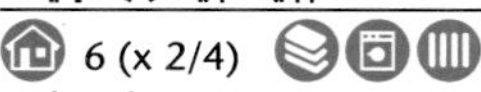

6 (x 2/4)

1 - 7 - 1 100,00 7 600,00

AVELENGO/HAFLING

HINTERRAINERHOF

via Hinterdorf 9, 39010 Avelengo/Hafling (BZ)
Tel. 0473279479 Fax 0473212621
Web: www.hinterrainer.com

Just 10 km from Merano, on the Avelengo Plateau, noted for the raising of horses, this old South Tyrolean house has been renovated to provide accommodation.

-

1 - - - -

-

1 - - - -

2(x 2)

1 - 7 - 1 51,00 7 -

NUSSERHOF

via Falzeben 7, 39010 Avelengo/Hafling (BZ)
Tel. 0473279401 Fax 0473279401

This recently renovated house in traditional style stands on the edge of a wood, about a kilometre from the village.

-

1 - - - -

-

1 - - - -

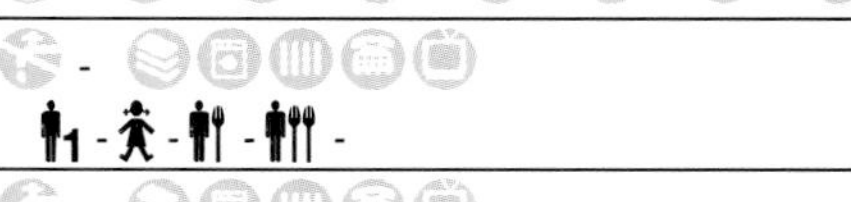

4(x 2)

1 - 7 - 1 40,00 7 -

BADIA/ABTEI

MOZL

at La Villa/Stern, via Rottonara 22,
39036 Badia/Abtei (BZ)
Tel. 0471847448

In the upper Val Badia, on the banks of the Gadera stream, a beautiful basin contains the hamlet of La Villa, a summer and winter resort with excellent facilities.

-
1 - - -
-
1 - - -
1(x 4)
1 - 7 - 1 25,80 7 -

Taelahof

at San Cassiano/Sankt Kassian, via Costadedoi 69, 39030 Badia/Abtei (BZ)
Tel. 0471849301 Fax 0471849340
Web: www.interpromotion.com/taela

San Cassiano is a well-known resort for both summer holidays and winter sports; the accommodation is located just one kilometre from the village.

-
1 - - -
-
1 - - -
4 (x 2/4)

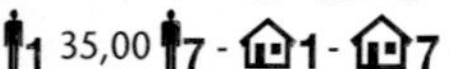
1 35,00 7 - 1 - 7 -

Bosentino

Maso Fosina

at Maso Fosina 5, 38040 Bosentino (TN)
Tel. 0461848468

In the upper Brenta Valley, amid woods rich in fauna, accommodation is available in an old maso. It's possible to tour the mountain huts on foot, on horseback or by mountain bike.

-
1 - - -
-
1 - - -
5(x 2)
1 16,00 7 - 1 - 7 -

Braies/Prags

Waidachhof

at Braises di Dentro/Innerprags 59, 39030 Braies/Prags (BZ)
Tel. 0474748655

The Val di Braies offers many opportunities for excursions and winter sports. The accommodation is in a house with a modern appearance.

-
1 - - -
6 (x 1/4)
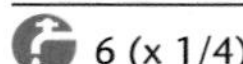

1 17,00 - - -

 -

1 - 7 - 1 - 7 -

BRENTONICO

MORTIGOLA

at Mortigola, 38060 Brentonico (TN)
Tel. 0464391555 Fax 0464391555

This plateau overlooks the Val Lagarina from the side rising up towards Monte Baldo. The farm is surrounded by market gardens, trees and a small lake for angling.

1 - - - -

1 - - - -

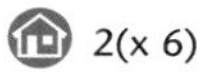 2(x 6) 

1 - 7 - 1 - 7 380,00

BRESIMO

ANNA POZZATTI

at Bevia 47, 38020 Bresimo (TN)
Tel. 0463539042 Fax 0463539042

From the balconies decked with geraniums, there's a splendid view of the valley bottom and the mountain peaks. This oasis of peace in the Ortles Group is an excellent base for easy hikes in the mountains.

1 - - - -

-

1 - - - -

 2(x 4)

1 18,00 7 - 1 - 7 -

BRESSANONE/BRIXEN

GFADERHOF

at Tecelinga/Tötschling 61,
39042 Bressanone/Brixen (BZ)
Tel. 0472852506 Fax 0472852506
E-mail: schatzerfranz@dnet.it

Located at the confluence of the Val Pusteria and the Valle Isarco, the accommodation is some distance from the village, in a recently built maso.

1 - - - -

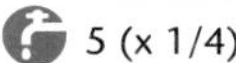 5 (x 1/4)

1 19,00 - - -

2 (x 2/4)

1 - 7 - 1 52,00 7 -

HÖRMANNHOF

at Sant'Andrea in Monte/Sankt Andrä 59,
39042 Bressanone/Brixen (BZ)
Tel. 0472831078 Fax 0472831078

Bressanone is the most important city in South Tyrol from an artistic point of view. The accommodation is close to the town, in a house that, although built recently, is traditional in style.

- 1 - - -

4 (x 2/4)

1 20,70 - - -

1(x 2)

1 - 7 - 1 82,60 7 -

BRUNICO/BRUNECK

STIENERHOF

at San Giorgio/Sankt Georgen, via Pipen 25, 39031 Brunico/Bruneck (BZ)
Tel. 0474550294

Situated on the edge of a wood, this typical South Tyrolean house has recently been renovated. From the meadows in front of it there's a view towards the deep Valle di Tures.

- 1 - - -

- 1 - - -

2(x 2)

1 - 7 - 1 49,10 7 -

CALAVINO

LA TORESELA

via Garibaldi 56, 38072 Calavino (TN)
Tel. 0461564231 Fax 0461564231

There's a friendly welcome and furnishings in Tyrolean style in a rustic house in the lower Sarca Valley. Within 25 km are Lake Garda and the ski slopes of Monte Bondone.

7 (x 2/4)

1 - - 31,00 -

- 1 - - -

- 1 - 7 - 1 - 7 -

CALDARO SULLA STRADA DEL VINO KALTERN AN DER WEINSTRASSE

EICHHOF

at Kalterer Höhe 10, 39052 Caldaro sulla Strada del Vino/Kaltern an der Weinstrasse (BZ)
Tel. 0471962634

Renowned for its wines and the lake, Caldaro is the main centre of the west bank of the Adige. Comfortable accommodation is available in this recently built maso set amid orchards and vineyards.

- 1 - - -

3 (x 2/4)

1 20,00 - - -

2(x 2)

1 - 7 - 1 54,00 7 -

STEFLHOF

Penegalweg 8, 39052 Caldaro sulla Strada del Vino/Kaltern an der Weinstrasse (BZ)
Tel. 0471964955 Fax 0471964955

Those staying with this family of wine-growers are assured of a friendly welcome: the red, made from Schiava grapes, and the fragrant whites alone make the trip worthwhile.

\-

1 - - -

\-

1 - - -

3(x 4)

1 - 7 - 1 55,00 7 -

Zur Traube

at Pozzo/Pfuss 7, 39052 Caldaro sulla Strada del Vino/Kaltern an der Weinstrasse (BZ)
Tel. **0471963369**
E-mail: **florian.bertol@dnet.it**

Pleasantly located on the valley floor, with its orchards and vineyards, this accommodation is in a modern house with a small open-air swimming pool.

\-

1 - - -

5 (x 2)

1 18,50 13,00 - -

\-

1 - 7 - 1 - 7 -

Caldes

Sottoilmelo

at Bordiana, via del Brenz 40, 38022 Caldes (TN)
Tel. **0463901632** Fax **0463901632**
Web: **www.agritursottoilmelo.it**

From this recently opened establishment at the mouth of the Val di Sole there are views of the peaks of the Stelvio National Park and the Adamello and Brenta ranges.

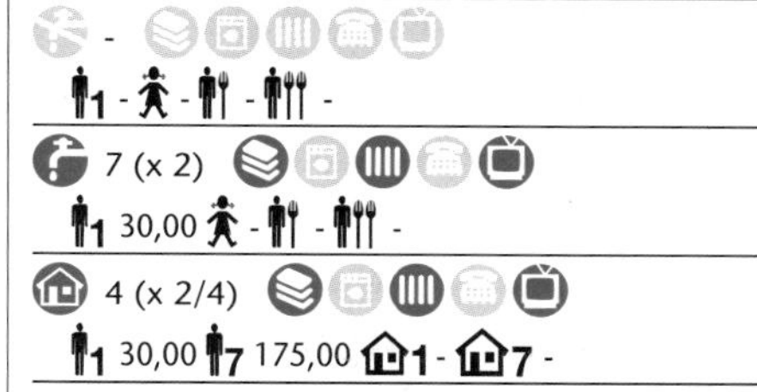

\-

1 - - -

7 (x 2)

1 30,00 - - -

4 (x 2/4)

1 30,00 7 175,00 1 - 7 -

Campo Tures/Sand in Taufers

Niederunterer

at Riva di Tures/Rein in Taufers 35, 39030 Campo Tures/Sand in Taufers (BZ)
Tel. **0474672508** Fax **0474672508**

Ideal for summer and winter holidays, this typical South Tyrolean house is located in a basin above the confluence of the Val di Riva with the Valle Aurina.

\-

1 - - -

\-

1 - - -

2(x 2)

1 - 7 - 1 52,00 7 -

Weißgarberhof

at Molini di Tures, am Anger 17, 39032 Campo Tures/Sand in Taufers (BZ)
Tel. **0474659009**

Tourist accommodation is available, on the edge of the village, in a house in the traditional style of the valley. Excursions may be made to the Vedrette di Ries Nature Park.

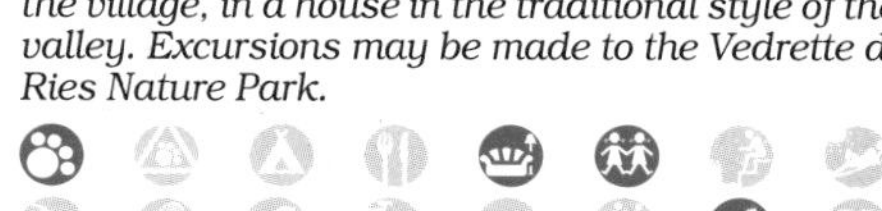

\-

1 - - -

5 (x 2/4)

1 18,60 - - -

1(x 2)

1 - 7 - 1 32,00 7 -

Canal San Bovo

Maso Paradisi

at Giaroni 1/P, 38050 Canal San Bovo (TN)
Tel. 0439719071

At the foot of the Lagorai Range, this renovated chalet is in a tranquil position with easy access to the nearby Paneveggio-Pale di San Martino Nature Park.

 -

 1 - - -

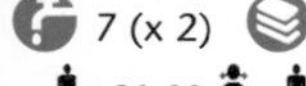 7 (x 2)

 1 31,00 - 42,00 -

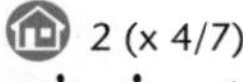 2 (x 4/7)

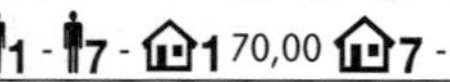 1 - 7 - 1 70,00 7 -

Capriana

Carbonare

at Carbonare 16, 38030 Capriana (TN)
Tel. 0462816329 Fax 0462816329
E-mail: carlo.signorini3@tin.it

This old house in stone and wood has been renovated by a family who, in addition to renting comfortable rooms, farm using organic methods (they are among the first in the valley to do so).

 -

1 - - -

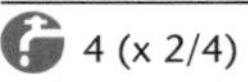 4 (x 2/4) 

1 20,00 18,00 38,00 -

-

1 - 7 - 1 - 7 -

Carano

Gottardini Rosa

at Solaiolo, 38033 Carano (TN)
Tel. 0462230312

This accommodation is ideal for a relaxing holiday, with visits to the Monte Corno Nature Park in the summer and skiing on the slopes at Cavalese in the winter.

 -

1 - - -

 -

1 - - -

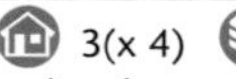 3(x 4) 

1 - 7 - 1 35,00 7 260,00

Castelbello/Kastelbell

Hochhueb

at Ciardes/Tschars, via Freiten 11,
39020 Castelbello/Kastelbell (BZ)
Tel. 0473624138 Fax 0473624746

In the lower Val Venosta, a castle dominates the valley floor: accommodation is available in this elegant house surrounded by orchards and vineyards.

-

1 - - -

5 (x 2/4)

1 23,00 - 35,00 -

-

1 - 7 - 1 - 7 -

Castello-Molina di Fiemme

Iellici Mariateresa

at Castello di Fiemme, via Avisio 26,
38030 Castello-Molina di Fiemme (TN)
Tel. 0462230137

The village of Castello is perched on a terrace high above the Avisio. This modern establishment offering accommodation is also in a splendid position.

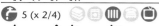

-

1 - - -

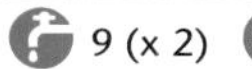

9 (x 2)

1 25,00 - - -

-

1 - 7 - 1 - 7 -

Maso Corradini

at Castello di Fiemme, via Milano 30,
38030 Castello-Molina di Fiemme (TN)
Tel. 0462231010 Fax 0462231010
E-mail: agri.corradini@tin.it

This establishment is near the village, in a tranquil area. From Cavalese a cable car goes up towards the Lagorai Range and, in winter, it's possible to ski for dozens of kilometres.

-

1 - - -

6 (x 2)

1 18,00 - - -

-

1 - 7 - 1 - 7 -

Castelrotto/Kastelruth

Oberlanzin

at Telfen Lanzin 61,
39040 Castelrotto/Kastelruth (BZ)
Tel. 0471706575

Accommodation is available in this recently built maso set amid the pastures on the slopes of Monte Bullaccia, a couple of kilometres from the village.

-

1 - - -

6 (x 2)

1 26,00 - - -

-

1 - 7 - 1 - 7 -

Patenerhof

at San Valentino/Sankt Valentin, via Patener 11,
39040 Castelrotto/Kastelruth (BZ)
Tel. 0471706033 Fax 0471706033
Web: www.patenerhof.com

This recently built house in traditional style is surrounded by the pastures at the foot of the dolomitic rocks of the Sciliar, a popular area for hikes along the high trails.

\-

1 - - -

\-

1 - - -

3(x 2)

1 - 7 - 1 87,80 7 -

Cavedago

Mirella Zeni

via Croce 8, 38010 Cavedago (TN)
Tel. 0461654208

This accommodation in the lower Val di Non is located in the village in a modern building, functionally furnished. There's a peaceful and friendly atmosphere.

2 (x 2)

1 28,41 - -

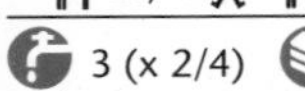

3 (x 2/4)

1 28,41 - -

1(x 3)

1 - 7 - 1 - 7 413,17

Chienes/Kiens

Radmüllerhof

via Monghezzo 17, 39030 Chienes/Kiens (BZ)
Tel. 0472868037

Located between Bressanone and Brunico, Chienes (784 m) offers various possibilities: in the summer, hiking in four nature parks; in the winter, skiing at Plan de Corones.

\-

1 - - -

\-

1 - - -

1(x 2)

1 - 7 - 1 90,00 7 -

Chiusa/Klausen

Feilerhof

at Gudon/Gufidaun 15,
39043 Chiusa/Klausen (BZ)
Tel. 0472847930

Chiusa on the Isarco, Gudon at the mouth of the Valle di Funes: on one side are woods, on the other, meadows and pastures, with the soaring pinnacles of the Dolomites in the background.

\-

1 - - -

\-

1 - - -

2(x 2)

1 - 7 - 1 76,50 7 -

Coredo

Giuseppe Rizzi

via Apena 8, 38010 Coredo (TN)
Tel. 0463536310

On the Predaia Plateau, this establishment, located near the village, offers accommodation in apartments furnished in rustic style.

1 - - - -

- -

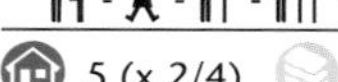

5 (x 2/4)

1 - 7 - 1 - 7 360,00

Mascotti Nicola

via IV Novembre 47, 38010 Coredo (TN)
Tel. 0463536319 Fax 0463536319

In a peaceful position on a terrace facing the Brenta Dolomites, the house, surrounded by orchards, is close to a wood.

1 - - - -

1 - - - -

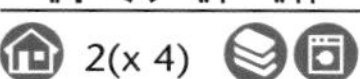

2(x 4)

1 - 7 - 1 100,00 7 420,00

Renzo Widmann

via IV Novembre 59, 38010 Coredo (TN)
Tel. 0463536927

The accommodation is in a modern house in a verdant setting with excellent views of the surrounding mountains.

1 - - - -

1 - - - -

3 (x 3/4)

1 25,00 7 - 1 - 7 -

Cortina sulla Strada del Vino Kurtinig an der Weinstrasse

Angerhof

via del Doss 1, 39040 Cortina sulla Strada del Vino/Kurtinig an der Weinstrasse (BZ)
Tel. 0471817021 Fax 0471817021

Halfway between Trento and Bolzano, at the point at which the Adige flows at the foot of Monte Craunel, this typical farmhouse is surrounded by vineyards and orchards.

1 - - - -

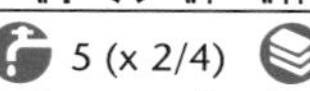

5 (x 2/4)

1 20,00 - - -

1 - 7 - 1 - 7 -

Curon Venosta Graun im Vinschgau

Haus Edith-Tanilenzhof

at Resia, via Principale 25,
39027 Curon Venosta/Graun Im Vinschgau (BZ)
Tel. 0473633238 Fax 0473633238

At the point where the frontiers of Italy, Switzerland and Austria meet, this accommodation has views over the Lago di Resia, where windsurfing is possible, and the snow-clad peaks of Ortles.

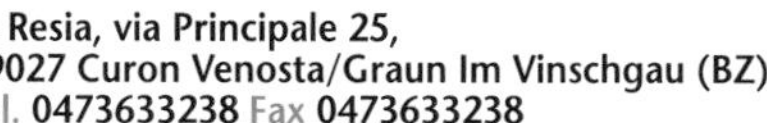

1 - - - -

2 (x 2)

20,00 - - -

3(x 2)

20,00 - - -

Rieglhof

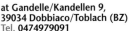

at Vallelunga/Langtaufers 44,
39020 Curon Venosta/Graun Im Vinschgau (BZ)
Tel. 0473633266 Fax 0473633266
Web: www.rieglhof.it

In the upper Val Venosta, at a high altitude on the shore of the Lago di Resia, accommodation is available in a maso surrounded by meadows and woods, and also in a new building.

\-

\- - - -

\-

\- - - -

4(x 2)

\- - 82,00 -

Dobbiaco/Toblach

Baumannhof

via Pusteria 19, 39034 Dobbiaco/Toblach (BZ)
Tel. 0474972602
Web: www.geocities.com/hotspring/falls/2367

In the upper Val Pusteria, some distance from the main town, the accommodation is in a house built in the traditional South Tyrolean style.

\-

\- - - -

\-

\- - - -

2(x 4)

\- - 83,00 -

Pahlerhof

at Gandelle/Kandellen 9,
39034 Dobbiaco/Toblach (BZ)
Tel. 0474979091

In the splendid setting of the valley, this typical Alpine chalet was constructed recently. From the village, it is possible to go up the Val di Landro as far as Cortina.

\-

\- - - -

1 (x 2)

15,00 - - -

3 (x 4/2)

15,00 - - -

Egna/Neumarkt

Kuckuckshof

at Mazon, via del Monte 1,
39044 Egna/Neumarkt (BZ)
Tel. 0471812405 Fax 0471812405

In the Adige Valley, above the Salorno narrows, accommodation is available in a recently constructed maso, for non-smokers only.

-

1 - - -

5 (x 2/4)

1 18,00 - -

-

1 - 7 - 1 - 7 -

Faedo

Ai Molini

via Molini 8, 38010 Faedo (TN)
Tel. 0461651088
Web: www.comune-faedo.it/agriturmolini

On the west side of the village, this holiday accommodation, which is ideal for families, is only half an hour's drive from the ski slopes of Andalo and Fai.

-

1 - - -

5 (x 2)

1 18,00 - -

-

1 - 7 - 1 - 7 -

Maso Nello

via Pineta 3, 38010 Faedo (TN)
Tel. 0461650384 Fax 0461650384
Web: pagina.de/masonello

In the Adige Valley, opposite the mouth of the Val di Non, this maso providing tourist accommodation is surrounded by vineyards on the edge of a wood.

-

1 - - -

4 (x 2)

1 26,00 - 39,00 -

2(x 4)

1 - 7 - 1 - 7 490,00

Fiè allo Sciliar Völs am Schlern

Merlhof

via Sciliar 9,
39050 Fiè allo Sciliar/Völs am Schlern (BZ)
Tel. 0471725552 Fax 0471725552
Web: www.merlhof.it

Located 16 km from Bolzano, in the lower Valle Isarco, dominated by the Sciliar, this renovated building is surrounded by an Alpine garden and orchard.

\-
1 - - -

\-
1 - - -

4 (x 2/4)
1 - 7 - 1 80,00 7 -

Pulserhof

at Aica di Sopra/Oberaicha 17/A,
39050 Fiè allo Sciliar/Völs am Schlern (BZ)
Tel. 0471601080 Fax 0471601080
Web: www.pulserhof.com

A building constructed recently in traditional style stands amid the splendid scenery at the approach to the dolomitic vastness of the Sciliar Nature Park.

\-
1 - - -

5 (x 2)
1 22,50 - - -

1(x 2)
1 - 7 - 1 62,00 7 -

Funes/Villnöss

Unterkantiolerhof

at Santa Maddalena/Sankt Magdalena 42,
39040 Funes/Villnöss (BZ)
Tel. 0472840219 Fax 0472840219
E-mail: unterkantiolerhof@libero.it

In the upper village of Santa Maddalena (1398 m), the accommodation is surrounded by pastures, woods and the dolomitic needles of the Puez-Odle Nature Park.

\-

1 - - -

\-
1 - - -

4(x 2)
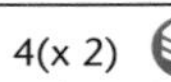  
1 - 7 - 1 80,00 7 -

Giovo

Emilio Ress

at Ceola, via Nazionale 48, 38030 Giovo (TN)
Tel. 0461684061 Fax 0461684061
E-mail: cristina.ress@tin.it

In the delightful setting of the Val di Cembra, this accommodation is in a recently refurbished building surrounded by vineyards, orchards and woods.

\-
1 - - -

9 (x 2)

1 26,00 21,00 34,00 -

LACES/LATSCH

SCHNALSERHOF

via Giovo 1, 39021 Laces/Latsch (BZ)
Tel. 0473623223 Fax 0473623223
E-mail: rinner.schnalserhof@rolmail.net

In the central Val Venosta, below the confluence with the Val Martello, this typical South Tyrolean house, which has been renovated, is just a stone's throw from the historic centre.

-

1 - - -

 1 (x 2)

1 18,00 - -

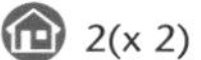 2(x 2)

1 - 7 - 1 70,00 7 -

LAGUNDO/ALGUND

HUBER-HOF

at Plars di Sopra 4, 39022 Lagundo/Algund (BZ)
Tel. 0473448353 Fax 0473447295
E-mail: huberhof-plars@web.de

Just a few kilometres from Merano, this establishment is located amid the orchards, with beautiful views and a pleasant Stube where breakfast or snacks are served.

-
1 - - -

 3 (x 2) 
1 18,10 - -

-
1 - 7 - 1 - 7 -

PLONERHOF

via Peter Thalguter 11,
39022 Lagundo/Algund (BZ)
Tel. 0473448728 Fax 0473448728

In the traditional style of the valley, this old building is located in the windy setting of the Burgraviato, at the point where the Val Venosta opens into the basin of Merano.

-

1 - - -

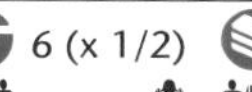 6 (x 1/2) 
1 26,00 - -

 1(x 2)

1 - 7 - 1 60,00 7 -

LAION/LAJEN

PRANTSCHURHOF

at San Pietro/Sankt Peter 51/A,
39040 Laion/Lajen (BZ)
Tel. 0471655653 Fax 0471656333
Web: www.agritursimoinitalia.com

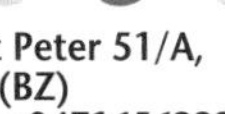

In the lower Val Gardena, near a village with an old centre, this recently constructed rural house stands amid flowery meadows and fir woods.

-

1 - - -

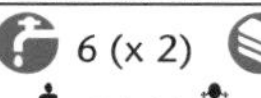 6 (x 2) 
1 24,00 - -

-
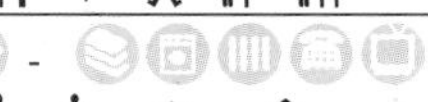
1 - 7 - 1 - 7 -

Laives/Leifers

Tschuffenerl

via La Costa/Seit 34, 39055 Laives/Leifers (BZ)
Tel. 0471250716

Just a few kilometres from Bolzano, with fine views towards Merano and the Gruppo di Tessa on the horizon, accommodation is available in a traditional house in a verdant setting.

-
1 - - -

-
1 - - -

2(x 2)

1 - 7 - 1 56,00 7 -

Lana/Lana

Köstenholzerhof

via Rena 11/A, 39011 Lana/Lana (BZ)
Tel. 0473562236 Fax 0473562236
E-mail: koestenholzerhof@rolmail.net

Towards Merano, the Adige Valley, with its vineyards and orchards, widens out. These surroundings are pleasant and stimulating, thanks also to the swimming pool.

-
1 - - -

-
1 - - -

4(x 2)

1 - 7 - 1 72,30 7 -

Leilichhof

via Monte Luco 3/12, 39011 Lana/Lana (BZ)
Tel. 0473563065

The apple tree is the symbol of South Tyrol, from its white blossom in the spring to the colours of autumn; and, of course, its fruit is the delicious filling of the ubiquitous strudel.

-
1 - - -

-
1 - - -

3 (x 2/4)

1 - 7 - 1 45,00 7 -

Mair am Turm

at Foiana, vicolo S. Maddalena 3,
39011 Lana/Lana (BZ)
Tel. 0473568009 Fax 0473568009

Not far from Merano is the wilderness of the Stelvio National Park, with excursions extending from the thickly wooded Val d'Ultimo to the glaciers of Cevedale.

 -

 -

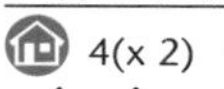 4(x 2)   

 1 - 7 - 1 67,10 7 -

Lasa/Laas

Untertröghof

at Alliz 33, 39023 Lasa/Laas (BZ)
Tel. 0473626170 Fax 0473626170
Web: www.geocities.com/untertroeghof

This accommodation is in a typical South Tyrolean house, next to the old maso, amid the meadows on a high terrace overlooking the central Val Venosta.

 -

 -

 2(x 2)  

1 - 7 - 1 77,00 7 -

La Valle/Wengen

Lüch da Ciurnadù

via Ciurnadù 204, 39030 La Valle/Wengen (BZ)
Tel. 0471843145 Fax 0471842389
Web: www.ciurnadu.it

This is a picturesque holiday centre, amid the meadows of the Val di Spessa and the central Val Badia. The accommodation is in a modern building, overlooking the valley floor.

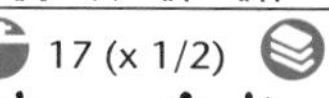 -

1 - - -

17 (x 1/2)

1 24,00 - 39,00 -

-

1 - 7 - 1 - 7 -

Lomaso

Maso Marocc

at Poia, 38077 Lomaso (TN)
Tel. 0465702098 Fax 0465702098

The main road to the lakes Molveno and Tenno runs along the valley of the Dalo. The accommodation is in a maso amid apple orchards, with rustic furnishings and flower-decked balconies.

-

1 - - -

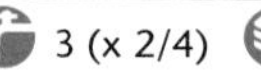 3 (x 2/4) 

1 30,00 - 35,00 -

 4(x 4) 

1 - 7 - 1 - 7 600,00

LUSERNA

AGRITUR GALENO

via Cima Nora 34, 38040 Luserna (TN)
Tel. 0464789723 Fax 0464789723
E-mail: gianfranconicolussigalen@virgilio.it

With Monte Cimon and the Cima di Vezzena forming a backdrop, the accommodation is in a modern family-run establishment furnished in traditional Alpine style.

-

1 - - - -

 13 (x 2)

1 26,00 - 46,00 -

-

1 - 7 - 1 - 7 -

MALLES VENOSTA MALS IM VINSCHGAU

MONTECIN

at Monteschino 66,
39024 Malles Venosta/Mals Im Vinschgau (BZ)
Tel. 3355627210 Fax 33505627210
Web: www.montecin.com

The upper Val Venosta: Ortles and Palla Bianca, Castel Coira and Glorenza, the abbey of Monte Maria and Malles - they're all just a few kilometres from Tarces.

-

1 - - - -

-

1 - - - -

 4(x 1)

1 - 7 - 1 76,00 7 -

RAMEISHOF

at Prämajur 12,
39024 Malles Venosta/Mals Im Vinschgau (BZ)
Tel. 0473830282 Fax 0473830282
E-mail: rameishof@dnet.it

This typical South Tyrolean house, which has been renovated, stands amid meadows and firs on the road going up the Valle Slingia from Burgusio towards the Rifugio Rasass.

-

1 - - - -

5 (x 2/4)

1 24,00 - - -

-

1 - 7 - 1 - 7 -

MARTELLO/MARTELL

NIEDERHOF

at Selva/Waldberg 222,
39020 Martello/Martell (BZ)
Tel. 0473744534 Fax 0473744534

Pleasant accommodation is available in a new maso on a grassy slope near a wood. Two self-contained apartments will be ready soon.

-

1 - - -

6 (x 2/4)

1 24,00 - 38,00 -

-

1 - 7 - 1 - 7 -

Meltina/Mölten

Kastnerhof

at Salonetto/Schlained 10,
39010 Meltina/Mölten (BZ)
Tel. **0471668004** Fax **0471668004**

Above the Adige Valley are beautiful plateaux with meadows and woods. One of these is the Meltina Plateau, the ideal setting for a delightful summer holiday.

-

1 - - -

5 (x 2)

1 23,20 - - -

3(x 2)

1 - 7 - 1 59,40 7 -

Merano/Meran

Köstbamerhof

at Quarazze, via Laurin 81,
39012 Merano/Meran (BZ)
Tel. **0473200909** Fax **0473200909**

Merano boasts splendid walks, including the famous Passeggiata Tappeiner, leading to Quarazze, where this farm with a beautiful view is located.

-

1 - - -

3 (x 2/4)

1 24,00 - - -

2(x 2)

1 - 7 - 1 60,00 7 -

Sittnerhof

via Verdi 60, 39012 Merano/Meran (BZ)
Tel. **0473221631** Fax **0473206520**
Web: **www.bauerhofurlaub.it**

This fine rural house is just 10 minutes' walk from a café in the centre or the attractive shop windows in the main street.

-

1 - - -

5 (x 2/4)

1 28,50 - - -

-

1 - 7 - 1 - 7 -

MONGUELFO/WELSBERG

GEIGERHOF

at Tesido, via Prati 25,
39035 Monguelfo/Welsberg (BZ)
Tel. 0474950078

This centre stands at the mouth of the Val di Casies. In one of the first hamlets above it, a renovated traditional stone and wood house is set amid meadows and woods.

 -

 1 - - -

-

1 - - -

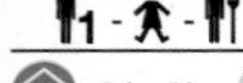 2(x 2)

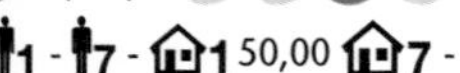 1 - 7 - 1 50,00 7 -

LANDHOF

at Tesido/Taisten, via del Sole 15,
39035 Monguelfo/Welsberg (BZ)
Tel. 0474950031 Fax 0474950031
E-mail: mairhofer.landhof@dnet.it

The main town faces the Fanes-Sennes-Braies Nature Park. The accommodation is in a large chalet; modern and family-run, it stands amid the pastures.

 -

 1 - - -

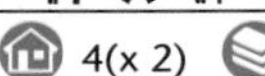 -

 1 - - -

4(x 2)

1 16,00 7 - 1 - 7 -

MONTAGNA/MONTAN

KLAUSENHOF

at Gleno/Glen 64, 39040 Montagna/Montan (BZ)
Tel. 0471819702

This refurbished traditional building, surrounded by the abundant flowers of an Alpine garden, offers accommodation in a rural setting.

-

1 - - -

 5 (x 2/4)

1 17,00 - - -

 -

1 - 7 - 1 - 7 -

Nalles/Nals

Kösslerhof

strada del Vino 37/17, 39010 Nalles/Nals (BZ)
Tel. 0471678456 Fax 0471678456
E-mail: koesslerhof@gmx.net

A path bordered by roses and low fruit trees leads to this house built in the traditional style of the valley.

-

1 - - -

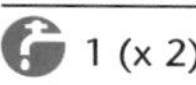 1 (x 2)

1 23,00 - -

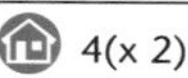 4(x 2)

1 - 7 - 1 67,00 7 -

Nova Levante/Welschnofen

Vöstlhof

via Cisgolo 2,
39056 Nova Levante/Welschnofen (BZ)
Tel. 0471613174
E-mail: voestlhof@dnet.it

This accommodation is in a renovated maso where the local speck is on sale. Beyond the meadows and woods rise the rock faces of Catinaccio and the Latemar Range.

-

1 - - -

 4 (x 2)

1 22,00 - -

3 (x 2/5)

1 22,00 7 - 1 - 7 -

Nova Ponente/Deutschnofen

Bachnerhof

at Unterwinkl 2,
39040 Nova Ponente/Deutschnofen (BZ)
Tel. 0471615163

Offering splendid views of Catinaccio and the Latemar Range, this accommodation is located at Monte San Pietro, close to Nova Ponente and the sanctuary of the Madonna di Pietralba.

-

1 - - -

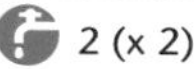   2 (x 2)

1 21,00 - 32,00 -

 2(x 2)

1 - 7 - 1 55,00 7 -

Ora/Auer

Trogerhof

via Stazione 82, 39040 Ora/Auer (BZ)
Tel. 0471811430 Fax 0471811430

The Adige Valley is a patchwork of vineyards and orchards. In front are the villages and castles of the Strada del Vino; behind, the Monte Corno Natural Park.

-

1 - - -

-

1 - - -

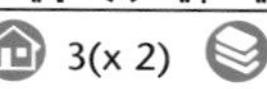  3(x 2)

1 - 7 - 1 67,00 7 -

Pergine Valsugana

Armanda Bernardi Bortolotti

via Montesei 2, 38057 Pergine Valsugana (TN)
Tel. 0461530125

In the upper Valsugana there are fast-flowing streams, lakes, thermal springs, mountain peaks and woods. The accommodation, on the first floor of a farmhouse, is ideal for families.

\-

1 - - -

\-

1 - - -

2(x 3)

1 - 7 - 1 - 7 181,00

Ettore Fontanari

at Canale, via Chimelli 25,
38057 Pergine Valsugana (TN)
Tel. 0461530023

This roomy renovated cottage is a couple of kilometres from the village in the countryside under orchards between the Brenta and the Fersina.

\-

1 - - -

\-

1 - - -

3 (x 4/5)

1 - 7 - 1 - 7 260,00

Prato allo Stelvio Prad am Stilfser Joch

Grösshof

at Montechiaro/Lichtenberg 1, 39026 Prato allo Stelvio/Prad am Stilfser Joch (BZ)
Tel. 0473616363

This accommodation is in a house in traditional style with flower-decked balconies. It is surrounded by Italy's largest national park.

\-

1 - - -

\-

1 - - -

2(x 2)

1 - 7 - 1 51,60 7 -

Renon/Ritten

Flachenhof

at Collalbo/Klobenstein, via Tann 31,
39054 Renon/Ritten (BZ)
Tel. 0471352782 Fax 0471352782
Web: www.flachenhof.it

One of the great features of a holiday here is that you can travel without a car through the meadows, woods and villages thanks to a little train and the cable car that goes down to the town.

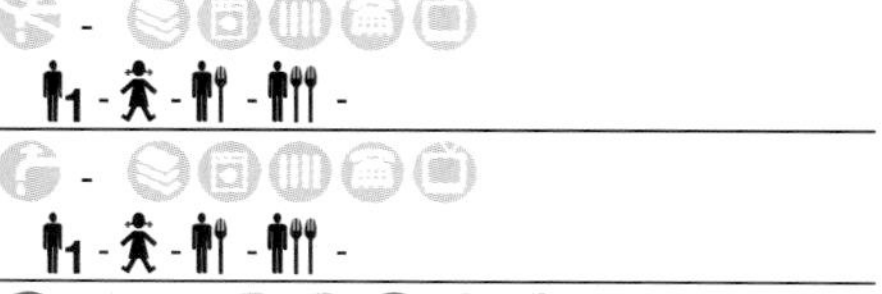

-

1 - - - -

-

1 - - - -

2(x 2)

1 - 7 - 1 79,00 7 -

Vogelhauserhof

at Pietra Rossa 111, 39054 Renon/Ritten (BZ)
Tel. 0471349091 Fax 0471349091
E-mail: mair_wolfgang@dnet.it

Located on the vast Renon Plateau, this is a maso offering comfortable apartments where families with children are welcome.

-

1 - - - -

-

1 - - - -

2(x 2)

1 - 7 - 1 57,00 7 -

Rio di Pusteria/Mühlbach

Brunnerhof

at Spinga/Spinges 5,
39037 Rio di Pusteria/Mühlbach (BZ)
Tel. 0472849591 Fax 0472849591

In the lower Val Pusteria, this renovated traditional building, next to a church in the centre of a charming village, is ideal for summer holidays.

-

1 - - - -

8 (x 1/4)

1 16,00 - 28,00 -

-

1 - 7 - 1 - 7 -

Roncegno

Agritur Rincher

at Prese, 38050 Roncegno (TN)
Tel. 0461764797
Web: www.rincher.com

Amid the pastures and woods of the upper Valsugana, with the Lagorai Range in the background, the accommodation is in a traditional maso, with wood-panelled rooms.

3 (x 1)

1 20,00 16,00 30,00 -

3 (x 2)

1 20,00 16,00 35,00 -

-

1 - 7 - 1 - 7 -

Montibeller

via Prose 1, 38050 Roncegno (TN)
Tel. 0461764355 Fax 0461773349
E-mail: valter.montibeller@tin.it

Surrounded by orchards near the village, with its thermal baths, this establishment has a friendly atmosphere. Guests are accommodated in modern rooms and apartments.

-

1 - - - -

4 (x 1/4)

1 23,00 - 35,00 -

7 (x 2/5)

1 - 7 - 1 - 7 452,00

San Candido/Innichen

Asthof

via Waidach 1, 39038 San Candido/Innichen (BZ)
Tel. 0474913270 Fax 0474913806
E-mail: rainer.asthof@dnet.it

This accommodation is just a stone's throw from the centre of one of the best organised summer and winter resorts in the area.

-

1 - - -

-

1 - - -

4 (x 2/4)

1 17,50 7 - 1 - 7 -

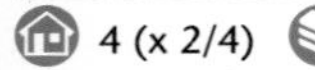 

GADENHOF

via Elzenbach 1,
39038 San Candido/Innichen (BZ)
Tel. 0474913523
Web: www.gadenhof.it

The setting of this renovated traditional building is the spectacular Dolomiti di Sesto Nature Park, dominated by Cima Nove (2581 m).

-

1 - - -

-

1 - - -

3(x 2)

1 - 7 - 1 93,00 7 -

SAN GENESIO ATESINO/JENESIEN

MALGORERHOF

at Cologna/Glaning 21,
39050 San Genesio Atesino/Jenesien (BZ)
Tel. 0471351960 Fax 0471351960

San Genesio can be reached from Bolzano by road or cable car, while Cologna (764 m), where this accommodation is located, is six kilometres from the centre of the city.

-

1 - - -

2 (x 2)

1 22,00 - - -

2 (x 2/6)

1 - 7 - 1 60,00 7 -

SAN LEONARDO IN PASSIRIA SANKT LEONHARD IN PASSEIER

HASLINGERHOF

at Schweinsteg 5, 39015 San Leonardo in Passiria/Sankt Leonhard in Passeier (BZ)
Tel. 0473645402 Fax 0473645402

In the lower Val Passiria, between Merano and San Leonardo, accommodation is available in comfortable rooms from spring, with its apple blossoms, to autumn, with the grape-harvest.

  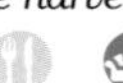 

-

1 - - -

6 (x 2/4)

1 16,20 - - -

-

1 - 7 - 1 - 7 -

San Lorenzo di Sebato
Sankt Lorenzen

Gschlier

at Sares/Saalen 20, 39030 San Lorenzo di Sebato/Sankt Lorenzen (BZ)
Tel. 0474403220
Web: www.gschliererhof.com

This village is located in the central Val Pusteria, at the mouth of the Val Badia. Accommodation is available in a building in traditional style that has been renovated.

\-

1 - - -

\-

1 - - -

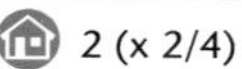 2 (x 2/4) 

1 - 7 - 1 62,00 7 -

San Martino in Badia
Sankt Martin in Thurn

Dasserhof

via Ponte Nuovo 107, 39030 San Martino in Badia/Sankt Martin in Thurn (BZ)
Tel. 0474523224
Web: www.pradel.it

In the central Val Badia, accommodation is available in a modern chalet, just a few hundred metres from the village, in sight of Castel Torre and Sasso della Croce.

\-

1 - - -

6 (x 2/4)

1 25,00 - 47,00 -

1(x 2)

1 30,00 7 - 1 - 7 -

Lüch de Vanc

at Longiarù Seres 36, 39030 San Martino in Badia/Sankt Martin in Thurn (BZ)
Tel. 0474590108 Fax 0474590173
Web: www.vanc.it

In the Valle di Longiarù, dominated by the Puez Range, with its high trails, the accommodation is in a renovated maso or in a nearby modern building.

\-

1 - - -

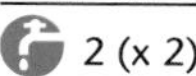 2 (x 2)

1 20,70 - 36,10 -

2(x 4)

1 - 7 - 1 82,60 7 -

San Martino in Passiria
Sankt Martin in Passeier

Untersaltaushof-Marteller

at Saltusio/Saltaus, via Passiria 10, 39010 San Martino in Passiria/Sankt Martin in Passeier (BZ)
Tel. 0473645454 Fax 0473645454

This typical Alpine house, which has been renovated and has a pergola and lawn, stands amid orchards and vineyards. Excursions and climbing are possible in the Gruppo di Tessa Nature Park.

\-

1 - - -

\-

1 - - -

4(x 2)

1 - 7 - 1 70,00 7 -

San Pancrazio/Sankt Pankraz

Ausserreggmannhof

at Foresta 23,
39010 San Pancrazio/Sankt Pankraz (BZ)
Tel. 0473563402 Fax 0473563402
Web: www.uab.it/ausserreggmannhof

The Val d'Ultimo is one of the most fascinating ways to reach the Stelvio National Park; at first it is thickly wooded, then it opens out, with vast expanses of grassland.

1 - - -

1 - - -

4(x 2)

1 - 7 - 1 57,00 7 -

San Vigilio di Marebbe Sankt Vigil in Enneberg

Lüch de Cone da Val

at San Vigilio/Sankt Vigil, via Chi Vai 10, 39030 San Vigilio di Marebbe/Sankt Vigil in Enneberg (BZ)
Tel. 0474501262
E-mail: atrebo@inwind.it

Between the Badia, Marebbe and San Vigilio valleys, towards the Fanes-Sennes-Braies Nature Park, accommodation is available in an attractive rural house.

1 - - -

1 - - -

4 (x 2/3)

1 - 7 - 1 78,00 7 -

Lüch dl'Ombolt

at Fordora 7, 39030 San Vigilio di Marebbe/Sankt Vigil in Enneberg (BZ)
Tel. 0474501306

Accommodation is available in a typical stone and wood building on the road that climbs up from San Vigilio to the Rifugio Furcia and Plan de Corones.

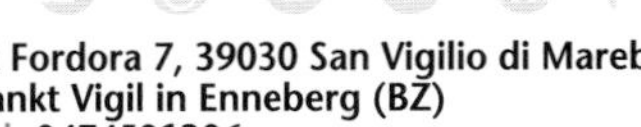

1 - - -

1 - - -

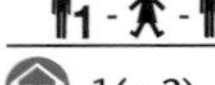

1(x 2)

1 12,90 7 - 1 - 7 -

Sarentino/Sarntal

Niederhauserhof

at Stetto/Steet 12, 39058 Sarentino/Sarntal (BZ)
Tel. 0471623285 Fax 0471623285

Accommodation at a high altitude is available in a maso in stone and wood; this is a base for interesting walks in the meadows and woods of the upper Val Sarentina.

\-

1 - - -

2 (x 1/2)
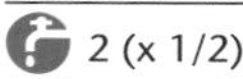
1 18,10 - -

2(x 2)
1 - 7 - 1 51,60 7 -

SCENA/SCHENNA

TORGGLERHOF

via S. Giorgio 12, 39017 Scena/Schenna (BZ)
Tel. 0473945744 Fax 0473945744

From Merano, the road climbs up to Scena, where accommodation is available amid meadows and vineyards on the slopes of the Picco di Ivigna. Cable cars ascend to Montescena (1445 m).

\-
1 - - -

\-
1 - - -

3 (x 2/4) 
1 - 7 - 1 72,30 7 -

SELVA DEI MOLINI/MÜHLWALD

TASSGASTEIGERHOF

via Centro 17/A,
39030 Selva dei Molini/Mühlwald (BZ)
Tel. 0474653219

Relaxing holidays are possible just 20 kilometres from Brunico in a modern building offering apartments with large flower-decked balconies.

\-
1 - - -

\-
1 - - -

2(x 4) 
1 12,90 7 - 1 - 7 -

SELVA DI VAL GARDENA WOLKENSTEIN IN GRÖDEN

SOLEIGAHOF

strada Daunei 77, 39048 Selva di Val Gardena/Wolkenstein in Gröden (BZ)
Tel. 0471795576 Fax 0471795576
E-mail: soleiga@val-gardena.com

Accommodation is available in a recently built maso, in a tranquil position amid meadows; nearby is the Puez-Odle Nature Park.

\-
1 - - -

5 (x 2) 
1 29,00 20,00 - -

\-
1 - 7 - 1 - 7 -

TUBLÀ

strada Daunei 100, 39048 Selva di Val Gardena/Wolkenstein in Gröden (BZ)
Tel. 0471795360 Fax 0471795360
E-mail: tubla@rolmail.net

For holidays amid meadows and conifers rising gently towards the rock faces of the Dolomites, accommodation is available in a well-equipped chalet, with its own pasture.

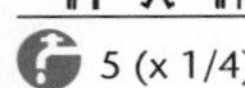  

5 (x 1/4)  

25,00

2(x 2) 

75,00

SESTO/SEXTEN

WEBER

at Ferrara/Schmieden, via Sonnwend 25,
39030 Sesto/Sexten (BZ)
Tel. 0474710081

A blaze of colourful flowers gladdens the hearts of guests at this modern house on the valley floor. Other delights await them during their mountain walks.

2 (x 2/5) 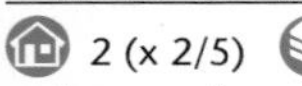   

20,60

SILANDRO/SCHLANDERS

MAREINHOF

  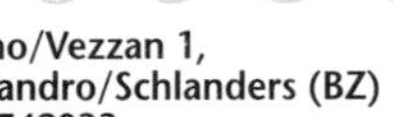

at Vezzano/Vezzan 1,
39028 Silandro/Schlanders (BZ)
Tel. 0473742033

Standing near a fir wood, this farmhouse with its balconies, is reassuringly solid. Not far away, the Val Martello leads up towards the peaks of Cevedale.

4 (x 2) 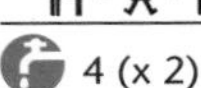

19,60

SLUDERNO/SCHLUDERNS

PALIHOF

at Gschneir 15, 39020 Sluderno/Schluderns (BZ)
Tel. 0473615010

In upper Val Venosta, accommodation is available in a traditional maso in a village some distance from the main town.

6 (x 2/4) 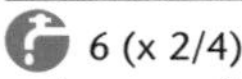  

19,60

TASSULLO

ODORIZZI MICHELE

at Rallo, via F.lli Pinamonti 52,
38010 Tassullo (TN)
Tel. 0463450294
Web: www.agriturismo.com/odorizzi

The accommodation is in an old, but renovated, house with a terrace and courtyard. Cles and the main centres of the Brenta Dolomites are within easy reach.

\-

1 - - -

7 (x 1/2)

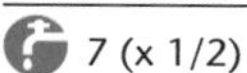

1 20,00 - -

3 (x 4/5)

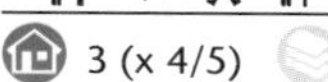

1 20,00 7 135,00 1 - 7 -

Terento/Terenten

Huberhof

via Walderlaner 1, 39030 Terento/Terenten (BZ)
Tel. 0472546177

In a sunny position on a terrace overlooking the lower Val Pusteria, Terento is the ideal place for a really peaceful holiday.

\-

1 - - -

2 (x 2)

1 16,50 - -

3(x 2)

1 - 7 - 1 49,00 7 -

Tesimo/Tisens

Weckhof

at Grissiano 9, 39010 Tesimo/Tisens (BZ)
Tel. 0473920880 Fax 0473920880

Located in the Val Venosta, also known as the 'apple garden', this is a maso with an old wood-fired oven for baking bread, from which its name probably derives.

\-

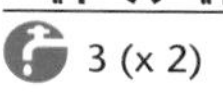
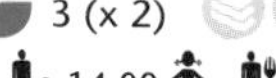

1 - - -

3 (x 2)

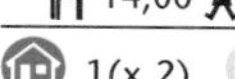

1 14,00 - -

1(x 2)

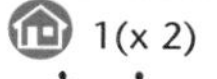

1 - 7 - 1 39,00 7 -

Tires/Tiers

Mühlhof

via S. Giorgio 47, 39050 Tires/Tiers (BZ)
Tel. 0471642256 Fax 0471642256
E-mail: muehlhof@volmail.net

Catinaccio, with the Torri del Vaiolet, forms the splendid backdrop to the holiday. Surrounded by open grassland, Tires is on the road going up to the Costalunga Pass.

\-

1 - - -

\-

1 - - -

2(x 2)

1 - 7 - 1 72,00 7 -

Tirolo/Tirol

Oberortsgut

via Aslago 21, 39019 Tirolo/Tirol (BZ)
Tel. 0473923409 Fax 0473923409

The symbol of this region, Castel Tirolo, stands amid the woods of the so-called Monte di Merano. It's in striking contrast to the attractive village, surrounded by vineyards and orchards.

-
1 - - -

-
1 - - -

4(x 2)
1 - 7 - 1 49,10 7 -

Tonadico

Agritur Broch

at Passo di Cereda, 38054 Tonadico (TN)
Tel. 043965028 Fax 0439652007

This is a peaceful locality that is, however, only a few kilometres from San Martino di Castrozza, one of the main summer and winter resorts in the area.

-
1 - - -

-
1 - - -

5 (x 4/6)
1 - 7 - 1 - 7 200,00

Tuenno

Agritur Tretter Giorgio

via E. Quaresima 13, 38019 Tuenno (TN)
Tel. 0463451276 Fax 0463451276
E-mail: agritur.tretter@libero.it

The accommodation is on the top floor, with balconies overlooking orchards. There's the possibility of excursions in the Dolomites for all tastes, from dinners in mountain huts, to bivouacking and skiing.

-
1 - - -

-
1 - - -

4(x 4)
1 - 7 - 1 - 7 465,00

Dallago Rodolfo

via Androna Snao 7, 38019 Tuenno (TN)
Tel. 0463451318

Just a few kilometres from Cles, in a village at the mouth of the Valle di Tovel, this accommodation consists of refurbished apartments with terraces or in an attic.

-
1 - - -

-
1 - - -

3 (x 2/5)
1 - 7 - 1 - 7 280,00

VALDAORA/OLANG

BULANDHOF

at Valdaora di Sopra/Oberolang, via Salla 3, 39030 Valdaora/Olang (BZ)
Tel. 0474496047 Fax 0474496047
E-mail: monthaler@jumpy.it

The accommodation is in an old maso at the foot of the mountains of the Fanes-Sennes-Braies Nature Park. In winter, it's possible to ski at Plan de Corones.

 -

1 - - -

-

1 - - -

 4(x 2)

1 - 7 - 1 77,00 7 -

WINKELPEINTE

at Valdaora di Sotto/Niederolang, via dei Campi 2, 39030 Valdaora/Olang (BZ)
Tel. 0474496610 Fax 0474496610

This is one of the most beautiful points of the Val Pusteria: on one side is the mouth of the Valle di Anterselva; on the other, the way to the Rifugio Furcia and San Vigilio di Marebbe.

 -

1 - - -

-

1 - - -

 2(x 2)  

1 - 7 - 1 90,00 7 -

VAL DI VIZZE/PFITSCH

BOARER

at San Giacomo/Sankt Jakob 75, 39049 Val di Vizze/Pfitsch (BZ)
Tel. 0472630143

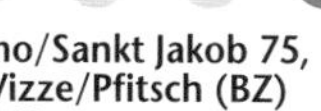

In the verdant upper Val di Vizze, below the Gran Pilastro (3510 m), accommodation is available in an Alpine chalet, the original appearance of which has been preserved.

-

1 - - -

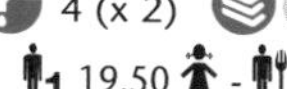 4 (x 2)

1 19,50 - - -

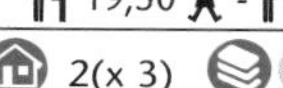 2(x 3)  

1 - 7 - 1 56,00 7 -

VALFLORIANA

MALGA SASS

at Malga Sass, 38040 Valfloriana (TN)
Tel. 0462910002

Surrounded by meadows and woods, this is a typical mountain hut built of wood without the use of stone (in the local dialect, sass means "knowledge").

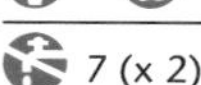 7 (x 2) 

1 - - 31,00 -

-

1 - - -

-

1 - 7 - 1 - 7 -

VALLE AURINA/AHRNTAL

PARRAINERHOF

at San Giacomo/Sankt Jacob 18,
39030 Valle Aurina/Ahrntal (BZ)
Tel. 0474650180

This resort is busy both in summer, when visitors head towards the Cima Dura and the Vetta d'Italia, and in winter, when they ski on the nearby slopes.

-

1 - - -

-

1 - - -

4(x 2)

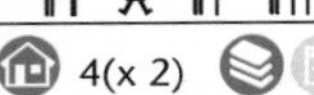

1 - 7 - 1 41,30 7 -

VALLE DI CASIES/GSIES

MUDLERHOF

at San Martino/Sankt Martin 5,
39030 Valle di Casies/Gsies (BZ)
Tel. 0474978446 Fax 0474978446
Web: www.mudlerhof.it

In the village of San Martino, this refurbished complex offers accommodation in the house and the adjacent former cowshed and hayloft.

-

1 - - -

-

1 - - -

4(x 2)

1 - 7 - 1 100,00 7 -

VANDOIES/VINTL

LANDMANN

at Vandoies di Sotto/Niedervintl, Haslach 3,
39030 Vandoies/Vintl (BZ)
Tel. 0472869383 Fax 0472869383
Web: www.landmann.it

From Vandoies, the road goes up the Valle di Fundres; more adventurous souls may continue to the mountain hut at the Ponte di Ghiaccio Pass, at the foot of the Gran Pilastro (3510 m).

-

1 - - -

6 (x 2)

1 23,00 - - -

-

1 - 7 - 1 - 7 -

VILLABASSA/NIEDERDORF

LEXERHOF

via H. Wassermann 20,
39039 Villabassa/Niederdorf (BZ)
Tel. 0474745026 Fax 0474745297
E-mail: petra.bachmann@raiffeisen.it

This traditional building has been converted into tourist accommodation. One could just relax here, but it would be a pity not to go out and explore the area!.

This charming house in stone and wood, with panoramic balconies and furnishings in the Alpine tradition, is surrounded by pastures and imposing mountains.

- 1 - - -

- 1 - - -

3(x 2)

1 - 7 - 1 77,50 7 -

-

1 - - -

7 (x 1/2)

1 33,60 - 43,90 -

-

1 - 7 - 1 - 7 -

Ziano di Fiemme

Maso Val Averta

E D

via del Prenner 11, 38030 Ziano di Fiemme (TN)
Tel. 0462571463 Fax 0462570445
E-mail: valaverta@cr-surfing.net

UMBRIA

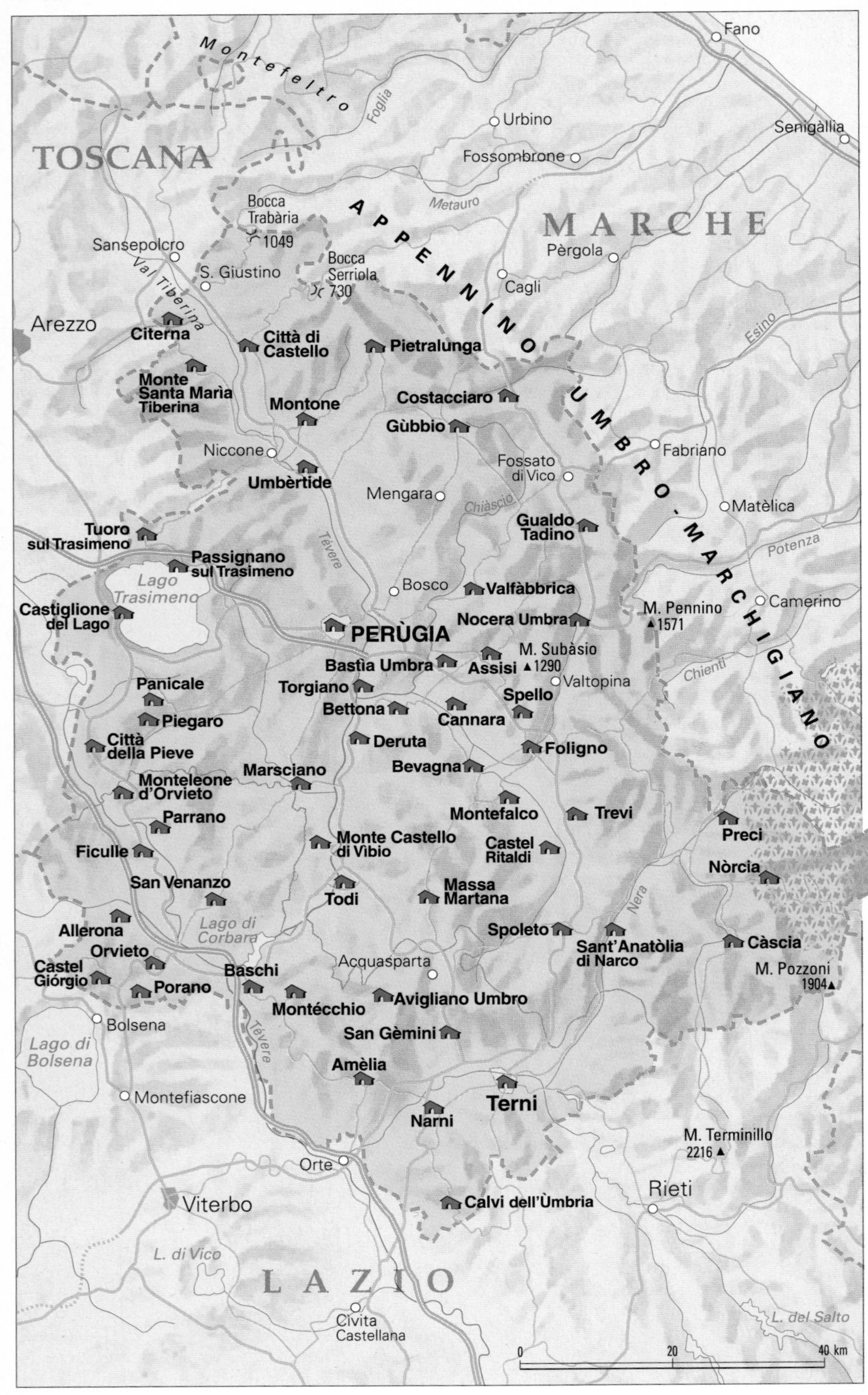

Montefeltro
Foglia
Fano
Urbino
Senigàllia
TOSCANA
Fossombrone
Bocca Trabària 1049
Metauro
APPENNINO UMBRO-MARCHIGIANO
MARCHE
Sansepolcro
Pèrgola
S. Giustino
Bocca Serriola 730
Cagli
Val Tiberina
Arezzo
Citerna
Città di Castello
Pietralunga
Esino
Monte Santa Marìa Tiberina
Montone
Costacciaro
Gùbbio
Niccone
Fabriano
Fossato di Vico
Umbèrtide
Mengara
Chiàscio
Matèlica
Gualdo Tadino
Tuoro sul Trasimeno
Tévere
Potenza
Passignano sul Trasimeno
Lago Trasimeno
Bosco
Valfàbbrica
Castiglione del Lago
M. Pennino 1571
Camerino
Nocera Umbra
PERÙGIA
M. Subàsio 1290
Bastìa Umbra
Assisi
Valtopina
Panicale
Chienti
Torgiano
Spello
Bettona
Cannara
Piegaro
Città della Pieve
Deruta
Foligno
Bevagna
Marsciano
Monteleone d'Orvieto
Montefalco
Trevi
Parrano
Preci
Monte Castello di Vibio
Castel Ritaldi
Ficulle
Nòrcia
San Venanzo
Massa Martana
Todi
Nera
Allerona
Lago di Corbara
Spoleto
Sant'Anatòlia di Narco
Càscia
Orvieto
Castel Giórgio
Baschi
Acquasparta
M. Pozzoni 1904
Porano
Montécchio
Avigliano Umbro
Bolsena
San Gèmini
Lago di Bolsena
Amèlia
Montefiascone
Terni
Narni
M. Terminillo 2216
Orte
Rieti
Viterbo
Calvi dell'Ùmbria
L. di Vico
LAZIO
Civita Castellana
L. del Salto
0
20
40 km

Allerona

Selvella

at Selvella 5, 05011 Allerona (TR)
Tel. 0763628166 Fax 0763628166
Web: www.argoweb.it/agriturismoselvella

This accommodation is amid the woods near Orvieto, in an area extending from the Paglia Valley and Monte Amiata to Lake Bolsena.

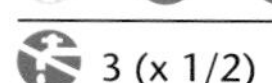  

3 (x 1/2)

1 36,00 - 55,00 -

5 (x 2) 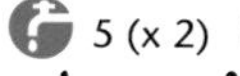 

1 39,00 - 60,00 -

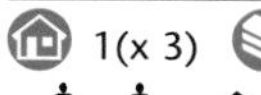 

1(x 3)

1 - 7 - 1 120,00 7 600,00

Amelia

Oliveto

strada Scendone 8, 05022 Amelia (TR)
Tel. 0744981101 Fax 0744981101
Web: www.agriturismooliveto.it

The position, between the Tiber and Nera valleys, is both pleasant and strategically placed for excursions to places of natural or cultural interest in Umbria and Lazio.

-

1 - - -

-

1 - - -

6 (x 2/4)

1 - 7 - 1 70,00 7 -

San Cristoforo

strada San Cristoforo 16,
05022 Amelia (TR)
Tel. 0744988249 Fax 0744988459
Web: www.sancristoforo.it

In the hills dividing the Tiber and Nera Valley, accommodation is available in the farmhouses of a small medieval village clustered round a church.

-

1 - - -

14 (x 2)

1 41,00 - 61,00 -

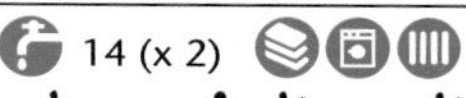

7 (x 2/5)

1 - 7 - 1 205,00 7 -

Assisi

Brigolante Guest Apartments

via Costa di Trex 31, 06081 Assisi (PG)
Tel. 075802250 Fax 075802250
Web: www.brigolante.com

Signora Rebecca offers accommodation in a solid, recently renovated farmhouse 6 km from Assisi, in the Monte Subasio Nature Park.

-

1 - - -

-

1 - - -

3(x 2)

1 - 7 - 1 70,00 7 440,00

Casa Faustina

at Mora 28, 06080 Assisi (PG)
Tel. 0758039377 Fax 0758039377
Web: www.casafaustina.it

There's a friendly welcome in eight small apartments in a converted 19th-century farmhouse and the adjacent building. The garden is shaded by pines, cypresses and olives.

-

1 - - - -

-

1 - - - -

8 (x 2/4)

1 - 7 - 1 85,00 7 124,00

Il Noceto Umbro

at Petrignano, via Campagna 43,
06081 Assisi (PG)
Tel. 0758000838 Fax 0758000838
Web: www.ilnocetoumbro.com

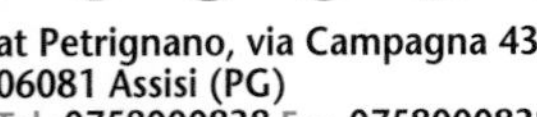

The rooms, furnished in simple style and with separate entrances, give onto the large garden; all the cooking is produced in-house. A swimming pool is located on the edge of the fields.

-

1 - - - -

7 (x 1/2)

1 39,00 19,50 57,00 -

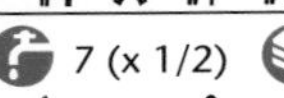

-

1 - 7 - 1 - 7 -

La Castellana

at Costa di Trex 4, 06081 Assisi (PG)
Tel. 0758019046 Fax 0758019046
Web: www.agriturismolacastellana.it

This farm, which comprises two recently renovated stone farmhouses, is in the Monte Subasio Nature Park. There's a splendid view of the Topino Valley.

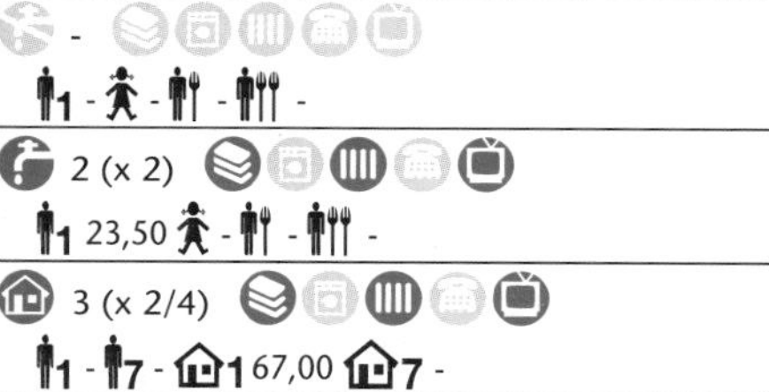

Le Querce di Assisi

at Pian della Pieve, 06081 Assisi (PG)
Tel. **075802332** Fax **0758025000**
Web: **www.lequerce.it**

Excellent accommodation is available in this group of restored houses surrounding a 14th-century mill in the Monte Subasio Nature Park. Wholesome local dishes are served here.

\-
1 - - -
12 (x 1/4)
1 60,00 - 80,00 -
5 (x 4/6)
1 - 7 - 1 - 7 1.260,00

Longetti

via S. Pietro Campagna 35, 06081 Assisi (PG)
Tel. **075816175** Fax **0759869562**
Web: **www.agriturismolongetti.com**

This recently refurbished stone farmhouse is located in the peaceful, verdant hills near Assisi. The interiors are full of atmosphere and the surroundings are fabulous.

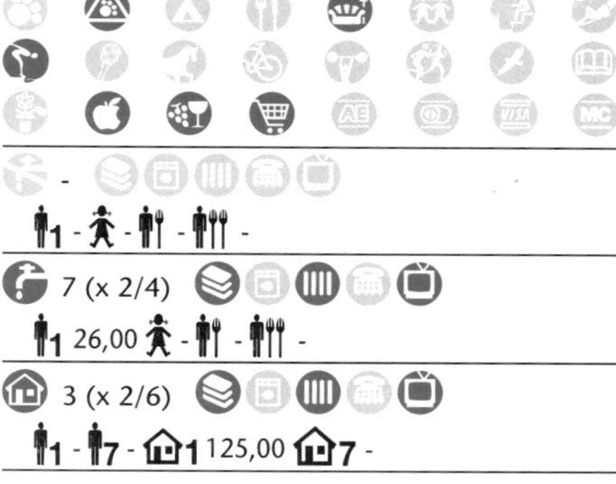

Malvarina

at Capodacqua, via S. Apollinare 32, 06081 Assisi (PG)
Tel. **0758064280** Fax **0758064280**
Web: **www.malvarina.it**

The farmhouse is named after an old spring between Assisi and Spello. Four stone buildings, with rustic and antique furnishings, are available for the guests.

\-
1 - - -
12 (x 1/4)
1 52,00 - 70,50 -
3(x 4)
1 - 7 - 1 98,00 7 -

Podere la Fornace

at Tordibetto di Assisi, via Ombrosa 3, 06081 Assisi (PG)
Tel. **0758019537** Fax **0758019630**
Web: **www.lafornace.com**

Despite their ancient appearance, these two stone cottages standing on opposite sites of the farmyard have modern conveniences and a pleasant atmosphere.

\-
1 - - -

2 (x 2)

1 67,00 - -

6 (x 2/4)

1 - 7 - 1 160,00 7 1.030,00

Santa Maria della Spina

at Santa Maria della Spina, 06080 Assisi (PG)
Tel. **0759869100** Fax **0759869100**
Web: **digilander.libero.it/patriziaepierluigi**

Between Assisi and the Ose, this peaceful accommodation of medieval origin, which has been carefully renovated, offers rooms and rustic apartments.

\-

1 - - -

3 (x 2)

1 23,00 20,00 - -

3(x 4)

1 - 7 - 1 103,00 7 -

Avigliano Umbro

Piano Grande

via S. Egidio 20, 05020 Avigliano Umbro (TR)
Tel. **0744933774** Fax **0744933774**
E-mail: **agrit.pianogrande@tiscali.it**

Set in a large garden, a carefully renovated 18th-century farmhouse has rooms and an apartment with period furniture.

\-

1 - - -

5 (x 2)

1 30,00 20,00 60,00 -

1(x 5)

1 - 7 - 1 120,00 7 580,00

Baschi

Pomurlo Vecchio

vocabolo Pomurlo Vecchio, 05023 Baschi (TR)
Tel. **0744950190** Fax **0744950500**
Web: **www.pomurlovecchio-lecasette.it**

Not far from Lake Corbara, accommodation is available in three renovated stone farmhouses furnished in traditional rural style.

\-

1 - - -

13 (x 1/2)

1 37,50 - 60,00 -

4(x 2)

1 - 7 - 1 75,00 7 -

Bastia Umbra

Il Morino

via Spoleto 8, 06083 Bastia Umbra (PG)
Tel. **0758010839** Fax **0758010839**

Not far from the village, but already in the countryside, this modern house has a garden with a mini-golf course.

\-

1 - - -

10 (x 2)

1 28,00 - 42,00 -

\-

1 - 7 - 1 - 7 -

BETTONA

IL POGGIO DEGLI OLIVI

at Montebalacca, 06080 Bettona (PG)
Tel. 0759869023 Fax 0759869023
Web: www.poggiodegliolivi.com

In the middle of a vast farm, this superb complex surrounds an 17th-century house: it has rustic furnishings, a swimming pool with a Jacuzzi and tennis courts.

\-

1 - - -

6 (x 2)

1 52,00 31,00 73,00 -

12 (x 2/6)

1 - 7 - 1 165,00 7 1.033,00

IL SAMBRO

at Passaggio, via S. Illuminata, 06084 Bettona (PG)
Tel. 075987109 Fax 0758019842
Web: www.edisons.it

This farmhouse commands views of the Valle Umbria and Assisi. Nearby, in the medieval village of Bettona, guests can discover the art and delicious cuisine of the region.

\-

1 - - -

\-

1 - - -

4 (x 3/4)

1 - 7 - 1 - 7 605,00

NATURA AMICA

at Fratta di Bettona, via dei Cacciatori 7,
06084 Bettona (PG)
Tel. 075982828 Fax 075982922

Rooms with a view over the Valle Umbra are available in a group of renovated buildings surrounding an old farmhouse. Horseback tours are also possible.

\-

1 - - -

6 (x 2)

1 26,00 - - -

4(x 4)

1 26,00 7 - 1 - 7 -

TORRE BURCHIO

vocabolo Burchio, 06084 Bettona (PG)
Tel. 0759885017 Fax 075987150
Web: www.torreburchio.it

Accommodation is available in a 19th-century farmhouse in a nature reserve of 600 hectares. Tourism on horseback is organised at all levels; groups of schoolchildren and adults are also welcome.

\-

1 - - -

16 (x 2)
46,50 32,50 67,50 -

13 (x 2/6)
- - 124,00 826,00

Bevagna

Il Corbezzolo

at Castelbuono, vocabolo S. Sisto 59/60,
06031 Bevagna (PG)
Tel. **0742361933** Fax **0742369042**
Web: **www.ilcorbezzolo.it**

The many delights on offer here include summer festivals, the grape-harvest, country walks, the new olive oil and outings in search of mushrooms and truffles.

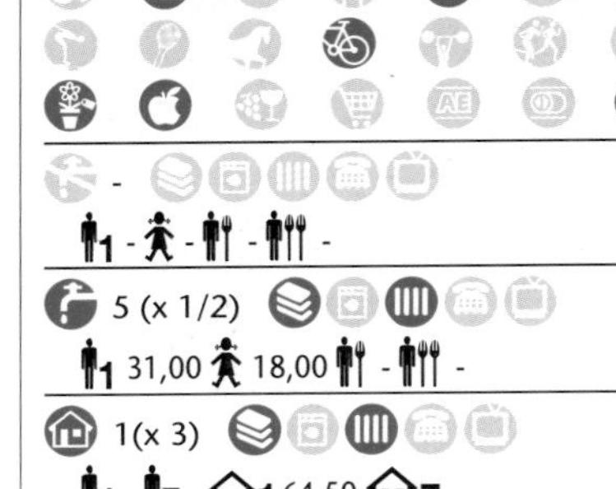

- - - -

5 (x 1/2)
31,00 18,00 - -

1(x 3)
- - 64,50 -

La Fonte

at Fiaggia, 06031 Bevagna (PG)
Tel. **0742360968** Fax **0742360968**
Web: **web.tiscali.it/agrifonte**

The position is excellent and the accommodation superb in old farmhouses with modern comforts and traditional furnishings.

\-

1 - - - -

\-

1 - - - -

8 (x 2/4)

1 25,00 7 - 1 - 7 -

Calvi dell'Umbria

San Martino

at Colle San Martino 10,
05032 Calvi dell'Umbria (TR)
Tel. **0744710644** Fax **0744710644**
E-mail: **louisecb@katamail.com**

From this handsome farmhouse there's a magnificent view of the Monti Sabini, the Umbrian hills and the Tiber Valley. The rooms are comfortable and characteristic.

\-

1 - - - -

\-

1 - - - -

4 (x 2/4) 

1 - 7 - 1 140,00 7 -

Cannara

La Fattoria del Gelso

vocabolo Bevagna 16, 06033 Cannara (PG)
Tel. **074272164** Fax **074272164**

In the countryside of the large valley of Assisi, accommodation is available in an old, but renovated, farmhouse and various self-contained units surrounding it.

\-

1 - - - -

11 (x 2/4)

1 40,00 - 65,00 -

\-

1 - 7 - 1 - 7 -

Cascia

Casale Sant'Antonio

at Casali Sant'Antonio, 06043 Cascia (PG)
Tel. **074376819**

In the Valnerina, this old farmhouse is ideal for those fond of holidays in the mountains. On the farm, visitors can see a collection of old agricultural implements and follow a nature trail.

\-

1 - - - -

1 (x 2) 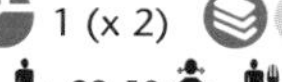

1 23,50 - - -

3 (x 2/4)

1 23,50 7 - 1 - 7 -

Castel Giorgio

Poggio del Miglio

at Poggio del Miglio 5,
05013 Castel Giorgio (TR)
Tel. 0763627449 Fax 0763627449
Web: www.poggiodelmiglio.de.vu

From the farm, a path leads to Lake Bolsena. Surrounded by organic crops, the farmhouse is ideal for a country holiday in a beautiful setting.

-

1 - - -

-

1 - - -

3 (x 2/6)

1 30,00 7 - 1 - 7 -

Castel Ritaldi

Torre Allori

at Colle del Marchese,
06044 Castel Ritaldi (PG)
Tel. 074351389 Fax 074351389
Web: www.torreallori.com

On a hill amid olive trees, this 18th-century farmhouse in brick and stone has been splendidly renovated in order to offer accommodation with all modern comforts.

2 (x 2)

1 28,00 15,00 44,00 -

4 (x 2)

1 30,00 15,00 46,00 -

2(x 2)

1 - 7 - 1 55,00 7 350,00

Castiglione del Lago

Casal de' Cucchi

at Petrignano, vocabolo I Cucchi,
06061 Castiglione del Lago (PG)
Tel. 0759528116 Fax 0755171244
Web: www.fanini.net

This award-winning wine-growing estate is located in the hills near Lake Trasimene. The complex consists of a number of buildings arranged around a swimming pool.

-

1 - - -

3 (x 2)

1 33,00 23,00 59,00 -

8 (x 3/4)

1 - 7 - 1 - 7 908,96

Le Quattro Stagioni

at Palareto-Castagni,
06061 Castiglione del Lago (PG)
Tel. 0759652892 Fax 0759652454

The name evokes rustic pleasures in various periods of the year: bathing and fishing in Lake Trasimene in the summer; hunting on the huge estate in the winter.

-

1 - - -

-

1 - - -

6(x 3)
1 - 7 - 1 85,00 7 600,00

Podere Bello

at Pineta 57, 06061 Castiglione del Lago (PG)
Tel. 0759680283 Fax 0759680283
Web: www.poderebello.it

Welcoming accommodation is available in the main house in stone, in a splendidly renovated 18th-century farmhouse and in cottages surrounded by the greenery of the park.

       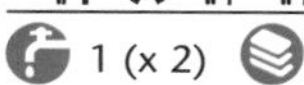  

\-
1 - - -

1 (x 2)
1 36,00 - 59,00 -

8 (x 2/4)
1 - 7 - 1 - 7 1.300,00

Poggio del Sole

at Ceraso 33, 06060 Castiglione del Lago (PG)
Tel. 0759680221 Fax 0759680221
Web: terreumbre.it

The rooms, their position, the careful management: all this helps to make the holiday as relaxing as possible. The Dionisi family also runs the Poggio Verde establishment.

\-
1 - - -

\-
1 - - -

7 (x 2/4)
1 - 7 - 1 100,00 7 750,00

Romitorio

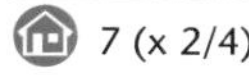     

at Pozzuolo, 06067 Castiglione del Lago (PG)
Tel. 075959517 Fax 075959517
Web: www.romitorio.com

Located in the hills, the accommodation is in stone and brick buildings surrounding a piazza with a small church adjacent. A baby-sitting service is also available.

\-
1 - - -

\-
1 - - -

13 (x 2/4)
1 - 7 - 1 - 7 900,00

Villa Osvaldo

at Salticchio 7, 06060 Castiglione del Lago (PG)
Tel. 0759527241 Fax 0759527241

Olives, cypresses, vines and cornfields surround this 17th-century farmhouse. Self-contained apartments are available in two separate buildings furnished in rustic style.

\-
1 - - -

\-
1 - - -

8 (x 2/4)
1 - 7 - 1 - 7 982,00

Citerna

Podere Casenove

at Fighille, via della Fonte 14, 06010 Citerna (PG)
Tel. 0575742705 Fax 0575742705
Web: www.poderecasenove.it

In the upper Tiber valley, this is an excellent base for visiting the historic towns nearby; guests will be delighted by the tastefully furnished house and the functional apartments.

\-

1 - - -

\-

1 - - -

2(x 4)

1 - 7 - 1 125,00 7 -

Città della Pieve

Madonna delle Grazie

vocabolo Madonna delle Grazie 6,
06062 Città della Pieve (PG)
Tel. 0578299822 Fax 0578299822
Web: www.madonnadellegrazie.it

In this traditional farmhouse with a splendid view, a young family greets the guests by offering them the farm's produce. It's a member of the ANTE, and has a guide.

\-

1 - - -

5 (x 2)

1 55,00 - - -

1(x 2)

1 - 7 - 1 - 7 840,00

Città di Castello

La Terrazza sul Macchietto

at Morra, via S. Crescenziano 1,
06012 Città di Castello (PG)
Tel. 0758574102
Web: www.laterrazzasulmacchietto.com

The accommodation is in the large 19th-century hose belonging to the Nicasi family, with its stone fireplaces and washbasins, floors of terracotta tiles and period furniture.

\-

1 - - -

\-

1 - - -

2(x 4)

1 - 7 - 1 248,00 7 1.000,00

Monterosello

at San Maiano, vocabolo Seripole,
06012 Città di Castello (PG)
Tel. 0758577031 Fax 0758550690
Web: www.monterosello.it

The accommodation is in two well-arranged farmhouses and a number of chalets. Guests may go bathing, fishing, boating and canoeing on the small lakes on the farm.

1 - - -

 14 (x 2/4) 

62,00 - 48,00 -

5(x 4)

105,00 700,00

Villa Bice

at Cerbara, villa Zampini 43/45,
06011 Città di Castello (PG)
Tel. 0758511430 Fax 0758511430
Web: www.villabice.it

In the romantic setting of the huge park surrounding an 18th-century villa, the two farmhouses flanking it contain delightful apartments.

7 (x 2/4)

130,00 755,00

Costacciaro

Pian d'Isola

at Pian d'Isola, 06021 Costacciaro (PG)
Tel. 0759170567 Fax 0759172014
Web: www.piandisola.it

This old, but renovated, farmhouse stands on the edge of the Monte Cucco Nature Park; it has simple but comfortable rooms, beautiful gardens and a riding-school.

9 (x 1/4)

35,00 - 50,00 -

Deruta

Antica Fattoria del Colle

strada del Colle delle Forche 6,
06053 Deruta (PG)
Tel. 075972201 Fax 075972201
Web: www.anticafattoriadelcolle.it

These two traditional farmhouses have been splendidly refurbished. In addition to its excellent cuisine, the farm has two sitting rooms with fireplaces and an attractive garden.

5 (x 2/4)

1 48,00 - 80,00 -

2 (x 4/3)

1 - 7 - 1 - 7 1.035,00

Ficulle

La Casella-Antico Feudo di Campagna

strada La Casella 4, 05016 Ficulle (TR)
Tel. **076386588** Fax **076386684**
Web: **www.lacasella.com**

This vast holiday village surrounds a central group of facilities (including horse-riding and fitness centres). The accommodation is in renovated farmhouses.

-

1 - - -

15 (x 2/4)

1 - - 90,50 -

-

1 - 7 - 1 - 7 -

Foligno

Rocca Deli

at Scandolaro, 06034 Foligno (PG)
Tel. **0742651249** Fax **074370273**
Web: **www.seeumbria.com**

Dating from the 12th century, this old fortress contains a few comfortable rooms and a charming country-style restaurant; outside are woods, an olive grove and a truffle-ground.

-

1 - - -

5 (x 1/4)

1 36,00 - 54,00 -

-

1 - 7 - 1 - 7 -

Gualdo Tadino

Bonomi Fabrizia

at San Pellegrino a Monte Camera,
06023 Gualdo Tadino (PG)
Tel. **075918145**

This pleasant hamlet in the hills has a little church and two late 19th-century farmhouses. It is surrounded by 30 hectares of land with oak-woods, olive groves and cultivated fields.

-

1 - - -

-

1 - - -

2(x 4)

1 25,00 7 - 1 - 7 -

GUBBIO

ABBAZIA DI VALLINGEGNO

at Scritto, 06024 Gubbio (PG)
Tel. 075920158 Fax 0759227007
Web: www.abbaziadivallingegno.it

This fascinating Benedictine monastic complex dates from the 12th century. In the houses where the farmers lived, the rustic rooms have beamed ceilings.

-

1 - - -

-

1 - - -

6(x 4)

1 - 7 - 1 180,00 7 1.250,00

IL CERRONE

at Nogna 40, 06024 Gubbio (PG)
Tel. 0759241041 Fax 0759241041
E-mail: ilcerrone@libero.it

This large estate under woods, pastures and cultivated fields extends over the hills around Gubbio. The accommodation is in a perfectly restored stone cottage.

-

1 - - -

-

1 - - -

3 (x 2/4)

1 - 7 - 1 106,00 7 500,00

LA GINESTRA

at Valmarcola Santa Cristina, 06024 Gubbio (PG)
Tel. 075920088 Fax 0759220197
Web: www.agriturismolaginestra.com

An 19th-century country house, a tower- house and a stone farmhouse, all meticulously restored, provide accommodation for nature lovers in a protected area.

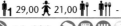

-

1 - - -

4 (x 2/4)

1 29,00 21,00 - -

4 (x 2/4)

1 - 7 - 1 34,00 7 930,00

OASI VERDE MENGARA

at Mengara 1, 06024 Gubbio (PG)
Tel. 0759227004 Fax 075920049
Web: www.oasiverdemengara.it

In the hills surrounding the little town, large rooms are available, furnished in rustic style, in a 17th-century stone farmhouse and its adjacent hayloft.

\-

1 - - - -

15 (x 2)

1 33,00 20,00 50,00 -

\-

1 - 7 - 1 - 7 -

Sant'Erasmo

at Padule, vocabolo Sant'Erasmo 37, 06020 Gubbio (PG)
Tel. **0759271024** Fax **0759291017**
Web: **www.agrisanterasmo.it**

Five kilometres from the centre, a large renovated farmhouse has five spacious apartments with all modern comforts. There's also a garden and playground.

\-

1 - - - -

\-

1 - - - -

5 (x 3/4)

1 26,00 7 - 1 - 7 -

Semidimela

at Petroia 36, 06020 Gubbio (PG)
Tel. **075920039** Fax **075920039**
Web: **www.semidimela.com**

This 16th-century stone farmhouse has been renovated without altering the original structure. The rooms have beams and floors with terracotta tiles.

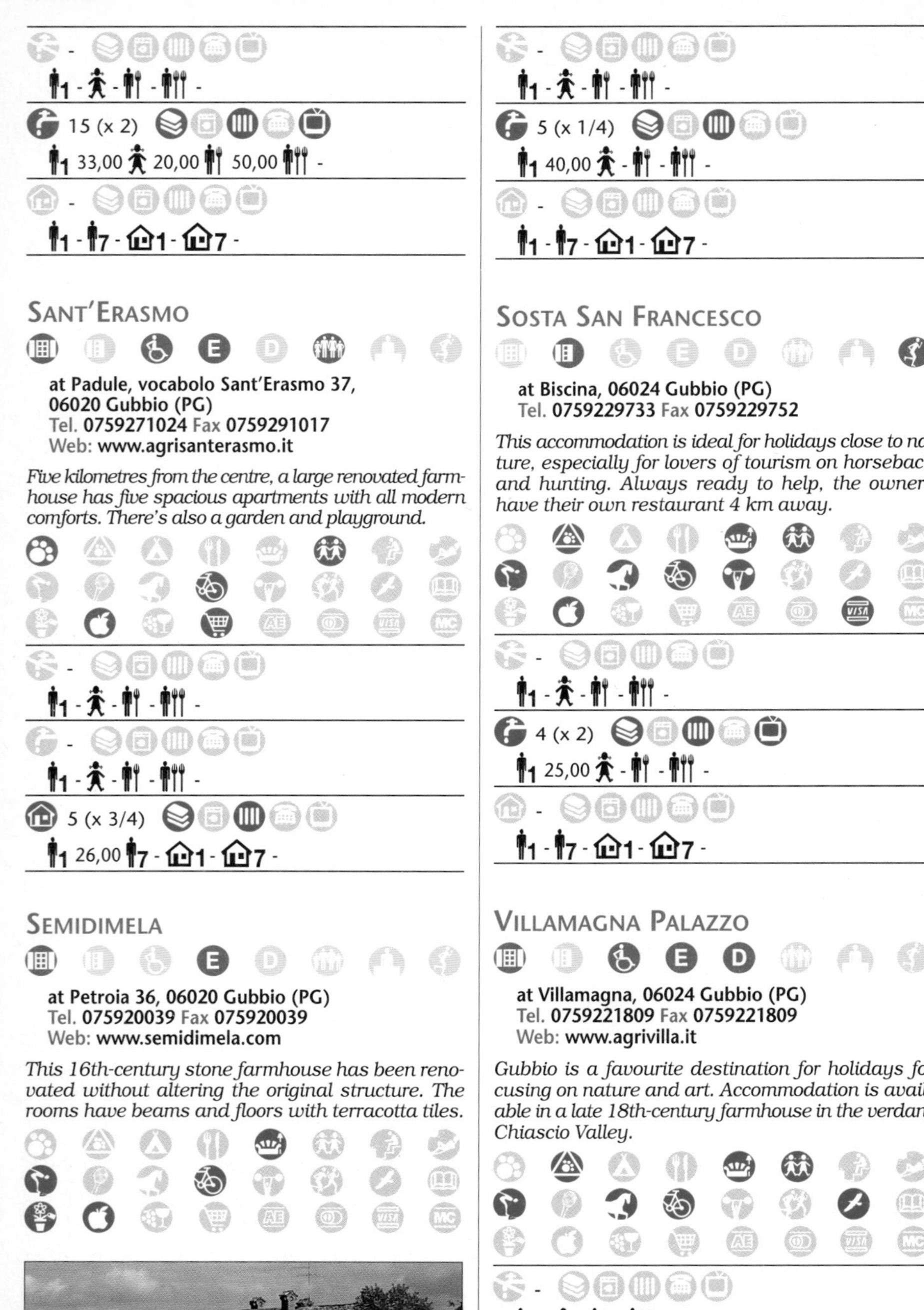

\-

1 - - - -

5 (x 1/4)

1 40,00 - - -

\-

1 - 7 - 1 - 7 -

Sosta San Francesco

at Biscina, 06024 Gubbio (PG)
Tel. **0759229733** Fax **0759229752**

This accommodation is ideal for holidays close to nature, especially for lovers of tourism on horseback and hunting. Always ready to help, the owners have their own restaurant 4 km away.

\-

1 - - - -

4 (x 2)

1 25,00 - - -

\-

1 - 7 - 1 - 7 -

Villamagna Palazzo

at Villamagna, 06024 Gubbio (PG)
Tel. **0759221809** Fax **0759221809**
Web: **www.agrivilla.it**

Gubbio is a favourite destination for holidays focusing on nature and art. Accommodation is available in a late 18th-century farmhouse in the verdant Chiascio Valley.

\-

1 - - - -

\-

1 - - - -

5 (x 2/5)

1 35,00 7 - 1 - 7 -

VILLA MOZART

at Ponte d'Assi, 06024 Gubbio (PG)
Tel. 0759272269 Fax 0759272269
Web: www.villamozart.it

Originally this was large monastery. Today, adapted to the needs of those wishing to spend a holiday in the country, it offers peaceful, very comfortable accommodation.

-

1 - - -

-

1 - - -

8(x 4)

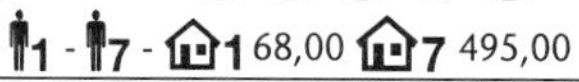

1 - 7 - 1 68,00 7 495,00

MARSCIANO

FATTORIA TEVERACCIO

at Cerro, 06055 Marsciano (PG)
Tel. 0758743787 Fax 0758744049

In a carefully renovated farmhouse dating from 1620, the former kitchen is now a living-room with a cooking area and fireplace. An annexe is also available.

-

1 - - -

10 (x 1/4)

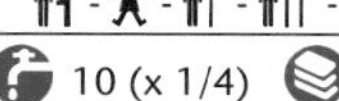

1 36,00 - - -

-

1 - 7 - 1 - 7 -

TORRE COLOMBAIA

at San Biagio della Valle, 06055 Marsciano (PG)
Tel. 0758787381 Fax 0758787381
Web: www.torrecolombaia.it

A hundred hectares of woods, formerly a game reserve, and 60 hectares under organic crops supply the produce used by the restaurant and on sale to the public.

-

1 - - -

5 (x 2)

1 45,00 - 62,00 -

3(x 4)

1 - 7 - 1 150,00 7 840,00

MASSA MARTANA

DA GIUSEPPINA

at Viepri, vocabolo Collalto 115,
06056 Massa Martana (PG)
Tel. 0758947429 Fax 0758947429
Web: www.bellaumbria.net

A young family has renovated this old stone cottage in a tranquil position on a hill to provide simple, comfortable accommodation.

-

1 - - -

5 (x 2)

1 37,00 - 55,50 -

1(x 4)

1 - 7 - 1 - 7 495,00

ORSINI

at S. Maria in Pantano, vocabolo Casa Fanello,
06056 Massa Martana (PG)
Tel. 075889140 Fax 0758950498
Web: www.orsiniagriturismo.it

This farm, in an area of historical and artistic interest, has made available small apartments with kitchenettes in the converted storerooms.

-

1 - - -

\-
1 - - - -

7(x 2)
1 - 7 - 1 105,00 7 -

Monte Castello di Vibio

Agrincontri

at Doglio, S. Maria Apparita,
06057 Monte Castello di Vibio (PG)
Tel. 0758749610 Fax 0758780014
Web: www.agrincontri.com

This rural complex on a farm where large game is raised offers accommodation that will meet a wide range of different requirements.

\-
1 - - - -

12 (x 2/4)
1 50,00 - 70,00 -

\-
1 - 7 - 1 - 7 -

Fattoria di Vibio

at Doglio, vocabolo Buchella 9,
06057 Monte Castello di Vibio (PG)
Tel. 0758749607 Fax 0758780014
Web: www.fattoriadivibio.com

In the Monte Peglia Nature Park, splendidly restored stone farmhouses offer their guests well-kept gardens, an elegant restaurant and a warm welcome.

\-
1 - - - -

14 (x 2)
1 - - 90,00 -

\-
1 - 7 - 1 - 7 -

Montecchio

Le Casette

vocabolo Le Casette, 05020 Montecchio (TR)
Tel. 0744957645 Fax 0744950500
Web: www.pomurlovecchio-lecasette.it

This hill farm includes a number of renovated stone farmhouses surrounded by large well-kept gardens with roses and other colourful flowers.

\-
1 - - - -

18 (x 1/4)
1 - - 60,00 -

1 - 7 - 1 - 7 -

Montefalco

Camiano Piccolo

via Camiano Piccolo 5, 06036 Montefalco (PG)
Tel. 0742379492 Fax 0742371077
Web: www.camianopicolo.com

These 16th-century farmhouses have been renovated without spoiling their original appearance; the carefully furnished rooms and apartments are located in the converted furnace area and barn.

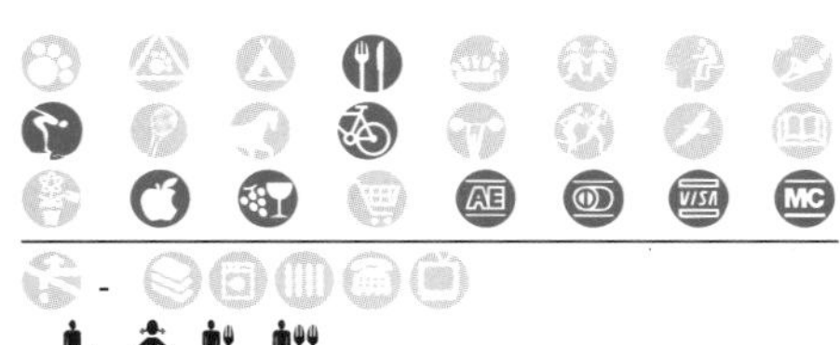

1 - - -

8 (x 1/2)

1 60,00 40,00 72,00 -

3(x 4)

1 - 7 - 1 - 7 1.000,00

Monteleone d'Orvieto

Miravalle

at Cornieto 2,
05017 Monteleone d'Orvieto (TR)
Tel. 0763835309 Fax 0763835309
Web: www.poggiomiravalle.com

In the open countryside, the accommodation is in a carefully renovated and very peaceful stone farmhouse, surrounded by olives, vines and woods.

1 - - -

1 - - -

6 (x 2/3)

1 - 7 - 1 114,00 7 725,00

Monte Santa Maria Tiberina

Petralta

at Petralta 15,
06010 Monte Santa Maria Tiberina (PG)
Tel. 0758570228 Fax 0758570228
E-mail: agripetralta@libero.it

There's a warm welcome in this typical Umbrian stone farmhouse; the rooms have panoramic views and are furnished in the traditional rural style.

2 (x 2/4)

1 31,00 - 55,00 -

2 (x 2/4)

1 34,00 - 62,00 -

2(x 4)

1 - 7 - 1 104,00 7 -

Montone

Civitella di Montone

at Carpini, vocabolo Civitella,
06014 Montone (PG)
Tel. 0759306358 Fax 0759306358
Web: www.agriturismo-civitella.com

'Relaxation, peace and a magnificent view'. This farmhouse, originally a 13th-century castle, preserves its original atmosphere, but offers its guests all modern comforts.

-

1 - - -

7 (x 2)

1 - - 61,00 -

-

1 - 7 - 1 - 7 -

Narni

Colle Abramo delle Vigne

at Vigne, strada di Colle Abramo 34,
05030 Narni (TR)
Tel. 0744796428 Fax 0744796428
Web: www.colleabramo.com

This establishment has accommodation in rooms and apartments furnished in traditional Umbrian style with verandas giving onto the garden.

-

1 - - -

2 (x 2)

1 50,00 - - -

7 (x 2/4)

1 50,00 7 - 1 - 7 -

Poder Novo

at San Liberato, strada Ortana Vecchia 2/V,
05027 Narni (TR)
Tel. 0744702005 Fax 0744702006
Web: www.podernovo.com

This farmhouse, set amid olives and an oak-wood, has rooms with a pleasant atmosphere and rustic furniture, and is also equipped for holidays for groups.

-

1 - - -

-

1 - - -

10 (x 2/4)

1 - 7 - 1 145,00 7 930,00

Nocera Umbra

La Lupa

at Colpertana, 06025 Nocera Umbra (PG)
Tel. 0742813539 Fax 0742813679
Web: www.agriturismo.com/lalupa

In this beautiful stone building standing on a hill there are rustically refined rooms for a holiday where the accent is on peace and quiet, and good food.

-

1 - - -

6 (x 2/4)

1 36,50 - 62,00 -

-

1 - 7 - 1 - 7 -

NORCIA

IL CASALE NEL PARCO

at Fontevena, 06046 Norcia (PG)
Tel. **0743816481** Fax **0743816481**
Web: **www.casalenelparco.com**

This elegant establishment is located close to the Monti Sibillini National Park, with a splendid view of Monte Patino. It's ideal for a holiday with the emphasis on all things authentic.

\-

1 - - -

8 (x 1/2)   

1 35,00 - 55,00 -

\-

1 - 7 - 1 - 7 -

ORVIETO

FATTORIA DI TITIGNANO

at Prodo, via Centro 7, 05018 Orvieto (TR)
Tel. **0763308000** Fax **0763308002**
Web: **www.titignano.it**

In a medieval village with a 12th-century castle, furnished rooms in rustic style are available; the management is professional and delicious local dishes are served.

\-

1 - - -

8 (x 2/4)  

1 45,00 - 57,00 -

\-

1 - 7 - 1 - 7 -

LA CACCIATA

at La Cacciata 6, 05010 Orvieto (TR)
Tel. **0763305481** Fax **0763300892**
Web: **www.argoweb.it/cacciata**

The establishment has a number of carefully restored farm buildings, a splendid swimming pool and a first-rate centre for tourism on horseback.

2 (x 2)

1 29,70 - 51,65 -

11 (x 2)

1 29,70 - 51,65 -

\-

1 - 7 - 1 - 7 -

LOCANDA ROSATI

at Buonviaggio, 05010 Orvieto (TR)
Tel. **0763217314** Fax **0763217314**
Web: **www.locandarosati.orvieto.tr.it**

The road that climbs up from Orvieto to Lake Bolsena passes this 19th-century farmhouse, which combines the rustic fascination of wood and stone with elegant furnishings.

\-

1 - - -

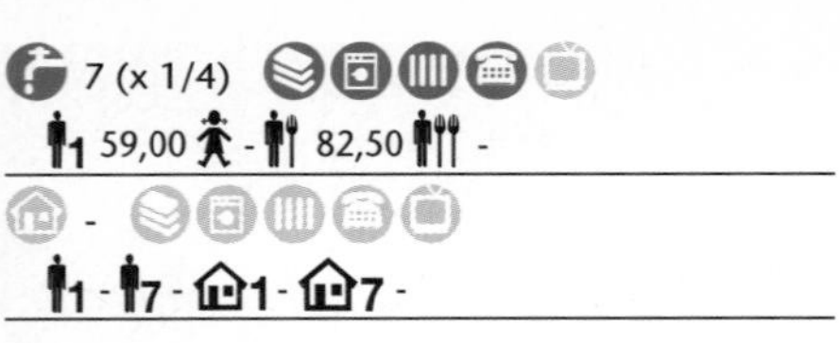

San Giorgio

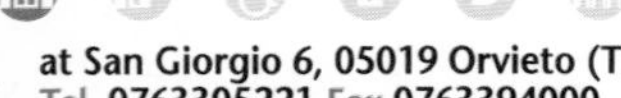

at San Giorgio 6, 05019 Orvieto (TR)
Tel. 0763305221 Fax 0763394000
Web: www.bellaumbria.net/agriturismo_sangiorgio

The apartments - in the main building, its outbuildings, a cottage near the little lake and a former mill - have recently been renovated and furnished with good taste.

-
-
9 (x 2/4)
1 - 7 - 1 130,00 7 -

Tenuta di Corbara

at Corbara 7, 05019 Orvieto (TR)
Tel. 0763304003 Fax 0763304152
Web: www.tenutadicorbara.it

In unspoilt natural surroundings, accommodation is available in large stone farmhouses that have been renovated; the comfortable rooms have period furniture and splendid views.

11 (x 1/2)
1 36,00 - 57,00 -
3(x 4)
1 - 7 - 1 191,00 7 1.343,00

Panicale

La Fonte

at Migliaiolo, via Vannucci 15,
06064 Panicale (PG)
Tel. 075837469 Fax 075837737
Web: www.agriturismolafonte.it

In the countryside near Panicale, this large farm, with the owner's house and a series of outbuildings, has apartments varying in size and style.

6(x 4)
1 - 7 - 1 - 7 800,00

La Rosa Canina

at Casalini, via dei Mandorli 23,
06064 Panicale (PG)
Tel. 0758350660 Fax 0758350660
Web: www.larosacanina.it

Simplicity and good food are the main attractions of this charming cottage adorned with roses and climbing plants, and furnished in traditional rural style.

8 (x 2)
1 - - 60,00 -

- 1 - 7 - 1 - 7 -

Montali

at Tavernelle, via Montali 23, 06068 Panicale (PG)
Tel. 0758350680 Fax 0758350144
Web: www.montalionline.com

The excellent vegetarian food, prepared by two professional chefs, and the rather oriental atmosphere give this establishment a truly unique character.

- 1 - - -

10 (x 2/4)

1 - - 77,50 -

- 1 - 7 - 1 - 7 -

Parrano

Il Poggiolo di Parrano

contrada Bagno 43, S.P. (provincial road) Parranese at km 8,5, 05010 Parrano (TR)
Tel. 0763838471 Fax 0763838776
Web: www.ilpoggiolo.com

This 19th-century farmhouse has four large apartments, with period furniture, a rustic kitchen and a fireplace; there's also a Jacuzzi.

- 1 - - -

1 (x 2)

1 50,00 - - -

4(x 2)

1 - 7 - 1 100,00 7 -

Passignano sul Trasimeno

Casale Poggio Colpiccione

at Col Piccione 39,
06065 Passignano sul Trasimeno (PG)
Tel. 075845371 Fax 075845371
Web: www.poggiocolpiccione.it

This farm is in a panoramic position just behind Passignano; the atmosphere is rustic, while the welcome is particularly warm.

- 1 - - -

- 1 - - -

10 (x 2/3)

1 35,00 7 - 1 - 7 -

Locanda del Galluzzo

at Trecine 12/A,
06060 Passignano sul Trasimeno (PG)
Tel. 075845352 Fax 075845352
Web: www.locandadelgalluzzo.it

This is a fine modern building modelled on the old Umbrian farmhouses. The guests are accommodated in the main block or in the adjacent one-room apartments.

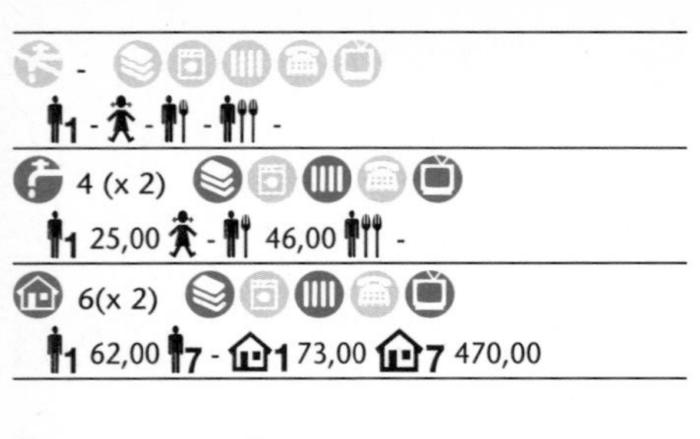

-
1 - - -

4 (x 2)

1 25,00 - 46,00 -

6(x 2)

1 62,00 7 - 1 73,00 7 470,00

Poggio del Belveduto

at Campori di Sopra, via S. Donato 65,
06065 Passignano sul Trasimeno (PG)
Tel. 075829076 Fax 0758478014
Web: www.poggiodelbelveduto.it

A stay at this establishment is an inviting prospect for those fond of touring on horseback. The restaurant-cum-bar serves delicious local dishes.

-
1 - - -

-
1 - - -

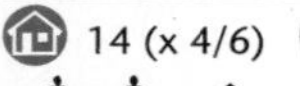
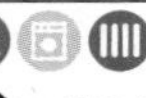

14 (x 4/6)

1 - 7 - 1 - 7 750,00

Perugia

Agricola Arna

at Civitella d'Arna, 06080 Perugia
Tel. 075602896 Fax 068083617
Web: www.agricolarna.it

This accommodation is in a fine country house with period furniture and a large 'English garden'. The main town and its attractions are just ten minutes' drive away.

-
1 - - -

5 (x 2/4)

1 31,00 - - -

5(x 3)

1 31,00 7 - 1 - 7 -

Case della Nonna

at Fratticiola Selvatica, 06080 Perugia
Tel. 0755915347 Fax 0755915322
Web: www.casedellanonna.com

In the hills, a farmhouse is surrounded by olive groves, oak-woods and large pastures. The rooms and apartments are comfortable, while the cuisine is homely, but carefully prepared.

-
1 - - -

12 (x 1/2)

1 45,00 - 65,00 -

1(x 3)

1 - 7 - 1 - 7 600,00

Il Covone

at Ponte Pattoli, strada Fratticiola 2, 06085 Perugia
Tel. 075694140 Fax 075694503
Web: www.covone.com

Guests eat with the owners in this beautiful medieval villa with frescoes, valuable paintings and a patio shaded by ancient trees.

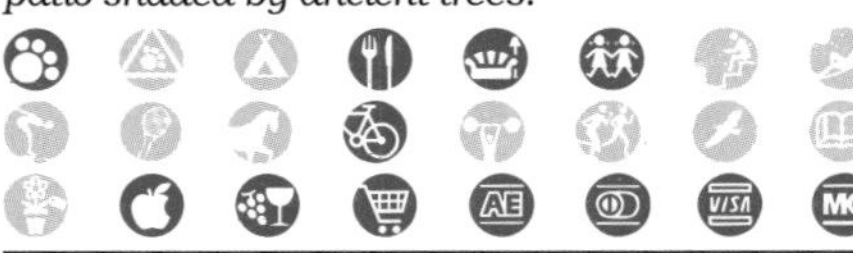

-
1 - - -

12 (x 2)

1 42,00 - 65,00 -

-
1 - 7 - 1 - 7 -

Il Mandoleto

E

at Capanne, strada Mandoleto 15, 06071 Perugia
Tel. 0755293119 Fax 0755294090
Web: www.mandoleto.it

A renovated farmhouse in the peaceful Umbrian countryside has tastefully furnished apartments and rooms with modern comforts.

\-

1 - - -

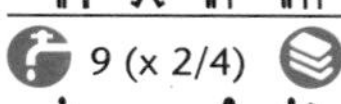

9 (x 2/4)

1 37,50 - - -

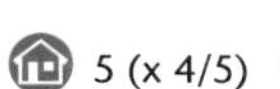  

5 (x 4/5)

1 - 7 - 1 95,00 7 630,00

Poggiolo

E D

at Poggio delle Corti, 06072 Perugia
Tel. 075695236 Fax 0758787222
Web: www.viadelsole.it

Shaded by old trees, the various buildings where the guests stay are scattered in the park, which is surrounded by 45 hectares of woods. Weeks of tourism on horseback are organised for children.

\-

1 - - -

5 (x 2)

1 46,00 - 68,00 -

7 (x 2/4)

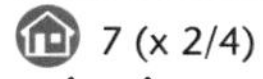  

1 - 7 - 1 - 7 1.343,00

Piegaro

Bulletta

E

at Castiglion Fosco, 06060 Piegaro (PG)
Tel. 075839259 Fax 0758397035
Web: web.tiscali.it/castiglionfosco

This rural accommodation is in three comfortably renovated 17th-century cottages, with large open spaces reserved for the guests.

\-

1 - - -

\-

1 - - -

7(x 3)

1 - 7 - 1 - 7 430,00

Piazzola alla Quercia

E D

vocabolo Piazzola 48,
06066 Piegaro (PG)
Tel. 0758358455 Fax 0758359621
Web: www.piazzola.it

Two stone cottages splendidly restored are at the centre of a large farm where the crops are grown with organic methods. The pork served by the restaurant is obtained from the Cinta Senese pig.

 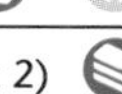 

2 (x 2)

1 25,00 - 47,00 -

5 (x 2)

1 27,00 - 52,00 -

4 (x 2/3)

1 - 7 - 1 - 7 598,00

Pietralunga

La Cerqua

E

case San Salvatore, 06026 Pietralunga (PG)
Tel. 0759460283 Fax 0759462033
Web: www.cerqua.it

Set amid pasture-land, organic crops and oak-woods, this former monastery, dating from the 14th century, houses the 'Magician's Garden', an open-air ecological workshop.

\-

1 - - -

8 (x 2/4)

1 37,00 - 54,00 -

2 (x 2/4)

1 - 7 - 1 100,00 7 -

Porano

L'Uva e le Stelle

at Boccetta, 05010 Porano (TR)
Tel. **0763374781** Fax **0763375923**
Web: **www.uvaelestelle.com**

On this estate, the production of the famous Orvieto wine dates back to the time of the Etruscans; accommodation is available in a stone farmhouse, furnished tastefully.

\-

1 - - -

\-

1 - - -

6(x 3)

1 - 7 - 1 147,19 7 759,20

Preci

Il Collaccio

at Collaccio, 06047 Preci (PG)
Tel. **0743939084** Fax **0743939094**
Web: **www.ilcollaccio.com**

There's accommodation to suit everybody here, ranging from the fascinating Locanda del Porcellino to ridge tents; in the Casale Grande there's a restaurant, with local produce on sale.

\-

1 - - -

11 (x 2/4)

1 40,00 - 55,00 -

5(x 4)

1 - 7 - 1 - 7 805,00

San Gemini

Valle Antica e Prata Prima

strada di Valle Antica, 05029 San Gemini (TR)
Tel. **0744241441** Fax **0744430210**
Web: **space.tin.it/viaggi/xpontegg**

The two farmhouses, surrounded by vineyards, olive groves and woods, look out over the beautiful countryside extending from San Gemini to Narni.

-
1 - - -

-
1 - - -

8(x 4)
1 - 7 - 1 90,00 7 -

SANT'ANATOLIA DI NARCO

LE VAIE

at Vaie 1/A,
06040 Sant'Anatolia di Narco (PG)
Tel. **0743613269** Fax **0743613269**

Surrounded by woods of downy and turkey oaks, those who stay in this recently renovated house have direct contact with life on the farm and the animals.

-
1 - - -

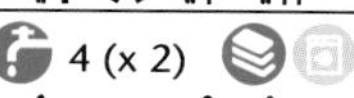

4 (x 2)
1 18,00 - 31,00 -

-
1 - 7 - 1 - 7 -

SAN VENANZO

BELVEDERE

at Pornella, vocabolo Belvedere 27,
05010 San Venanzo (TR)
Tel. **075875411** Fax **075875411**
E-mail: **agribelvedere@iol.it**

For a holiday close to nature, accommodation is available in a modern house that's large and comfortable, and ideal for groups.

-
1 - - -

-
1 - - -

1(x 10)
1 - 7 - 1 - 7 700,00

SANTA MARIA

vocabolo Cerreto Alto 57,
05010 San Venanzo (TR)
Tel. **075875331** Fax **0758790291**
Web: **www.agrisantamaria.it**

Located on a large hill farm close to the main road from Perugia to Orvieto, this 17th-century house has been renovated, combining tradition with the principles of ecological architecture.

-
1 - - -

1 (x 2)
1 30,00 - - -

6 (x 2/6)
1 - 7 - 1 60,00 7 -

SPELLO

LE DUE TORRI

at Limiti di Spello, via Torre Quadrano 1,
06038 Spello (PG)
Tel. **0742651249** Fax **0743270273**
Web: **www.seeumbria.com**

Accommodation is available in two white and pink stone farmhouses that have been carefully renovated, with special attention being given to the furnishings.

1 - - -

9 (x 2/4)

1 40,00 - 65,00 -

6 (x 2/3)

1 - 7 - 1 100,00 7 697,00

Spoleto

Cirimpiccolo

at Madonna di Lugo 42, 06049 Spoleto (PG)
Tel. 0743223780 Fax 0743223782
Web: www.spoletorurale.it

Just a short distance from the town, famous for the Festival dei Due Mondi, this tranquil modern farmhouse with all modern comforts is ideal for a rural holiday.

-

1 - - -

15 (x 2/4)

1 28,50 - - -

1(x 8)

1 - 7 - 1 155,00 7 -

Convento di Agghielli

at Pompagnano, 06049 Spoleto (PG)
Tel. 0743225010 Fax 0743225010
Web: www.agghielli.it

Just a few kilometres from Spoleto, in a hundred hectares of meadows and woods, a monastic complex is now used for tourist accommodation; the rooms are large and elegant.

-

1 - - -

16 (x 2/4)

1 - - 105,00 -

-

1 - 7 - 1 - 7 -

Il Casale Grande

at Beroide, 06040 Spoleto (PG)
Tel. 0743275780 Fax 0743270273
Web: www.seeumbria.com

This large 19th-century house, which has been carefully renovated, is in the middle of a large farm where guests can see how olive oil is produced.

-

1 - - -

-

1 - - -

4(x 2)

1 - 7 - 1 109,00 7 671,00

Il Pecoraro

at Strettura, S.S. (state road) Flaminia at km 110, 06040 Spoleto (PG)
Tel. 0743229697 Fax 0743229697
Web: www.ilpecoraro.it

The farm is an excellent base for sports activities: the area is ideal for hiking and speleology, as well as canyoning and rafting on the River Nera.

-

1 - - -

11 (x 2)

1 31,00 - 47,00 -

-

1 - 7 - 1 - 7 -

La Miniera

at Cascinano, 06049 Spoleto (PG)
Tel. 0743261298 Fax 37423931183
Web: www.agrispoleto.it

On this large farm (about 200 hectares), guests may wander amid olives, vines and chestnut trees, orchards and cornfields, pigs and scurrying poultry.

-

1 - - -

-

1 - - -

6(x 3)

1 - 7 - 1 100,00 7 650,00

L'Ulivo

at Bazzano Inferiore, 06049 Spoleto (PG)
Tel. 074349031 Fax 074349031
Web: www.agrulivo.com

This is an area of great historical and environmental interest. Accommodation is available in a cottage that has been tastefully renovated by the owner and is surrounded by a large garden.

-

1 - - -

2 (x 1/2)

1 40,00 - - -

4 (x 2/4)

1 - 7 - 1 140,00 7 750,00

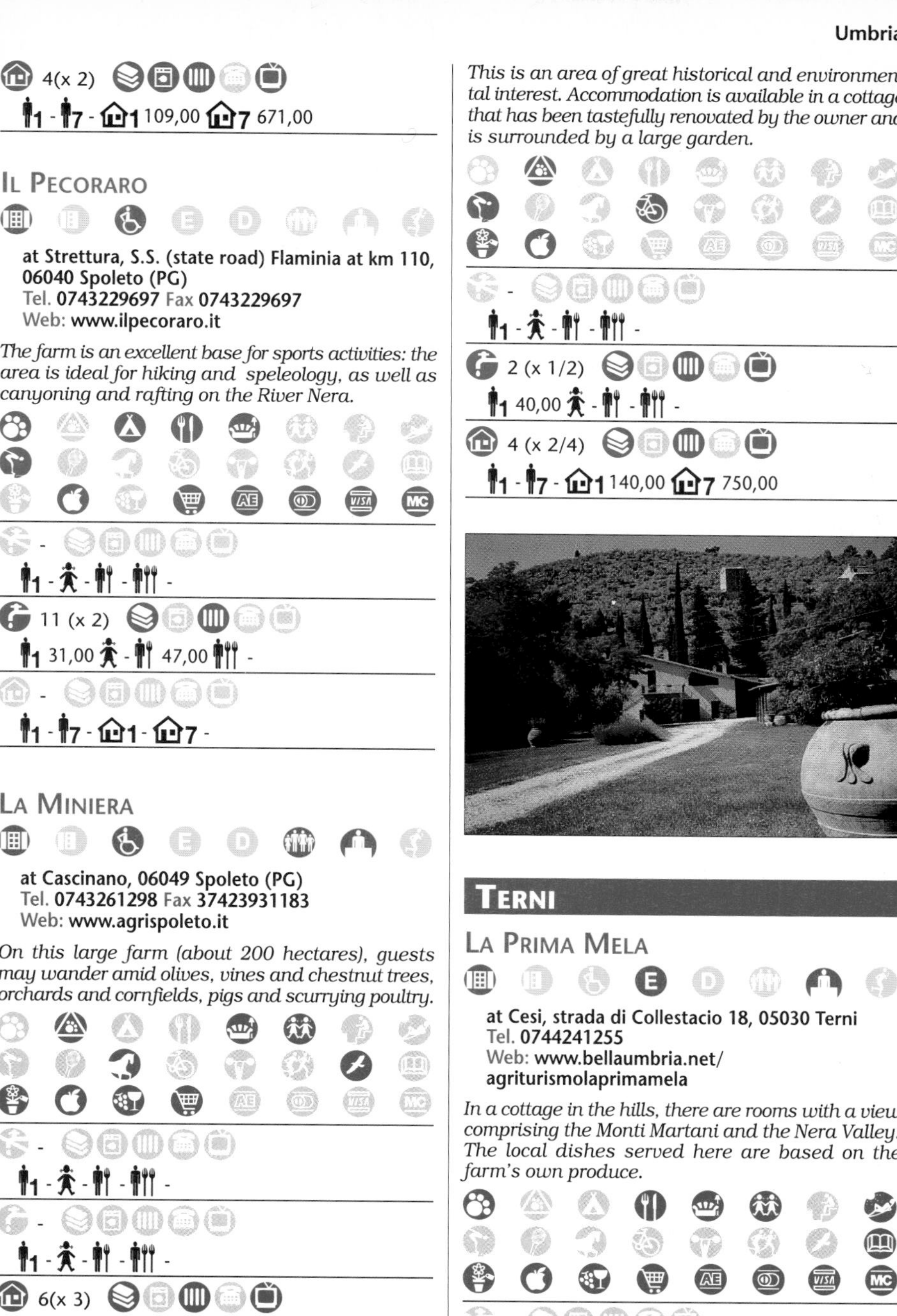

Terni

La Prima Mela

at Cesi, strada di Collestacio 18, 05030 Terni
Tel. 0744241255
Web: www.bellaumbria.net/agriturismolaprimamela

In a cottage in the hills, there are rooms with a view comprising the Monti Martani and the Nera Valley. The local dishes served here are based on the farm's own produce.

-

1 - - -

5 (x 1/2)

1 33,00 - 52,00 -

-

1 - 7 - 1 - 7 -

Todi

Castello di Porchiano

at Porchiano, 06059 Todi (PG)
Tel. 0758853127 Fax 0635347308
Web: agriturismotodi.umbria.com/porchiano

In a panoramic medieval village, a number of carefully renovated stone buildings have been converted into simple but elegant self-contained apartments.

-

1 - - -

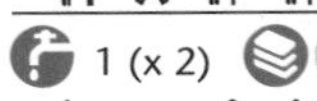

1 (x 2)

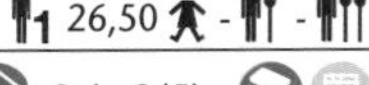

1 26,50 - - -

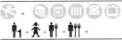

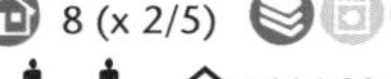

8 (x 2/5)

1 - 7 - 1 104,00 7 -

Piantoneto II

at San Damiano 5,
06059 Todi (PG)
Tel. 0758944524 Fax 0758944524
Web: www.agriturismotodi.umbria.com

Set amid olive groves, this late 19th-century farmhouse offers its guests a kitchen and living-room furnished in traditional style.

-

1 - - -

4 (x 1/2)

1 28,50 - 41,50 -

-

1 - 7 - 1 - 7 -

Tenuta di Canonica

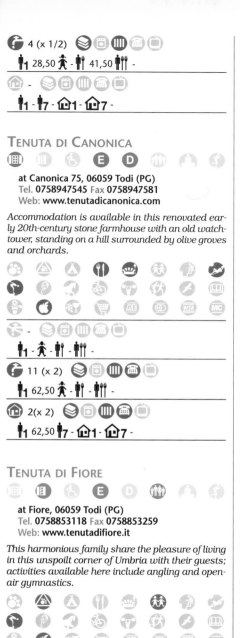

at Canonica 75, 06059 Todi (PG)
Tel. 0758947545 Fax 0758947581
Web: www.tenutadicanonica.com

Accommodation is available in this renovated early 20th-century stone farmhouse with an old watchtower, standing on a hill surrounded by olive groves and orchards.

-

1 - - - -

11 (x 2)

1 62,50 - - -

2(x 2)

1 62,50 7 - 1 - 7 -

Tenuta di Fiore

at Fiore, 06059 Todi (PG)
Tel. 0758853118 Fax 0758853259
Web: www.tenutadifiore.it

This harmonious family share the pleasure of living in this unspoilt corner of Umbria with their guests; activities available here include angling and open-air gymnastics.

-

1 - - - -

-

1 - - - -

4 (x 2/4)

1 - 7 - 1 155,00 7 1.085,00

Torgiano

I Mori Gelsi

via Entrata 37, 06089 Torgiano (PG)
Tel. 075982192 Fax 0744421819
Web: www.spinolaonline.it

Part vineyard and part game farm, this establishment offers accommodation in an old, but splendidly renovated, oratory and in a number of well-kept cottages.

-

1 - - - -

-

1 - - - -

3 (x 2/6)

1 - 7 - 1 - 7 910,00

Poggio alle Vigne

via Montespinello, 06089 Torgiano (PG)
Tel. 075982994 Fax 0759887014
Web: www.lungarotti.it

Accommodation is available in a 17th-century farmhouse converted into ten attractive apartment without altering the original forms and materials in any way.

-

1 - - - -

-

1 - - - -

10(x 3)

1 - 7 - 1 - 7 796,00

TREVI

I MANDORLI

at Bovara, Fondaccio 6, 06039 Trevi (PG)
Tel. 074278669 Fax 074278669
Web: www.seeumbria.com/mandorli

The former owner's house is in the centre of a rural complex comprising a number of cottages built around a square with small grassy areas dotted with flowers.

\-

1 - - -

3 (x 2)

1 35,00 - 55,00 -

3 (x 2/4)

1 - 7 - 1 135,00 7 -

VILLA SILVANA

at Parrano, via Fonte Pigge 6, 06032 Trevi (PG)
Tel. 0755053642 Fax 0755053642
Web: www.villasilvana.it

Surrounded by an olive grove close to the walls of a medieval village, this establishment has three cottages and wooden chalets available for its guests.

\-

1 - - -

3 (x 2)

1 40,00 28,00 - -

12 (x 2/6)

1 - 7 - 1 140,00 7 840,00

TUORO SUL TRASIMENO

LA DOGANA

via Dogana 4, 06069 Tuoro sul Trasimeno (PG)
Tel. 0758230158 Fax 0758230252
Web: www.agriturismodogana.it

The stone farmhouses surrounding the complex have been renovated and divided into small apartments furnished with period furniture.

\-

1 - - - -

\-

1 - - - -

13 (x 2/3)

1 - 7 - 1 75,00 7 500,00

Montemelino

via Fonte Sant'Angelo 15,
06069 Tuoro sul Trasimeno (PG)
Tel. 0758230127 Fax 0758230156
E-mail: margret@inwind.it

In the centre of the farm, old stone farmhouses, with terraces and verandas, have been converted to provide six apartments where the accent is on tranquillity and comfort.

\-

1 - - - -

\-

1 - - - -

6 (x 2/4)

1 - 7 - 1 - 7 439,00

Parco Fiorito

at Piazzano, via C.S. Piazzano 33,
06069 Tuoro sul Trasimeno (PG)
Tel. 075825340 Fax 075825340
Web: www.parcofiorito.it/fiorito

The farm surrounds a renovated 16th-century former monastery, set amid woods. The accommodation is in three farmhouses, embellished with wood and terracotta.

\-

1 - - - -

4 (x 2)

1 50,00 25,00 73,00 -

6 (x 4/6)

1 - 7 - 1 - 7 886,00

Umbertide

Cignano I

at Preggio, vocabolo Cignano 147,
06060 Umbertide (PG)
Tel. 0759410292 Fax 0759410292
Web: www.cignano.com

In a peaceful, sunny position, these farm cottages are ideal for a relaxing holiday - although the social attractions of Perugia are only 25 kilometres away.

2 (x 1/2)

1 42,00 - - -

2 (x 2)

1 42,00 - - -

4 (x 2/4)

1 - 7 - 1 110,00 7 -

Fattoria del Cerretino

at Calzolaro, via Colonnata 3, 06010 Umbertide (PG)
Tel. 0759302166 Fax 0759302166
Web: www.cerretino.it

The three farmhouses form a small hamlet in the hills. Around the kitchen garden, which is at the guests' disposal, there are 20 hectares of cultivated land mixed with pine and chestnut woods.

-
1 - - -
3 (x 2)
1 35,00 - 61,00 -
7 (x 2/4)
1 - 7 - 1 - 7 830,00

La Chiusa

at Niccone, S.S. (state road) Niccone at km 2.3, 06019 Umbertide (PG)
Tel. 0759410848 Fax 0759410774
Web: www.lachiusa.com

This is a 19th-century farmhouse in a verdant setting. Accommodation is available in two suites and three small apartments. The Ristorantino serves dishes prepared with the farm's organic produce.

-
1 - - -
2 (x 4)
1 50,00 - 85,00 -
3 (x 2/4)
1 - 7 - 1 100,00 7 -

Nestore

at Verna, 06019 Umbertide (PG)
Tel. 0759302126 Fax 0759271001
Web: www.nestoreholidays.com

The Nestore stream flows between the hills, evoking both the domestic pleasures of the accommodation and the prospect of an active holiday.

-
1 - - -
-
1 - - -
8 (x 2/4)
1 - 7 - 1 180,00 7 800,00

Valfabbrica

Il Castello di Giomici

at Giomici, piazza Sant'Attanasio 1, 06029 Valfabbrica (PG)
Tel. 0755058028 Fax 0755003285
Web: www.ilcastellodigiomici.it

This romantic medieval castle dominates the Chiascio valley; the accommodation is in both the main building and the old stone farmhouses nearby.

-
1 - - -
-
1 - - -

14 (x 2/5)

1 - 7 - 1 255,00 7 1.240,00

La Fontanella

vocabolo Capanni 3,
06029 Valfabbrica (PG)
Tel. 075909065 Fax 075909065
Web: www.lafontanella.com

Surrounded by greenery in a panoramic position, guests stay in the simple rooms of a stone farmhouse, where they can enjoy the authentic dishes prepared by Signora Paola.

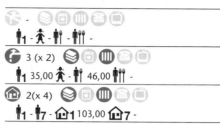

1 - - -

3 (x 2)

1 35,00 - 46,00 -

2(x 4)

1 - 7 - 1 103,00 7 -

The Martinelli Collection

Gian Lorenzo Bernini and the Roman Baroque context in the collection of a XX century scholar

Paintings, drawings, reliefs, medals of G.L. Bernini, A. Buonvicino, A. Algardi, A. Sacchi, C. Maratta

Times: 10,30-13,00 15,00-17,30; closed on tuesday
Tickets: Euro 3,00 / Euro 2,00 and Euro 1,00 reduced
free from 0 to 6 years of age
Guided tours and educational itineraries: infoline 199 101330

Information: Cultural Office of Perugia City Council: Tel. 0039 075 5772352
www.comune.perugia.it

AGRITURISMO TENUTA DI CORBARA

A vacation in the Agriturismo Tenuta di Corbara is just the occasion to discover Umbrian gastronomic tradition. We make all we offer to our hosts: meat, vegetables, extra virgin olive oil, Orvieto wine, honey, cheese, bread and pasta still hand made. Walking through ancient farms dominated bay large farmstead restructured following Umbrian peasant tradition, you'll discover our flavors and our nature. We are in Italy, near the city of Orvieto, in Umbria, an hour from Rome and Florence.

Orvieto - Terni - Umbria - Italy Tel. +39 0763.304003 Fax +39 0763.304152
Web: www.tenutadicorbara.it e-mail: info@tenutadicorbara.it

Loc. Cenerente
06134 Perugia - Italy
Tel. ++39. 075 690764
www.sanlorenzodellarabatta.com
E-mail: info@sanlorenzodellarabatta.com

Perched on a hiltop, set in the splendid Umbrian scenery of rolling hills, the whole complex is an ideal place to forget the stress of everyday life in one of Italy's most fascinating regions, renowned for its art, culture and scenery .
Its tranquil, evocative atmosphere make it the ideal place for the holiday of a lifetime.
At San Lorenzo della Rabatta guests can choose between accomrnodation of different sizes.
Each house tastefully recreates the environment of the past: vaulted ceilings, stone fireplaces, rooms painted in earth colours, co-ordinated country fabrics, rustic furniture and antiques.
On a more modern note, each house has a fully equipped kitchen and satellite TV. And of course, the views are stunning!

VALLE D'AOSTA

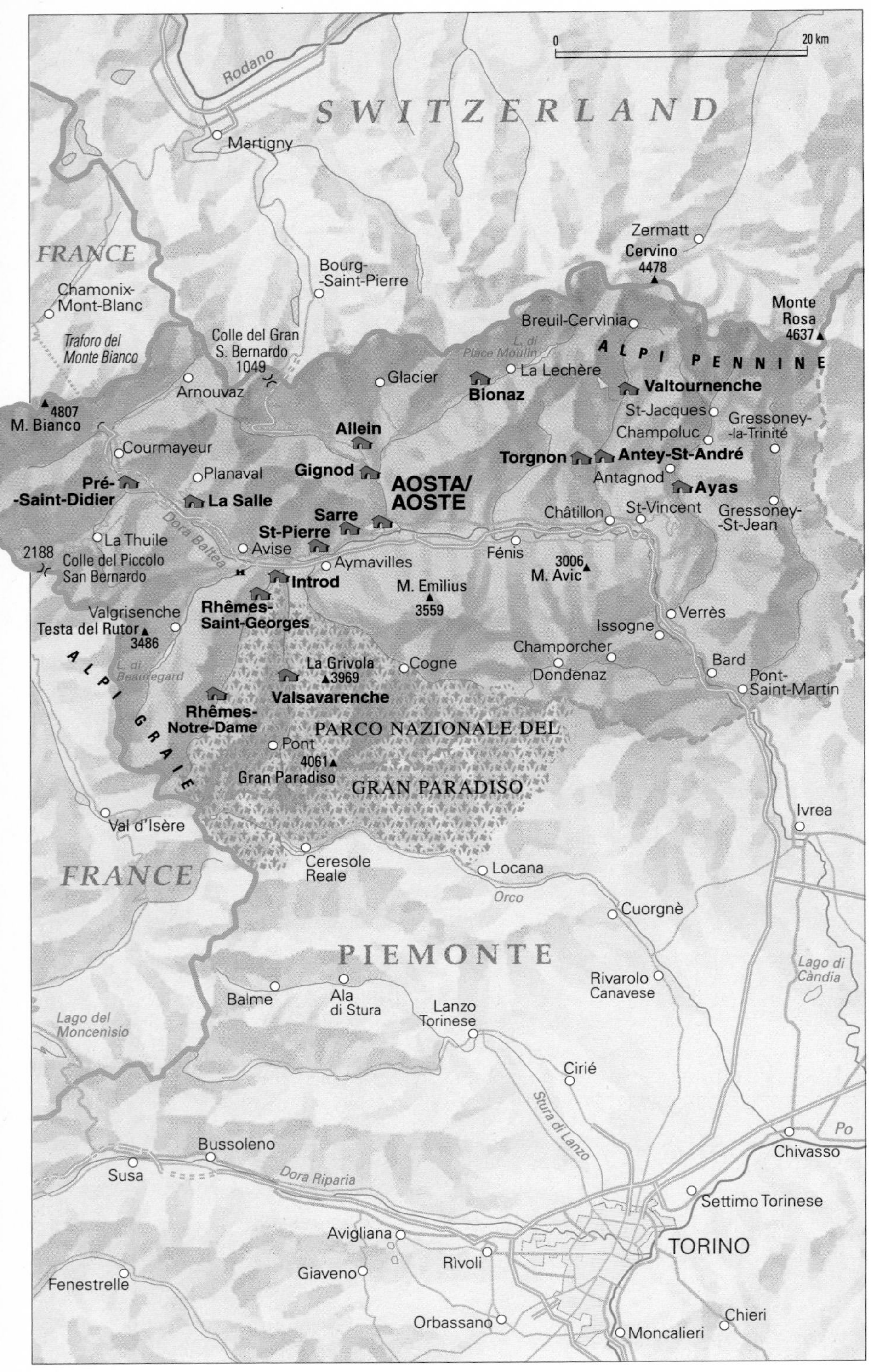

0
20 km
Rodano
SWITZERLAND
Martigny
FRANCE
Zermatt
Cervino
4478
Bourg-
-Saint-Pierre
Chamonix-
Mont-Blanc
Monte
Rosa
4637
Breuil-Cervìnia
Traforo del
Monte Bianco
Colle del Gran
S. Bernardo
1049
L. di
Place Moulin
ALPI PENNINE
La Lechère
Arnouvaz
Glacier
Bionaz
Valtournenche
4807
M. Bianco
St-Jacques
Gressoney-
-la-Trinité
Allein
Champoluc
Courmayeur
Torgnon
Antey-St-André
Gignod
Planaval
Antagnod
Pré-
-Saint-Didier
AOSTA/
AOSTE
Ayas
La Salle
Sarre
Châtillon
St-Vincent
Gressoney-
-St-Jean
St-Pierre
Dora Baltea
La Thuile
Avise
Fénis
2188
Colle del Piccolo
San Bernardo
Aymavilles
3006
M. Avic
Introd
M. Emilius
3559
Valgrisenche
Rhêmes-
Saint-Georges
Verrès
Testa del Rutor
3486
Issogne
ALPI GRAIE
Champorcher
L. di
Beauregard
La Grivola
3969
Cogne
Bard
Dondenaz
Pont-
Saint-Martin
Valsavarenche
Rhêmes-
Notre-Dame
PARCO NAZIONALE DEL
GRAN PARADISO
Pont
4061
Gran Paradiso
Ivrea
Val d'Isère
Ceresole
Reale
Locana
FRANCE
Orco
Cuorgnè
PIEMONTE
Rivarolo
Canavese
Lago di
Càndia
Balme
Ala
di Stura
Lanzo
Torinese
Lago del
Moncenisio
Ciriè
Stura di Lanzo
Po
Bussoleno
Chivasso
Susa
Dora Riparia
Settimo Torinese
Avigliana
TORINO
Rìvoli
Giaveno
Fenestrelle
Orbassano
Chieri
Moncalieri

Allein

Lo Ratelé

at Ville 33, 11010 Allein (AO)
Tel. 016578265 Fax 016578265

Accommodation is available in a three-storeyed farmhouse with flower-decked balconies. With its meadows, pastures and cultivated fields, the farm produces meat, eggs, butter and cheese.

\-

1 - - -

7 (x 2/4)

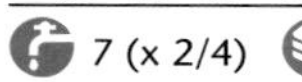

1 - - 39,00 -

\-

1 - 7 - 1 - 7 -

Antey-Saint-André

Au Jardin Fleuri

11020 Antey-Saint-André (AO)
Tel. 0166548372 Fax 0166548372

Set amid the imposing scenery of the Valtournenche, this farm, which has 22 hectares of land, produces milk, eggs, wine, vegetables and apples.

\-

1 - - -

\-

1 - - -

3 (x 4/6)

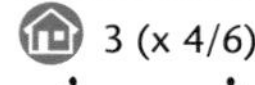

1 25,00 7 - 1 - 7 -

Aosta/Aoste

La Ferme

regione Chabloz 18, 11100 Aosta/Aoste
Tel. 0165551647

Just outside Aosta, amid market gardens, orchards and vineyards, an elegant chalet in stone and wood is located near the owner's house.

\-

1 - - -

\-

1 - - -

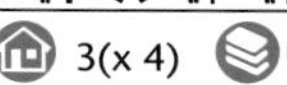

3(x 4)

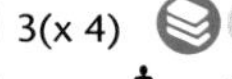

1 28,00 7 - 1 - 7 -

Plan d'Avie

at Arpuilles, 11100 Aosta/Aoste
Tel. 016551126

From the plateau, there's a splendid view of the mountains surrounding Aosta. A large white house accommodates guests in three large apartments on the first floor.

\-

1 - - -

\-

1 - - -

22,00 - 1 - 7 -

Ayas

Goïl

at Antagnod, 11020 Ayas (AO)
Tel. 0125306370

In a beautiful position on a slope with a view of Monte Rosa, this farm produces milk, butter and fontana cheese. The accommodation is in picturesque stone houses.

\-

1 - - -

3 (x 2/4)

1 - - 40,00 -

\-

1 - 7 - 1 - 7 -

Bionaz

La Renardière

at Perquis 3, 11010 Bionaz (AO)
Tel. 0165710887

In the charming Valpelline, this village is set amid the meadows of the Plan de Veyne. Guests sleep in a two-storeyed cottage and eat with the owners.

2 (x 2)

1 - - 40,00 -

2 (x 2/4)

1 - - 45,00 -

\-

1 - 7 - 1 - 7 -

Gignod

Le Myosotis

at Arliod 9, 11010 Gignod (AO)
Tel. 0165256893

The name (Myosotis) is Latin for forget-me-nots: it's an excellent choice for this large 19th-century house, which has been tastefully renovated to provide accommodation.

\-

1 - - -

4 (x 2)

1 35,00 - - -

\-

1 - 7 - 1 - 7 -

Introd

Plantey

at Villes Dessus 65, 11010 Introd (AO)
Tel. 016595531 Fax 0165920991

On the edge of the Gran Paradiso National Park, this white building stands in the middle of a small farm with a vegetable garden, orchard and meadows.

1 - - -

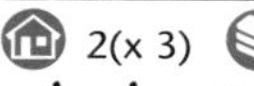

1 - - -

2(x 3)

1 - 7 - 1 46,00 7 -

La Salle

Le Perce Neige

at Château 39, 11015 La Salle (AO)
Tel. 0165862422

In the upper valley of the Dora Baltea, the farm stands on a mountainside in a panoramic position. The accommodation is in two charming buildings.

1 - - -

6 (x 2)

1 29,00 - -

1 - 7 - 1 - 7 -

Pré-Saint-Didier

Petit Mont Blanc

at Verrand, avenue Dent du Geant 24,
11010 Pré-Saint-Didier (AO)
Tel. 0165845083 Fax 0165845083

Near to Courmayeur, this farm has a view of Mont Blanc and opportunities for a wide range of excursions. Guests may take part in the haymaking or help to look after the vegetable garden and animals.

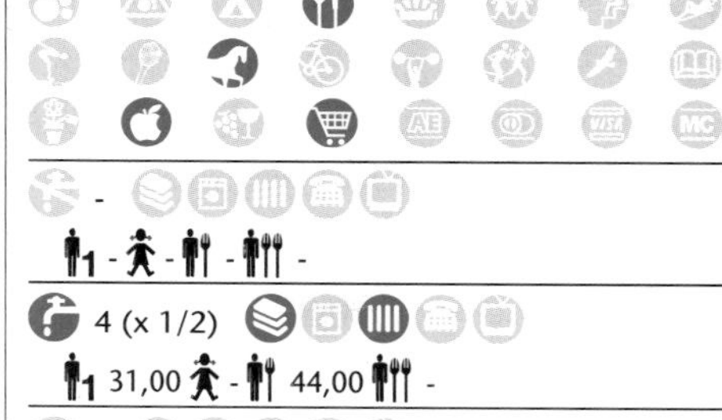

1 - - -

4 (x 1/2)

1 31,00 - 44,00 -

1 - 7 - 1 - 7 -

Rhêmes-Notre-Dame

Lo Sabot

at Bruil, 11010 Rhêmes-Notre-Dame (AO)
Tel. 0165936150

In the centre of the village, located in a large basin full of meadows in the Valle di Rhêmes, is this large chalet with balconies and a splendid display of geraniums.

1 - - -

4 (x 2)

1 25,00 - 35,00 -

1 - 7 - 1 - 7 -

Rhêmes-Saint-Georges

Edelweiss

at Melignon, 11010 Rhêmes-Saint-Georges (AO)
Tel. 0165767160
Web: www.aostanet.com/edelweiss

In a hamlet with just a few houses amid the larches, this old stone building offers accommodation to tourists coming to the Valle di Rhêmes to experiece life on a farm.

\-
1 - - -
\-
1 - - -
3(x 3)
1 18,08 7 - 1 - 7 -

Le Vieux Creton

at Creton, 11010 Rhêmes-Saint-Georges (AO)
Tel. 0165907612
E-mail: r.therisod@netvallee.it

Located in the Gran Paradiso National Park at the point where the woods give way to the high pastures, this accommodation is ideal for nature-lovers.

\-
1 - - -
\-
1 - - -

4 (x 2/5)
1 20,00 7 - 1 - 7 -

Saint-Pierre

L'Abri

at Vetan Dessous 83, 11010 Saint-Pierre (AO)
Tel. 0165908830 Fax 0165908228
E-mail: abri.agriturist@tiscali.it

On the plateau overlooking the Dora Baltea, this romantic stone cottage has rooms with period furniture, a small dining-room and a kitchenette.

\-
1 - - -

6 (x 1/2)

1 28,00 - - -
\-
1 - 7 - 1 - 7 -

Les Ecureuils

at Homené Dessus 8, 11010 Saint-Pierre (AO)
Tel. 0165903831 Fax 0165909849
Web: www.lesecureuils.it

Accommodation is available in a remarkably well-kept 18th-century rural complex where the main activity is stock-raising; it supplies the restaurant with wholesome produce.

5 (x 1/2)
1 28,00 - 41,00 -
\-
1 - - -
\-
1 - 7 - 1 - 7 -

Sarre

La Grandze de Moueine

at Lalex 1, 11010 Sarre (AO)
Tel. 0165257092 Fax 0165257092
E-mail: lamouein@tin.it

Within sight of Sarre Castle, this 18th-century house (the name, in patois, means the 'nun's farmhouse') still has some elements of its original architecture.

-

1 - - -

-

1 - - -

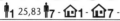

3(x 4)

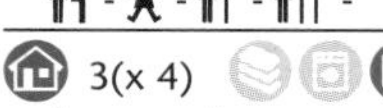

1 25,83 7 - 1 - 7 -

Torgnon

Boule de Neige

at Mazod, 11020 Torgnon (AO)
Tel. 0166540617 Fax 0166540956
E-mail: ferme.perrin@tiscali.it

At an altitude of 1300 m, this small hameau (hamlet) stands on a very well positioned plateau. This fine rural building is in stone with wooden balconies.

-

1 - - -

2 (x 2)

1 28,00 - 38,00 -

2(x 4)

1 - 7 - 1 - 7 413,00

Valsavarenche

Lo Mayen

at Bien, 11010 Valsavarenche (AO)
Tel. 0165905735

The farm comprises 40 hectares of meadows, pastures and woods in the heart of the Gran Paradiso National Park. Located near the river, the farmhouse is surrounded by larches and firs.

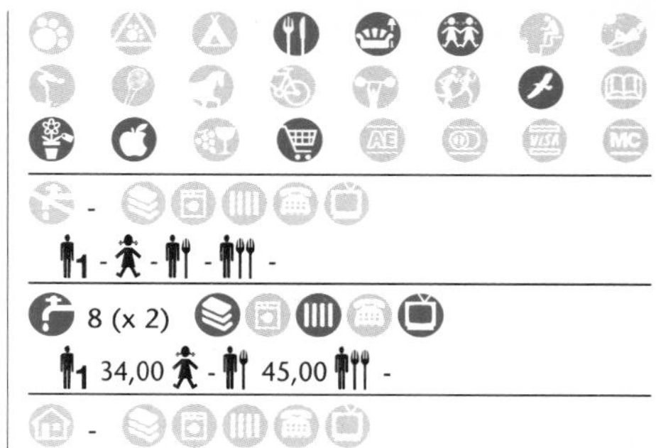

-

1 - - -

8 (x 2)

1 34,00 - 45,00 -

-

1 - 7 - 1 - 7 -

Valtournenche

La Péra Doussa

at Loz 31, 11028 Valtournenche (AO)
Tel. 016692777 Fax 016692767

Set amid the woods and pastures of the Valtournenche, this large chalet with a lift offers large rooms on the first floor, and also has a welcoming restaurant.

-

1 - - -

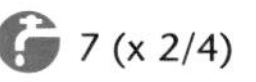  

7 (x 2/4)

1 30,00 - 46,00 -

-

1 - 7 - 1 - 7 -

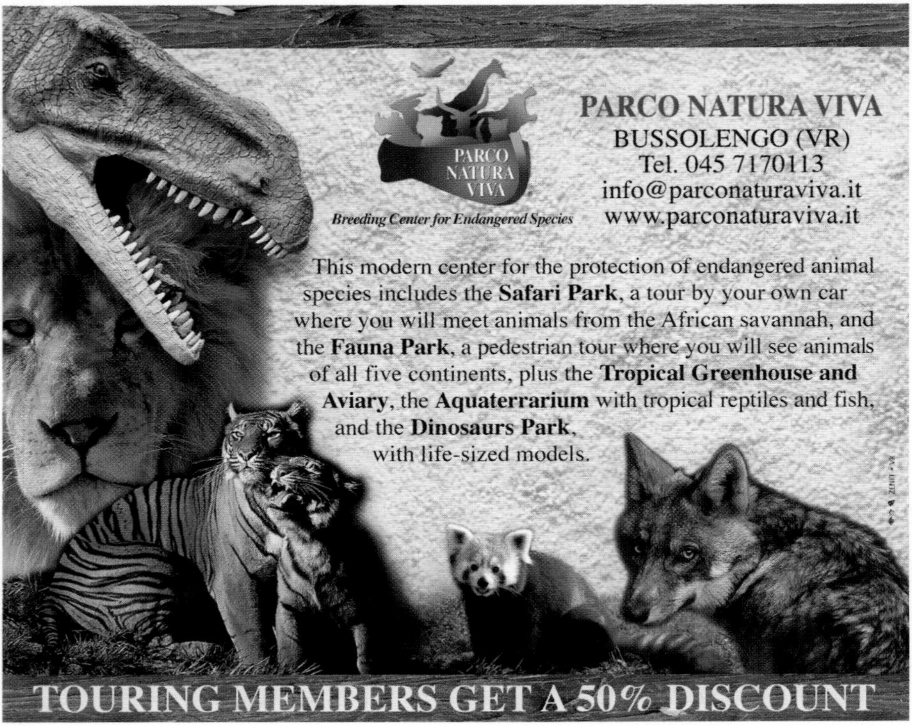

VENETO

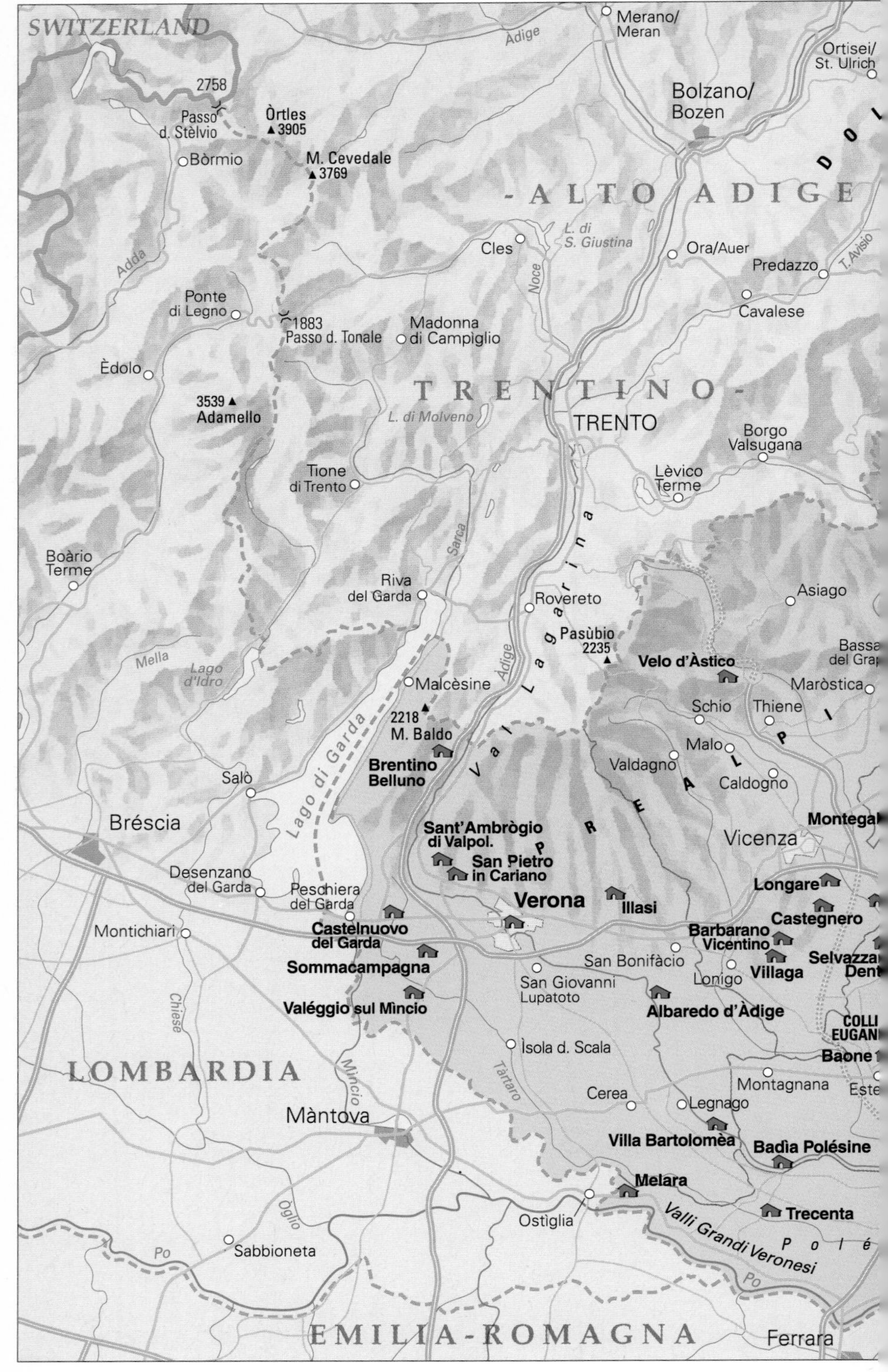

SWITZERLAND
Merano/
Meran
Àdige
Ortisei/
St. Ulrich
2758
Passo
d. Stèlvio
Òrtles
3905
Bolzano/
Bozen
Bòrmio
M. Cevedale
3769
- ALTO ADIGE
L. di
S. Giustina
Cles
Ora/Auer
Predazzo
T. Avisio
Adda
Noce
Ponte
di Legno
1883
Passo d. Tonale
Madonna
di Campiglio
Cavalese
Èdolo
TRENTINO-
3539
Adamello
L. di Molveno
TRENTO
Borgo
Valsugana
Tione
di Trento
Lèvico
Terme
Sarca
Boàrio
Terme
Riva
del Garda
Rovereto
Asiago
Pasùbio
2235
Mella
Lago
d'Idro
Velo d'Àstico
Malcèsine
Adige
Val Lagarina
Maròstica
Schio
Thiene
2218
M. Baldo
Malo
Brentino
Belluno
Valdagno
Caldogno
Lago di Garda
Salò
Bréscia
PREALPI
Sant'Ambrògio
di Valpol.
Vicenza
San Pietro
in Cariano
Desenzano
del Garda
Peschiera
del Garda
Longare
Verona
Illasi
Castegnero
Montichiari
Castelnuovo
del Garda
Barbarano
Vicentino
Sommacampagna
San Bonifàcio
Villaga
San Giovanni
Lupatoto
Lonigo
Chiese
Valéggio sul Mincio
Albaredo d'Àdige
Ìsola d. Scala
LOMBARDIA
Mincio
Tàrtaro
Montagnana
Cerea
Legnago
Màntova
Villa Bartolomèa
Badìa Polésine
Melara
Ostìglia
Valli Grandi Veronesi
Trecenta
Òglio
Sabbioneta
Po
Po
EMILIA-ROMAGNA
Ferrara

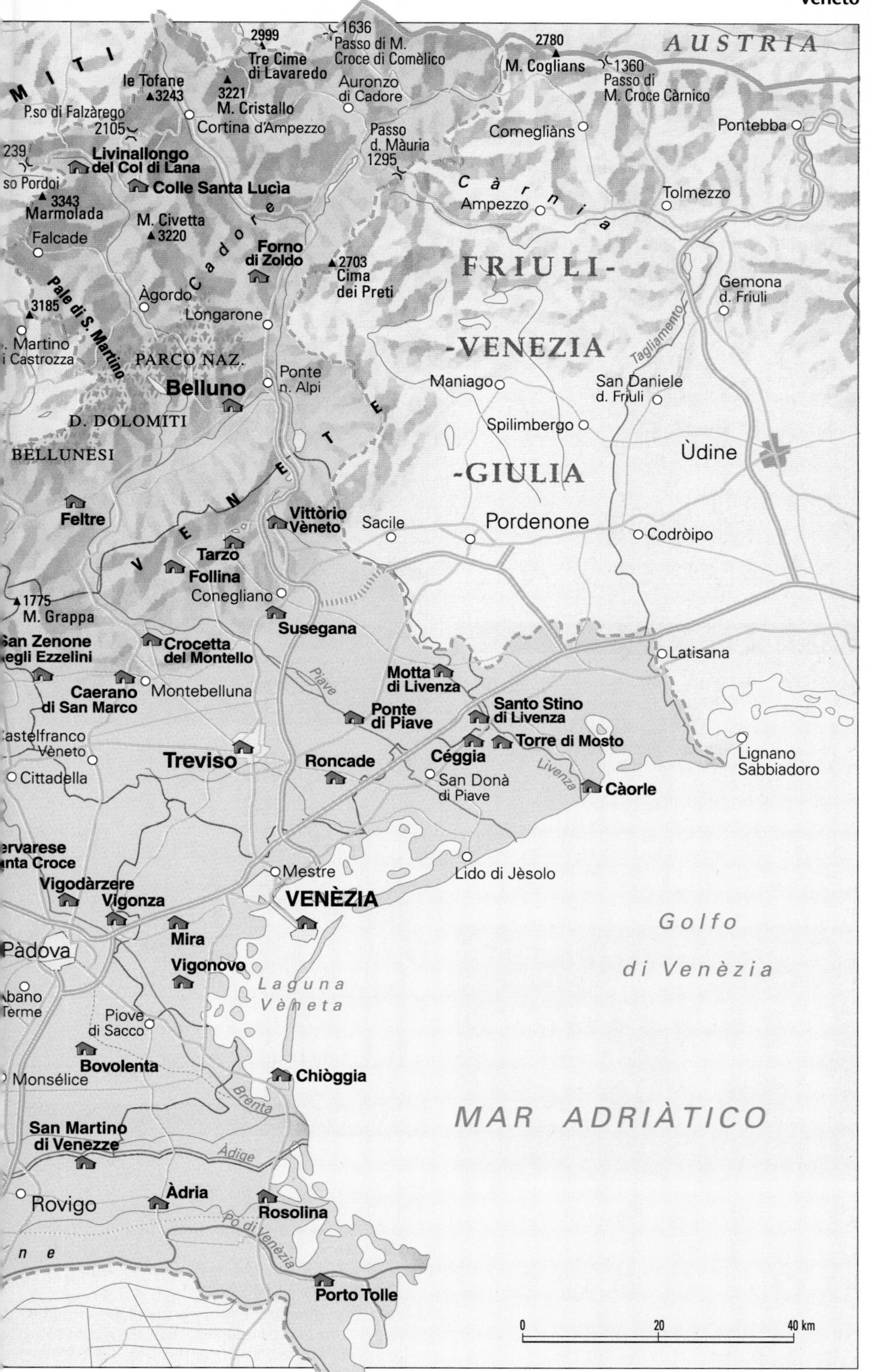
AUSTRIA
2999
Tre Cime di Lavaredo
1636
Passo di M. Croce di Comèlico
2780
M. Coglians
1360
Passo di M. Croce Càrnico
le Tofane
3243
3221
M. Cristallo
P.so di Falzàrego
2105
Cortina d'Ampezzo
Auronzo di Cadore
Passo d. Màuria
1295
Comegliàns
Pontebba
Livinallongo del Col di Lana
Colle Santa Lucìa
3343
Marmolada
M. Civetta
3220
Falcade
Càrnia
Ampezzo
Tolmezzo
Cadore
Forno di Zoldo
2703
Cima dei Preti
FRIULI-
-VENEZIA
-GIULIA
Gemona d. Friuli
Pale di S. Martino
3185
Àgordo
Longarone
Tagliamento
PARCO NAZ.
D. DOLOMITI
BELLUNESI
Belluno
Ponte n. Alpi
Maniago
San Daniele d. Friuli
Spilimbergo
Ùdine
VENETE
Feltre
Vittòrio Vèneto
Sacile
Pordenone
Codròipo
Tarzo
Follina
Conegliano
1775
M. Grappa
Susegana
San Zenone degli Ezzelini
Crocetta del Montello
Latisana
Caerano di San Marco
Montebelluna
Piave
Motta di Livenza
Ponte di Piave
Santo Stino di Livenza
Torre di Mosto
Castelfranco Vèneto
Cittadella
Treviso
Roncade
Céggia
San Donà di Piave
Livenza
Càorle
Lignano Sabbiadoro
Mestre
Lido di Jèsolo
Vigodàrzere
Vigonza
VENÈZIA
Mira
Pàdova
Golfo di Venèzia
Vigonovo
Laguna Vèneta
Piove di Sacco
Bovolenta
Monsélice
Chiòggia
Brenta
MAR ADRIÀTICO
San Martino di Venezze
Àdige
Rovigo
Àdria
Rosolina
Po di Venèzia
Porto Tolle
0
20
40 km

Adria

Scirocco

at Voltascirocco 3, 45011 Adria (RO)
Tel. **042640963**
E-mail: **agri.scirocco@katamail.com**

In a mid-18th-century country house, large fireplaces and floors of terracotta tiles give the flavour of a bygone age to the holiday.

 2 (x 4) 

1 20,66 - 36,00 -

\-

1 - - -

 1(x 4)

1 - 7 - 1 - 7 260,00

Albaredo d'Adige

Ca' dell'Acqua

at Coriano Veronese, via Zurlare 27,
37050 Albaredo d'Adige (VR)
Tel. **0457025008** Fax **0457025133**
Web: **web.tiscali.it/villabrena**

Accommodation is available in an early 20th-century villa in Palladian style. With rows of poplars and box hedges, this is also a prestigious setting for conferences and ceremonies.

\-

1 - - -

4 (x 2)

1 30,00 15,00 40,00 -

\-

1 - 7 - 1 - 7 -

Badia Polesine

Le Clementine

via Colombano 1239/B, 45021 Badia Polesine (RO)
Tel. **0425597029** Fax **0425589273**
Web: **www.leclementine.it**

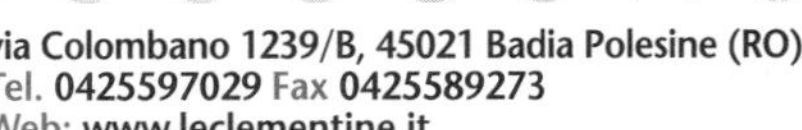

This farmhouse is located close to the banks of the Adige, the main focus for recreational activities. The rooms have period furniture and frescoed festoons.

\-

1 - - -

7 (x 2/4)

1 26,00 - - -

\-

1 - 7 - 1 - 7 -

Baone

Alba

at Ca' Barbaro, via Madonnetta 14,
35030 Baone (PD)
Tel. **04294480** Fax **04294480**
Web: **www.agriturismoalba.it**

 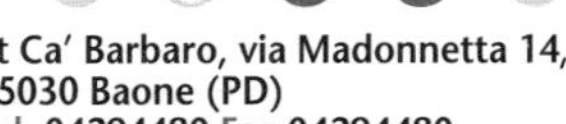

A holiday on this farm offers plenty of opportunities for excursions to the Euganean Hills (Este and Monselice) and Padua, with of course, the ever-popular Venice not so far away.

4 (x 4)

1 25,00 15,00 40,00 -

1 (x 2)

1 27,00 15,00 41,00 -

\-

1 - 7 - 1 - 7 -

Le Pesare

at Rivadolmo, via Ca' Bianche, 35030 Baone (PD)
Tel. 0498803032 Fax 0498803032
E-mail: fracanzani3@supereva.it

This farmhouse has a friendly atmosphere and it's an excellent base for visits to the Euganean Hills Regional Park, Este, Monselice, Montagnana and the Brenta Canal.

\-

1 - - -

\-

1 - - -

1(x 4)

1 - 7 - 1 - 7 550,00

Barbarano Vicentino

Il Castello

via Castello 6, 36021 Barbarano Vicentino (VI)
Tel. 0444886055 Fax 0444777140
Web: www.castellomarinoni.it

Elegant accommodation is available in a renovated 18th-century house forming part of the complex of a large villa in the Berici Hills.

\-

1 - - -

1 (x 2)

1 23,00 20,00 - -

3(x 2)

1 26,00 7 - 1 - 7 -

Belluno

Fulcio Miari Fulcis

at Modolo Castion, 32024 Belluno
Tel. 0437927198 Fax 0437927198

There's a refined atmosphere in this accommodation for lovers of horse-riding and winter sports; the rooms have four-poster beds.

5 (x 2/4)

1 30,00 - - -

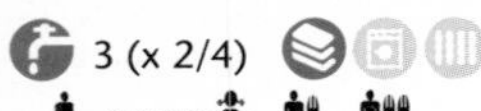

3 (x 2/4)

30,00 - - -

\-

\- - - -

Sant'Anna

at Castion, via Pedecastello 27, 32024 Belluno
Tel. 0437272491 Fax 043727491
Web: www.dolomiti.it/santanna

Close to the Belluno Dolomites National Park, the accommodation is in a strategic position between a city with a pleasant atmosphere and the mountains.

\-

\- - - -

1 (x 2)

35,00 - - -

3 (x 2/4)

\- - 85,00 520,00

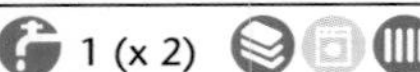

Bovolenta

Venturato

at Fossaragna, via Argine Destro 29,
35024 Bovolenta (PD)
Tel. 0495347010 Fax 0495347914

The accommodation is on the banks of the Bacchiglione, in a renovated 18th-century house with attic rooms fitted with air-conditioning.

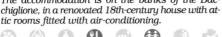

\-

\- - - -

7 (x 1/4)

40,00 20,00 60,00 -

\-

\- - - -

Brentino Belluno

Fugatti Rolando

at Belluno Veronese, via Mama 5,
37020 Brentino Belluno (VR)
Tel. 0457230110 Fax 0457230110
E-mail: vini-fugatti-r@libero.it

In the central Adige Valley, not far from the mild climate of Lake Garda, with Monte Baldo behind and vineyards everywhere, there's love for the land and a friendly welcome.

\-

\- - - -

7 (x 2)

27,50 - 39,50 -

\-

\- - - -

Caerano di San Marco

Col delle Rane

via Mercato Vecchio 18,
31031 Caerano di San Marco (TV)
Tel. 0423650085 Fax 0423650652
Web: www.coldellerane.it

Between the plain and the hills, towards Asolo and Possagno, this handsome country house is an excellent base for a tour of the villas of the Veneto.

-

1 - - -

14 (x 1/2)

1 35,00 - - -

1(x 2)

1 - 7 - 1 60,00 7 -

CAORLE

LEMENE

at Marango, strada Durisi 16,
30021 Caorle (VE)
Tel. **0498759470** Fax **049666237**
Web: **www.agriturismolemene.it**

This house in the country is "extremely tranquil, hospitable and well-kept, ideal for families with children and young couples".

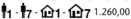

-

1 - - -

-

1 - - -

4(x 3)

1 - 7 - 1 - 7 1.260,00

CASTEGNERO

L'ALBARA

at Villaganzerla, via Pasine 22,
36020 Castegnero (VI)
Tel. **0444639715** Fax **0444738595**
Web: **www.agriturismoalbara.com**

This farmhouse is typical of the Veneto, as are the family, who tend the vegetable gardens and vineyards, and provide accommodation and meals; guests also have a swimming pool and riding-school at their disposal.

-

1 - - -

6 (x 2)

1 40,00 20,00 56,00 -

-

1 - 7 - 1 - 7 -

CASTELNUOVO DEL GARDA

FINILON

at Finilon 7, 37014 Castelnuovo del Garda (VR)
Tel. **0457575114**

Dating from the late 18th or early 19th centuries, this farmhouse stands round a large courtyard. Lake Garda is just a few kilometres away, the hills near the Mincio are even closer.

5 (x 1/4)

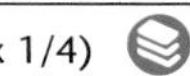

1 20,00 6,00 - -

-

1 - - -

2(x 2)

1 - 7 - 1 52,00 7 -

Ceggia

Pra' d'Arca

via Caltorta 18, 30022 Ceggia (VE)
Tel. 0421329755 Fax 0421329755
Web: users.iol.it/pradarca

Located between the Piave and the Livenza, this farmhouse, with a glazed veranda and a large lawn, is perfect for seaside holidays as it is situated close to Jesolo and Caorle.

4 (x 1/2)

1 25,00 - 30,00 -

1 (x 4)

1 25,00 - 30,00 -

-

1 - 7 - 1 - 7 -

Cervarese Santa Croce

La Buonaterra

at San Martino, via Repoise 73,
35030 Cervarese Santa Croce (PD)
Tel. 0499915497 Fax 0499915497
Web: www.buonaterrabio.it

The owners involve the guests in the work on the farm - such as looking after the herb garden, orchards and Paduan hens - and introduce them to the delights of the cuisine of the Veneto.

-

1 - - -

5 (x 2/4)

1 40,00 - 55,00 -

-

1 - 7 - 1 - 7 -

Chioggia

Ca' Rustica

at Ca' Lino, via Ca' de Luca 15, 30015 Chioggia (VE)
Tel. 0415200562 Fax 0415209061
E-mail: carustica@libero.it

This excellently renovated farmhouse with a large garden is well-placed for visits to Venice, Padua and Ravenna.

-

1 - - -

-

1 - - -

1(x 5)

1 30,00 7 - 1 80,00 7 -

Colle Santa Lucia

Eredi Frena Luigi

via Pian 1, 32020 Colle Santa Lucia (BL)
Tel. 0437720084
E-mail: gusty65@libero.it

This recently built chalet is open almost all the year round, with the most famous ski slopes of the Belluno Dolomites just half an hour's drive away.

\-

1 - - -

\-

1 - - -

2(x 12)

1 - 7 - 1 - 7 500,00

CROCETTA DEL MONTELLO

MONTELLO

at Ciano del Montello, via Generale Vaccari presa 16/A, 31035 Crocetta del Montello (TV)
Tel. **042384838** Fax **0423848388**
Web: **www.agriturismoitalia.com**

Surrounded by the woods of the Montello, with its splendid views and beautiful landscape, this establishment has rooms and apartments in rustic style.

\-

1 - - -

4 (x 2/4)

1 28,40 - 43,90 -

2(x 4)

1 48,40 7 - 1 - 7 -

FELTRE

MENEGUZ AURELIA

at Villabruna, via Arson 113, 32032 Feltre (BL)
Tel. **043942136** Fax **043942136**

This farm in the Belluno Dolomites National Park provides accommodation in a renovated stone building with wood-panelled interiors.

3 (x 2)

1 12,91 - 15,49 -

-

1 - - -

-

1 - 7 - 1 - 7 -

Follina

La Bella

via Ligonto 45, 31051 Follina (TV)
Tel. 0438970309 Fax 0438974301
Web: www.agriturismolabella.com

At Follina, in the Prosecco production area, where the vineyards are tended like gardens, there's a refined welcome in a villa made even more pleasant by the excellent local cuisine.

-

1 - - -

17 (x 1/2) 

1 30,00 20,00 - -

-

1 - 7 - 1 - 7 -

Forno di Zoldo

La Sloda

at Pralongo, via S. Andrea 20,
32012 Forno di Zoldo (BL)
Tel. 0437787696 Fax 043778190
E-mail: lasloda@hotmail.com

Located on the edge of the Belluno Dolomites National Park, this farmhouse, renovated in accordance with the principles of ecological architecture, has a warm, typically Alpine atmosphere.

-

1 - - -

5 (x 1/4)

1 30,00 20,00 - -

-

1 - 7 - 1 - 7 -

Illasi

Centro Ippico Agrituristico

at Deserto 1, 37030 Illasi (VR)
Tel. 0457834441 Fax 0457834441
E-mail: lara-andreis@tin.it

Set amid the hills sloping towards the Adige, this accommodation is in a 19th-century farmhouse, with a centre for tourism on horseback that issues FISE (Federazione Italiana Sport Equestri) certificates.

-

1 - - -

7 (x 2/4)

1 28,00 24,00 - -

3(x 4)

1 - 7 - 1 100,00 7 -

Livinallongo del Col di Lana

El Cirum

at Grone di Masarei 25,
32020 Livinallongo del Col di Lana (BL)
Tel. 043679422

In a panoramic position in beautiful surroundings, the maso (farmhouse) has been built recently, but with a traditional appearance and furnishings.

\-

1 - - -

2 (x 4)

1 23,24 - -

2(x 4)

1 23,24 7 - 1 - 7 -

Longare

Costozza dei Conti da Schio

at Costozza, piazza da Schio 4,
36023 Longare (VI)
Tel. 0444555099 Fax 0444555099
E-mail: giuliodaschio@libero.it

In the splendid setting of the Ville Da Schio, with a spectacular terraced garden, there are natural caverns used for storing wine.

\-

1 - - -

\-

1 - - -

1(x 10)

1 - 7 - 1 - 7 1.300,00

Le Vescovane

via S. Rocco 19, 36023 Longare (VI)
Tel. 0444273570 Fax 0444273265
Web: www.levescovane.com

In the verdant setting of the Berici Hills, first-rate accommodation and food are available. The main building is a tranquil hillside restaurant with rooms.

\-

1 - - -

9 (x 2)

1 42,00 - 58,00 -

1(x 4)

1 - 7 - 1 180,00 7 870,00

Melara

Ca' del Nonno

via Corno 35, 45037 Melara (RO)
Tel. 042589785

On one side are the Valli Grandi Veronesi, on the other the banks of the Po, ideal for trips by bicycle. The accommodation is in a renovated farmhouse.

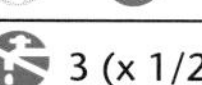
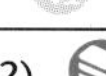

3 (x 1/2)

1 30,00 - -

\-

1 - - -

\-

1 - 7 - 1 - 7 -

Mira

Santa Barbara

at Gambarare, via Seriola Veneta destra 130,
30030 Mira (VE)
Tel. 041428929 Fax 041428929
Web: www.agriturismovenezia.it

This accommodation is in a handsome farmhouse that has been renovated and equipped with period furniture; it also has conference facilities.

\-
1 - - -

\-
1 - - -

2(x 4)

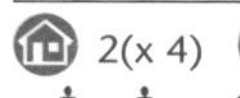

1 - 7 - 1 - 7 680,00

Montegalda

Il Palazzone

via G. Roi 33, 36047 Montegalda (VI)
Tel. 0444635001 Fax 0444737040
Web: www.brunello.it

Accommodation is available in this rustic building that has been carefully renovated; the cuisine is basically vegetarian, with the exception of cured pork products.

\-
1 - - -

6 (x 1/4)
1 31,00 - - -

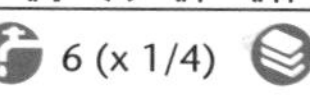

\-
1 - 7 - 1 - 7 -

Motta di Livenza

La Casa di Bacco

via Callalta 52, 31045 Motta di Livenza (TV)
Tel. 0422768488 Fax 0422765091
Web: www.casadibacco.it

This renovated cottage is in the middle of a vast wine-growing estate. The beaches of Caorle and Jesolo are 20 km away, those of Lignano Sabbiadoro and Bibione 50 km away.

\-
1 - - -

13 (x 2)
1 40,00 20,00 30,00 -

\-
1 - 7 - 1 - 7 -

Ponte di Piave

Rechsteiner

at San Nicolò, via Montegrappa 3,
31047 Ponte di Piave (TV)
Tel. 0422807128 Fax 0422752155
Web: www.rechsteiner.it

In the renowned wine-producing area flanking the Piave, accommodation is available in a farmhouse with an attractive arcade and large terrace.

- -
1 - - -

11 (x 2)
1 36,00 - 55,00 -

4(x 3)
1 - 7 - 1 120,00 7 -

Porto Tolle

Caprissio

at Ca' Mello, via C. Terranova 1,
45018 Porto Tolle (RO)
Tel. 042680053 Fax 042680053

This large building is rustic but modern, with grassy spaces and areas suitable for camping. An airfield for ultra-lights is adjacent.

-
1 - - -

3 (x 1/2)
1 23,50 - 36,00 -

-
1 - 7 - 1 - 7 -

Roncade

Castello di Roncade

E D

via Roma 141, 31056 Roncade (TV)
Tel. 0422708736 Fax 0422840964
Web: www.castellodironcade.com

This wine-growing estate centres on the 16th-century Villa Giustinian. The renovated towers housing the tourist accommodation stand on the perimeters of the estate.

-
1 - - -

5 (x 1/2)
1 50,00 35,00 - -

6(x 4)
1 50,00 7 - 1 - 7 -

Rosolina

San Gaetano

via Moceniga 20, 45010 Rosolina (RO)
Tel. **0426664634** Fax **0426664589**

Guests staying in this establishment, which opened in 1990, can enjoy holidays lazing on splendid beaches or exploring the surrounding countryside.

\-

1 - - -

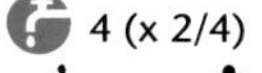 4 (x 2/4) 

1 25,82 - 38,73 -

\-

1 - 7 - 1 - 7 -

\-

1 - - -

4 (x 2)

1 52,50 - -

3(x 4)

1 - 7 - 1 - 7 980,00

San Martino di Venezze

Tenuta Castel Venezze

at Ca' Venezze 420,
45030 San Martino di Venezze (RO)
Tel. **042599667** Fax **042599667**
Web: **www.tenutacastelvenezze.it**

This huge farm, dating from the 15th century, is set in the peaceful countryside through which the Adige flows towards the Adriatic.

San Pietro in Cariano

Fioravante

at San Floriano, via Don C. Biasi 7,
37020 San Pietro in Cariano (VR)
Tel. **0457701317** Fax **0457701317**
E-mail: **fioragri@hotmail.com**

In the plain at the mouth of the Adige Valley, accommodation is available in a recent building in the verdant surroundings of the tree plantations.

\-

1 - - -

12 (x 1/4)  

1 41,00 - -

\-

1 - 7 - 1 - 7 -

Sant'Ambrogio di Valpolicella

Coop. Agricola 8 Marzo-Ca' Verde

at Ca' Verde,
37010 Sant'Ambrogio di Valpolicella (VR)
Tel. **0456862272** Fax **0456887952**
E-mail: **agricaverde@hotmail.com**

This farmhouse of 16th-century origin, located in the countryside close to the Monti Lessini, offers accommodation that is ideal for families with children.

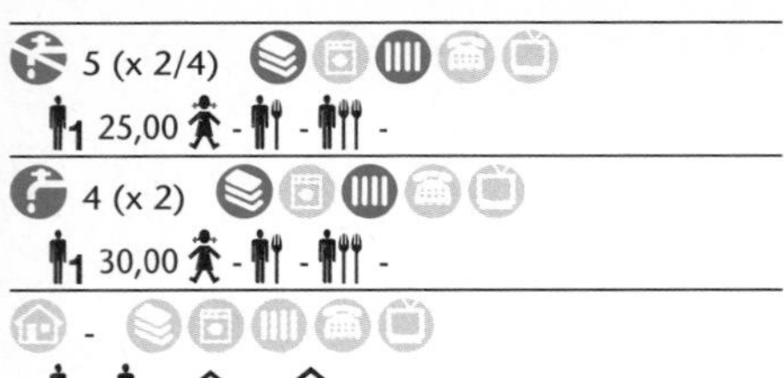

5 (x 2/4)

1 25,00 - - -

4 (x 2)

1 30,00 - - -

-

1 - 7 - 1 - 7 -

Santo Stino di Livenza

Al Cantinon

E D

at Corbolone, via Pordenone 2,
30029 Santo Stino di Livenza (VE)
Tel. 0421310211 Fax 0421310211
Web: www.lampo.it

This farm providing accommodation belongs to Mazzarotto (Cantina Dialma wines) and, at the same time, supplies meat, vegetables and so on to company canteens.

-

1 - - - -

3 (x 2)

1 25,82 - - -

-

1 - 7 - 1 - 7 -

San Zenone degli Ezzelini

Ca' Roer

E

at La Roggia, via Vallorgana 1,
31020 San Zenone degli Ezzelini (TV)
Tel. 042353042
E-mail: mariaelena.locatelli@libero.it

The Ca' Roer, named after the family (Roero) who have owned it since the 18th century, has apartments furnished with antiques.

-

1 - - - -

-

1 - - - -

2(x 4)

1 30,00 7 - 1 - 7 -

Selvazzano Dentro

Castello della Montecchia

E D

at Montecchia, via Montecchia 16,
35030 Selvazzano Dentro (PD)
Tel. 049637294 Fax 0498055826
Web: www.lamontecchia.it

This large wine-growing estate is dominated by the Villa Emo Capodilista. The accommodation gives onto a courtyard, where a tower is all that remains of a medieval castle.

-

1 - - - -

-

1 - - - -

3(x 4)

1 - 7 - 1 - 7 980,00

Sommacampagna

La Fredda

D

via Fredda 1, 37066 Sommacampagna (VR)
Tel. 045510124 Fax 045510127
Web: www.lafredda.com

In the plain, halfway between the Mincio, marking the border between the Veneto and Lombardy, and Verona, accommodation is available in the one-storeyed main house or in new bungalows.

-
1 - - -

12 (x 2/4)
1 36,00 - - -

-
1 - 7 - 1 - 7 -

Susegana

Collalto

via XXIV Maggio 1, 31058 Susegana (TV)
Tel. 0438738241 Fax 043873538
Web: www.collalto.it

In the immediate vicinity of the Collato estate, accommodation is available in a cottage with elegant furnishings and open spaces with recreational facilities.

-
1 - - -

-
1 - - -

2(x 6)
1 - 7 - 1 - 7 1.550,00

Tarzo

Mondragon

at Arfanta, via Mondragon 1, 31020 Tarzo (TV)
Tel. 0438933021 Fax 0438933867
Web: www.mondragon.it

Accommodation is available in a fine stone building in the woods of the Alpine foothills near Treviso, with customised offers of a historical or naturalistic character.

    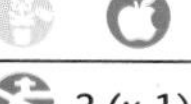  

2 (x 1)
1 21,00 - 33,00 -

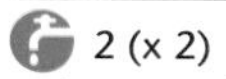  

2 (x 2)
1 21,00 - 33,00 -

-
1 - 7 - 1 - 7 -

Torre di Mosto

La Via Antiga

at Staffolo, via S. Martino 13,
30020 Torre di Mosto (VE)
Tel. 042162378 Fax 0421317014
E-mail: cirozanin@libero.it

Not far from the sea at Caorle, between the Piave and the Livenza, an organic farm provides accommodation and dishes prepared with its own produce.

-
1 - - -

2 (x 2)
1 25,00 - - -

4(x 2)
1 - 7 - 1 - 7 350,00

Trecenta

Ca' Pozza

via Tenuta Spalletti 41, 45027 Trecenta (RO)
Tel. 0425700101 Fax 0425700101
E-mail: agr.ca'pozza@libero.it

Art lovers will want to visit the magnificent villas of the Veneto, naturalists, the marshes known here as gorghi. The accommodation is in a renovated farmhouse.

\-

1 - - -

4 (x 2/4)

1 26,00 - - -

\-

1 - 7 - 1 - 7 -

Treviso

Il Cascinale

via Torre d'Orlando 6/B, 31100 Treviso
Tel. **0422402203** Fax **0422346418**
Web: **www.agriturismoilcascinale.it**

Just a stone's throw from the centre, stands this large rural building recently converted into holiday accommodation.

\-

1 - - -

8 (x 1/4)  

1 40,00 - - -

\-

1 - 7 - 1 - 7 -

Valeggio sul Mincio

Gian Galeazzo Visconti

at Borghetto, via Monte Borghetto 3,
37067 Valeggio sul Mincio (VR)
Tel. **0457952086** Fax **0456379912**
Web: **www.ggvisconti.it**

This group of old farmhouses has accommodation in rooms located in the carefully converted barchessa (arcaded storehouse), hayloft, barn and cowshed.

\-

1 - - -

\-

1 - - -

8 (x 2/5)  

1 - 7 - 1 82,00 7 -

Velo d'Astico

Villa Gianfranco

at Lago, via Canova 7, 36010 Velo d'Astico (VI)
Tel. **0445742180** Fax **0445742020**
Web: **www.agriturvillagianfranco.com**

This villa offers accommodation and meals, as well as walks in the park. In this area, from Monte Pasubio to the Asiago Plateau, traces of the First World War battlegrounds are still visible.

\-

1 - - -

5 (x 2)
32,00 - 40,00 -

-
1 - 7 - 1 - 7 -

VENEZIA

LE GARZETTE

at Malamocco, lungomare Alberoni 32, 30100 Venezia
Tel. 041731078 Fax 0412428798
Web: welcome.to/legarzette

The island of the Lido is the thin strip of land separating the Venetian Lagoon from the sea. This accommodation has direct access to the sea.

-
1 - - - -

5 (x 1/4)
1 45,00 - 70,00 -

-
1 - 7 - 1 - 7 -

ORTO ARCOBALENO

at Zelarino, via Parolari 88, 30174 Venezia
Tel. 041680341 Fax 041680341
E-mail: castelligalvan@tin.it

This area rich in hedges and water is the ideal setting for this farmhouse. Surrounded by market gardens and organic beehives, it has a warm, pleasant atmosphere.

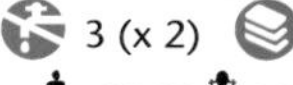
3 (x 2)
1 18,00 10,00 - -

-
1 - - - -

-
1 - 7 - 1 - 7 -

VERONA

SAN MATTIA

via Santa Giuliana 2/A, 37100 Verona
Tel. 045913797 Fax 045913797
E-mail: francescamorassutti@libero.it

Just outside Verona, on the road leading to the hills, this country establishment is ideal for those also wishing to visit the city. The rooms have modern furniture.

-
1 - - - -

6 (x 4)
1 35,00 - - -

-
1 - 7 - 1 - 7 -

VIGODARZERE

ELFIÒ

at Tavo, via Fornace 1, 35010 Vigodarzere (PD)
Tel. 049767647 Fax 049767885

The river flowing beyond the trees is ideal for romantic boat trips or riding along its banks. Venice is just 20 minutes away. The rooms have period furnishings.

-
1 - - - -

2 (x 1/2)
1 45,00 - - -

4 (x 3/6)

1 35,00 7 - 1 - 7 -

Vigonovo

Le Meridiane

at Tombelle, via Piovego 17, 30030 Vigonovo (VE)
Tel. 049503960 Fax 049503960
E-mail: fpplemeridiane@hotmail.com

In this carefully restored group of farmhouses located in the plain, accommodation is available for a very tranquil holiday.

3 (x 1/4)

1 23,24 - -

1 (x 2)

1 25,83 - -

\-

1 - 7 - 1 - 7 -

Villa Serena

at Pava, via Nogia 28, 30030 Vigonovo (VE)
Tel. 0499830957 Fax 0499830957
E-mail: villaserena.ve@libero.it

In the area of the Brenta Canal, this is a recent building surrounding a courtyard, with wooden structures and rustic finishings. There's a safari park and a nursery for ornamental plants.

\-

1 - - -

15 (x 1/2)

1 24,00 15,50 45,00 -

\-

1 - 7 - 1 - 7 -

Vigonza

Villa Selvatico

at Codiverno, via Selvatico 1,
35010 Vigonza (PD)
Tel. 049646092 Fax 049646092
Web: www.villaselvatico.com

Just a few kilometres from Padua and the Brenta Canal, a 16th-century villa surrounded by a magnificent park is the ideal place for holidays in style.

\-

1 - - -

\-

1 - - -

4 (x 2/4)

1 - 7 - 1 225,00 7 1.550,00

Villa Bartolomea

Tenuta La Pila

at Spinimbecco, via Pila 42,
37049 Villa Bartolomea (VR)
Tel. 0442659289 Fax 0442658707
Web: www.tenutalapila.it

Not far from the Adige, this group of old farmhouses standing around a rice mill offers the pleasures of the rural life, with bicycle trips and, nearby, the historic cities.

-
1 - - -

5 (x 2)

1 33,00 16,50 - -

2(x 4)

1 - 7 - 1 132,00 7 715,00

Villaga

Le Mandolare

via Mandolare 6, 36020 Villaga (VI)
Tel. 0444776072 Fax 0444787453
E-mail: lemandolare@libero.it

The heart of the establishment is an old building, while the adjacent outbuildings house the excellent restaurant and accommodation in pleasant rooms.

-
1 - - -

4 (x 2/4)

1 30,00 - - -

2(x 4)

1 - 7 - 1 60,00 7 -

Vittorio Veneto

Le Colline

at Cozzuolo, via San Mor 13,
31029 Vittorio Veneto (TV)
Tel. 0438560282 Fax 0438560282
E-mail: agriturismolecolline@libero.it

This farmhouse, renovated in a rustic style, stands on a hilltop with a splendid view of the Prosecco vineyards sloping down gradually towards the Adriatic coast.

-
1 - - -

5 (x 1/4)

1 25,00 - 35,00 -

2(x 2)

1 - 7 - 1 30,00 7 -

Index of places

C

I

J

K

L

M

N

O

P

Q

R

S

W

Z